The Economic Organization of the Household
Second Edition

Surveying the field of the economics of the hortion of this text reviews the theory of the consu undergraduate level. The text applies and ext sumer demand and expenditures; consumptior cation among market work, home work, and emphasizing investment in education, children ., .ιιιιιty; marriage; and divorce. Influenced by Gary Becker and his associates, the models developed are used to help explain modern U.S. trends in family behavior. Topics are discussed with the aid of geometry and a little algebra. For those with a background in calculus, mathematical endnotes provide the models on which the text discussions are based and interesting applications beyond the scope of the text. The work is suitable for upper-level undergraduates in economics, consumer economics, and public policy programs. The text is also useful as an introduction to the economics of the family for graduate students in sociology, demography, and the policy sciences.

W. Keith Bryant is Professor Emeritus, Department of Policy Analysis and Management, Cornell University, where he also chaired that department and the Department of Consumer Economics and Housing. He previously taught at the University of Minnesota. Professor Bryant served as President of the American Council on Consumer Interests, is a Distinguished Fellow of the Council, and also served as a staff member of President Lyndon Johnson's National Advisory Commission on Rural Poverty. He has published in journals such as the *Journal of Marriage and Family*, *Review of Economics of the Household*, *Journal of Business*, *Journal of Consumer Research*, *American Journal of Agricultural Economics*, *Journal of Consumer Affairs*, and the *Journal of Family and Economic Issues*. His current research focuses on the economics of the household with special interest in time use and household production.

Cathleen D. Zick is Professor and Chair of the Department of Family and Consumer Studies at the University of Utah. Her research focuses on the economic and socio-demographic factors that affect family well-being. Professor Zick's work has been published in numerous scholarly journals including *Demography*, the *Journal of Marriage and Family*, *Journal of Gerontology: Social Sciences*, *Journal of Consumer Affairs*, *Social Science Research*, and the *Journal of Family and Economic Issues*. She serves on five editorial boards and is currently the President-Elect of the American Council on Consumer Interests.

The Economic Organization of the Household

Second Edition

W. KEITH BRYANT

Cornell University

CATHLEEN D. ZICK

University of Utah

CAMBRIDGE UNIVERSITY PRESS
Cambridge, New York, Melbourne, Madrid, Cape Town, Singapore, São Paulo

Cambridge University Press
40 West 20th Street, New York, NY 10011-4211, USA

www.cambridge.org
Information on this title: www.cambridge.org/9780521801416

First published 2006

Printed in the United States of America

A catalog record for this publication is available from the British Library.

Library of Congress Cataloging in Publication Data

Bryant, W. Keith (Wilfrid Keith), 1934–
The economic organization of the household / W. Keith Bryant, Cathleen D. Zick. – 2nd ed.
p. cm.
Includes bibliographical references and index.
ISBN-13: 978-0-521-80141-6 (hardback)
ISBN-10: 0-521-80141-9 (hardback)
ISBN-13: 978-0-521-80527-8 (pbk.)
ISBN-10: 0-521-80527-9 (pbk.)
1. Consumption (Economics) – United States. 2. Income – United States.
3. Households – United States. 4. Family – Economic aspects – United States.
5. Consumption (Economics) 6. Income. 7. Households.
8. Family – Economic aspects. I. Zick, Cathleen D. II. Title.
HC110.C6.B79 2005
332.024′0068 – dc22 2005018307

ISBN-13 978-0-521-80141-6 hardback
ISBN-10 0-521-80141-9 hardback

ISBN-13 978-0-521-80527-8 paperback
ISBN-10 0-521-80527-9 paperback

To our spouses and children
Ken, Marty, Nathan, Frances, and Mike

Contents

Figures

ix

Preface to the Second Edition

In 1987, when we began writing the first edition of *The Economic Organization of the Household* in earnest, there had been no attempt to gather the threads of the research and discussion on the economics of the family, weave them together, and present them as a whole cloth to either the undergraduate or beginning graduate student. Since then, a flood of research has been published in response to the trends in family behavior, some of which raised puzzling social policy questions. Simultaneously, a host of national cross-section and panel data sets that could be used to test hypotheses about family behavior became available. *The Handbook of Population and Family Economics*, edited by Mark Rosenzweig and Oded Stark (1997), has provided researchers and advanced graduate students with useful discussions of models, hypotheses, and empirical research on the subject from both economics and demography. But to our knowledge, with all its faults, *The Economic Organization of the Household* remains the single source of an integrated treatment of the economics of the family at the senior undergraduate and first-year graduate student level. It seemed worthwhile, therefore, to revise it: by including the research done since 1989 as well as some earlier research neglected in the first edition, by including some topics not covered in the first edition, and by dropping a few topics that teachers have said were less useful or dated.

Like the first edition, this revised edition is a textbook on the economics of the family for students who have completed a semester of introductory microeconomics. It is intended as a text for a junior-senior semester-long course. Because of the mathematical notes, it can also be used by first-year graduate students in economics programs, especially applied economics programs like consumer economics, and by students of the family in other social science or public policy programs who want a survey and introduction to the subject. This was the market for the first edition and we hope this revised edition continues to serve it well.

Comparative static analysis is used throughout and, with only minor exceptions, perfect foresight and certainty are assumed in the belief that a firm grounding in the basics is the goal. The discussions use English, geometry, and algebra, with calculus relegated to mathematical notes following each chapter. Indifference curve diagrams are used whenever possible to cement the basic hypothesis that family behavior arises out of attempts to maximize satisfaction subject to resource, legal, social, and technological constraints. Demand and supply diagrams are used periodically where appropriate. Chapters 2 and 3 review neoclassical consumer theory at the intermediate level. The results of empirical research estimating the demand functions for a variety of goods and services are used as examples. The basic theory presented in Chapters 2 and 3 is used and extended in succeeding chapters with the level of the discussion rising somewhat given that students have mastered the earlier material. There are eight chapters in the revised edition and we were each responsible for revising four chapters. Both of us edited every chapter.

Textbooks are the products of authors and the myriad of influences upon them: some from associates and students, others from the environments that authors inhabit. Michigan State University and the Universities of California-Davis, Chicago, Minnesota, and Wisconsin have provided one or both of us with stimulating environments in which we could grow intellectually. The faculties and students of Cornell University and the University of Utah, in particular, have been immensely important to the development of both authors.

Our spouses, Marty and Ken, provided space, time, computer skills, encouragement, and nudging without which this revision would never have been completed. We owe them immense debts that can never be repaid (and they know it!). Our children, Nathan, Michael, and Frances, also played important parts. Growing up as the first edition developed, Michael and Frances suffered through years of family dinners at which the topics in the book were discussed and debated. They were grateful to be grown and gone during the writing of the revised edition. Nathan was not so lucky. Discussions of various topics in the revised edition crowded out subjects (e.g., basketball, track and field) much more important to him many evenings.

Scott Parris, Economics Editor for Cambridge University Press, encouraged us to revise the book and had infinite patience as writing deadline after deadline came and went. We appreciate his ultimate faith in us and in the project. Simina Calin, his assistant, also had infinite patience with authors writing a book using WordPerfect in a Microsoft Word world. Katie Greczylo of TechBooks guided us through the production process from "final" manuscript through copyediting, indexing, and page proofs to published book. We wrote the manuscript. They transformed it into a book.

ONE

Introduction

The Economic Organization of the Household is an introduction to the economics of the family. It uses the economic theory of production as well as the economic theory of the consumer to better understand the behavior of individuals and families. By behavior we mean more than just consumers' purchases of market goods and services as explained by neoclassical consumer theory. The economics of the family also sheds light on individual and family investments in monetary assets and human capital, the use of householders' time in market work, household work, and other nonmarket activities. Economics of the family goes further in providing an understanding of the effects economic forces have on the fertility, marriage, and divorce decisions of individuals and families.

The economics of the family has been called the "new home economics" in partial recognition of the long history of empirical studies of family behavior conducted by home economists. By the 1930s, "family economics and home management" had become a separate field of study within home economics. Purchasing behavior, family time use, and financial management were among the topics studied and taught. Home management theory was developed to provide a unified framework within which all family decision making could be understood (Deacon and Firebaugh 1988). As such, it was multidisciplinary in its attempt to integrate economics, sociology, and psychology into a single framework for the empirical study of family behavior. It utilized psychology and sociology more than it did economics, in part because economics at that time was focused almost exclusively on explaining the behavior of markets for consumer goods and services. Exceptions were Margaret Reid's 1934 treatise, *The Economics of Household Production*, dealing extensively with the productive activities carried out by the household, and Wesley Clair Mitchell's 1912 article, "The Backward Art of Spending Money," focusing on the purchasing agent role performed by household members. Although both studies were used extensively by home economists, neither stimulated sufficient interest by economists to develop an economics of the family. Theory building by economists had to await the changes in consumer and family behavior that occurred after World War II and economists' struggles to understand them.

Traditionally, economists made use of the economic theory of the consumer primarily for the purpose of understanding the market demands for consumer goods and services. In the face of the failure of Keynesian macroeconomics to explain the surge in aggregate consumption after World War II, consumer theory was used to provide an adequate microeconomic grounding for the study of aggregate consumption and saving (Friedman 1957; Modigliani and Brumberg 1954). Inadequate explanations of national economic growth in the twentieth century led to the formal recognition within economic theory that people create human capital by investing in themselves and that human capital is itself an important generator of economic growth (Schultz 1974; Becker 1975).

The puzzling rapid rise in the labor force participation rate of married females beginning in the 1940s also stimulated labor economists to look within the household for answers. Jacob Mincer's (1963) recognition that married females made choices between market work and household work began to shed light on their market work behavior. Gary Becker (1965) recognized the productive activities of households, emphasized the time spent by individuals and families in household production (i.e., nonmarket work), and formally incorporated the economic theory of production into consumer theory. The baby boom of the 1940s and 1950s, the subsequent baby bust of the 1960s, along with the interconnections between the labor force participation of married females and fertility, stimulated the use of consumer theory in explanations of fertility (Becker and Lewis 1974). Similar inadequacies in the economic explanations of trends in marriage and divorce led to the application of consumer theory to the problems of explaining the marriage and divorce decisions individuals make (Becker 1973–1974; Becker et al. 1977; Manser and Brown 1979; McElroy and Horney 1981).

The economics of the family, therefore, has been largely a theoretical and empirical response to the demand for better explanations of the new or markedly changed individual and family behavior of the past forty to fifty years. As such, the economics of the family has joined sociology and demography in attempting to provide better explanations of the important trends in household behavior: the important changes in consumption and savings patterns in the past half century, the increasing education and training of the population (especially females), the rising labor force participation rate of married women, the decline in fertility, the decline in marriage rates, the rise in divorce rates, and the connections among these diverse trends.

INDIVIDUALS, HOUSEHOLDS, AND FAMILIES

The focus of the text is on the behavior of individuals and families. These terms, individuals and families, are by their nature vague and in need of clarification. For our purposes a household is a small group of people who use their collective resources to pursue the same goals. A household, therefore, can be an individual, a family (by which we mean a group of individuals living together and related by marriage, birth, or adoption), or a small group of families or unrelated individuals (so long as they jointly use their resources to pursue the same goals). Empirically, the U.S. Census Bureau's definition comes about as close as possible to defining the concept: a household is "all persons who ... occupy separate living quarters. ... A household includes related family members and all unrelated persons who share the separate living quarters" (U.S. Bureau of the Census 1982, p. 4). According to this definition, a household, then, may be an individual living alone and conducting her own affairs, a family, or a household. In the text, we use the terms consumer, individual, family, and household as synonyms unless otherwise noted. The term consumer is used in Chapters 2, 3, and 4 because the subject under discussion is the demand for consumer goods and services and for saving. The consumer in this context can be either an individual, a family, or a potentially larger entity like the Census-defined household. In Chapters 5, 6, 7, and 8, dealing with household time use, human capital, fertility, marriage, and divorce, the terms individual, family, and household are used more frequently.

AN OVERVIEW OF THE ECONOMIC ORGANIZATION
OF THE HOUSEHOLD

Goals

Economists, whether studying households or firms, posit that decision makers make decisions among alternative courses of action so as to further their goals. The decisions make a difference because of the different consequences each of the alternatives possesses. For economics to be relevant, then, decision makers must have goals they wish to pursue, there must be alternative courses of action that can be taken to further the goals, the decision makers must be able to choose among the alternatives, and the choices must matter in the sense that each alternative is costly and hence some alternatives further the goals better than others (i.e., more cheaply for a given degree of goal fulfillment or by increasing the degree of goal fulfillment at the same cost).

Rather than attempt to distinguish among the amazing welter of specific goals individuals and families have (e.g., to clean house today, complete a report at the office, potty train one's child, pass an algebra test), economists focus on what can be termed high-level goals to which the attainment of each of the myriad of lower-level goals contributes. In the case of individuals and families, the high-level goal is "satisfaction." The goal of individuals and families is said to be "maximizing satisfaction." Happiness and well-being are common synonyms for satisfaction. It is difficult to deny that individuals and families don't attempt to be as happy as possible or have as much well-being as possible given their resources and the constraints on their use. Thus, the assumption that individuals, families, and households act to maximize satisfaction seems to be a reasonable one.

Activities

Individuals and family members set about increasing satisfaction or their well-being by engaging in a set of activities. These activities are as diverse as the welter of lower-level goals. For the purpose of analysis, however, economists have grouped them in recognizable aggregate categories. Market work, household work, voluntary work, child care, and leisure are typical categories. Each of these aggregate activities yield satisfaction directly or indirectly. Market work yields income, which, in turn, is used to better one's life. Market work may also yield satisfaction directly in that some market work is pleasurable. Household work produces a set of household goods and services that, in turn, yield satisfaction: a clean house, a groomed lawn, laundered clothes, a shiny car, a fixed appliance, and so on. Like market work, household work may also yield satisfaction directly – as anyone who enjoys working in the garden or preparing a nice dinner will tell you. Voluntary work yields the satisfaction one obtains from furthering someone else's goals or the goals of an agency one regards as worthwhile. Through voluntary work one may also gain the experience necessary to get more rewarding or higher paid market work. Child care develops socially and economically independent children as well as yielding the immediate fulfillment one gets from looking after one's own children. Leisure, whether watching TV, reading, playing a sport, or going to dinner and the theater, yields satisfaction directly.

Individuals, then, choose among the variety of activities open to them in their attempts to be as happy as possible. For instance, economists posit that an individual will choose to marry only if being married will make her/him happier than being single. Some activities are preferred more than others and these preferences partly determine which activities are chosen and how much of each is done. However, since resources must be employed to engage in any activity and, since engaging in one set of activities precludes the possibility of engaging in others, no activity is pursued to the exclusion of all others and no one does everything.

Resource Constraints

To engage in activities, one must have resources: if an activity takes no other resources, it at least takes time. Resources are at once the means by which activities are conducted and also an important constraint on the number and extent of activities performed. The resources are of several sorts, including monetary, physical, and human. A household's monetary resources include its monthly income, its savings and investments, and its credit. Physical resources are the myriad of multi-use household goods. Included are the house, the set of appliances and furniture, audio-visual systems, clothes, linens, cars, tools, and athletic equipment. Human resources are of two sorts: the knowledge and skills embodied in the individuals and the time of each individual in the household. Until the 1950s, consumer theory focused almost entirely on income as the resource constraining individual and household behavior. The recent insight that physical and human resources also constrain behavior stems from the challenges economists faced in explaining the rather dramatic shifts in time allocation, marriage, and fertility over the past forty to fifty years.

Technological Constraints

Each activity has an underlying technology that is employed to engage in the activity. An activity's technology can be viewed as a recipe by which the resources required are employed. For example, the amount of time and skill required and the piano, piano bench, sheet music, and physical setting of the piano produce the activity of playing the piano. The more skill, sheet music, and time with the same piano, the longer and better the piano concert. Likewise, the more soiled clothes, laundry detergent, hot water, electricity, and time with the same washer and dryer, the more clean clothes. Thus, the technology of the activities form important constraints on the activities the household engages in as well as the amount of satisfaction yielded directly or indirectly by the activities.

Legal and Socio-Cultural Constraints

The behavior of households is as bounded by legal and socio-cultural constraints as it is by technology and the resources at the households' disposal. Legal constraints are of two sorts: they enjoin households from engaging in some activities or from using some resources. Thievery, murder, and the consumption of certain substances are prohibited, while other substances can only be consumed by adults. We all are subject to being taxed. While such laws can be broken provided one is prepared to pay the possible consequences, we do not in this text discuss these possibilities. They are left for a text on the economics of crime. However, we do discuss tax and welfare policies that impinge on households' choices.

Socio-cultural constraints are likewise important in ordering the economic organization of the household. The roles socio-cultural constraints play in ordering behavior is the natural purview of family sociologists and, as such, are de-emphasized or neglected in this text. We do not dwell on the roles that cultural and religious factors play in constraining household choice. No text can do everything. However, since religion does feature importantly in fertility, marriage, and divorce decisions, we devote some space to this subject in Chapters 7 and 8.

The Organization of the Chapters

In writing this book, we begin by describing a simple economic model of the household and we add layers of complexity to this model as we move from chapter to chapter. Chapters 2 and 3 present a static, one-period economic model of consumer demand for goods and services. In these two chapters, we also examine the role that income and prices play in facilitating and constraining the household's purchase decisions. In Chapter 4, we move to a multiperiod model that can be used to examine questions of saving, borrowing, and consumption. This allows us to use the model to examine the hypothesis that past actions and expected future conditions and actions help to determine present behavior. With Chapter 5, we up the ante even more by introducing time and production technologies as additional constraints that affect behavioral choices. Chapter 5 develops the concept of the production function as the representation of household technology and by so doing we gain new insights about the household as a producer of goods and services. Chapter 6 introduces the economic concept of human capital, its creation, and its implications for both market and household production. Finally, Chapters 7 and 8 utilize the household production function and the concept of investment in human capital to enhance our understanding of households' fertility and marriage behavior.

While the economic models build in their complexity as we move from Chapter 2 to Chapter 8, we endeavor to use graphical presentations of the models whenever possible, reserving much of the more complex mathematical modeling for the mathematical notes sections at the ends of the chapters. In this way, we hope this text will be useful for both junior- or senior-level economics seminars and first-year graduate seminars.

TWO

Household Equilibrium

INTRODUCTION

We are now ready to begin the economic analysis of the household. This chapter is devoted to developing the basic economic model of the household that underlies the remaining discussion. The model is set up to analyze the household's demand for goods and services, which will prepare for the discussion in Chapter 3. The model abstracts from the many household attributes and environmental factors, concentrating on two important attributes: (1) the set of goods and services the household can afford, given its income and market prices, and (2) the goals of the household expressed in terms of the preferences it has for goods. The former attribute – what the household can have – is described by the household's budget constraint; the latter – its goals – is described by the household's preference map and utility function. We discuss each in turn. To add concreteness to the analysis we will use food as an example. Hence, we are interested in developing a model of the household that will allow us to analyze the demand for food. The analysis will be general, however, and applicable to the demand for any good.

THE BUDGET CONSTRAINT

In each period (say, a year) we suppose the household to enter the marketplace to purchase those quantities of food and other goods and services that will maximize the family's satisfaction. In doing so it faces market prices for food and other things along with the limited income it possesses.

Its choices are necessarily made in the light of these facts. We can gain great insight into the choice environment faced by the household by organizing and representing these facts both algebraically and geometrically. We do the algebraic representation first.

Let the market price at which a unit of food may be purchased during the time period under consideration be p_f dollars per unit of food. Likewise, let p_o be the price at which units of the composite good "all other goods" may be purchased. Similarly, let the quantities of food and "all other goods" purchasable per period by the family be q_f and q_o respectively.[1] And let the family's total income per period be Y.

There is no reason to suppose that the family will not use all of its income because, as we will see subsequently, using all of its income is the only way it can achieve the greatest satisfaction or well-being. Thus, the family spends all of its income on the two composite goods, food and "all other goods."[2] This concept called the budget constraint can be represented as

$$p_f q_f + p_o q_o = Y. \tag{2.1}$$

Definition: The budget constraint represents all the possible combinations of food and "all other goods" purchasable by the family, if it uses all of its income in the period of analysis.

By setting q_f at 0, the maximum quantity of "all other goods" purchasable by the family, q_o^m, can be found by solving equation (2.1) for q_o,

$$q_o^m = Y/p_o. \tag{2.2}$$

---

[1] The terms *price per unit quantity* and *quantity of food* are intentionally vague. For this analysis we cannot add pounds of beef, oranges, apples, and lettuce to obtain pounds of food. Such a measure is useless because we have added unlike things. Nor can we add the price per pound of beef to the price per pound of lettuce and get a meaningful price of food. Instead, price and quantity *indexes* for food must be developed in addition to price and quantity indexes for "all other goods" and services. Accomplishing this reduces all food items into one composite "good" we call food and "all other goods" and services into another composite good we will call "all other goods."

[2] The composite good "all other goods" includes any saving that the household does and thus really does encompass all the uses to which the household puts its income other than purchasing food. Thus, expenditures really do equal total family income. The price of the composite good "all other goods" is similar in concept and construction to the consumer price index (minus the food component) the U.S. Bureau of Labor Statistics uses to trace the general level of all consumer prices in the economy. Likewise, the price of food, p_f, is similar in concept and construction to the price index of the food component in the consumer price index.

Likewise, the maximum quantity of food purchasable by the family, q_f^m, is

$$q_f^m = Y/p_f. \tag{2.3}$$

Consequently, the family's budget constraint says that the family is able to purchase quantities of food between 0 and q_f^m and quantities of "all other goods" between 0 and q_o^m with its income of Y in the time period under study.

A geometric representation of the budget constraint can be obtained by solving equation (2.1) for q_o and plotting the resulting line on a graph with q_o measured along the vertical axis and q_f measured along the horizontal axis. The resulting equation is

$$q_o = Y/p_o - (p_f/p_o)q_f. \tag{2.4}$$

The shape of equation (2.4) is best illustrated in the following example. Suppose $Y = \$40$, $p_f = \$8/\text{unit}$, and $p_o = \$4/\text{unit}$. Then, we can use equation (2.4) to find the various quantities of food and "all other goods" that are possible for the household to purchase. In this case equation (2.4) is

$$q_o = 40/4 - (8/4)q_f = 10 - 2q_f.$$

The following tabulation gives the possible combinations open to the family:

q_f	q_o
0	10
1	8
2	6
3	4
4	2
5	0

These combinations are plotted in Figure 2.1 with the points joined to show the budget line. The line has as its vertical intercept the point $(q_o^m, 0)$, which represents the maximum quantity of "all other goods" purchasable by the family (i.e., 10 units) and the zero quantity of food it can purchase as a consequence. The line's horizontal intercept is at point $(0, q_f^m)$, representing the maximum quantity of food purchasable (i.e., 5 units) with the family's income of $40 and the consequent zero quantity of "all other goods."

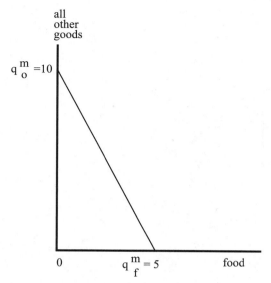

Figure 2.1. The budget line when $Y = \$40$, $p_f = \$8/\text{unit}$, and $p_o = \$4/\text{unit}$; that is, $q_o = 10 - 2q_f$.

Definition: The budget line, as $q_o^m q_f^m$ is called, represents all the possible combinations of food and "all other goods" purchasable by the family if it exhausts its income, Y.

The budget line has two properties: its slope and its location. Each has economic meaning and is discussed in turn.

Relative Prices

The slope is the gradient or steepness of the line. The equation for any straight line is represented as $y = b + mx$ where y is the variable plotted on the vertical axis, x is the variable plotted on the horizontal axis, b is the line's vertical intercept, and m is the line's slope. In equation (2.4), $b = Y/p_o$ is the intercept and $m = -(p_f/p_o)$ is its slope.

What economic concepts does the slope represent? The slope is the relative price of food in terms of "all other goods." The lower the relative price of food, the gentler the slope of the budget line; the higher the relative price of food, the steeper the budget line. Figure 2.2 shows three budget lines of varying steepness, or slope. The relative price of food in the budget line $q_o^m q_f^{m'}$ is lower than in $q_o^m q_f^m$ since the slope of the former is less than that of the latter.

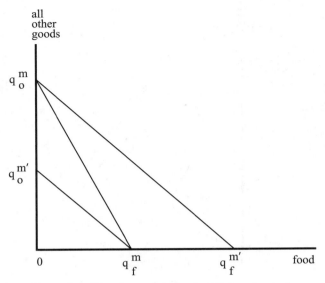

Figure 2.2. The slope of the budget line, $-(p_f/p_o)$.

The slope also represents the market exchange rate between food and "all other goods"; that is, the rate at which "all other goods" must be given in exchange for food. In the above numeric example, $p_f = \$8/\text{unit}$ of food and $p_o = \$4/\text{unit}$ of "all other goods"; therefore, $(p_f/p_o) = 2$, and 2 units of "all other goods" can be exchanged in the marketplace for 1 unit of food. Conversely, 1 unit of food can be exchanged for 2 units of "all other goods." If, however, $p_f = \$4/\text{unit}$ and $p_o = \$4/\text{unit}$, then the household would be able to exchange 1 unit of food for 1 unit of "all other goods" in the marketplace. The slope, therefore, represents the rate at which the household can exchange food for "all other goods" in the marketplace.

Changes in Prices

Take note of another feature of Figure 2.2. The vertical intercepts of two budget lines ($q_o^m q_f^m$ and $q_o^m q_f^{m'}$) are the same, q_o^m. Since the vertical intercept represents Y/p_o, this ratio must be the same for each of the two budget lines (see equation [2.4]). Furthermore, since only the horizontal intercepts of the two budget lines are different and, hence, the slopes differ, the only feature of the two budget lines that differs must be p_f. Consequently, these two budget lines in Figure 2.2 represent the change in a family's budget line if p_f changes, Y and p_o remaining the same. Likewise, budget lines $q_o^m q_f^m$ and $q_o^{m'} q_f^m$ in Figure 2.2 represent the budget lines facing a household before and after a change in p_o family income and the price of food remaining unchanged. A change from $q_o^m q_f^m$ to $q_o^{m'} q_f^m$ in Figure 2.2, thus, represents an increase in the price of "all other goods," Y and p_f held constant, whereas a change from $q_o^{m'} q_f^m$ to $q_o^m q_f^m$ in Figure 2.2 represents a decrease in the price of "all other goods," Y and p_f held constant.

Finally, note that budget line $q_o^m q_f^{m'}$ is longer than line $q_o^m q_f^m$ in Figure 2.2. Recall, also, that the former line represents a situation in which p_f is lower than in the latter, p_o being the same in both circumstances. Each point on $q_o^m q_f^{m'}$ represents a combination of food and "all other goods" available to the consumer if all income is spent. Consequently, the longer the budget line, the more choice afforded the consumer.[3] A drop in the price of food with the price of "all other goods" remaining unchanged, therefore, expands the choices open to consumers; the lower p_f, the more food and "all other goods" purchasable by the household.

Size of Income

The location of the budget line is the distance of the budget line from the origin. Its location represents the quantity of resources available to the family during the time period; that is, its income, Y. The further from the origin, the greater the income; the closer, the more meager the income. This is illustrated in Figure 2.2. The budget line $q_o^{m'} q_f^m$ represents half the family income represented by $q_o^m q_f^{m'}$. This is so because the distances $0 q_o^{m'}$ and $q_o^{m'} q_o^m$ are equal, as are $0 q_f^m$ and $q_f^m q_f^{m'}$, indicating that the family can purchase twice as much food and "all other goods" if its situation is represented by $q_o^m q_f^{m'}$ rather than by $q_o^{m'} q_f^m$.

Notice, also, that the slopes of the two budget lines $q_o^m q_f^{m'}$ and $q_o^{m'} q_f^m$ are equal in Figure 2.2, indicating that the price of food relative to "all other goods" is the same in each case. Consequently, the two budget lines differ only in the size of family income. Indeed, the shift from $q_o^{m'} q_f^m$ to $q_o^m q_f^{m'}$ represents a doubling of income, p_o and p_f being unchanged, because the latter budget line is twice as far from the origin as the former. Again, note that $q_o^m q_f^{m'}$ is much longer than $q_o^{m'} q_f^m$, indicating that a larger income affords more choices to the household than smaller incomes. Such

---

[3] Speaking intuitively. Mathematically, each line has an infinite number of points.

a change in the budget line could also take place if all prices, p_o and p_f, declined by half, with family income, Y, remaining unchanged. This, of course, is the opposite of inflation; that is, deflation.

An algebraic example of the effect of a change in income, with prices remaining unchanged, is if Y changes from \$40 to \$80 in the earlier example. The result of this change is to change the budget line from $q_o = 10 - 2q_f$ to $q_o = 20 - 2q_f$. An example of deflation is when p_f falls from \$8/unit to \$4/unit and p_o falls from \$4/unit to \$2/unit. The resulting budget equation with $Y = \$40$ is $q_o = 40/2 - (4/2)q_f = 20 - 2q_f$, the same as if income had doubled.

The location and slope of the household's budget line, therefore, represent the amount of real resources possessed by the household and relative market prices, respectively. Changes in income, provided prices remain constant, can be represented by parallel shifts in the budget line. Changes in relative prices can be represented by changes in the slope starting from either the vertical or the horizontal intercept, depending on which of the two prices changes.

PREFERENCES

To complete the simple model of the household for the purpose of analyzing its demand behavior, the household's preferences must be represented as well as its budget constraint. The household's preferences reflect its likes and dislikes, and its views as to what will increase and decrease its well-being – its goals, if you will. The inclusion of the household's preferences in our model of household demand behavior is crucial because the household's demands for goods and services are the results of the interaction between its preferences and its possibilities, the latter being represented by the budget constraint.

Economists are much less interested in the details of a household's preferences than with the structure of those preferences. What do we mean by the structure of a household's preferences? By structure we mean whether preferences follow certain logical rules, regardless of what the preferences are or how strongly they are held. If the structure or rules that govern preferences do not differ from household to household, then economists can say quite a lot about household demand and consumption behavior even though the details of households' preferences are likely very different. Let us be more specific.

With respect to any two combinations of goods – for instance, food and "all other goods" – assume that the household can tell us which of the two it prefers or whether it prefers each of the combinations equally. In short, we assume that *households can rank all the possible combinations of food and "all other goods."*

Next, it is assumed that *the household prefers more to less*: more food or more "all other goods" or more of both. You may wish to argue with this assumption, correctly pointing out that a household may prefer less to more of many things. Rather than invalidating the model we are building, we can make a distinction between things that are economic "goods" and those that are economic "bads." Economic "bads" are things that reduce well-being (e.g., garbage) whereas economic "goods" increase well-being. We can redefine economic "bads" to be goods simply by taking their negative. Thus, less garbage is a "good" as are less pollution and less sickness. Consequently, assuming that more is preferred to less is not an unduly restrictive assumption.[4]

The household is also presumed to be consistent in its preferences. If it prefers combination *A* to combination *B*, and combination *B* to combination *C*, then it cannot prefer combination *C* to combination *A*. In mathematical terms, consistent preferences are transitive preferences.

In sum, the structure of household preferences refers to the following three properties that we assume for each household: (1) the household can rank each combination of goods or services, (2) the household prefers more goods to fewer, and (3) the household is consistent in its preference ranking of goods and services.

We can summarize the household's preferences for goods algebraically with a *preference*, or *utility*, function. In particular, the utility function describing its preferences for food and "all other goods" would look like

$$U = U(q_f, q_o) \tag{2.5}$$

where U represents the amount of satisfaction gained from a particular combination of q_f and q_o (see mathematical note 1). The term *amount* need not be taken literally if one doubts that satisfaction or well-being can be measured cardinally. The variable U can merely be taken as a ranking or ordinal measure of the comparative satisfaction derived from combinations of q_f and q_o that the household prefers more and from

---

[4] "Goods" and "bads" have been referred to as economic goods and economic bads to emphasize the restricted meaning of the two terms. All that is meant by an economic good is something for which more is preferred to less. All that is meant by an economic bad is something for which less is preferred to more. No ethical connotations are implied when these terms are used.

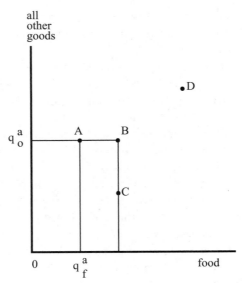

Figure 2.3. The household's preference for combinations A, B, C, and D.

combinations of q_f and q_o that it prefers less.[5] In words, equation (2.5) says that the household's satisfaction or well-being depends on the amount of food and "all other goods" that it purchases and consumes.

The household's utility function and the assumptions about the structure of preferences can be understood more easily and clearly geometrically than algebraically. Consequently, in Figure 2.3 we have again plotted q_o up the vertical axis and q_f along the horizontal axis. Any point within Figure 2.3, then, represents a particular combination of q_o and q_f. Take point A, for instance. It represents q_o^a of "all other goods" and q_f^a of food.

Consider combinations A, B, and C, where B contains the same quantity of q_o as A but more q_f, and it contains the same quantity of q_f as C but more q_o. The assumption that the household prefers more to less simply means that B is preferred to both A and C. Combinations represented by points farther from the origin in the northeasterly direction are always preferred to combinations represented by points closer to the origin in the southwesterly direction. Thus, the household prefers D to A, B, and C; and B to A and C. As yet we have no basis for telling whether it prefers A to C or C to A or likes A and C equally well.

---

[5] See Mansfield (1982), Chapter 3, or Hirshleifer (1976), Chapter 3, for discussions of the history and distinctions between ordinal and cardinal utility.

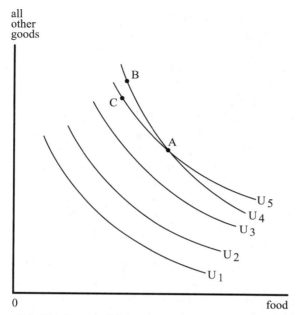

Figure 2.4. The household's preference map: indifference curves.

To tell whether the family prefers A to C or C to A or likes them equally well, we must introduce the geometrical concept of the indifference curve.

Definition: An indifference curve is the locus of points representing all the combinations of goods that the household prefers equally well (see mathematical note 2).

We know that indifference curves must be negatively sloped. Why? If one was positively sloped, of every two combinations joined, one would contain more of both q_f and q_o than the other. But this would violate the assumption that households always prefer more goods to less. Thus, indifference curves cannot be positively sloped. Neither can indifference curves be horizontal or vertical. A glance at Figure 2.3 will confirm this. Combinations B and A cannot be on the same indifference curve since B contains more q_f than A and the same amount of q_o. Consequently, B must be preferred to A. An analogous set of statements can be made about B and C (see mathematical note 3). Therefore, indifference curves have a negative slope.

Figure 2.4 is a household's preference map on which several indifference curves are shown. Each is negatively sloped as argued in the previous section. Recognize that the indifference curves in Figure 2.4 are simply a few of the many that could be drawn. Indeed, one must think of each point in Figure 2.4, each representing a combination of q_o and q_f, as having an indifference curve passing through it.

The assumption that the household prefers more to less means that indifference curves farther from the origin represent greater well-being or utility than those closer to the origin. Consequently, the location of indifference curves represents the extent of the satisfaction obtained by the household: indifference curve U_3 in Figure 2.4 represents more satisfaction than U_2. The household's preference map, therefore, appears more as a "hill of satisfaction," with its foot at the origin and its peak off the page somewhere in a northeasterly direction. Each indifference curve, then, is analogous to an isoaltitude line on a contour map.

Another characteristic of indifference curves is that they cannot intersect one another. Figure 2.4 also makes this clear. Indifference curves U_4 and U_5 intersect in this figure at point A. In this picture A and B are located on U_4, which means that they are equally preferred by the household. Similarly, A and C are on U_5 and are also, therefore, both equally preferred. But B is farther to the northeast than C and, thus, is preferred to C. Because B is as well liked as A and A is as well liked as C, to be consistent, then, B must not be preferred to C. Intersecting indifference curves imply, therefore, that the household simultaneously likes two combinations equally well and also prefers one of them over the other. This is a most inconsistent state of affairs and contrary to the assumptions made earlier.

Thus far it has been established that indifference curves are negatively sloped and do not intersect one another. Furthermore, we have established that their locations (i.e., their distances from the origin) represent levels of satisfaction or well-being. We now must discuss the economic interpretation of their slopes. The indifference curves in Figure 2.4 have all been drawn convex to the origin; this is their usual shape. Not only are indifference curves negatively sloped, almost all are convex to the origin. Two limiting cases (one in which the indifference curve is a downward-sloping straight line and one in which it has the shape of a right angle) will be discussed in a future section. Here we discuss the economic meaning of the convexity of indifference curves.

THE MARGINAL RATE OF SUBSTITUTION

Definition: The slope at any point on an indifference curve represents the rate at which the household is willing to exchange food for "all other

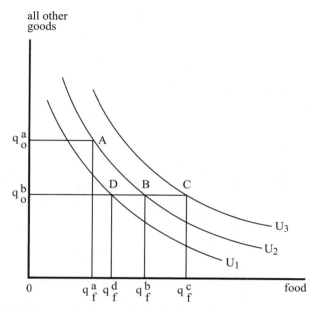

Figure 2.5. The marginal rate of substitution of food for "all other goods."

goods" (or vice versa), holding satisfaction constant. This "preferential" rate of exchange is called the marginal rate of substitution of food for "all other goods" (see mathematical note 4).

Figure 2.5 illustrates the marginal rate of substitution. Begin at point A on the indifference curve and consider whether the household would willingly give up $q_o^a q_o^b$ quantity of "all other goods" in exchange for $q_f^a q_f^d$ additional food. The answer is no because the household would be less well off at point D than at point A, D being on a lower indifference curve than A. Consider again whether the household would willingly give up $q_o^a q_o^b$ in order to get $q_f^a q_f^c$ additional food. The answer is yes. Since C is on a higher indifference curve than A, the exchange would make the household better off. Finally, consider whether the household would exchange $q_o^a q_o^b$ for $q_f^a q_f^b$ added food. The answer is that the family would be indifferent because combination A and combination B provide it with the same level of satisfaction.

Thus, the household would be willing to exchange $q_o^a q_o^b$ "all other goods" for $q_f^a q_f^b$ more food and still be as satisfied as it was before. Now move point B along the indifference curve closer and closer to point A. In the limit, as B approaches A, the ratio of the amounts the household

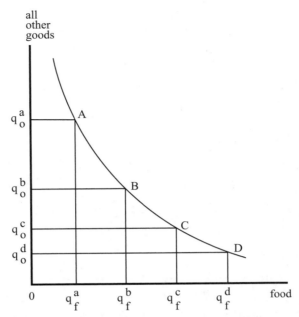

Figure 2.6. The decline in the marginal rate of substitution of food for "all other goods" as more food is substituted for "all other goods."

would be willing to exchange and be equally satisfied equals the slope of the indifference curve at point A. The slope at any point on an indifference curve, therefore, represents the rate at which the household would willingly exchange "all other goods" for food and be as satisfied after as before the exchange.

   Because any indifference curve changes slope throughout its length, the marginal rate of substitution is different at each point along its length. In fact, the marginal rate of substitution declines as the amount of food increases. This is illustrated in Figure 2.6. The figure is constructed so that $q_f^a q_f^b$, $q_f^b q_f^c$, and $q_f^c q_f^d$ are all of equal length, each representing a "unit" of food. Points A, B, C, and D are all on the same indifference curve. Begin at point A and note that the family is willing to give up $q_o^a q_o^b$ units of "all other goods" in order to get an added unit of food, $q_f^a q_f^b$. At B the household is willing to give up $q_o^b q_o^c$ units of "all other goods" in order to get another unit of food, $q_f^b q_f^c$. Note that the quantity of "all other goods" the household is willing to give up at B for an added unit of food was less than at point A. At C it is willing to give up $q_o^c q_o^d$ units of "all other goods" for yet another unit of food, $q_f^c q_f^d$. Again, the quantity of "all other goods" the family is willing to give up for an added unit of food is less at point *C* than at point *B*. Indeed, the smaller the quantity of "all other goods" the family possesses, the less it is willing to give up even more "all other goods" for an added unit of food: the marginal rate of substitution of food for "all other goods" declines.

A declining marginal rate of substitution is a property of indifference curves that are convex to the origin. Declining marginal rates of substitution reflect *relative satiation*. Relative satiation means that the more of something a family possesses relative to other goods, the less of other goods it will give up to acquire even more of the already abundant good. Alternatively, the more of something the family possesses relative to other goods, the more of that good it will be willing to give up in exchange for a good it has less of. Economists believe that the preferences of typical households exhibit relative satiation, and therefore, indifference curves that are convex to the origin are very representative of families in general.[6]

SUBSTITUTES AND COMPLEMENTS

There are two cases of nonconvex indifference curves worth discussing. One is the downward-sloping, *straight-line indifference curve* and the other is the *right-angled indifference curve*. The downward-sloping, straight-line indifference curve is illustrated in Figure 2.7.

Consider the straight-line indifference curve, U_1, first. Indifference curve U_1 exhibits constant marginal rates of substitution throughout its length: regardless of how much good *Y* the household possesses, it is always willing to give up the same amount of it in order to acquire an added unit of good *X*. Reflection on this situation will convince you that such goods must be perfect substitutes for one another. Goods that are substitutes for each other tend to be used by the household for the same purpose. A record player, tape player, and CD player are all substitutes for each other since each can be used to play music. The record player is an inferior substitute for a tape player. Similarly, the tape player is an inferior substitute for a CD player. Two identical CD players, however, are

---

[6] Preferences represented by indifference curves concave to the origin exhibit increasing marginal rates of substitution. Such preferences are pathological, at least if carried to the extreme. They imply that the more one has of a good relative to other things, the more of other things one is willing to give up to acquire even more of the good in question. This is like the mythical King Midas, who sacrificed everything, even his daughter, for more gold: the more gold he got, the more willing he was to give up other things for yet more gold. Typical households do not possess such preferences.

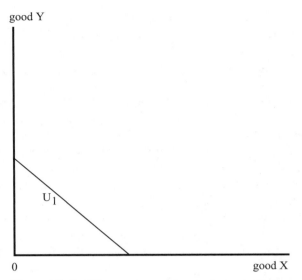

Figure 2.7. Indifference curves for perfect substitutes.

perfect substitutes for each other. The reason is that the household would be willing to give up one for the other at the rate of one for one, and the marginal rate of substitution would remain constant. Another example is regular and extra-strength aspirin tablets. They are perfect substitutes for each other even though the former has 325 mg of aspirin per tablet and the latter has 500 mg per tablet. The marginal rate of substitution of extra-strength for regular aspirin is $325/500 = 0.65$ and is constant. That is, 0.65 of an extra-strength aspirin is a perfect substitute for 1 regular aspirin.

At the other extreme are the right-angled indifference curves: U_2 and U_3 in Figure 2.8. Note that the points of the right-angled indifference curves lie along the straight line, $0AB$, emanating from the origin. Points along this line represent combinations of goods Y and X with the same proportions of Y to X. The family obtains the same satisfaction from $q_y^a q_x^a$ as it does from $q_y^a q_x^b$ (i.e., at C) or from $q_y^b q_x^a$. Adding $q_y^b q_y^a$ of Y to $q_y^a q_x^a$ of Y and X adds no satisfaction. Neither does adding $q_x^b q_x^a$ of X to $q_y^a q_x^a$ of X and Y augment utility. The only way the household is better off is if the quantities of Y and X are increased in the same proportion: $q_y^b q_y^a / q_x^b q_x^a$. Clearly, goods X and Y not only complement each other, they are perfect complements. They are used together for the same purpose. Examples are cereal and milk for those who like milk with their cereal, left and right

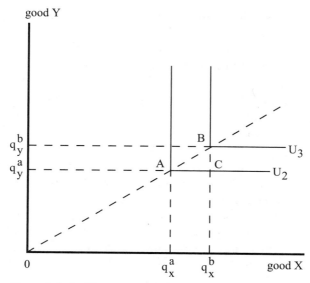

Figure 2.8. Indifference curves for perfect complements.

shoes for those with two feet, and tires and cars if the household wishes the car to provide transportation.

Most goods are neither perfect substitutes nor perfect complements. Consequently, the indifference curves describing the preferences for most goods will be neither downward-sloping straight lines nor right angles. Instead, they will be downward sloping and convex to the origin, representing diminishing marginal rates of substitution. The greater the convexity the indifference curves possess, the less satisfactory are the goods as substitutes for each other; the less convex, the better are the goods as substitutes for each other.

If we are to know the shapes and locations of the indifference curves of any particular household, we must ask the household many detailed questions about its preferences. Our purpose, however, is to explain and predict the economic behavior of households on the average, not the behavior of any particular household. For this limited purpose it is sufficient simply to know that household indifference curves exhibit diminishing marginal rates of substitution. A detailed knowledge of households' preference maps is not necessary.[7]

---

[7] A detailed knowledge of consumer preferences is useful, however, in market research and product development, in which products may be tailored to consumers with particular

We have discussed the household's budget constraint as if it were the only constraint facing the household. Yet, previously, we mentioned legal, technical, and socio-cultural constraints. In this simple model of consumer behavior the socio-cultural norms regarding the use of food and "all other goods" have already been taken into account by the household in forming its preferences. Likewise, it is presumed that the technical constraints governing the use of food and "all other goods" by the household also have been taken into account by the indifference curves of the household. Also, the composite goods (food and "all other goods") do not include any illegal commodities, such as cocaine or marijuana. In short, we presume that the legal, technical, and socio-cultural constraints upon the household's behavior have already been taken into account and have affected the shapes and slopes of the indifference curves. These constraints can be dealt with separately in more complex models, as we will see subsequently. But in this simple beginning model, they have been built into household preferences.

PUTTING THE PARTS TOGETHER: CONSUMER EQUILIBRIUM

The budget constraint, equation (2.1), and the utility function, equation (2.5), constitute two of the three elements of the algebraic model of the consumer aspects of a household. Likewise, the budget line and the indifference curves constitute two of the three geometric elements of the same model. It is left to put them together. This is done with the third element of the model, a *behavioral assumption*, or *hypothesis*. The hypothesis has been mentioned previously (it is, indeed, the major economic hypothesis about the way households behave): in any period of time households attempt to maximize satisfaction or well-being, subject to the resource, legal, technical, and socio-cultural constraints on their behavior. Simply stated, among the choices open to it, the household will choose the alternative that most furthers its goals. That is, among all the possible combinations of goods available to the household, it will choose the combination that makes it better off or more satisfied than any other combination. As was pointed out in Chapter 1, such behavior is part and parcel of being goal directed, the behavioral assumption shared by all the social sciences.

preferences or advertising campaigns may be directed to consumers with particular tastes. Such detailed knowledge of consumer preferences is sought by marketing managers and consumer psychologists. The knowledge is obtained through extremely detailed questionnaires filled out by sample consumers.

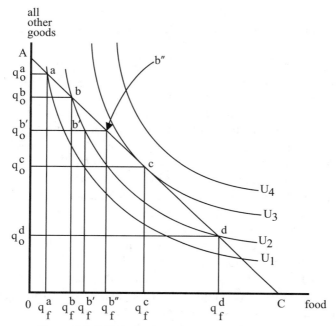

Figure 2.9. Maximization of satisfaction at point *c*.

The satisfaction-maximizing combination of food and "all other goods" can be found by putting the household's indifference curves together in the same figure as its budget constraint. Obviously, the satisfaction-maximizing combination of "all other goods" and food will be somewhere on the budget line. The fact that households prefer more to less ensures that there are combinations on the budget line the family prefers to any given point to the southwest of the budget line. Combinations to the northeast of the budget line are unattainable given the household's income and the market prices of food and "all other goods." The combination that maximizes satisfaction, therefore, will be represented by the point on the budget line that rests on the highest indifference curve touching the budget line. The purchase and consumption of no other combination of food and "all other goods" will bring the household as much satisfaction.

These points are illustrated in Figure 2.9, in which a household's indifference curves have been superimposed over its budget line. Which combination of food and "all other goods" will maximize this household's satisfaction? The question may be approached by supposing the household initially is at point *a* at the intersection of AC and U_1. Suppose the household experiments with other combinations of food and "all other goods" by trying combinations with less food and more "all other goods" than at point a. By doing so it will reach increasingly lower indifference curves, signifying that it gets increasingly less satisfaction from such substitutions. Consequently, it will at least return to the combination of food and "all other goods" represented by point a.

Now suppose it experiments in the opposite direction, choosing instead combinations along the budget line to the right of point a. For example, say it moves to point b, where it consumes q_o^b of "all other goods" and q_f^b of food. Because point b is on U_2 and point a is on U_1, the household will be more satisfied with combination b than with combination a.

Given that the household increased its satisfaction (i.e., came closer to achieving its goals) by substituting food for "all other goods," assume that it continues to experiment by increasing its purchases of food at the expense of "all other goods," moving to point c on the budget line. Again, it is more satisfied at c than it was at b.

If it again tries to substitute more food for "all other goods" and moves to, for instance, point d, it finds that it has moved to a combination of food and "all other goods" that is not as satisfying as the combination at point c. Inspection of Figure 2.9 reveals that no point between d and c or between b and c will yield as much satisfaction as the combination at point c – all of them except c being on indifference curves inferior to U_3. The combination of food and "all other goods" represented by point c is unique: of those attainable by the household, no other point makes the household as satisfied. The combination represented by point c, therefore, is the combination that maximizes the household's satisfaction and will be the combination chosen by the household. Geometrically, point c is the *point of tangency* between the budget line and the highest attainable indifference curve, U_3. At point c the household's marginal rate of substitution of food for "all other goods" (represented by the slope of U_3 at point c) equals the rate at which food and "all other goods" exchange for each other in the marketplace (represented by the slope of the budget line). Recall that the marginal rate of substitution is the rate at which the household is willing to exchange "all other goods" for food. Recall also that the exchange rate between food and "all other goods" in the marketplace represents the rate at which the household is able to exchange "all other goods" for food. At point c, then, the rate at which the household is willing to exchange "all other goods" for food equals the rate at which it is able to exchange these two goods. At point c and at no other point are these two rates equal.

If the rate at which the household is willing to exchange and the rate at which it is able to exchange goods are not equal, then the household is not maximizing satisfaction and could be "doing better" at some other point. If the rate at which it is willing to substitute food for "all other goods" is greater than the rate at which it is able to in the marketplace, then surely it pays the household in terms of satisfaction to substitute food for "all other goods." This is so because the rate at which a family is willing to exchange "all other goods" for food is the maximum price that it is willing to pay for more food, whereas the rate at which it is able to exchange "all other goods" for food is the market price for food. If the price it is willing to pay for food is greater than the market price of food, food can be said to be "a good buy" and the household will increase its satisfaction by buying more food and less "all other goods."

This idea is represented in Figure 2.9 by the fact that at points a and b (and at any point on the budget line northwest of point c) the slopes of the indifference curves are greater than the slopes of the budget line. Look at point b in particular. By substituting $q_f^b q_f^{b'}$ of food for $q_o^b q_o^{b'}$, it can remain as satisfied as it was before. But by exchanging the same quantity of "all other goods," $q_o^b q_o^{b'}$, for food in the marketplace, it can get $q_f^b q_f^{b''}$ food, $q_f^{b'} q_f^{b''}$ more food than the $q_f^b q_f^{b'}$ it would be willing to take. At point b, therefore, food is priced more cheaply than it is worth to the household, and the household will increase its satisfaction by purchasing more food and less of "all other goods." The opposite situation exists at point d (and all other points on the budget line to the southeast of point c).

When the household purchases and consumes the combinations of goods and services that maximize its satisfaction (i.e., allows it most nearly to achieve its goals), the household is said to be in equilibrium.

Definition: A household is in equilibrium when it has no incentive to change its purchase pattern.

Clearly, this is the case at point c because to change its purchase pattern and move to any other point would lead to a reduction in its satisfaction. The household will continue its purchase pattern of q_o^c of "all other goods" and q_f^c of food per period so long as the market price of food in terms of "all other goods" remains equal to the price of food in terms of "all other goods" that it is willing to pay. These two prices will remain equal so long as its preferences, its income, and market prices remain unchanged.

There is another useful way to interpret equilibrium. At point c

$$MU_f/p_f = MU_o/p_o \qquad (2.6)$$

(see mathematical note 5). In equation (2.6) MU_f represents the *marginal utility of food* and MU_o denotes the *marginal utility of "all other goods."*

Definition: The marginal utility of any good is the added utility that a household can obtain from purchasing and consuming an added unit of the good, holding the consumption of "all other goods" constant.

Thus, the marginal utility of food is the added satisfaction the household can obtain from purchasing an added unit of food, holding the consumption of "all other goods" constant.

What, then, does equation (2.6) say? The ratio of the marginal utility of a good to its price is the marginal utility of an added dollar spent on that good. Equation (2.6) can be read, then, as follows: in equilibrium an added dollar spent by the household on any good (in this case, on food or on "all other goods") must yield the same added satisfaction. On reflection this must be so because consider, instead, a situation in which

$$MU_f/p_f > MU_o/p_o; \qquad (2.7)$$

that is, an added dollar spent on food yields more satisfaction than an added dollar spent on "all other goods." Then the household would be more satisfied if it shifted its purchase pattern by spending a dollar less on "all other goods" and by spending it instead on more food. If that were the case, the household would have the incentive to do so and, consequently, cannot be said to be in equilibrium. Equilibrium, recall, is when the household has no incentive to alter its purchase pattern in any way.

Figure 2.9 illustrates a kind of equilibrium in which the household demands some food and some of "all other goods." This kind of equilibrium is called an *interior solution* because equilibrium occurs somewhere on the budget line rather than at either end. Another kind of equilibrium exists in circumstances in which the household demands none of the good being analyzed. This kind of equilibrium is called a *corner solution*. When this occurs, the marginal rate of substitution is less than the market rate of exchange between the good being analyzed and "all other goods."

Figure 2.10 illustrates a corner solution equilibrium. Suppose we are interested in the household's demand for a global positioning system (GPS). Some people own GPSs and some don't. Figure 2.10 has the quantity of GPSs, q_g, plotted on the horizontal axis and "all other goods" plotted on the vertical axis. Line AC is a particular household's budget line. The slope of AC is the ratio of the price of GPSs to the price of "all other goods," p_g/p_o. U_0, U_1, and U_2 are three of the household's indifference

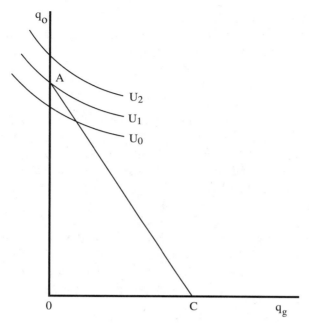

Figure 2.10. A corner solution.

curves representing its preferences for GPSs and "all other goods." Given the household's budget line, the highest indifference curve it can reach is at point A, representing the situation in which the household spends all its income on "all other goods" and does not buy a GPS. Point A is the point of maximum satisfaction. It is an equilibrium position because no other point on AC would be more satisfying to the household, and therefore, the household has no incentive to move from point A. However, note that at point A, equation (2.6) does not hold. Instead,

$$MU_g / MU_o < p_g / p_o \qquad (2.8)$$

holds (see mathematical note 6).

At point A the slope of the indifference curve U, is less than the slope of the budget line. This represents the fact that the price the household is willing to pay for one GPS (in terms of the quantity of "all other goods" it would be willing to give up to get a GPS and be as satisfied as it was before) is less than the market price of a GPS. Consequently, although it is able to buy a GPS, it is not willing to do so. Its demand for a GPS is zero and the household is in equilibrium. All households that do not purchase particular goods are at corner solutions, with respect to those goods. Because all households do not buy all goods in any given year, all households are at corner solutions, with respect to some goods, all the time. Corner solutions, therefore, are ubiquitous.[8]

SUMMARY

If the economist knew the family's preference map to be as pictured by the indifference curves in Figure 2.9, and if the economist knew that the household's income in conjunction with the market prices of food and "all other goods" would result in a budget line as pictured in Figure 2.9, then the economist would predict that the family's purchase pattern was q_o^c of "all other goods" and q_f^c of food. If that were not the family's purchase pattern, the economist would predict that it soon would be, because the family would be in *disequilibrium* and would have the incentive to change it to q_f^c of food and q_o^c of "all other goods." Figure 2.9 (or Figure 2.10), consequently, answers the first of two major questions asked by the economist:

(1) What is the household's purchase pattern?
(2) How would it change if other things change?

The first question is often phrased a little differently and is focused on the particular good under study, in this case food. The alternative way of asking the first question is:

(1) What is the household's demand for food?

The answer provided by Figure 2.9 is:

The quantity of food demanded by the household is q_f^c, given its income is Y and the market prices of food and "all other goods" are p_f and p_o, respectively.

The answer to the analogous question about the demand for a GPS provided by Figure 2.10 is:

---

[8] There are also cases of corner solutions that do not occur at one of the axes and result in a nonzero demand by the household for a particular good. They occur when the budget line is not straight but, instead, "kinked." Kinked budget lines arise for several reasons, one of which is "quantity discount pricing." In such circumstances, the consumer may maximize satisfaction at the kink, where the highest attainable indifference curve intersects the budget line at the kink. In such situations equation (2.6) will not hold. See Chapter 3, where such situations are analyzed.

The number of GPSs demanded by the household is zero, given its income and the market prices of GPSs and "all other goods" represented by the budget line *AC*.

These answers, however, pertain to a particular household given a knowledge of its preferences, its income, and market prices. Economists don't often know enough about a particular family's preferences to be able to make such a prediction. Of what use is the model then? The usefulness comes in the ability to predict the economic behavior, not of the individual household, but rather of the representative or average household. And more important, the usefulness comes in the ability to predict whether the average household will increase or decrease its purchases of food, GPSs, or other goods or activities being analyzed in response to changes in prices, incomes, or preferences via changes in the technical, legal, or socio-cultural constraints facing households. Typically, it is sufficient to know far less about preferences to explain the behavior of the representative household than is required to explain the behavior of any particular household. We elaborate on this model and draw out further implications in Chapter 3.

Mathematical Notes

1. Equation (2.5), $U = U(q_f, q_o)$, is general and represents a very wide class of algebraic forms. Each household's preferences can be represented by a specific algebraic version of equation (2.5). In order to do empirical research on household behavior, economists frequently assume that similar households share the same utility function. This is analogous to the sociologist's assumption that people in the same social class share the same values. One specific functional form for the utility function is

$$U = a_f(lnq_f - b_f) + a_o(lnq_o - b_o) \qquad (1)$$

   where $a_f + a_o = 1$, $a_i > 0$ ($i = o, f$), and $b_i \geq 0$. The b_i's are interpreted as the subsistence levels of food and other things. This functional form is called a Stone-Geary function after the economists who first used it. From it is derived the Linear Expenditures System, a system of demand equations widely used in empirical research. See Deaton and Muellbauer (1981).

2. Algebraically, the indifference curve can be formed in the following fashion. Set the satisfaction level, U, equal to a constant, say U_c, and substitute U_c for U in equation (2.5). Then the function

$$U_c = U(q_f, q_o) \qquad (2)$$

   is the equation for an indifference curve because it gives all the combinations of q_o and q_f that yield the same level, U_c, of satisfaction.

3. What a horizontal (vertical) indifference curve really means is that the good measured along the horizontal (vertical) axis does not affect the hosuehold's well-being at all; that is,

$$\partial U/\partial q_x = MU_x = 0 \tag{3}$$

where q_x is the good measured along the horizontal (vertical) axis. If someone says about a particular good, for instance, cherries, "I can take them or leave them," the person is saying that cherries don't affect his or her well-being at all.

4. The slope of the indifference curve can be found in the following fashion. Take the total differential of the indifference equation (2):

$$dU_c = (\partial u/\partial q_o)dq_o + (\partial u/\partial q_f)dq_f. \tag{4}$$

Now, set dU_c equal to 0 (because movement along the indifference curve keeps the level of utility constant) and solve for dq_o/dq_f to get

$$dq_o/dq_f = -(\partial u/\partial q_f)/(\partial u/\partial q_o) = -(MU_f/MU_o). \tag{5}$$

Equation 5 is the equation for the marginal rate of substitution of food for "all other goods," where MU_f and MU_o are marginal utilities of food and "all other goods," respectively.

5. The calculus of maximizing satisfaction is as follows. Mathematically, maximizing satisfaction amounts to finding values of q_o and q_f for which the utility function $U = U(q_f, q_o)$ is a maximum subject to the budget constraint

$$p_o q_o + p_f q_f = Y. \tag{6}$$

   The budget constraint can be solved for q_o (see equation [2.4]) and inserted into the utility function to get

$$U = u([Y/p_o) - (p_f/p_o)q_f], q_f). \tag{7}$$

The utility function is now a function of q_f only (Y, p_f, and p_o being considered constants).

   To maximize utility it remains to differentiate U with respect to q_f, set the derivative equal to 0, and solve the resulting equation for the value of q_f. The resulting equation, called a first-order condition, is

$$\partial u/\partial q_f - (\partial u/\partial q_o)[-(p_f/p_o)] = 0 \tag{8}$$

or

$$(\partial u/\partial q_f)/(\partial u/\partial q_o) = -(p_f/p_o). \tag{9}$$

In these equations $\partial u/\partial q_f$ is interpreted as the marginal utility of food, MU_f, and $\partial u/\partial q_o$ is interpreted as the marginal utility of "all other goods," MU_o. The ratio of these two marginal utilities is clearly the marginal rate of substitution of food for "all other goods" (equation [5]). Thus, this equation says no more than is said by the tangency between the highest attainable indifference curve and the budget line. Both specify the equilibrium combination of food and "all other goods" given household income and market prices for the two goods.

Equation (8) can be rephrased in still another useful way:

$$MU_f/p_f = MU_o/p_o. \tag{10}$$

This is the form of the equation interpreted in the text.

6. The calculus of the corner solution is as follows. The consumer maximizes $U = u(q_g, q_o)$ subject to the budget constraint $p_g q_g + p_o q_o = Y$ and the provisos $q_o \geq 0$ and $q_g \geq 0$. Form the Lagrangean expression

$$L = u(q_g, q_o) - \lambda_y(p_g q_g + p_o q_o - Y) + \lambda_o(q_o \geq 0) + \lambda_g(q_g \geq 0) \tag{11}$$

where $\lambda_i = 0$ if $q_i > 0$ $(i = o, g)$, otherwise $\lambda_i > 0$; and $\lambda_y > 0$ when $p_g q_g + p_o q_o - Y = 0$, otherwise $\lambda_y = 0$. L is a function of $q_o, q_g, \lambda_y, \lambda_o,$ and λ_g. To find the maximum of L and hence maximum satisfaction differentiate L successively by $q_o, q_g, \lambda_y, \lambda_o,$ and λ_g, setting each partial derivative to 0 yields

$$u_o - \lambda_y p_o + \lambda_o = 0 \tag{12}$$
$$u_g - \lambda_y p_g + \lambda_g = 0 \tag{13}$$
$$-p_o q_o - p_g q_g + Y = 0 \tag{14}$$
$$q_o \geq 0 \tag{15}$$
$$q_g \geq 0. \tag{16}$$

If $q_g = 0$ and $q_o > 0$, then equations (12) and (13) become

$$u_o - \lambda_y p_o = 0 \tag{17}$$

and

$$u_g - \lambda_y p_g + \lambda_g = 0. \tag{18}$$

Solving equations (17) and (18) each for λ_y and equating yields

$$(u_g + \lambda_g)/p_g = u_o/p_o \tag{19}$$

or

$$(u_g + \lambda_g)/u_o = p_g/p_o. \tag{20}$$

Because $q_g = 0$, $\lambda_g > 0$ and

$$u_g/u_o < p_g/p_o; \tag{21}$$

that is, the price the household is willing to pay for a GPS, u_g/u_o, is less than the market price, p_g/p_o, and therefore no GPS will be purchased.

The price at which the household is indifferent to buying or not buying a good (GPSs in this case), $u_g/u_o|_{q_g=0}$, is called the household's reservation price for the good. Retailers must charge prices somewhat lower than households' reservation prices for goods in order to induce them to buy.

THREE

The Analysis of Consumer Demand

INTRODUCTION

This chapter deals with the analysis of consumer demand. The model of the household developed in Chapter 2 is used to examine the effects of several types of changes in the economic environment on the household's demand for a good. The discussion is suggestive rather than exhaustive, with the possibilities for analysis and application being very large. Beginning with an analysis of income effects, the chapter progresses to a discussion of price effects and then to analyses of several applications depicting several different price schemes with which consumers are commonly faced. Finally, the effects of preferences on demand are discussed.

The discussion is couched in terms of hypothetical experiments. The model of the household is observed in equilibrium given an initial set of conditions (e.g., income, prices, and preferences). Then a change in one of these conditions (e.g., income) is introduced and the model altered to include the change. The model's new equilibrium is found and compared with the initial equilibrium. The comparison of the prechange and postchange equilibria leads to conclusions about how the change affected the equilibrium combinations of goods demanded by the modeled household. The conclusions become hypotheses as to how typical households' demands for the good in question would change given a change in the factor (e.g., income, price) being analyzed. Finally, the findings from a few empirical economic studies are reported to give the flavor of the actual demand behavior of households in response to the changes in the conditions discussed. This type of analysis is called comparative statics and is the analytical technique used throughout the chapter.

Before beginning the analysis it is useful to get an intuitive notion of the dimensions of consumer demand in the United States. Table 3.1 provides a picture for 2002. This table shows mean income before taxes in 2002. Table 3.1 also shows, on average, how Americans spent their before-tax income in 2002 and how expenditure patterns vary by income quintile.

The focus of this chapter is the analysis of the demands for consumption goods and services. Consumption goods and services are often broken down into the categories included in Table 3.1. As of 2002, on average 27.27 percent of before-tax income was spent on shelter, utilities, household operations, and household furnishings, 11.35 percent on food (both at home and away from home), 16.15 percent on transportation, 4.88 percent on health care, 4.38 percent on entertainment, 3.79 percent on clothing, and smaller amounts on personal care, recreation, private education and reading, and insurance.

If we focus on expenditures by income quintiles in Table 3.1, we see that consumption varies considerably by income level. For instance, households in the highest income quintile spend twice as much on food at home and four times as much on food away from home as do households in the lowest income quintiles. Indeed, in Table 3.1, expenditures on virtually all categories of consumption increase as income increases.

Goods and services can also be classified into the three categories of durables, nondurables, and services. According to the U.S. Department of Commerce, durables are goods with storage lives of over three years (Seskin and Parker 1998). Examples are cars, car parts, furniture, and appliances. Nondurables are goods with storage or inventory lives of less than three years (e.g., food, clothing and shoes, and gasoline and oil). Services are commodities that cannot be stored and this category includes the rental value of owner-occupied housing, house rents, household operation expenses (e.g., electricity and domestic services), financial services (e.g., banking and insurance), transportation, health care, recreation, and private education. From 1990 to 2002, *real* expenditures on durables per household rose 22 percent, while expenditures on nondurables per household rose 5.3 percent, and expenditures on services per household rose 31 percent (U.S. Bureau of Economic Analysis 2004). Relatively speaking, Americans increased their consumption of services and durables more than they did nondurables over the course of the 1990s.

Clearly, American consumption patterns vary both in the cross-section and over time. What factors could be responsible for these consumption differences? In the remainder of this chapter, we will demonstrate how the economic model of consumer demand can help us answer this question.

Table 3.1. *Average Consumer Expenditures and Expenditures by Income Quintile for U.S.: 2002*

	Average Expenditures in 2002 (All Consumer Units)	Expenditures as a Percent of Before-Tax Income, 2002 (All Consumer Units)	Expenditures by Income Quintile, 2002				
			Lowest 20%	Second 20%	Third 20%	Fourth 20%	Highest 20%
Income before taxes	$49,430		$8316	$21,162	$36,989	$59,177	$121,367
Food at home	$3217	6.50%	$2144	$2677	$3073	$3660	$4528
Food away from home	$2395	4.85%	$1042	$1464	$1998	$2914	$4554
Alcoholic beverages and tobacco	$749	1.51%	$410	$565	$779	$4875	$1113
Shelter	$7854	15.89%	$3891	$5161	$6771	$8743	$14,690
Utilities	$2683	5.43%	$1661	$2209	$2585	$3106	$3851
Household operations and supplies	$1342	2.71%	$543	$843	$1111	$1697	$2515
Household furnishings and equipment	$1602	3.24%	$544	$904	$1277	$1795	$3484
Apparel and services	$1872	3.79%	$953	$1168	$1526	$2094	$3617
Transportation	$7984	16.15%	$3285	$5013	$7472	$10,369	$13,769
Health care	$2410	4.88%	$1402	$2183	$2506	$2692	$3262
Entertainment	$2167	4.38%	$813	$1103	$1644	$2659	$4608
Personal care products and services	$562	1.14%	$306	$417	$493	$644	$947
Reading and education	$916	1.85%	$732	$461	$557	$830	$2000
Cash contributions	$1366	2.76%	$449	$862	$1121	$1558	$2834
Life and other personal insurance	$425	0.86%	$159	$243	$340	$477	$903
Misc.	$846	1.71%	$373	$625	$756	$1020	$1456

Sources: U.S. Bureau of the Census (2004-2005); U.S. Bureau of Labor Statistics (2004a). Table excludes interest paid on consumer loans, contributions to pension plans and social security, and savings.

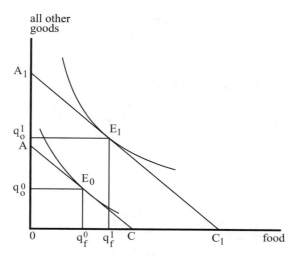

Figure 3.1. The effect of an increase in income on the family's purchase pattern.

INCOME EFFECTS

We begin our discussion with the model of the household developed in Chapter 2, which focused on the household's food demand and consumption behavior. Because of the focus on food, all other goods demanded by the household were collapsed into one composite good called "all other goods."[1] This example will be used again.

In Figure 3.1 the typical household is represented by its indifference curves and its budget line, which considers its annual cash income, Y_0, and the market prices for food and "all other goods," p_f^0 and p_o^0, respectively. Its initial equilibrium is at E_0. At E_0 it purchases q_f^0 amount of food and q_o^0 amount of "all other goods" per year. In so doing, it is as well off as it can be given its income and market prices.

Suppose, now, that the household experiences an increase in income from Y_0, to Y_1 per year. This increase in income causes the budget line to change from

$$q_o = (Y_0/p_o^0) - (p_f^0/p_o^0) q_f \qquad (3.1)$$

to

$$q_o = (Y_1/p_o^0) - (p_f^0/p_o^0) q_f. \qquad (3.2)$$

---

[1] In order to collapse all goods except one (in this case food) into one composite good, we must assume that the prices of all the goods that are part of "all other goods" change proportionately. This requirement is demonstrated by the Hicks' Composite Good Theorem. (See mathematical note 1.)

Note that the only difference between the two equations is in the intercept: before the change it was (Y_0/p_o^0); after the change it is (Y_1/p_o^0), the latter intercept being bigger. The slopes of the two budget lines, $-(p_f^0/p_o^0)$, are the same.

This change is represented in Figure 3.1 by the shift in the budget line from AC to A_1C_1. Faced with the expansion of its opportunities, the household responds by choosing to purchase and consume more of both food and "all other goods." Given the higher income, the family reaches its new equilibrium at E_1, purchasing and consuming q_f^1 amount of food and q_o^1 amount of "all other goods." The effect of the change in income, $Y_1 - Y_0$, on the annual demand for food has been an increase of $q_f^1 - q_f^0$ units. Likewise, the effect of the increase in income on the demand for "all other goods" has been an increase of $q_o^1 - q_o^0$ units (see mathematical note 2).

It is important to note that because income is the only element of the household's environment that changed, the changes in the demands for food and for "all other goods" are solely attributable to the change in income. In particular, note that the household's preferences did not change, because the shape and location of the indifference curves remained unchanged. All that the increase in income did was to expand the family's consumption opportunities. Given the expanded opportunities, the household took advantage of them for its own betterment, reestablishing equilibrium at E_1.[2]

Both preferences and market prices can modify the effects of income on demand. One would expect that a \$100 increase in income would affect a family's demand for food differently if food were cheap relative to "all other goods" than if it were expensive. If food were relatively cheap, then the budget lines facing families would be relatively flat (compared with the slopes of budget lines if food were relatively expensive). Being flat, food would tend to bulk large in the equilibrium purchase patterns of typical families. Given the concept of relative satiety (i.e., diminishing marginal

---

[2] The assertion that changes in income alter household consumption alternatives but do not change their preferences is different from the hypothesis typically made in sociology and anthropology. To sociologists and anthropologists income represents an important component of "social class." As such, an increase in income not only expands the alternatives open to the household, it also tends to put the household into the next higher social class. Once in the new social class, the household's consumption preferences are altered; the household tends to adopt the preferences of the new class and cast off the preferences of the old class. The hypothesis of "stable preferences," then, marks an important difference between economics on the one hand and sociology and anthropology on the other. Note that to test the hypothesis of changing preferences it is necessary to know the households' preferences to observe whether they change in the face of changes in income. Furthermore, the change in income must be large enough to ensure that the household enters the next higher "social class," as operationally defined by sociology.

rates of substitution of food for other things), an increase in income might affect the demand for food less than if food were relatively expensive.

Likewise, even though the "average" family may increase its demand for food by X amount in the face of a $100 increase in annual income, the response of individual families, all with Y_0, initially and all experiencing a $100 increase in annual income, can be expected to vary because each family's preferences differ in major or minor ways from that of others.

Figure 3.1 depicts a situation in which an increase in income has increased the demands for both food and "all other goods." However, if the family had begun with Y_1 income and then experienced a decline in income to Y_0, then Figure 3.1 also shows that its demand for food will decline from q_f^1 to q_f^0. Thus, the income effect is positive: an increase in income increases food demand whereas a decline in income occasions a decline in the demand for food.

Definition: If the demand for a good increases as income increases and decreases as income decreases, prices and preferences held constant, then the good is called a normal good.

Figure 3.2 illustrates a case in which the demand for good X declines as income increases. In Figure 3.2 the family's preferences are such that as income rises, expanding its consumption alternatives from AC to A_1C_1, the demand for good X actually declines; the income effect on its demand is

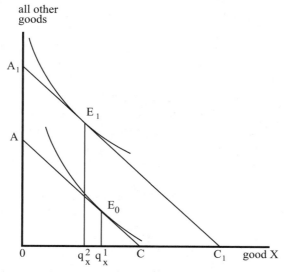

Figure 3.2. Budget lines and indifference curves for an inferior good.

negative: as income increases, demand for X falls. Carbohydrate-rich food products are examples of inferior goods. As income increases, holding prices constant, we know that people demand more protein in their diets and less carbohydrates (Adrian and Daniel 1976). Protein is, therefore, a normal good. Goods like carbohydrates, however, with negative income effects are called inferior goods.

Definition: If the demand for a good decreases as income increases and increases when income decreases, prices and preferences held constant, then the good is called an inferior good.

Engel Curves

Usually, the analyst is particularly interested in the relationship between the demand for a specific good and income. The Engel curve is a simple representation of this relationship.

Definition: An Engel curve is the locus of all points representing the quantities demanded of the good at various levels of income, with prices and preferences held constant.

Figure 3.3 illustrates an Engel curve for food and shows how it is derived from the indifference curve diagram. Panel A of Figure 3.3 is an indifference curve diagram representing the equilibrium purchase patterns of a family at two levels of income, Y_0 and Y_1, holding the family's preferences and relative prices constant.

In panel B is a diagram with income, Y, on the vertical axis and the quantity of food demanded, q_f, on the horizontal axis. Panels A and B are aligned so that the quantities of food demanded in the equilibrium purchase patterns in the upper panel can be projected down to the lower panel. The incomes, Y_0, and Y_1, are represented by the budget lines, AC and A_1C_1, respectively. F_0F_1 is the Engel curve. Theoretically, Engel curves begin at the origin or intersect the income axis. With zero income, the quantity demanded must be zero since the household can afford no purchases.[3] At very low incomes, however, the demand for particular goods may also be zero.[4]

---

[3] This point illustrates the difference between demand and need. Demand is defined as the quantity of a good the household is willing and able to purchase and consume, whereas the concept of need is independent of the ability to purchase. Certainly a household needs both food and "all other goods" to survive and prosper. But with no income, it has no demand because it is unable to make any purchases.

[4] Recall Figure 2.9, which depicted a corner solution in which the household maximized satisfaction by demanding no GPSs and devoting all its income to the purchase of "all other goods."

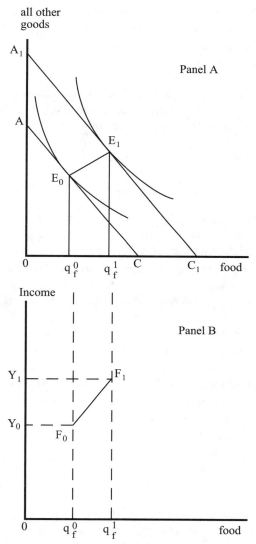

Figure 3.3. Deriving the Engel curve.

The Income Elasticity of Demand

We have just shown that the responses of a household to changes in its income vary across goods. In some instances, the household responds to an increase in its income with a large increase in the quantities demanded. In other instances, the response in quantities demanded is quite small. The magnitude of the response in demand to changes in income is frequently measured by the income elasticity of demand. Since the income elasticity is measured in percentage terms, the response in demand for one good to changes in income can be compared with the responses in the demand for others.

Definition: The income elasticity of demand for a good is the percentage change in the quantity demanded due to a 1 percent change in income, with preferences and relative prices constant.

In general, the formula is

$$N_x = (\Delta q_x/q_x)\,100/(\Delta Y/Y)\,100 = (\Delta q_x/\Delta Y)(Y/q_x) \qquad (3.3)$$

where Δq_x is the change in the quantity demanded of good X due to the change in income, ΔY is the change in income, and q_x and Y are the pre-change values of the quantity of X demanded and income, respectively.

There are two computing formulas for the income elasticity: the point and the arc income elasticity. The former formula is used to compute the income elasticity at a specific point on an Engel curve, and the latter is used when the change in income is large. The differences between point and arc elasticities can be more easily understood when discussed in terms of a diagram. Figure 3.4 illustrates the Engel curve $0E$ for good X. Consider the income elasticity at point A, where the household demands q_x^a amount of good X when its income is Y_a. The slope of the Engel curve at point A represents the change in income, ΔY, divided by the change in q_x, Δq_x; that is, $\Delta Y/\Delta q_x$. It can be found by taking the slope of the tangent to the Engel curve at A. Straight line $d_a AA'$ is the tangent to $0E$ at point A. Suppose the equation for the tangent is

$$Y = d_a + n_a q_x; \qquad (3.4)$$

d_a is the vertical intercept of $d_a AA'$ and n_a is the slope, $\Delta Y/\Delta q_x$, at A. Now, draw a straight line from point A to the origin; that is $0A$. It has slope Y_a/q_x^a. The point income elasticity of demand for X at point A can then be phrased in terms of the slopes of these two lines:

$$N_x^a = \frac{\text{slope of the straight line from A to the origin}}{\text{slope of the tangent to the Engel curve at A}} \qquad (3.5)$$

or

$$N_x^a = (Y_a/q_x^a)/n_a = (Y_a/q_x^a)/(\Delta Y/\Delta q_x) = (\Delta q_x/\Delta Y)(Y_a/q_x^a). \qquad (3.6)$$

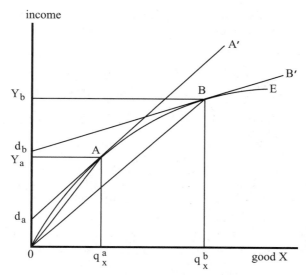

Figure 3.4. The income elasticity of demand for X derived from the Engel curve for X.

Likewise, the point income elasticity of demand for X at point B is

$$N_x^b = (Y_b/q_x^b)/n_b = (Y_b/q_x^b)/(\Delta Y/\Delta q_x) = (\Delta q_x/\Delta Y)(Y_b/q_x^b) \quad (3.7)$$

where n_b is the slope of $d_b BB'$, which is tangent to the Engel curve at B and Y_b/q_x^b is the slope of $0B$.

Suppose, instead, one does not know the Engel curve for X but only has the following facts: when income is Y_a, the quantity of X demanded is q_x^a, and when income is Y_b, the quantity of X demanded is q_x^b. In other words, there is no knowledge of the slope of the Engel curve either at point A or at point B. The income elasticity can still be computed but it will be an approximation. There are three approximation formulas: one at point A, one at point B, and one at the average of the two points, at income $(Y_a + Y_b)/2$ and quantity $(q_x^a + q_x^b)/2$.

The approximate measure of the point elasticity of demand at point A is

$$N_x^a = [(q_x^b - q_x^a)/(Y_b - Y_a)](Y_a/q_x^a).$$

Likewise, the approximate measure of the point income elasticity at point B is

$$N_x^b = [(q_x^b - q_x^a)/(Y_b - Y_a)](Y_b/q_x^b).$$

The approximation made at the average of the two points is called an arc elasticity (the arc between points A and B). To compute it, take the change in quantity as $q_x^b - q_x^a$ and the income change as $Y_b - Y_a$. The arc income elasticity formula is

$$N_x = \left[(q_x^b - q_x^a) / (Y_b - Y_a) \right] \left[(Y_a + Y_b) / (q_x^a + q_x^b) \right]. \qquad (3.8)$$

The arc elasticity will lie between the point elasticities at A and B.

An Example

An example of the use of these formulas is as follows. Suppose that with an income over the school year of $10,500 after tuition and fees are paid, Doug purchases ten books per school year. After his school-year income rose to $11,000 per school year, he purchased twelve books per year. His income elasticity of demand for books at the lower income was

$$N_b^l = [(12 - 10)/(11{,}000 - 10{,}500)](10{,}500/10) = 4.20.$$

This means that when his income rose by 1 percent, he increased his demand for books by 4.2 percent. His income elasticity of demand for books at the higher income is

$$N_b^h = [(12 - 10)/(11{,}000 - 10{,}500)](11{,}000/12) = 3.67.$$

This means that when his income rose by 1 percent, he increased his demand for books by 3.67 percent. Finally, his arc income elasticity of demand for books is

$$Arc\ N_b = [(12 - 10)/(11{,}000 - 10{,}500)](21{,}500/22) = 3.91.$$

Translated, as Doug's income rose by 1 percent, he increased his demand for textbooks by 3.91 percent. Note that these are all approximations of Doug's income elasticity of demand for books and that the arc income elasticity does fall between the two point elasticities.

Interpreting Income Elasticities

An income elasticity of demand greater than 1 indicates that the percentage response in the demand for X is greater than the percentage change in income. This indicates great responsiveness and such goods are said to be income elastic. Income-elastic goods are also sometimes called luxury goods for obvious reasons. Examples of income elastic goods and services include food consumed away from home ($N = 1.2$) (Tyrrell and

Mount 1987) ($N = 1.54$) (Fan and Lewis 1999), motor vehicles and parts ($N = 2.7$) (Bryant and Wang 1990a), new cars ($N = 1.70$) (McCarthy 1996), education ($N = 1.50$) (Fan and Lewis 1999), apparel ($N = 1.53$) (Fan and Lewis 1999), and recreation ($N = 1.42$) (Falvey and Gemmell 1996).

An income elasticity of demand for a good less than 1 indicates that the percentage response in demand is less than the percentage change in income. This indicates that the demand for the good is not very responsive to changes in income and such goods are said to be income inelastic. Income-inelastic goods are sometimes called necessities, again for obvious reasons. Examples of income-inelastic goods are food eaten at home ($N = 0.4$) (Tyrrell and Mount 1987), furniture and household equipment ($N = 0.69$) (Bryant and Wang 1990a), alcohol (N ranging from 0.132 to 0.353) (Yen and Jensen 1996), and apparel (N ranging from 0.404 to 0.621) (Wagner and Mokhtari 2000). Examples of income-inelastic services include health care among those who have health insurance ($N \sim 0$) (Getzen 2000) and residential electricity ($N = 0.23$) (Branch 1993) ($N = 0.32$) (Wilder, Johnson, and Rhyne 1992).

Finally, consider the case in which the income elasticity is exactly 1. At 1 the income elasticity of demand for X is unitary: a 1 percent increase in income engenders a 1 percent increase in the demand for good X. There are, perhaps, no goods for which the demands are exactly unitary income elastic. The demand for "other durables" (i.e., durable toys, sports equipment, boats and motors, yard and garden equipment, home repair equipment) in the United States, however, has been estimated at 1.05 (Bryant and Wang 1990a). Thus, a 1 percent increase in consumer income increases the demand for "other durables" in the United States by about 1 percent. In addition, a study that made use of data from sixty countries found an income elasticity of demand for services as an aggregate category to also be close to unity at 0.965 (Falvey and Gemmell 1996).

Uses of Income Elasticities

Income elasticities of demand are used by corporations to predict changes in the demands for the consumer products they produce as consumers' incomes rise and fall. Governmental policy agencies use income elasticities of demand to predict how different industries producing different consumer goods and services will be affected by changes in consumers' incomes when income tax rates are altered. Income elasticities are also used to predict how families eligible for particular types of governmental income subsidies will change their demands when the income subsidy is altered. For instance, the income elasticity of demand for food is frequently used to predict the change in the demand for food by recipients of food stamps when a program change alters the amount of food stamps they receive. Likewise, the income elasticity of demand for housing is used in calculating the changes in the demand for low-income housing resulting from changes in welfare benefits from, for example, the Temporary Assistance for Needy Families Program.

PRICE EFFECTS

As with income effects, we analyze price effects in the absence of any other change that would affect the purchase pattern of the household. There are two prices in our simple model of demand, the price of good X and the price of "all other goods." Either price could change and affect the demand for X. The effect of a change in the price of a good on the demand for the same good is called the own-price effect. The effect of a change in the price of a good on the demand for another good is called a cross-price effect. We will discuss the own-price effect first.

The Own-Price Effect

As before, the analysis begins by assuming that a household is in equilibrium given its income, the relative prices at which goods can be purchased, and its preferences. Then the price of one of the goods is changed (raised or lowered) and the household's response to that change is observed. The difference between the equilibrium quantities demanded of the good whose price changed is the own-price effect. This is illustrated in Figure 3.5.

Figure 3.5 depicts a typical household's purchase pattern involving good X and "all other goods." Good X is plotted on the horizontal axis. Prior to any change in p_x, the household is in equilibrium at E_0, purchasing and consuming q_x^0 of good X and q_o^0 of "all other goods." The price of X then falls, shifting the budget line from AC to AC_1.

The decline in the price of X does two things. It lowers the relative price of X, making X cheaper relative to "all other goods." The falling price also expands choice, making possible many more purchase pattern alternatives than were open to the household before the price change. Of course, a price increase would reverse each of these two phenomena.

After the fall in p_x, the household maximizes satisfaction at E_1, purchasing and consuming q_x^1 of X and q_o^1 of "all other goods." Clearly, the own-price effect X on the demand for X is $q_x^1 - q_x^0$.

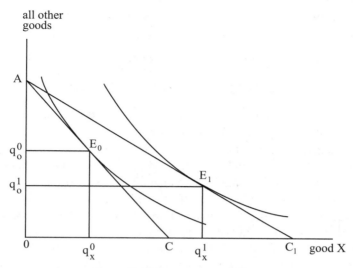

Figure 3.5. The own-price effect.

Definition: The own-price effect is the change in the demand for a good in response to a change in that good's own price, holding income, other prices, and preferences constant.

The own-price effect of p_x on the demand for X is negative: as p_x falls, the demand for X rises. This is the almost-universal response. Of course, each household's own-price response will differ from those of other households because preferences can be expected to differ among households. Real income can also alter the household's own-price effect. It is reasonable that a change in the price of food might affect a poor family's demand for food differently than that of a rich family. Indeed, the response of a poor family's demand for food to a decline in the price of food might be expected to be larger than the response of a rich family. The reason is that the rich family will already be relatively sated with food whereas the poor family will not.

The Own-Price Elasticity of Demand

Just as the income effect was measured by the income elasticity, the own-price response is measured by the own-price elasticity. The elasticity measurement is useful because elasticities of different goods can be compared since they are measured in percentages.

Definition: The own-price elasticity of demand for a good is the absolute value of the percentage change in the quantity demanded of the good due to a 1 percent change in its price, holding other prices, income, and preferences constant.

Algebraically the own-price elasticity of demand can be stated as

$$E_x = |(\Delta q_x/q_x) \, 100/(\Delta p_x/p_x) \cdot 100| = |(\Delta q_x/\Delta p_x)(p_x/q_x)| \quad (3.9)$$

where Δq_x is the change in the quantity of X demanded in response to the change in price, Δp_x. Even though the own-price response is almost universally negative, there may be the very rare case in which the own-price response is positive. To allow for this possibility, the own-price elasticity is defined to be positive; that is, the negative sign is ignored. In reporting estimates of own-price elasticities of demand for particular goods, we will always include the negative sign as a reminder that as the price of a good rises, the demand for it falls and vice versa.

Like income elasticities, price elasticities fall into three categories. Goods may be deemed to be price elastic or price inelastic, or they may have unitary price elasticity. Let's begin with the case of a unitary price-elastic good. When a good is unitary price elastic, its own price elasticity of demand is said to be equal to 1. In this special case, expenditures on X remain unchanged in the face of a decline in p_x. With no change in $p_x q_x$ in the face of a fall in the price of X, the quantity of X demanded must have increased by an amount just sufficient to offset the fall in p_x. This occurs when the percentage change in the price generates an identical percentage change in the quantity, that is, $E_x = 1$.

Goods whose own-price elasticities are less than 1 are said to be own-price inelastic. The demands for such goods are not very responsive to changes in their prices. In the case of own-price inelastic goods, the rise in the demand for X in response to the fall in p_x is insufficient to prevent expenditures on X from falling. A fall in $p_x q_x$ in response to a 1 percent decline in p_x must mean that q_x rose by less than 1 percent. Consequently, the own-price elasticity of demand for X must be less than 1, that is, $E_x < 1$.

Although the demands for few, if any, goods are exactly unitary-price elastic, there are many that are price inelastic. The demand for all food is very price inelastic, about -0.17, although individual foods like beef are less price inelastic (Mann and St. George 1978). Other price-inelastic goods and services include housing ($E = -0.55$) and fuels and utilities ($E = -0.27$ to -0.41) (Fan and Lewis 1999), gasoline ($E = -0.86$) (Puller and Greening 1999), automobiles ($E = -0.87$) (McCarthy 1996), health care ($E = -0.84$) and education ($E = -0.54$)

(Falvey and Gemmell 1996), and electricity in the short run ($E = -0.11$) (Beierlein, Dunn, and McCornon 1981).

Finally, take the case of own-price elastic goods. Here, expenditures on X, $p_x q_x$, must rise in response to a fall in p_x. For expenditures on X to rise due to a 1 percent fall in p_x, the increase in the demand for X must have been greater than 1 percent. The own-price elasticity of demand for X in such a case, therefore, is greater than 1, $E_x > 1$. Goods possessing own-price elasticities of demand greater than 1 are said to be price elastic.

Price-elastic goods show great responsiveness to price. Some examples are hamburger ($E = -1.5$) (Capps and Havlicek 1987), communications ($E = -1.85$) (Falvey and Gemmell 1996), electricity in the long run ($E = -1.2$) (Taylor 1975), education ($E = -2.81$ to -3.56), and apparel ($E = -1.61$ to -1.78) (Fan and Lewis, 1999).

The formula for the own-price elasticity of demand for a good,

$$E_x = |(\Delta q_x / \Delta p_x)(p_x / q_x)| \qquad (3.10)$$

is definitionally correct, but computing formulas are needed when one is confronted with real data. Suppose we know that the demand for good X is q_x^a when the price is p_x^a and the demand for X is q_x^b when the price is p_x^b. One can estimate the own-price elasticity either at point A or at point B with a point own-price elasticity formula.

The point own-price elasticity at A can be estimated by

$$E_x^a = |[(q_x^b - q_x^a)/(p_x^b - p_x^a)](p_x^a / q_x^a)| \,.$$

Likewise, the point own-price elasticity or demand for X at point B is estimated by

$$E_x^b = |[(q_x^b - q_x^a)/(p_x^b - p_x^a)](p_x^b / q_x^b)| \,.$$

If the price change is large or if an average price elasticity is desired between points A and B, then the arc own-price elasticity is relevant. The formula for the arc price elasticity is

$$Arc\ E_x = |[(q_x^b - q_x^a)/(p_x^b - p_x^a)][(p_x^a + p_x^b)/(q_x^a + q_x^b)]| \,.$$

An Example

Suppose that at a price for apartments in Collegetown of $1.25 per square foot per month, Doug and his two friends rent an apartment with 700 square feet (three bedrooms of 10 feet × 10 feet each, a kitchen of 10 feet × 10 feet, and living room, bathroom, and hallway space equal to another

300 square feet). Then, suppose the price of Collegetown apartments rises to \$1.50 per square foot per month. At the higher price Doug and his friends move to an apartment with 600 square feet of space. Their point price elasticity measured at the lower price is $E_h^l = |[(700 - 600)/(1.25 - 1.50)](1.25/700)| = 0.71$.

Their price elasticity of demand for housing at the higher price is $E_h^h = |[(700 - 600)/(1.25 - 1.50)](1.50/600)| = 1.00$. Their arc price elasticity of demand is Arc $E_h = |[(700 - 600)/(1.25 - 1.50)](2.75/1,300)| = 0.85$. As with point and arc income elasticities, the arc own-price elasticity lies between the two point elasticities. Not knowing Doug's responses to price changes smaller than from \$1.25 to \$1.50 per square foot, the arc own-price elasticity is, perhaps, the better estimate to use. Using it, the demand for housing by Doug and his friends is, therefore, own-price inelastic. For each 1 percent increase in the price of Collegetown housing, Doug and his friends will reduce their demand for housing by 0.85 percent. This means that Collegetown landlords can increase their gross profits from renting to Doug and his friends by raising rents. If their demand for Collegetown housing had been own-price elastic, however, Collegetown landlords would be able to increase gross profits from renting by lowering rents.

Uses of Price Elasticities

Price elasticities of demand are used by firms to assess what will happen to their revenue if they lower or raise prices. If a good is price inelastic then the firm knows that if the price is increased (decreased), revenue (i.e., price × quantity) will increase (decrease) because the percentage decline in demand will be less than the percentage increase in the price (i.e., $|E| < 1$). In contrast, if a good is price elastic (i.e., $|E| > 1$) then if its price is increased (decreased), revenue will decrease (increase) because the percentage decline in demand will be greater than the percentage increase in the price.

Government also makes use of price-elasticity information, particularly when assessing the impact of sales tax policies on demand for specific goods and services. A sales tax essentially raises the price of a good and governments thus selectively use sales taxes to discourage consumption of specific commodities. For example, health economists have estimated that the price elasticity of demand for initiating cigarette smoking among young people is approximately −0.7 (Institute of Medicine 1998).

That is, for every 10 percent increase in the price of cigarettes, 7 percent fewer young people will take up smoking. This has precipitated the recommendation that increasing the sales tax on cigarettes would be an effective method of reducing teen smoking. Recently, however, research by DeCicca, Kenkel, and Mathios (2002) has sparked a debate regarding whether the own-price elasticity for initiating cigarette smoking is this large.

THE HOUSEHOLD'S DEMAND CURVE

Usually, the relationship between the price of a good and the quantity demanded is studied and graphed directly rather than studied in the context of the household's indifference diagram. This relationship between the quantity of X demanded and the price of X is called the demand curve for X. It is derived from the household indifference diagram in Figure 3.6.

In the top panel of Figure 3.6, three equilibrium purchase patterns are depicted at three different prices for X, with income, other prices, and preferences held constant. In the bottom panel is a diagram with the price of X plotted on the vertical axis and the quantity of X demanded plotted along the horizontal axis such that quantities of X in the equilibrium purchase patterns in the top panel can be dropped vertically down the horizontal axis on the bottom panel. As the price of X falls from p_x^o to p_x^1 to p_x^2, the demand for X increases from q_x^o to q_x^1 to q_x^2. The curve so mapped out is the demand curve for X.

Definition: The demand curve for a good is the schedule of quantities the consumer is willing and able to consume at different prices, holding income, other prices, and consumer preferences constant.

Note that the slope at any point on the demand curve in the bottom panel of Figure 3.6 is $(\Delta p_x / \Delta q_x)$; that is, the rise over the run. Note also that if one were to draw a line from the point on the demand curve to the origin, the slope of that line would be (p_x / q_x). Because the own-price elasticity of demand has been defined as $E_x = |(\Delta q_x / \Delta p_x)(p_x / q_x)|$ (equation [3.10]), it is clear that the own-price elasticity of demand can be estimated from the demand curve as $E_x = |(p_x / q_x)/(\Delta p_x / \Delta q_x)| = |(\Delta q_x / \Delta p_x)(p_x / q_x)|$; that is,

$$E_x = \frac{\text{slope of the line from the origin to the point on the demand curve}}{\text{slope of the demand curve at the point}}.$$

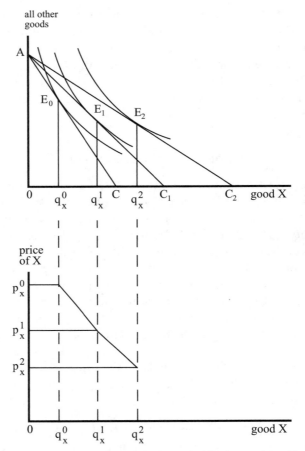

Figure 3.6. Derivation of the household's demand for X.

Income and Substitution Effects

It was stated previously that a price change evokes two different changes in the environment of a household: it makes the good that's price changed more or less expensive relative to other goods, and it alters the alternatives open to the household, reducing choice if the price increases, and increasing choice if it falls. Not surprisingly, then, the own-price effect of any price change can be decomposed into two effects: the one due to the relative price change and the other due to the change in the choices open to the household. The part due to changing relative prices is called the substitution effect, and the part due to changing alternatives induced by the price change is called the income effect.

The substitution effect can be explained in the following way. Suppose the price of good X falls. Even if the household was neither more nor less satisfied after the price change than before, the fact that the price of X has fallen relative to the prices of all other things creates an incentive for the household to substitute the now cheaper X for some of the now relatively more expensive "all other goods" that it had been buying. That is to say, at the prechange equilibrium purchase pattern, the price that the household is willing to pay for X is more than the new, lowered price of X. Consequently, it will buy more of X and less of "all other goods."

Definition: The substitution effect of a price change is the effect of a change in a good's price on the demand for that good, holding satisfaction constant.

The income effect is quite simple. The decrease in the price of X opens up consumption alternatives not available at the old price. This is exactly what an increase in real income does, and the household responds in the same manner: by increasing its consumption of both X and "all other goods" (so long as both are normal goods).

Definition: The income effect of a price change is the effect on the demand for X of the change in "income" brought about by the change in the price of X.

The Geometry of Income and Substitution Effects

Figure 3.7 illustrates the geometry of income and substitution effects. The household's pre-price-change budget line is AC, and given its preferences, its equilibrium purchase pattern of X and "all other goods" is E_0. Now suppose p_x falls, the new budget line being AC_1. The postchange demand for X is q_x^1, so that the own-price effect is $q_x^1 - q_x^0$.

Now suppose, instead, that at the same time p_x fell, sufficient income was (hypothetically) taken away from the household so that it was no better and no worse off at the new, lower price of X than it was before the price fell. If the household is no better and no worse off at the new relative price of X than it was at the old relative price, it must be on the same indifference curve. If the household faces the new price of X rather than the old, and if it is no better off than before, its budget line must be tangent to the same indifference curve it was on before the price fell and some of its income had been taken away. This budget line is $A'C'$ in Figure 3.7. It has been drawn parallel to AC_1, reflecting the new relative

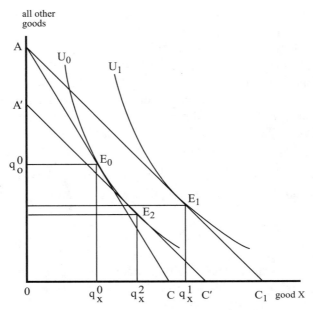

Figure 3.7. Decomposing the own-price effect.

price of X, and tangent to U_o, reflecting the fact that the household is no better and no worse off than it was before. At the pre-price-decline equilibrium, E_0, the slope of U_0 (i.e., the [marginal rate of substitution]$_{xo}$) is greater than the slope of $A'C'$, indicating that the relative price the household is willing to pay for X is higher than the new market price of X. Consequently, the household alters its purchase pattern by substituting X for "all other goods" until it reaches E_2, where the marginal rate of substitution of X for "all other goods" is equal to the relative market price of X. The substitution effect of the fall in p_x is, therefore, an increase of $q_x^2 - q_x^0$ in the amount of X demanded.

Note that so long as the indifference curve is convex to the origin, the substitution effect is negative: the quantity demanded of X rising as its price falls and vice versa. Because indifference curves are usually convex to the origin, we will assume that the substitution effect is always negative.

Having identified the substitution effect, we can now return to the household the income we (hypothetically) took away from it. Returning the income is equivalent to expanding the household's alternatives, shifting the budget line from $A'C'$ to AC_1. With the increase in real income the household maximizes its satisfaction on AC_1 at E_1, where q_x^1 is demanded.

The income effect of the price change, therefore, is $q_x^1 - q_x^2$. This is the effect (measured at the new relative price of X) of the expanded alternatives opened to the household due to the fall in p_x.

Notice that so long as good X is a normal good, the income effect and the substitution effect augment each other, making for a larger own-price effect. If, however, good X is an inferior good (i.e., the income effect is negative), then the substitution effect and the income effect of the price change tend to offset each other, making the total price effect smaller.

The own-price effect is equal to the sum of the substitution effect and the income effect. This can be expressed algebraically as[5]

$$\Delta q_x / \Delta p_x = [(\Delta q_x / \Delta p_x)|_{u=c}] - [q_x(\Delta q_x / \Delta y)|_{p_x=p_k}] \qquad (3.11)$$

where

$\Delta q_x / \Delta p_x$ = the own-price effect,
$(\Delta q_x / \Delta p_x)|_{u=c}$ = the own-substitution effect, and
$-q_x(\Delta q_x / \Delta Y)|_{p_x=p_k}$ = the income effect of the price change.

The minus sign on the income effect adjusts the income effect for the direction of the price change. A price increase reduces real income, whereas a price decline increases real income.

Several propositions follow from the decomposition of the own-price effect into its substitution and income effect components.

Proposition 1: The more and better substitutes good X has, the larger the substitution effect of any own-price effect and, *ceteris paribus*, the larger the own-price effect.

Proposition 1 relates to the own-substitution effect in equation (3.11). The more and better substitutes good X has (and, therefore, the larger the own-substitution effect), the easier it will be for the household to substitute other goods for X if p_x rises, holding satisfaction constant. Likewise, the better a substitute X is for other goods, the easier it will be for the household to increase its consumption of X at the expense of other things should p_x fall. Thus, the bigger the own-substitution effect, the larger the own-price effect.

---

[5] Equation (3.11) is an approximation to the Slutsky equation (Slutsky 1915) expressed in terms of first derivatives. See mathematical note 3 for its derivation. The Slutsky equation is the fundamental equation in demand theory and was first published in 1915. It and the economics of the household are, therefore, not new.

As an example, compare the price elasticities of hamburger and of all food (E about -1.5 and -0.17, respectively) (Mann and St. George 1978; Capps and Havlicek 1987). Hamburger has many good substitutes (e.g., chicken, pork, fish, beans, tofu), whereas all food does not. One might be able to substitute some clothing and housing for a little food in order to burn fewer calories to stay warm, but the scope for substitution is quite narrow. Consequently, the demand for hamburger will be more price elastic than the demand for all food.

The geometry of the proposition is straightforward. Recall from Chapter 2 that the extent of the curvature of the indifference curves reflects the substitutability of X for other things: the shallower the indifference curve, the better X substitutes for other things. Finding the substitution effects with indifference curves of different curvature will readily establish that the shallower the indifference curve, the greater the substitution effect, thus illustrating Proposition 1.

Proposition 2: The more responsive the demand for a good is to income, the larger the income effect of any price change and the larger the total price effect.

This proposition deals with the $(\Delta q_x/\Delta Y)|_{p_x=p_k}$, part of the term representing the income effect in equation (3.11). Suppose p_x^1 falls. The household no longer has to use as much of its income as it did before to buy the same quantity of X. The "extra" income it has is an approximate measure of the increase in real income brought about by the fall in p_x. The consumer will respond to this increase in income in the same fashion as if income had increased through any other means, and the extent of the response will depend on the income effect: the larger the income effect, the larger the own-price effect.

Examples are easy to find. Take hamburger and pork, for instance. The income and own-price elasticities of these two meats are as follows (Capps and Havlicek 1987):

	Income elasticity	Own-price elasticity
Hamburger	1.38	-1.58
Pork	1.11	-1.30

The demand for hamburger is more own-price elastic than the demand for pork in part because it is more income elastic, in accordance with Proposition 2.

Proposition 3: The more X is demanded prior to the change in its price, the larger the change in income caused by any price change, and the larger the own-price effect.

This proposition relates to the $-q_x$ part of the income effect, $-q_x(\Delta q_x/\Delta Y)|_{p_x=p_k}$, in equation (3.11). The point is roughly this. Consider a $0.05/unit fall in the price of X. If the consumer had purchased 100 units of X prior to the price decline, the same 100 units would cost $5.00 less after the price drop than before. The extra $5.00 could be spent on more X or more "all other goods." If, however, only 50 units of X were consumed prior to the price decline, the price drop would yield only $2.50 of additional real income. Given that the income effect, $\Delta q_x/\Delta Y$, is on a per-dollar basis, the greater the increase in real income brought about by the price decline, the greater its income effect, and, in turn, the greater the own-price effect.

One implication of Proposition 3 is that because rich people demand more of most goods and services than poor people (because most goods and services are normal goods), rich people's demands for goods and services will have larger own-price effects than poor people's, *ceteris paribus*. We, therefore, might expect rich people "to take advantage" of sales more than poor people.

SOME EXAMPLES: BRINGING THEORY CLOSER TO REALITY

The circumstances and changes that have been discussed have been simplifications of reality, the simplifications being made for the purposes of exposition. If the discussion were left here, one might be able to accuse the theory of not being able to handle the complexities of the real world. In this section, several examples are discussed in an attempt to show the scope and power of simple demand theory.

Quantity Discounts: The Case of College Classes

Quantity discounts abound in many different markets. In grocery stores often the per-unit price for products varies by the size of the package. For example, a 16-ounce box of laundry detergent typically has a higher per-ounce price than a 48-ounce box of laundry detergent. Likewise, a 12-ounce soft drink sold in a convenience store may sell for $0.49 (approximately 4 cents per ounce) while the largest size, 48 ounces, sells for $0.89 (approximately 1.9 cents per ounce). Yet another example of quantity

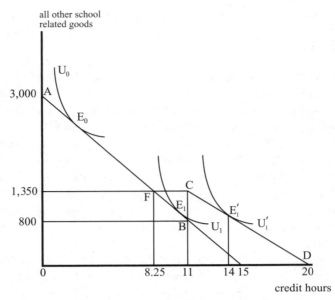

Figure 3.8. The case of quantity discounts on college classes.

discounts occurs when museums charge one admission price for a single adult, say $6.00, and another admission price, say $15.00, for a family of three or more (i.e., $5.00 per person or less). Clearly, quantity discounts are a common feature of a number of different markets. Here we present an example of quantity discounts, what they do to consumer choice, and what typical consumer responses are.

Suppose tuition for classes at a college is priced in the following way. The price per credit hour (ch), p_{ch}, is $200 if no more than 11 credit hours of course work are purchased. But if more than 11 credit hours are purchased, $p_{ch} = $150. Further suppose that the consumer has budgeted $Y = $3000 to be spent on schooling for one semester and suppose, for simplicity, that the price of "other school-related things," p_o, is $1.00/unit.

This type of quantity discount has a startling effect on the budget line confronting the consumer. Figure 3.8 illustrates it. The AB part of the budget line is found in the following way. If no credit hours are purchased, then $Y/p_o = $3000/$1 = 3000$ units of "other school-related things" can be purchased. This is point A in the diagram. If 11 credit hours of course work are purchased, then $p_d q_d = $200 \times 11 = 2200 is spent on course credit hours, leaving $800 to be spent on "other school-related things," which, since $p_o = $1.00/unit, comes to 800 units. This is represented by

B in Figure 3.8. *AB* is, then, the budget line facing consumers who enroll for (i.e., buy) no more than 11 credit hours of course work.

The *CD* portion of the budget line is found as follows. If all that the consumer buys is credit hours, then all of the credit hours can be purchased at the lower price of \$150/ch and $Yp_d = 3000/150 = 20$ ch of course work can be purchased. This is point *D*. Finally, suppose (contrary to fact) that the consumer can buy 11 ch of course work at \$150/ch; then if \$1650 is spent on credit hours, \$1350 can be spent on "other school-related things." This point (1350, 11) is point *C* in Figure 3.8. Although point *C* does not represent an option available to the consumer, because the \$150/ch price applies only to quantities greater than 11 credit hours, it does represent the lower limit of what can be attained at the discounted price. *CD*, then, is the budget line if the consumer buys more than 11 credit hours of course work.

Two different consumers are illustrated in Figure 3.8, both of whom face budget line *ABCD*: consumer 0 with indifference curve U_0 and consumer 1 with indifference curves U_1 and U_1'. Consumer 0 has a very small demand for college courses and maximizes satisfaction at E_0, demanding fewer than 11 credit hours of course work. For consumer 0 to maximize satisfaction on the *AB* part of the budget line, the indifference curve to which *AB* is tangent must pass above point *C*; otherwise, buying more than 11 credit hours would bring greater satisfaction. This is the situation in which consumer 1 finds himself. *AB* is tangent to indifference curve U_1 at E_1, but maximum satisfaction is attained at point E_1' on the higher U_1', at which consumer 1 buys more than 11 credit hours and, hence, can take advantage of the quantity discount.

Notice how the vertical part of the budget line, *BC*, "shades" the *FB* portion of *AB*. It is shaded in the sense that there are points on *CD* that dominate any point on *FB*. For the same income (i.e., \$3000) the consumer can buy more credit hours and the same amount of "all other goods" at points on *CD* than he can on *FB*. Because more is preferred to less, no consumer will be in equilibrium on *FB*. Thus, no consumer will enroll for between 8.25 and 11 credit hours. To do so would place them in the *FB* portion of the *AB* budget line. This is precisely the situation of consumer 1. If there had been no quantity discount, consumer 1 would have maximized satisfaction at E_1. With the quantity discount, however, consumer 1 finds it in his own best interest to demand 14 credit hours of course work at E_1'.

Quantity discounts, then, spur the demand for the discounted product in a fashion not simply the result of a conventional price effect: the discontinuity in the budget line caused by the quantity discount is an additional inducement. Such discontinuities and the effect they have in making uneconomic the purchase of quantities slightly smaller than the quantity at which the discount begins may be part of the reason for odd package sizes. An equally cogent reason is that odd package sizes tend to confuse the consumer to the store's benefit.

Another way of looking at the quantity discount is that it is a species of price discrimination practiced by manufacturers and stores: the higher price for small sizes being the advantage the store takes of the consumer with the small demand. Perhaps the consumer with the small demand works full time but also wants to further his education. To enroll for 12 or more credit hours would mean that he would not be able to meet both his work and schooling commitments. Paying the higher per unit price when taking fewer credit hours is the price paid for being able to pursue work and schooling simultaneously. Or the consumer with the small demand might be the poor consumer for whom other demands on income force purchasing many items in quantities too small to be able to exploit quantity discounts.

Cash versus In-Kind Transfers: The Food Stamps Example

Several federal entitlement programs provide direct cash payments to eligible households while others provide a so-called in-kind payment – typically a voucher that can be used to purchase only certain goods or services. Examples of cash programs include Social Security, Supplemental Security Income, and Unemployment Compensation. Examples of the in-kind transfer programs include food stamps, child care subsidies, and the Supplemental Nutrition Program for Women, Infants, and Children. What are the implications of providing in-kind transfers rather than direct cash payments to households? Here we provide an example of one in-kind transfer, the Food Stamp Program, and how it alters consumer choices relative to a direct cash payment.

The Food Stamp Program is a federal program that provides an in-kind transfer (typically in the form of coupons or a debit card) to low-income consumers so that they can purchase food to enhance their diets. To be eligible to participate in the Food Stamp Program a household must meet both an assets and an income test.

Suppose a low-income household has an income Y of \$1000 per month and is eligible for \$200 in supplemental food stamp benefits. For the sake

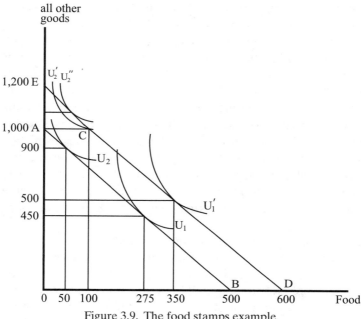

Figure 3.9. The food stamps example.

of simplicity, let's say that the price of food, p_f, is $2.00/unit and the price of "all other goods," p_o, is $1.00/unit. Figure 3.9 illustrates how the receipt of food stamps alters the budget constraint faced by this household. AB represents the household's initial budget constraint. Under the food stamp budget constraint, expenditures on items other than food are still limited to $1000 (point A). But, if the household spends all $1000 on commodities other than food, it can still use the $200 in food stamps to purchase 100 units of food (point C). If a household chose to spend all of its income on food, however, it could now purchase 600 rather than 500 units of food (point D). Thus, with a food stamp entitlement of $200 that can only be used to purchase food, the budget constraint shifts from AB to ACD.

Two sets of household preferences have been drawn on Figure 3.9. Both reflect a preference set where food is viewed as a normal good. U_1 represents the preferences of household 1 that initially maximizes satisfaction by purchasing 275 units of food and 450 units of "all other goods." In the presence of the Food Stamp Program, this household moves from U_1 to U_1' where it consumes 350 units of food and 500 units of "all other goods." Thus, this household increases its consumption of both food and "all other goods" given the enlarged budget constraint provided by the Food Stamp Program. In this situation, the household uses all $200 in food stamps to purchase food but it shifts some of the cash it would have otherwise spent on food (i.e., $50) to increase its consumption of "all other goods."

U_2 represents the preferences of household 2 that initially maximizes its satisfaction at 50 units of food and 900 units of "all other goods." Under the food stamp budget constraint this household moves from U_2 to U_2' and now maximizes its satisfaction by consuming 100 units of food and 1000 units of "all other goods." Note that household 2 has also increased its purchases of both food and "all other goods." But, this household maximizes its satisfaction at the kink point on the budget constraint (i.e., point C).

Suppose the Food Stamp Program were changed so that it provided a $200 cash transfer rather than an in-kind transfer. This cash transfer is represented by the budget line ECD in Figure 3.9. It is clear that the consumption behavior of household 1 is the same regardless of whether the transfer comes in the form of an in-kind transfer or a cash benefit. That is, in the presence of either a cash or equivalent in-kind transfer program, household 1 maximizes its satisfaction by purchasing 350 units of food and 500 units of "all other goods." In contrast, household 2 would elect to consume less food and more of "all other goods" under a cash benefit program compared to the in-kind transfer. This point is illustrated by indifference curve U_2'', which is tangent to the budget line ECD and higher than indifference curve U_2'. At U_2'', the household would spend $1000 on "all other goods" and it would also use some of its cash benefits to buy "all other goods" rather than food. Note that household 2 increases its consumption of food under the cash transfer program but not by as much as it would if an in-kind transfer program were in place.

With an in-kind transfer program, household 1 is said to be unconstrained in its consumption choices while household 2 is said to be constrained. Thus, the model suggests that by offering an in-kind food supplement program, the government encourages greater consumption of food for the fraction of households that are food constrained than would otherwise occur in a cash benefit program. More generally, by earmarking the funds for only certain types of expenditures, governments can use in-kind transfer programs to encourage greater consumption of particular goods.

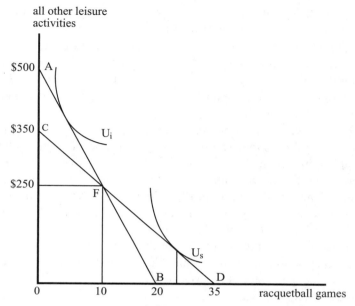

Figure 3.10. The case of a racquetball club's annual membership fees and lower hourly court rent.

Two-Part Prices: The Racquetball Club Racket

Racquetball, tennis, and general fitness centers have all become quite popular in recent years. Typically, the individual interested in such activities has the following alternatives. One can "pay as you play" by renting courts or exercise equipment by the hour. Alternatively, by joining a club, one is able to pay lower fees for the use of courts. Joining a club, however, involves paying an annual membership fee.

Suppose for example, that an individual has $500 per month that can be allocated to all leisure activities ($Y = \$500$) and she can play racquetball on pay-as-you-play courts at the rate of $25/hour. Or she can join a racquetball club for a monthly membership fee of $150/month and play on the club's courts at the rate of $10.00/hour. For convenience, suppose that the price of "other leisure" is $p_l = \$1.00$/unit.

The pay-as-you-play budget line is line AB in Figure 3.10. If no racquetball is played, 500 units of "other leisure" can be purchased, hence, point A. If the consumer does nothing but play racquetball on pay-as-you-play courts, $Y/p_r = \$500/\$25 = 20$ hours per month can be played.

This is point B. Membership in the club with no racquetball played allows the individual to buy $500 - 150 = 350$ units of "other leisure," point C. Belonging to the club and doing nothing but playing racquetball allows the consumer to play racquetball for ($\$500 - \$150$)/$10/hour = 35 hours per month, point D. Line AB is the pay-as-you-play consumer's budget line, whereas point A and the segment CD (excluding C) is the racquetball club member's budget line.

The pay-as-you-play budget line lies above the club member's budget line in the AF region. The reverse is true in the FD region. Point F, the point of intersection, is at (250, 10). It is not in the best interest of the individual to join the club unless that person plans to play at least 10 hours of racquetball per month. The implication for consumer behavior, of course, is that only serious racquetball players (e.g., the possessor of indifference curve U_s) will join a club, whereas infrequent players (e.g., the individual represented by U_i) will pay as they play. Serious players are induced to play more racquetball than if club memberships were unavailable. Infrequent players play less often than if the lower hourly court rentals available only with membership were available.

Electricity Rates: Block Rate Pricing

Historically, residential energy consumers have faced what is known as "block rate pricing" for electricity. Under a block rate price structure, households are charged a relatively high price per unit for consuming small amounts of electricity. Once their demand exceeds a particular threshold, however, then they pay a lower price per unit for electricity. Increased emphasis on energy conservation coupled with recent energy shortages have caused many state regulatory commissions to revisit the issue of electricity pricing. As a consequence, some states now have a single rate or even an inverted block rate structure. Here, we show how household demand varies under simplified versions of each of these three electricity pricing schemes.

For the purposes of discussion, suppose a household has a monthly income of $500 and that the price of "all other goods" is $p_o = \$1.00$/unit. With respect to electricity, suppose that the household must pay a minimum monthly hookup charge of $25, even if it uses no electricity at all during the month. We begin with a single price system where the household pays a price, $p_e^o = \$0.20$/ kilowatt-hour (kWh) for each unit of electricity it uses. If the household chooses to consume no electricity and is not hooked up, it can spend $500 on "other goods." This is point A in Figure 3.11. If

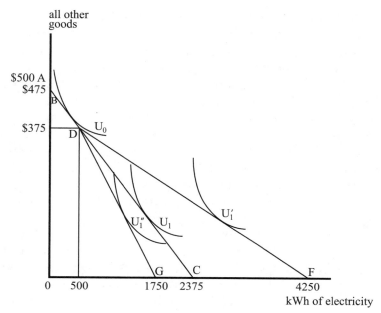

Figure 3.11. Block rate pricing.

the household elects to be hooked up but consumes no electricity for the month, the household pays the hookup fee of $25, leaving $475 to be spent on "all other goods." This is point *B*. If the household chooses to consume nothing but electricity, it can purchase 2375 kWh, which is point *C*.

Now suppose there is a block rate pricing structure rather than a single price. Specifically, suppose the household pays a price of $p_e^0 =$ $0.20/kWh for any electricity used up to (and including) 500 kWh. And, the household pays $p_e^1 =$ $0.10/kWh for all kWh used greater than 500 kWh. Up to 500 kWh, the budget constraint remains the same as it was under a single rate pricing structure. At 500 kWh, the price of electricity changes. If a household uses exactly 500 kWh during the month, it spends $25 on the hookup plus $0.20 × 500 = $25 + $100 = $125 on electricity, leaving $375 to be spent on "other goods." This is point *D* in Figure 3.11. Finally, if the household buys electricity and nothing else, it consumes 500 kWh + ($500 − $25 − $100)/$0.10 = 500 + 3750 = 4250 kWh per year. This is point *F*. The budget line under the traditional block rate pricing system is thus point *A* and the line segments represented by *BDF*.

Finally, let's turn to an example of an inverted block rate pricing structure. Under this pricing structure, households are charged low rates when they consume relatively small amounts of electricity. If their demand exceeds a certain threshold, then they pay a higher price per unit for the additional electricity consumed. Again, suppose that the price is $p_e^1 = \$0.20/\text{kWh}$ for the first 500 kWh that a household consumes. But now, the household pays $p_e^2 = \$0.30/\text{kWh}$ for all kilowatt-hours used greater than 500 kWh. From 0 to 500 kWh, the budget constraint remains the same as it was under a single rate pricing structure. But, if the household buys only electricity and nothing else, it consumes $500\,\text{kWh} + (\$500 - \$25 - \$100)/\$0.30 = 500 + 1250 = 1750$ kWh per year. This is point G in Figure 3.11. The budget line is thus point A and the line segments represented by BDG.

Clearly, under a traditional block rate pricing scheme, small demanders of electricity pay higher per kilowatt-hour prices for electricity and, partly in consequence, are induced to consume less electricity than they would if the price were lower. Big users of electricity pay lower prices for the electricity they use and, again partly in consequence, consume more electricity than they otherwise would under a single pricing scheme. In contrast, an inverted block rate pricing structure reduces electricity consumption among heavy users relative to what they would consume under a single price system.

Indifference curves for two different households have been drawn tangent to the BDC budget constraint. The household associated with indifference curve U_0 is a small demander of electricity. In our example, households like this will consume the same amount of electricity regardless of which pricing scheme is put in place. In contrast, the household possessing indifference curve U_1 demands large amounts of electricity and this household's demand will be affected by the choice of pricing scheme.

Under the block pricing scheme, the large electricity user is rewarded by the declining price structure and in response increases its electricity consumption. In contrast, when an inverted block pricing structure is used, this same household is induced to reduce its consumption of electricity from what it would have been under a single pricing scheme.

It is now apparent why the block rate pricing structure for electricity has been criticized in recent years by those advocating for energy conservation. Clearly, conservationists would prefer an inverted block structure or even a single pricing scheme as both would encourage households to consume less than they do under the traditional block rate price structure.

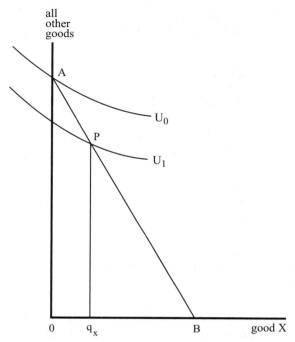

Figure 3.12. The zero purchase solution.

Interestingly, some electric companies have adopted a flat or inverted block rate structure for the summer months when they are often operating at peak capacity. Some of these same companies have a traditional block rate structure during the rest of the year.

PURCHASE VERSUS NONPURCHASE BEHAVIOR

Most textbook indifference curve diagrams are drawn with "interior solutions" in mind. That is, the illustrated situation is one in which some of each good X and "all other goods" are consumed. But at any point in time, some households are purchasers of good X and others are not. Because no household purchases every good in every period, the "corner solution" illustrated in Figure 3.12 is representative of every household for some goods. For the consumer depicted in Figure 3.12, satisfaction is maximized at point A and good X is not purchased.[6]

---

[6] Recall Figure 2.9 and the accompanying discussion.

Consider Figure 3.12 in more detail. The slope of the indifference curve through A (i.e., the slope of U_0 at A) is less than the slope of the budget line at A; that is,

$$MU_x/MU_o\,|_A = MU_x/MU_o|_{q_x=0} < p_x/p_o$$

where MU_x = marginal utility of X, MU_o = marginal utility of "all other goods," the $|_A$ notation means "at point A," and $|_{q_x=0}$ means "at $q_x = 0$." The ratio p_x/p_o is, of course, the market price of good X in terms of "all other goods." Recall that the slope of any indifference curve reflects the real price the consumer is willing to pay for more X, holding satisfaction constant. Recall, too, that the slope of the budget line is the real price the consumer must pay for the good in the marketplace.[7] At a price of $MU_x/MU_o|_A$, the consumer is indifferent between zero consumption of X and a small amount of X. $MU_x/MU_o|_A$ is called the consumer's *reservation price* of X. Because the consumer's reservation price for X is less than the market price of X, given the consumer's income and other prices, there is no incentive for the consumer to buy any X.

Now consider the firms selling good X. They are, of course, interested in changing the nonpurchaser into a purchaser of X if it can be done cheaply enough. The indifference curve diagram isolates the various options firms have to influence consumer behavior and, thus, presents a clear picture of the firms' marketing problem and the several ways of solving it. The options are to (1) raise the consumer's income if X is a normal good, (2) raise the price of "all other goods" and so make X relatively cheaper, (3) lower the price of X below the consumer's reservation price, and (4) raise the consumer's reservation price above the market price by changing preferences or by redefining the good. Neither raising consumer income nor raising other prices is feasible for individual firms. This leaves lowering the price of X or raising the consumer's reservation price as possible alternatives.

An obvious method is to reduce the price of X below the consumer's reservation price so as to draw the consumer into the market. A knowledge of the reservation prices of nonbuyers would tell firms how many added consumers of X would result from any given price decline. Although firms lack knowledge of the reservation prices of individual

---

[7] The adjective "real" is used to modify both the price the consumer is willing to pay and the market price because they are phrased in terms of the goods (i.e., the consumer's real resources) that must be given up to get good X.

consumers, they do have quite accurate general knowledge of the distribution of reservation prices of nonpurchasers. For example, through experience, car dealers know roughly how many added cars they will sell if they allow their salespeople to bargain with customers at lower prices. Part of the bargaining process employed by salespeople is intended to discover the individual consumer's reservation price and how it might be manipulated. Again through experience, department stores know reasonably accurately how much extra merchandise they will sell during a sale at which prices are slashed by a given amount. In both cases, a knowledge of the distribution of consumers' reservation prices allows firms to predict the effectiveness of price declines of different magnitudes.

Firms' price reductions may take a variety of forms.[8] The simplest scheme is to offer the good or service in question at a lower "sale" price for a limited time. A more complicated but common form of price reduction is the use of coupons that provide consumers with "cents off" or "buy one and get one free" opportunities if they purchase the product in question. Other somewhat less common price reduction schemes include refund offers, continuity plans (e.g., airlines that offer frequent flyer miles that can be redeemed for a free ticket or a seating upgrade), bonus packaging (i.e., increasing the amount of the good offered at the same price), and free samples. The hope of the seller is that if she can get nonpurchasing households to experience her product once, then perhaps they will continue to purchase the product even after the price is again raised. For this to occur, a household that initially does not purchase the good must have its preferences changed by the consumption experience.

From the firm's perspective, price reductions have the disadvantage that both loyal purchasers (i.e., those households for which prior to the sale $MU_x/MU_o = p_x/p_o$) and nonpurchasers (i.e., those households for which prior to the sale $MU_x/MU_o|_{q_x=0} < p_x/p_o$) usually get to take advantage of the lowered price. Thus, firms may be more eager to use price reduction policies when (1) they are introducing new products for which all households are initially nonpurchasers or (2) they observe that sales for an existing product have recently declined.

The other common way of turning nonpurchasers into purchasers is to raise the reservation prices of consumers; that is, to make consumers more willing to buy the good than before. Advertising is an important

---

[8] In the marketing literature, all of these price-reduction strategies fall under the title of "sales promotion" or "consumer promotion" efforts.

means of changing consumer preferences so as to raise reservation prices (i.e., increasing MU_x relative to MU_o). Geometrically, advertising good X rotates consumers' indifference curves clockwise and, therefore, steepens the slope of the indifference curve through point A. Marketing departments of firms seek information that will indicate how many added purchases a given expenditure on advertising will yield. The cost of changing customer preferences can then be balanced against the projected added sales revenue to be generated to determine the level of the advertising campaign.

A final way to raise the reservation price is to redefine the good being offered for sale. Instead of selling a box of breakfast cereal at price p_x, for instance, the firm will offer at the same price a box of breakfast cereal plus a magic decoder ring used to decode messages from Mars. The consumer's reservation price, thereby, changes from $MU_1 / MU_3|_{q_1=0}$ where MU_1 = marginal utility of the box of cereal and MU_3 = marginal utility of "all other goods," to $(MU_1 + MU_2)/MU_3|_{q_1=0\,\text{and}\,q_2=0}$ where MU_1 and MU_3 are defined as before and MU_2 = the marginal utility of the magic decoder ring (see mathematical note 4). So long as the consumer gets some positive utility from the magic decoder ring, the consumer's reservation price for the "tied sale" is higher than the reservation price for the box of cereal alone. If MU_2 is high enough (and that depends on the pressure the consumer's five-year-old son puts on him or her!), the consumer's reservation price may rise enough that it exceeds the market price and the consumer will become a purchaser. The firm must balance the cost of the magic decoder ring against the added revenue generated by the tied sale.[9]

CROSS-PRICE EFFECTS

Just as a change in the price of good X induces changes in the demand for X, so does a change in the price of a good other than X. The effect of a change in the price of another good, p_z, on the demand for X, holding p_x, income, and preferences constant, is called the cross-price effect of p_z on the demand for X.

Two illustrations will be given. In the first, the price of "all other goods" changes and the effect on good X is observed; in the second, there are

---

[9] Although the tied sale has been phrased in terms of breakfast cereal and the junk toys cereal companies include with the cereal, the principle is the same as that used by the car salesperson who "throws in" a stereo sound system rather than lowering the price as an inducement to have you buy the car.

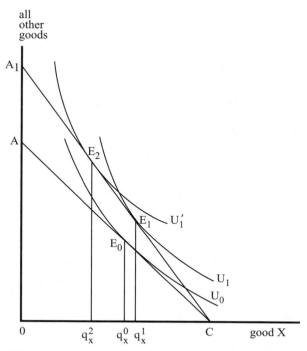

Figure 3.13. The cross-price effect of a decline in the price of "all other goods" on the demand for X.

more than two goods, and when the price of one of them changes, its effect on the demand for X is observed.

The first case is pictured in Figure 3.13, in which the household is at equilibrium at point E_0, at pre-change prices and income, demanding q_x^0. Then the price of "all other goods," p_o, falls, reducing the price of "all other goods" relative to X and expanding the purchase pattern alternatives open to the household. These changes are seen by comparing the initial budget line, AC, with the post-change budget line, A_1C. At the new prices and assuming the household to possess indifference curves U_0 and U_1, the household responds by demanding more X than before: q_x^1 rather than q_x^0. The total cross-price effect of the decline in p_o on X is $q_x^1 - q_x^0$, an increase in the demand for X. The cross-price effect on the demand for X need not be negative; that is, a fall in p_o inducing a rise in q_x. The total cross-price effect can just as easily be positive; that is, a fall in p_o inducing a fall in the demand for X. If the household possessed indifference curves U_0 and U_1', the decline in p_o would lead the family to reestablish equilibrium at

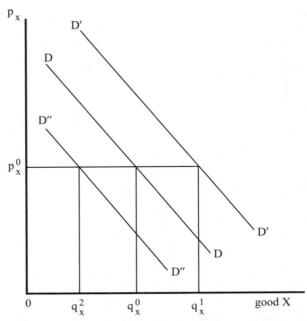

Figure 3.14. The cross-price effect of p_z on the demand for X when X and Z are substitutes and complements.

E_2 rather than at E_1. In this case, the family's demand for X falls from q_x^0 to q_x^2 in response to the fall in p_o. Here, then, the total cross-price effect is positive.

Figure 3.13 is an accurate representation of the effect on the demand for X when the prices of all goods other than X change (and in the same proportion). What if the price of one of the many goods and services available to the household changed? How would it affect the demand for X?

To analyze this situation, one must leave the indifference curve diagram, for it allows consideration of just two goods: X and "all other goods" combined. Instead, we must conduct the analysis in terms of a demand diagram. Figure 3.14 pictures the demand curve for X and the effect changes in the price of another good, Z, have on the demand for X. Line DD represents the quantities demanded of X at various possible prices of X, p_x, holding all other prices, family income, and preferences constant. Suppose the price of X is p_x^0. Then, at p_x^0 the household demands q_x^0 of X.

Now suppose that the price of good Z, p_z, falls. The fall in p_z will induce an increase in the quantity of Z demanded. What will be its effect on the demand for X? Its effect will differ depending on whether X and Z are substitutes or complements. Suppose they are substitutes for each other and, consequently, tend to be alternative ways of satisfying a particular want. As p_z falls, Z becomes cheaper relative to X than before, and because they are substitutes, the household will substitute added use of Z for some of its use of X. The demand for X will, therefore, fall. Consequently, the household's demand curve for X will shift to the left in Figure 3.14 to $D''D''$, indicating that regardless of the price of X, a fall in the price of Z will induce the family to demand less X than before. In particular, with the price of X at p_x^0, the fall in p_z leads to a fall in the quantity of X demanded from q_x^0 to q_x^2.

In contrast, suppose that X and Z are complements. That is, X and Z tend to be used in conjunction with each other to meet the same need. Then, as p_z falls and the quantity demanded of Z rises, the demand for X will also rise, because the two are complements of each other. Consequently, the family's demand curve for X will shift to the right in response to a fall in p_z, say to $D'D'$, indicating that the quantity demanded of X is larger as p_z falls, regardless of the price of X. In particular, at a price of X equal to p_x^0 the quantity of X demanded rises from q_x^0 to q_x^1 with a fall in p_z.

Substitutes and complements, then, can be defined in terms of the signs of their cross-price effects.

Definition: Two goods are substitutes if a rise in the price of one of the goods increases the demand for the other good.

Definition: Two goods are complements if a rise in the price of one of the goods reduces the demand for the other good.[10]

Cross-Price Elasticities

Cross-price effects can be measured in terms of elasticities just as can own-price effects. The advantage is the same; cross-price effects can be compared in elasticity terms because elasticities are defined in terms of percentage changes that are comparable across commodities. In

---

[10] The definitions given in the text are for gross cross-price effects. Substitutes and complements are also defined in terms of cross-substitution effects. (See mathematical note 5.)

contrast, cross-price effects, being defined in terms of the units in which the goods are sold, are not comparable, because the units are not commensurable.

Definition: The cross-price elasticity of demand for X with respect to the price of Z is the percentage change in the demand for X given a 1 percent change in the price of Z, holding other prices, income, and preferences constant.

The algebraic formula is $E_{xz} = (\Delta q_x / \Delta p_z)(p_z / q_x)$. This formula is for the point cross-price elasticity. The arc cross-price elasticity is analogous to the arc price and income elasticities: $Arc\ E_{xz} = (\Delta q_x / \Delta p_z)(p_z^0 + p_z^1)/$ $(q_x^0 + q_x^1)$, where the superscripts 0 and 1 denote the pre-change and post-change price levels, respectively. Computing formulas for point and arc cross-price elasticities are analogous to those for own-price elasticities and need not be given.

Empirical estimates of cross-price elasticities tend to be smaller than the estimates of the own-price elasticities for the same good. McCarthy (1996), for instance, estimates the own-price elasticity of demand for domestically produced automobiles to be −0.78, whereas the cross-price elasticity of demand for domestic cars with respect to the price of foreign cars is only 0.28. These broad categories of cars are substitutes for each other: an increase in the price of foreign cars increases the demand for domestically manufactured cars. More specifically, a 1 percent rise in the price of foreign cars can be expected to raise the demand for domestic cars by about 0.28 percent.

Another example of changes in the price of one good on the demands for other goods is the effect of the price of women's time on the household's purchase patterns. As the price of women's time has risen, married women increasingly have entered the labor market and, in consequence, have reduced the household work they do. Also in response, households have increased their demands for some goods and services and reduced their demands for others. Estimates indicate that the cross-price elasticity between the price of women's time (i.e., female wage rate) and the demand for housing is 0.29; for gasoline and motor oil, −0.62; for electricity and natural gas, −0.40; and for transportation services, −0.33 (Bryant and Wang 1990a). As female wage rates have risen and continue to rise, the demand for housing rises while the demands for gasoline and oil, electricity and natural gas, and transportation services all fall due to cross-price effects.

PREFERENCE EFFECTS

Changes in prices and income are not the only things affecting the demand for goods and services by households. Household preferences also affect demand. The economic model of the household, however, provides few insights about how preferences are formed or why they might change over time. This is because economists are interested in preferences only as they are revealed through household behavior (i.e., the household's demand for goods). To learn more about *why* preferences vary, one must turn to sociological, psychological, political, and anthropological treatments of the family – a task that is beyond the scope of this book.

Although economics cannot provide a thorough understanding of preference formation and change within the household, the economic model does recognize that "preference shifters" influence household demand. Preference shifters are observable characteristics that are associated with differences in underlying preference orderings. They typically are classified into two groups. The first group of preference shifters includes attributes of the purchase situation such as advertising or seasonality. For instance, Gould (1998) found that households that did not currently purchase butter were more likely to purchase butter during November and December when many households do extra baking for the winter holidays.

The second group includes socio-demographic and cultural features of the household. Household characteristics that are associated with variations in preferences include the age, education, and ethnicity of the adult(s) in the household, the household's religious affiliation, household size, and household composition. For example, households that affiliate with certain religions may have dietary restrictions that limit their consumption of certain foods or alcohol (e.g., members of the Church of Jesus Christ of Latter Day Saints are instructed to not drink alcohol).

Perhaps the two most powerful preference shifters that are used by economists to explain differences in the demands for goods and services among households are household size and composition. The following section discusses these preference shifters and reports some illustrative empirical estimates of such effects.

Household Size and Composition Effects

Differences in household size and composition have different effects on demand depending on the good or service in question. Furthermore, a change in composition may affect household size. The addition of a baby simultaneously changes a household's size as well as its composition. The aging of the baby, however, changes only the household's composition. Adding a baby to a household increases the household's demand for baby clothes, baby foods, baby furniture, and the like, whereas the arrival of a grandparent affects the demands for none of these goods and services but will affect the demands for others, such as medical services and food and perhaps television and telephone service. Adding either a baby or a grandparent increases the household's demand for housing but to different degrees.

The essential thing that a change in household size or composition does is alter the household's preferences for goods and services. Geometrically this means that the shapes of the household's indifference curves are altered, that is, such changes alter the household's marginal rates of substitution between goods and services. Prior to the arrival of a baby the household would be quite unwilling to give up any other good or service in order to increase its consumption of, say, diapers. The arrival of a baby changes this: the marginal rate of substitution of diapers for "all other goods" increases precipitously. Upon arrival of the baby, the household is much more willing to give up some other things in order to acquire diapers, holding satisfaction constant.

In a diagram with toys on the horizontal axis and "all other goods" on the vertical, a new baby alters the indifference curves so that they are steeper. This is illustrated in Figure 3.15. Indifference curve U_0 is one of the household's indifference curves between toys and "all other goods" prior to the arrival of a child. Assume that $q_t^1 - q_t^0$ measures one unit of toys. At point A on indifference curve U_0, then, the household would willingly give up $q_o^0 - q_o^1$ units of "all other goods" in exchange for an added unit of toys, holding satisfaction constant. In other words, points A and B are on U_0. When a child is added to the household, however, the household's preferences change. Now, it is willing to give up more of "all other goods" in exchange for another unit of toys and will still be as satisfied as it was before. Where before at point A it would have given up $q_o^0 - q_o^1$ for an added unit of toys, now it will give up $q_o^0 - q_o^2$ and still be as satisfied as it was before. If so, then, point C rather than B must now be on the same indifference curve as point A. Thus, the arrival of the child into the household served to "rotate" the household's indifference curves clockwise and make them steeper at point A.

The effect of the child-induced shift in preferences on the demand for toys is illustrated in Figure 3.16. Prior to the arrival of the child, the

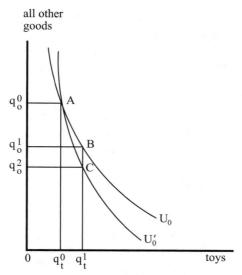

Figure 3.15. The effect of the arrival of a child on the household's preference map with respect to children's toys.

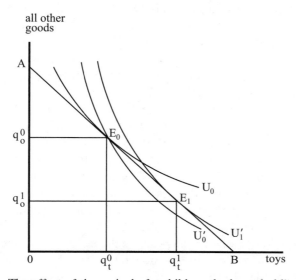

Figure 3.16. The effect of the arrival of a child on the household's demand for toys.

household's demand for toys was q_t^0, given prices and its income represented by the budget line AB, and given preferences represented by indifference curve U_0. The arrival of a child increases the marginal rate of substitution of toys for other things, shifting the indifference curves to U_0' and U_1'. At the pre-child equilibrium purchase pattern, E_0, the household is willing to pay a higher than market price for toys relative to "all other goals" things; that is, the marginal rate of substitution at point E_0 (i.e., the slope of U_0') is now steeper than the budget line. Consequently, in order to maximize satisfaction the household increases its demand for toys and reduces its demand for "all other goods" until it reaches E_1, at which it demands q_t^1 of toys and q_o^1 of "all other goods."

Note that neither relative market prices nor the household's income changed and, therefore, the budget line remained unchanged. Instead, the household's preferences changed with the arrival of the child and, in consequence, altered the household's purchase pattern of goods and services. In order to buy more toys for the child, the household had to reduce its demand for other things. This occurred because before and after the child arrived, the household's expenditures exhausted its income. Something had to make way for the added toys in the household's purchase pattern.

As the child grows, the needs and wants of the child (and of the parents for the child and for themselves) will change, and these, too, will alter the household's preference map. The marginal rates of substitution between some goods will increase while others will reduce. As they do, the household's demands for the individual goods and services will increase or decrease. These are household composition effects because household size remains constant.

The arrival of a child in the household (or some other individual, such as an older adult) has both size and composition effects. The two effects are difficult to separate empirically.

An example of household size and composition effects on demand is the change in demand for electricity. Branch (1993) examined the effects of household size and composition on the short-run residential demand for electricity and found them both to be important factors in explaining the variation in demand. For example, his analyses reveal that, on average, the addition of one individual to the household raises electricity demand by 8 percent (i.e., the household size effect). In addition, with each additional year that the reference person in the household ages, he found that electricity demand rises by 0.3 percent (i.e., the household composition effect). So, a household with a reference person who was 45 years old would consume 6 percent more electricity on average than an otherwise similar household in which the reference person was 25 years old.

SUMMARY

Three of the major determinants of household consumption patterns are prices, income, and preferences. As the real income of the consumer changes, more or fewer consumption alternatives become available depending on the direction of the real income change. In response, consumers alter their consumption patterns: increasing their demands for normal goods and reducing their demands for inferior goods with income increases. As some prices change relative to others, some consumer goods become cheaper and others more expensive. The price changes set up incentives for consumers to demand more of the cheaper goods and less of the more expensive ones. The price changes also alter the household's real income, inducing income effects.

Neither price nor income changes are hypothesized to alter consumers' preference patterns; that is, the shapes and locations of their indifference curves. Characteristics of the purchase situation and characteristics of the household can affect preferences. For instance, a change in household size alters the prices consumers are willing to pay for goods and services; that is, their marginal rates of substitution between goods. These changes in preferences, operating against a background of constant market prices and real income, lead the household to change its purchase pattern in favor of those goods for which the marginal rates of substitution have risen and away from those goods for which the marginal rates of substitution have fallen.

So, now we return to a question that was asked at the beginning of this chapter: What factors could be responsible for the shift in consumption patterns that was observed over the decade of the 1990s? The answers are now clear. Changes in consumption patterns are driven largely by changes in household income, market prices, and household preferences.

Mathematical Notes

1. Suppose there are only three goods in the market with quantities of the goods being q_1, q_2, and q_3, and their analogous prices being p_1, p_2, and p_3. The budget constraint, then, is

$$p_1 q_1 + p_2 q_2 + p_3 q_3 = Y \tag{1}$$

where Y represents total income. But suppose also that p_2 and p_3 move proportionately such that

$$p_2 = \alpha_2 p \quad \text{and} \quad p_3 = \alpha_3 p \tag{2}$$

where α_2 and α_3 are constants of proportionality and p can be regarded as a price analogous to the Consumer Price Index but excludes the price of good 1. Then, the budget constraint can be rephrased as

$$p_1 q_1 + p(\alpha_2 q_2 + \alpha_3 q_3) = Y \tag{3}$$

or as

$$p_1 q_1 + p q_0 = Y \tag{4}$$

where $\alpha_2 q_2 + \alpha_3 q_3 = q_o$. Then q_o is a price-weighted quantity index of all goods other than good 1. The utility function can, then, be defined as

$$U = u(q_1, q_o) \tag{5}$$

where q_1 is the good being analyzed and q_o is a composite good of "all other goods." If the prices of goods 2 and 3 don't move proportionately, then "all other goods" cannot be so collapsed into the composite good, q_o. This is Hicks' Composite Good Theorem.

2. The income effect is derived by the calculus in the following way. Find the conditions for maximizing the utility function,

$$U = u(q_x, q_o) \tag{6}$$

subject to the budget constraint,

$$p_x q_x + p_o q_o = Y \tag{7}$$

by forming the Lagrangean expression

$$L_g = u(q_x, q_o) - \lambda(p_x q_x + p_o q_o - Y) \tag{8}$$

(where $\lambda =$ the Lagrangean multiplier); differentiating equation (8) with respect to q_x, q_o, and λ; and setting the first derivatives to 0. This yields the following first-order conditions for a maximum:

$$u_x - \lambda p_x = 0 \tag{9}$$

$$u_o - \lambda p_o = 0 \tag{10}$$

$$-p_x q_x - p_o q_o + Y = 0. \tag{11}$$

Now, taking the total differential of equations (9)–(11) yields

$$u_{xx} dq_x + u_{xo} dq_o - p_x d\lambda = \lambda dp_x \tag{12}$$

$$u_{ox} dq_x + u_{oo} dq_o - p_o d\lambda = \lambda dp_o \tag{13}$$

$$-p_x dq_x - p_o dq_o - 0 d\lambda = q_x dp_x + q_o dp_o - dY. \tag{14}$$

Equations (12)–(14) can be solved for dq_x in terms of dp_x, dp_o, and dY employing matrix algebra to get

$$dq_x = \lambda(D_{xx}/D)dp_x + \lambda(D_{xo}/D)dp_o + (D_{x\lambda}/D)(q_x dp_x + q_o dp_o - dY)$$
(15)

where $D_{xi} (i = x, o, \lambda)$ is the cofactor of the xth element of the matrix

$$\begin{bmatrix} u_{xx} & u_{xo} & -p_x \\ u_{ox} & u_{oo} & -p_o \\ -p_x & -p_o & 0 \end{bmatrix}$$

and D is the determinant of the above matrix.

Equation (15) is the general form for the demand function for X expressed as a differential equation. That is, equation (15) tells us by how much the demand for X will change (i.e., dq_x) given small changes in p_x, p_o, and Y when they all occur at the same time.

The income effect on the demand for X, however, is the change in the demand for X when Y changes, holding p_x and p_o constant. To find the income effect on the demand for X, it remains to set dp_x and dp_o both equal to 0 (because prices are being held constant), divide through by dY, and change the "d" notation to the "∂" notation (in recognition of the fact that holding prices constant while income changes is a partial, not a total, derivative). Thus,

$$\partial q_x / \partial Y = -D_{x\lambda}/D.$$
(16)

From the second-order conditions for a maximum (see Henderson and Quandt 1958, Chapter 2, for a discussion of the second-order conditions), we know that $D > 0$, but we know nothing about the sign of $D_{x\lambda}$. Consequently, the income effect can be positive (a normal good), negative (an inferior good), or zero (income independent).

3. The Slutsky equation is derived from equation (15) in mathematical note 2. Recall that equation (15) is the total differential of q_x, showing the change in the demand for X given small changes in p_x, p_o, and Y all occurring simultaneously. To derive the own-price effect from equation (15), set dY and dp_o equal to 0 (because income and other prices are held constant), divide through equation (15) by dp_x, and change the "d" notation to "∂" in recognition of the fact that holding Y and p_o constant while changing p_x is a partial derivative. Thus,

$$\partial q_x / \partial p_x = \lambda(D_{xx}/D) + q_x(D_{x\lambda}/D).$$
(17)

How is equation (17) to be interpreted? Consider the second term on the right-hand side first. Since $\partial q_x / \partial Y = -D_{x\lambda}/D$ (see equation [16]), equation (17) can be rewritten as

$$\partial q_x / \partial p_x = \lambda(D_{xx}/D) - q_x(\partial q_x / \partial Y).$$
(18)

Clearly, the second term on the right-hand side of equation (18) is the "income effect" of the price change. As p_x falls, real income rises and the household increases its demand for X if X is normal. The more X the consumer purchased prior to the fall in p_x, the more income is saved at the lower price that can be spent on yet more X or other things. This is the explanation for the $-q_x$ term in the income effect part of equation (18). Furthermore, the more responsive the household is to any change in income (brought about in this case by a fall in p_x), the greater the income effect of the price change will be. Hence, the $\partial q_x / \partial Y$ term in equation (18).

Now consider the interpretation of the $\lambda(D_{xx}/D)$ term. One way of looking at $\lambda(D_{xx}/D)$ is to view it as the change in the demand for X due to a change in p_x, holding p_o constant and when $q_x dp_x + q_o dp_o - dY = 0$ in equation (15). Thus, we must find the conditions under which

$$q_x dp_x + q_o dp_o - dY = 0. \tag{19}$$

Along with the change in p_x, suppose income is (hypothetically) changed so that the household is neither better off nor worse off than before the price change. If so, household utility will not have changed and any change in utility brought about by price-induced changes in X must be exactly offset by changes in utility brought about by price-induced changes in "all other goods," O. Thus,

$$dU = u_x dq_x + u_o dq_o = 0. \tag{20}$$

But, since the household remains in equilibrium, equations (9) and (10) in mathematical note 2 still hold true. We can solve (9) for u_x and (10) for u_o and insert the results into equation (20) to get

$$\lambda p_x dq_x + \lambda p_o dq_o = 0$$

or, dividing through by $-\lambda$,

$$-p_x dq_x - p_o dq_o = 0. \tag{21}$$

Now, the total differential of the budget constraint is

$$-p_x dq_x - p_o dq_o = q_x dq_x + q_o dp_o - dY. \tag{22}$$

Since the left-hand side of equation (22) equals 0 according to equation (21), so must the right-hand side. Consequently, it must be the case that $\lambda(D_{xx}/D)$ is the change in the demand for X given a change in p_x, holding satisfaction (i.e., utility) constant. Thus,

$$\partial q_x / \partial p_x |_{u=c} = \lambda(D_{xx}/D). \tag{23}$$

The notation $\partial q_x / \partial p_x |_{u=c}$ is to be read as "the change in the demand for X due to a change in p_x, holding satisfaction (i.e., utility) constant." Clearly, then, equation (23) is the own-substitution effect. Substituting 23 into (18) yields

$$\partial q_x / \partial p_x = \partial q_x / \partial p_x |_{u=c} - q_x (\partial q_x / \partial Y) \tag{24}$$

which is the Slutsky equation. This presentation is an elaboration of the discussion in Henderson and Quandt (1958, p. 25).

4. The tied sale way of raising consumers' reservation prices above the market price can be modeled as follows. Supose the consumer's utility function is

$$U = u(q_1, q_2, q_3) \tag{25}$$

where q_1 is breakfast cereal, q_2 is magic decoder rings, and q_3 is "all other goods." Suppose, further, that the breakfast cereal firm creates a new good, q_z, by packaging magic decoder rings with the breakfast cereal such that one ring is packaged with each unit of cereal. Thus,

$$q_1 = q_z \quad \text{and} \quad q_2 = q_z. \tag{26}$$

Suppose, finally, the firm charges a price for the cereal plus the ring, p_z, equal to the price of the cereal, p_1. Form the budget constraint

$$p_1 q_1 + p_3 q_3 = Y. \tag{27}$$

Substitute (26) into (25) and (27) to get

$$U = u(q_z, q_z, q_3) \tag{28}$$

and

$$p_1 q_z + p_3 q_3 = Y. \tag{29}$$

Maximizing (28) subject to (29) yields the following equilibrium conditions:

$$(u_1 + u_2)/u_3 = p_1/p_3 \quad \text{for} \quad q_z > 0 \ \text{and} \ q_3 > 0; \tag{30}$$
$$(u_1 + u_2)/u_3 < p_1/p_3 \quad \text{for} \quad q_z > 0 \ \text{and} \ q_3 > 0. \tag{31}$$

The reservation price of good z is $(u_1 + u_2)/u_3|_{q_z=0}$. The addition of the ring to the cereal raises the reservation price of cereal by u_2, thus raising the likelihood that more consumers will purchase the cereal than in the absence of the tied sale.

5. The definitions of substitutes and complements given in the text are for *gross substitutes* and *gross complements*; that is, the definitions are in terms of the *total cross-price effects*. However, total cross-price effects can be *decomposed into cross-substitution and income effects* by means of a Slutsky equation just as *own-price effects* can be decomposed into *substitution and income effects*.

   The Slutsky equation for the cross-price effect is derived from equation (15) by setting $dp_x = dY = 0$, dividing through by dp_o, and changing the "d" notation to the "∂" notation to signify a partial derivative. This yields

$$\partial q_x/\partial p_o = \lambda(D_{xo}/D) + q_o(D_{x\lambda}/D) \tag{32}$$

where $\lambda(D_{xo}/D) = \partial q_x/\partial p_o|_{u=0}$ and is called the cross-substitution effect, and $-(D_{x\lambda}/D) = \partial q_x/\partial Y$ and is called the income effect (see equation [16]). Consequently, the cross-price Slutsky equation is

$$\partial q_x/\partial p_o = \partial q_x/\partial p_o|_{u=c} - q_o \partial q_x/\partial Y. \tag{33}$$

Even though equation (33) was derived from a two-good model, the Slutsky equation for the cross-price effect when there are more than two goods has the identical form.

Net substitutes and *net complements* are defined in terms of the cross-substitution effect. Two goods are net substitutes if the cross-substitution effect of a change in the price of one of the goods on the demand for the other is positive. Two goods are net complements if the cross-substitution effect of a change in the price of one of the goods on the demand for the other is negative. Unless otherwise stated in the text, the terms *substitutes* and *complements* will refer to gross complements and substitutes.

FOUR

Consumption and Saving

INTRODUCTION

In Chapters 2 and 3 a simple one-period model was developed and used to analyze household demands for goods and services at any point in time. In such a model the household has no memory and no foresight; it lives only in the present. Although terribly simple, the model is very helpful in understanding how families allocate their current income among the competing current demands for those resources.

But households are not so myopic as to confine their decision making to the present. They recognize that today is not a capsule with no yesterday and tomorrow. Rather, today's decisions must be made in recognition of what occurred before and what is expected to occur in the future. Commitments made in previous periods are honored in the present. Furthermore, not only do they expect to demand goods and services tomorrow, but households also expect to have added resources in the future. Consequently, one can expect that households will behave today in the light of their yesterdays and what they expect for their tomorrows.

That the consumption behavior of families has a past is reflected in the fact that families have debts from the past that they must pay off at least in part in the present and that they have resources from the past (financial assets like bank accounts, stocks and bonds, and physical assets, such as owned homes, cars, durables, and the like) that can be used to augment present consumption. That families' consumption behavior anticipates a future is reflected in the fact that families typically do save and borrow and do not consume all their assets in the present.

Table 4.1. *Income, Consumption, Saving, and Interest Payments in the United States: 1990–1998*

	Billions of Dollars			Percentage of PDI		
Item	1990	1995	2002	1990	1995	2002
Personal disposable income (PDI)	4179	5277	7816	100	100	100
Personal consumption expenditures	3839	4954	7304	91.9	93.9	93.5
Personal saving	221.3	180	291	5.3	3.4	3.7
Net personal transfers to rest of world	10	16	32.3	0.2	0.3	0.4
Interest paid by consumers	109	128	188.4	2.6	2.4	2.4

Source: U.S. Bureau of the Census 2003, Table 668.

These facts are well reflected in the national data on consumption and savings for the United States shown in Table 4.1. In 1990, $3839 billion was spent on consumption, $221 billion was saved, and $109 billion was used to pay the interest on consumer debt. These amounts accounted for 91.9 percent, 5.3 percent, and 2.6 percent of personal disposable income (PDI), respectively. By 2002, American consumers were consuming much more, saving much more, and paying much more interest on consumer debt absolutely. But the percentages of PDI show that by 2002, Americans were consuming more, paying less interest on consumer debt, and saving less relative to PDI than they did in 1990.

In each year, however, consumers saved in anticipation for consumption in the future, and made interest payments on debts incurred in the past in order to expand past consumption. Clearly, the past, present, and future are reflected in these patterns.

Making present decisions in the light of the past and the expected future is characteristic of all household economic behavior. In this, our first examination of the consequences of decision making over time, we will concentrate on the household's aggregate consumption and saving decisions: how much of current resources is devoted to present consumption and how much is used to pay for either past or future consumption. Consequently, both borrowing and lending will be analyzed because they are the principal ways by which households are able to transfer resources from one period to another. In brief, each household must decide what fraction of its current resources it will consume and what fraction it will save.

But what is consumption and what is saving? We need accurate definitions of these two concepts and a better understanding of how each is carried out.

Definition: Consumption is an activity in which goods are purchased and yield satisfaction in the current period.

Food purchased and consumed today is consumption. The purchase and use of a theater ticket or electricity today is consumption. What about purchases and use of CDs or clothing today? Certainly, consumption is involved because resources are being expended today that yield satisfaction today. But because the CDs can be listened to and the clothes worn tomorrow, too, resources are also being expended today that yield satisfaction tomorrow. This is the essence of saving.

Definition: Saving is an activity in which resources are used in the current period and yield satisfaction in future periods.

Purchases of CDs and clothing are examples of activities that are simultaneously consumption and saving. So is the purchase of a car or other durable good.[1] Pure saving occurs when households use some of their current resources to increase their bank balances, buy stocks and bonds, or lend money to an individual or firm. Indeed, increasing their bank balances is, in reality, simply lending money to the bank. In cases of pure saving the resources saved increase satisfaction in the period in the future when they are consumed.

Consumption-saving is, therefore, a continuum with pure consumption at one extreme and pure saving at the other. As with other continua, we will simplify matters by investigating only the extremes: pure consumption and pure saving. With an understanding of household behavior at each of the poles of the continuum, we can better understand the behavior at any point along the continuum.

We have discussed saving as if it were always either zero or some positive amount. Nothing can be further from the truth. Households can also dissave and frequently do. Dissaving is the reverse of saving.

---

[1] The U.S. government classifies cars, furniture, and household equipment as durables and includes them in personal consumption expenditures (see Table 3.1). Clothing and cassette tapes are judged to have lives of less than three years and are classified as nondurables but are also included in personal consumption expenditures (U.S. Bureau of Economic Analysis 1986). In reality, then, government statistics overestimate consumption and underestimate saving.

Definition: Dissaving involves the transfer of future resources to the present so as to increase current consumption.

Dissaving involves borrowing. When we borrow money to buy a house, a car, or an education, we transfer resources we expect to have in the future for use in the present period. If debts outstanding are subtracted from assets (i.e., total savings), the result is net assets or net worth. We can say, then, that saving occurs when net worth increases and dissaving occurs when net worth declines. Paying off debts, then, is just as much saving as increasing one's bank balances.

The major question addressed in this chapter is how the household allocates its resources through time: what factors determine its total consumption, and what factors determine its total saving. One of the important determinants of consumption and saving is income, and therefore space is devoted to it in this chapter. The relation of consumption to income has engaged the interests of economists since the Great Depression of the 1930s because of its implications for monetary and fiscal policy. We will also examine how household consumption and saving behavior responds to changes in both interest rates and prices (i.e., inflation and deflation). We also examine factors that account for the pattern of household consumption and saving over the household's life cycle.

A CONSUMPTION AND SAVING MODEL OF THE HOUSEHOLD

The factors from the past and the future that bear on a household's current consumption and saving decisions can be examined within a very simple model containing two periods: today and tomorrow. Interpret "today" as the current year and "tomorrow" as next year. Assume that the household will not exist "the day after tomorrow" and that it leaves no inheritances when it departs the scene. Assume, moreover, that the household knows for certain today what tomorrow will be like: that is, what its income tomorrow will be, what tomorrow's prices will be, and what its preferences will be tomorrow.

Such a circumstance is a gross caricature of the actual situation in which families must make their decisions. The restriction of the model to "today" and "tomorrow" is made so that we can represent the model on a two-dimensional diagram rather than with more complicated mathematics. The assumption that the household leaves no bequests is also made to contain the model to two dimensions. And presuming that the household knows the future with certainty allows us to ignore the much more complicated mathematics required to model uncertainty. Nonetheless, the model sheds much light on actual behavior, and its simplicity dispenses with much irrelevant detail.

The household is pictured at the beginning of year one faced with deciding how much to consume in years one and two, denoted by C_1 and C_2, respectively, such that it exhausts its total resources. Its total resources include its labor income in years one and two, denoted by Y_1, and Y_2, along with whatever net assets (assets minus debts), denoted by A_1, it brought into the current period from the past. A_1, therefore, is negative if the household's total debts exceed its total assets. A_1, is positive if its total assets exceed its total debts. The household will make its consumption and saving decisions so as to maximize its satisfaction over the two periods; that is, so as to achieve the goals it has set out for itself, subject to the total resources at its disposal.

As with the model in Chapters 2 and 3, the intertemporal household model contains three parts: the household's intertemporal budget constraint, the household's preferences, and the behavioral hypothesis that it makes decisions to maximize satisfaction. We deal with each in turn.

The Household's Intertemporal Budget Constraint

At this point we need an accurate representation of the resources at the household's disposal at the beginning of year one when it makes its decisions. Think about it in the following way. The household has its net assets, A_1, plus its current income, Y_1. In addition, it has the maximum amount of money it can borrow using year two's income, Y_2, as collateral. Let the maximum sum it can borrow be denoted by B_1^m. B_1^m can be viewed as the household's credit line. Thus total household resources at the beginning of year one, R_1, equal

$$R_1 = A_1 + Y_1 + B_1^m. \tag{4.1}$$

Can we be more precise about B_1^m? Anything the household borrows in year one must be paid back with interest in year two. Supposing the rate of interest to be r, then in year two B_1^m must be paid back plus the interest on B_1^m, which is rB_1^m. What will this amount to? No lender will loan more than the household can pay back with its income in year two. Consequently, the principal and interest on the maximum loan will equal year two's income, Y_2:

$$B_1^m + r B_1^m = Y_2. \tag{4.2}$$

Solving for B_1^m yields the maximum loan:

$$B_1^m = Y_2/(1+r). \tag{4.3}$$

For example, if the household's expected income in year two was \$100 and the rate of interest was 10 percent, then the household could borrow a total of \$ 100/1.10 = \$90.91 in year one. In year two the \$90.91 principle would be paid back along with \$9.09 in interest in year two. $Y_2/(1+r)$, then, is the value of year two's income in year one. Alternatively, $Y_2/(1+r)$ is referred to as the present value of Y_2, valued at the beginning of year one (see mathematical note 1). The total resources of the household at the beginning of year one then sum to

$$R_1 = A_1 + Y_1 + Y_2/(1+r). \tag{4.4}$$

Another way of looking at R_1 is to view it as representing the maximum expenditure on current consumption the household could make in year one if it spent its entire resources on current consumption and consumed nothing in year two. Thus,

$$p_c C_1^m = R_1 \tag{4.5}$$

where C_1^m represents the maximum quantity of goods and services the household could consume in year one, given that the price of goods and services was p_c.[2] Thus,

$$C_1^m = R_1/p_c. \tag{4.6}$$

On a graph with consumption in year one ("today") on the horizontal axis and consumption in year two ("tomorrow") on the vertical axis, $(C_1^m, 0) = D$ plotted on the horizontal axis represents the maximum possible consumption in year one and the minimum consumption in year two given the household's resources, the market rate of interest at which money can be borrowed, and the price of consumption goods. Such a graph is pictured in Figure 4.1.

Likewise, we can compute the maximum quantity of goods and services the household could consume in year two if it saved all of its year one

---

[2] The price of consumption goods and services, p_c, is assumed not to change between year one and year two. This assumption allows us to postpone discussing questions of inflation and deflation until later in the chapter.

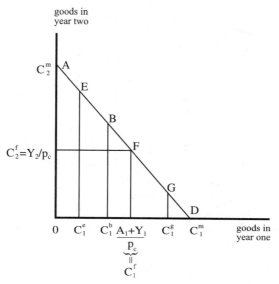

Figure 4.1. The household's budget line between consumption in year one and consumption in year two.

income and net assets. Saving this amount would yield $A_1 + Y_1$ in year two plus the interest on this sum, $r(A_1 + Y)$. Adding to this sum income received in year two, Y_2, the maximum expenditure on goods and services consumable in year two would be

$$p_c C_2^m = (1 + r)(A_1 + Y_1) + Y_2 \tag{4.7}$$

where C_2^m is the maximum quantity of goods and services consumable in year two, or

$$C_2^m = [(1 + r)(A_1 + Y_1) + Y_2]/p_c. \tag{4.8}$$

Plotting $(0, C_2^m) = A$ on the vertical axis of Figure 4.1 represents the maximum quantity of goods and services purchasable in year two and the minimum quantity purchasable in year one. A straight line joining A and D represents the household's budget line. It represents all the combinations of C_1 and C_2 available to the household if it exhausts its total resources between the two years. This budget line is exactly analogous to the budget lines that were developed in Chapter 2 and used to analyze demand in Chapter 3.

The slope of the budget line in Figure 4.1 represents the rate at which the household is able to exchange consumption in year one for consumption in year two in the market. Algebraically, the

$$\text{slope} = -\frac{\text{rise}}{\text{run}} = \frac{[(1+r)(Y_1 + A_1) + Y_2]/p_c}{[(Y_1 + A_1) + Y_2/(1+r)]/p_c} = -(1+r).$$

Thus, a dollars' worth of consumption in year one can be exchanged for $(1 + r)$ dollars' worth of consumption in year two. This is reasonable: giving up a dollar's worth of consumption in year one implies that $1.00 is saved. By year two, the saved dollar is worth $1.00 (1 + r)$ and thence can buy $(1 + r)$ dollars' worth of consumption in year two. Conversely, borrowing a dollar from year two for use in year one yields $1/(1 + r)$ dollars of purchasing power in year one since the dollar next year must pay off both the loan and the interest on the loan.

The intertemporal budget line in Figure 4.1 does more than illustrate possible consumption combinations in years one and two. It also illustrates regions of saving and borrowing. Saving is income minus consumption. If consumption in year one is C_1, saving is $S_1 = Y_1 - p_c C_1$. Suppose at point B in Figure 4.1, $C_1^b = Y_1/p_c$. Thus, $S_1 = 0$. Point E, lying to the left of point B, represents a situation in which consumption, C_1^e, is less than at point B, and therefore saving, S_1, must be positive. Point G, lying to the right of point B, represents a situation in which consumption, C_1^g, is greater than at point B, where it equals Y_1/p_c, and therefore saving, S_1, must be negative. Negative saving, of course, is the equivalent of borrowing. Point B, therefore, represents a situation in which the household represented by this budget line would be neither a saver nor a borrower. Any point on the budget line to the left of B is the saving region, whereas any point to the right of B is the borrowing region.

Point F and the region between B and F in Figure 4.1 are also of interest. Suppose at F, $C_1^f = (A_1 + Y_1)/p_c$ and $C_2^f = Y_2/p_c$. Thus, if the household were consuming at point F it would consume all of its year one resources in year one and all of its year two resources in year two. In this case, the household would be consuming all of its net assets, A_1. By consuming its net assets the household is, in a sense, borrowing from itself. This occurs at any point between B and F. To the right of F, say at G, the household consumes more than $(A_1 + Y_1)/p_c$ in year one and can only do so by borrowing in the credit market.

The Household's Time Preference Map

Just as the consumer has preferences among combinations of goods at any point in time (see Chapter 2), the consumer also has preferences

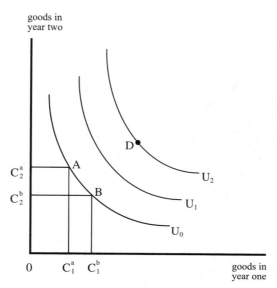

Figure 4.2. The household's time preference map.

among consumption in different years. Figure 4.2 illustrates a representative set of indifference curves between consumption in year one, C_1, and consumption in year two, C_2. Each of the indifference curves in Figure 4.2 is the locus of all points representing combinations of C_1 and C_2 among which the household is indifferent. The household, for instance, is indifferent between (C_1^a, C_2^a) and (C_1^b, C_2^b) on indifference curve U_0. It prefers combination D on U_2 to either A or B because D contains more consumption in both years.

The slope of each of these indifference curves represents the marginal rate of substitution of C_1 for C_2, $MRS_{1,2}$; that is, the rate at which the household is willing to substitute consumption in year one for consumption in year two and still be as satisfied as it was before. And, as with the marginal rate of substitution between goods at a single point in time, the marginal rate of substitution between consumption through time diminishes. Hence, the indifference curves in the household's time preference map are negatively sloped and convex to the origin.

Time Preference and Other Motives for Saving. The $MRS_{1,2}$ can be used to characterize a household's time preference. Households are said to be present oriented, future oriented, or have neutral time preference. The essential characteristic of a present-oriented household is that given no other motive to transfer resources between periods, such a household prefers to consume more in the current period than in future periods. Consequently, such a household will borrow against future income so as to consume more today. A future-oriented household will save in similar circumstances, whereas a household with neutral time preference will neither borrow nor lend.

From the information in previous sections, it is clear that an understanding of time preference and its rigorous definition requires a discussion of other motives for saving and the specification of conditions that remove all motives for saving except the relative preference for consumption now or in the future. Consequently, we must discuss other motives for saving.

EVENING OUT THE INCOME STREAM. The first motive arises because the receipt of one's resources through time is uneven and will not match the desired time path of consumption. By saving or borrowing, one can rearrange one's resources in time so that they match the desired time path of consumption.

This is an important reason for saving. It is common knowledge that an individual's income is low while that individual is young, rises after the completion of one's education, rises more with the pursuit of one's occupation, and subsequently falls in retirement. In the face of this life-cycle pattern of income, people commonly borrow against future income when young in order to finance educations, houses, and the like. In contrast, beginning somewhere in middle age, people typically save to increase their resources during retirement. During retirement, saving may fall as retirees live off their accumulated wealth. The earlier borrowing, followed by saving and then, in retirement, the possible running down of net wealth are attempts to even out the receipt of one's income stream over the life cycle to make it coincide more closely with desired consumption patterns.

CONSUMING WHEN GOODS ARE CHEAP. A second motive for saving and borrowing is to transfer resources into time periods when goods are relatively cheap and to transfer resources out of periods when goods are relatively expensive. High interest rates today mean that today's income can buy more goods tomorrow than they can today. Similarly, if prices are expected to be lower tomorrow than today, a dollar saved today can buy more goods tomorrow than if spent today. In contrast, low interest rates today or the expectation of higher prices tomorrow each create incentives to borrow from the high-priced future in order to consume more today when goods are cheaper. Rearranging one's income stream through time so that it coincides with the pattern of prices and interest rates through time is, then, the second motive.

BEQUESTS. An important reason to save is to leave an inheritance for one's heirs; that is, a bequest. However, this motive has been excluded at the outset by assuming that the consumer leaves nothing behind when she dies at the end of period 2.

HEDGING AGAINST UNCERTAINTY. A final reason to save is as a hedge against uncertainty. That is, to create a buffer against the possibility of a spell of unforseen unemployment or unexpected health care expenses. This kind of saving is typically called *precautionary saving*. Precautionary saving is excluded in the model by the assumption that the consumer is certain about the future.

TIME PREFERENCE, PER SE. The fifth motive, time preference, is simply the desire to rearrange one's consumption pattern through time – unaffected by, the expected pattern of prices, interest rates, and income through time, and also unaffected by uncertainty or the bequest motive. As such, time preference is reflected in the shapes of the indifference curves between consumption now and consumption then. Thus, the $MRS_{1,2}$ can reveal a consumer's time preference in circumstances in which the other motives for saving and borrowing are removed.

Motives for saving other than time preference are removed when a consumer's resources are distributed evenly through time (i.e., $A_1 = 0$ and $Y_1 = Y_2$), when interest rates provide no incentive either to borrow or to lend (i.e., when $r = 0$), and when the pattern of prices in time provides no incentive either to borrow or to lend (i.e., when $p_1 = p_2 = p_c$).

Definition: A consumer with neutral time preference will neither borrow nor lend when $A_1 = 0$, $Y_1 = Y_2$, $r = 0$, and $p_1 = p_2 = p_c$.

Definition: A present-oriented consumer will borrow when $A_1 = 0$, $Y_1 = Y_2$, $r = 0$, and $p_1 = p_2 = p_c$.

Definition: A future-oriented consumer will save when $A_1 = 0$, $Y_1 = Y_2$, $r = 0$, and $p_1 = p_2 = p_c$.

Such preferences are illustrated in Figure 4.3. Budget line AB is drawn with a slope of -1; that is, if $r = 0$ and p_c is constant through time, then the slope of $AB = -(1+r)/1 = -1$. Given that the household's resources are equal in the two years, $Y_1 = Y_2 = Y$ and $A_1 = 0$, the point at which the household neither borrows nor saves is $(Y_1/p_c, Y_2/p_c)$; that is, point N. Budget line AB, then, sets up the conditions under which the motives other than time preference are set aside.

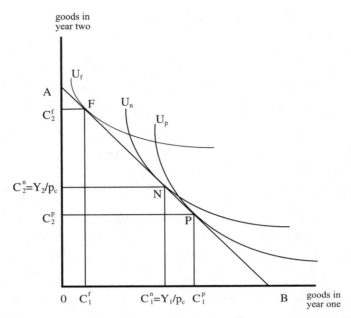

Figure 4.3. A present-oriented household, P, a future-oriented household, F, and a household with neutral time preference, N.

Three households, each with different time preferences and represented by U_p, U_n, and U_f are shown. Each maximizes satisfaction at a different point when faced with the same circumstances, AB. Household N, possessing indifference curve U_n, maximizes satisfaction at point N, where it consumes its income in each year and neither borrows or saves. It has *neutral time preference*. Household P, with indifference curve U_p, maximizes satisfaction between N and B at P. It borrows, $C_1^p - Y_1/p_c$, and so consumes more than its income in the present. It is *present oriented*. In short, household P is "impatient" and its impatience leads it to consume more in the present at the expense of less in the future. Household F, represented by indifference curve U_f, maximizes its satisfaction at point F between A and N. At point F its consumption in year one is C_1^f, less than its income. Consequently, it saves $(Y_1/p_c) - C_1^f$ so that it can consume C_2^f in year two, an amount more than its income in year two. Household F, therefore, is *future oriented*. Household F is "patient," preferring to consume more in the future than in the present.

If the $MRS_{1,2}$ of a family at point N is -1, the family has neutral time preference. If the $MRS_{1,2}$ of a family at N is less than -1 (i.e., the indifference curve through point N has less slope than AB), the family is future

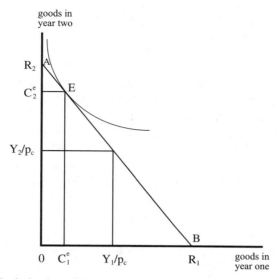

Figure 4.4. Maximization of intertemporal household satisfaction subject to the household's resource constraint.

oriented. If the family's $MRS_{1,2}$ at N is greater than -1 (i.e., the indifference curve through point N is steeper than AB), the family is present oriented.

The two-period, intertemporal utility function is written most generally as

$$U = u(C_1, C_2). \tag{4.9}$$

A very common, more specific algebraic representation is the additive function

$$U = v(C_1) + (1 + \delta)^{-1} v(C_2) \tag{4.10}$$

where $\partial v / \partial C_i = v_i > 0 \, (i = 1, 2)$, $\partial v_i / \partial C_i = v_{ii} < 0$, and $\delta = $ rate of time preference. (See mathematical note 2.)

Intertemporal Satisfaction Maximization

When faced with its current and expected future resources, the prices of consumption goods, and interest rates, the household will choose that combination of current consumption and net saving (positive, if saving exceeds borrowing; negative, if borrowing exceeds saving) that will maximize satisfaction (see mathematical note 3). This is illustrated in Figure 4.4.

The household represented by Figure 4.4 maximizes satisfaction at point E, where the budget line is tangent to the highest attainable indifference curve. At point E the family's marginal rate of time preference, as represented by the slope of the indifference curve, equals the rate at which goods in year one can be exchanged for goods in year two in the marketplace, as represented by the slope of the budget line. This family consumes C_1^e in year one and saves $Y_1 - p_c C_1^e = S_1^e$. In year two it consumes C_2^e, spending an amount in excess of its income in year two by the amount saved in year one, S_1^e, plus the interest on that saved, $r S_1^e$.

Figure 4.4 makes clear that the household's current consumption and saving depend on the household's present and future expected resources, R_1, the price of consumption goods, p_c, and the interest rate, r, in addition to its rate of time preference, that is, whether it prefers current consumption to future consumption or the reverse. We now turn to a discussion of the role played by the household's resources in determining its consumption and saving.

THE RESOURCE-CONSUMPTION-SAVING RELATION

Households with different total resources will devote different amounts to current consumption and to saving. A household's total resources, R_1, are composed of current income, Y_1, future expected income, Y_2, and net assets, A_1. If current consumption is a normal good, an increase in Y_1, Y_2, or A_1, holding interest rates and prices constant, will increase current consumption. This means that a household's current consumption can be expected to increase if its future expected income rises even though the family experiences no increase in its current income. Likewise, two families, each with the same current and expected future incomes, will have different current consumptions and savings if one has borrowed more in the past and enters the current period with smaller net assets. The fewer total resources depresses the family's current consumption.

The effect of one such change in resources, an increase in future expected income, on current consumption and saving is illustrated in Figure 4.5. To simplify the diagram, net assets are assumed to be zero ($A_1 = 0$). Initially, the household faces budget line AB given its resources of Y_1 and Y_2, the interest rate r, and the price level, p_c. Given these conditions, the family maximizes satisfaction at point E_o, involving current consumption of C_1^0 and saving of $S_1^0 = (Y_1/p_c) - C_1^0$.

Now suppose that the family gains information on the basis of which it can expect income in the future to be Y_2^1 rather than Y_2. The increase

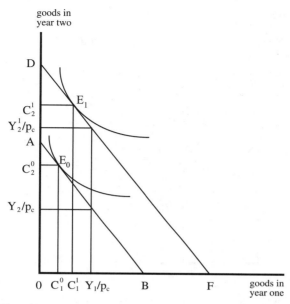

Figure 4.5. The effect of an increase in expected future income on current consumption and saving.

in future expected income increases the household's total resources and, thus, expands its opportunities, shifting the budget line from AB to DF. Given that present and future consumption are both normal goods (which is, in fact, the case empirically), the family's current consumption and future consumption will both increase. The increase in current consumption to C_1^1 brought about by the increase in future expected income from Y_2 to Y_2^1 leads to a decline in current saving to $S_1^1 = (Y_1/p_c) - C_1^1$.

The logic of this decline in current saving is that the increase in current consumption necessarily results in a decline in current saving because the increase in income will not actually occur until year two. Moreover, with the increase in future expected income the family needs to save less currently to provide for desired future consumption. This is exactly the behavior of a household that learns of a previously unexpected increase in future income via, for instance, a previously unforeseen future promotion or a previously unforeseen future inheritance. Current consumption rises and current savings falls.

A more likely change in a household's resources is a change in its current income. As a result of a rise in current income, its total resources increase, expanding consumption opportunities in both the present and

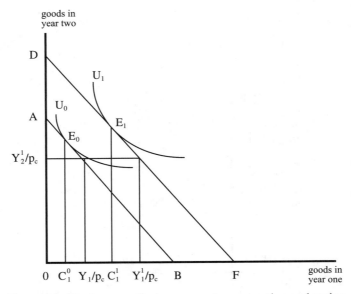

Figure 4.6. The income effect on current consumption and saving.

the future periods. Current consumption and current saving will both rise as long as consumption does not rise more than current income rises (which empirically is the case). If the household was a net borrower prior to the increase in current income, the increase in saving will take the form of a decline in net borrowing; that is, the household will pay some of its debts down. Figure 4.6 illustrates such a situation. When current income, Y_1, rises to Y_1^1, current consumption increases from C_1^0 to C_1^1 and saving increases to $(Y_1^1/p_c) - C_1^1$.

Economists have long had an interest in the relation between income and consumption because the relation has been a basis of policies combating depressions and unemployment. Some governmental policies seek to stimulate consumption by increasing people's income in the expectation that the increased consumption will stimulate an increase in employment. Such policies and the relationships underlying them are discussed in macroeconomics courses. Suffice it to say here that crucial to the effectiveness of such policies is the relationship between income and consumption, or the so-called consumption function.

The simple framework that has just been introduced is well suited for a discussion of the consumption function. The relation between income and consumption is the familiar Engel curve that was introduced and discussed in Chapter 3. There, the Engel curve was used to examine the relation between income and the demand for particular goods such as food, toys, or electricity. Here in Chapter 4, we use it to examine the relationship between consumption and income, where consumption is expenditures on all the goods the household buys.

We begin the discussion of the income-consumption relation with the absolute income hypothesis. Discussions of the permanent income and the life-cycle income hypotheses follow. The discussion ends with some of the modifications to the permanent income hypothesis that have been stimulated by events in the past twenty-five years. The history of these several hypotheses is included, in part, to show the student the interplay between theoretical and empirical research.

THE ABSOLUTE INCOME HYPOTHESIS

The first conception of the consumption function was the absolute income consumption function introduced by John Maynard Keynes in 1936. Keynes did not begin with the framework we have laid out in this chapter. Instead, he postulated that the "fundamental psychological law ... is that men are disposed as a rule and on the average to increase their consumption as their income increases but not by as much as the increase in their income" (1936, p. 96). This hypothesis implies that there is a positive relationship between current income and current consumption and that the change in current consumption due to a change in current income, $\Delta C_1 / \Delta Y_1$ in terms of the notation introduced in Chapter 3, is between 0 and 1; that is,

$$0 < \Delta C_1 / \Delta Y_1 < 1.$$

Keynes called $\Delta C_1 / \Delta Y_1$ the *marginal propensity to consume* (MPC), and subsequent authors have followed him.

Keynes's hypothesis, that the *MPC* is between 0 and 1, has been borne out by all subsequent empirical studies: the *MPC* has been found to be between 0.7 and 0.8 in most cross-section empirical studies. That is, if the current consumption expenditures of two groups of otherwise similar families are compared, one with current income $1000 higher than the other, the higher income families will have current consumption expenditures about $700 to $800 higher than the lower income families.

Keynes also hypothesized that high-income people save a higher fraction of their current income than low-income people. Again, this hypothesis is borne out by studies comparing the saving/income ratios of otherwise-similar rich and poor families.

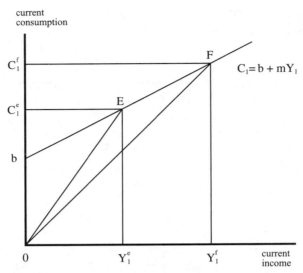

Figure 4.7. An example of a consumption function based on the absolute income hypothesis.

The absolute income consumption function is illustrated by the Engel curve in Figure 4.7. Current consumption, C_1, and current income, Y_1, are plotted on the vertical and horizontal axes respectively. The consumption function

$$C_1 = b + mY_1$$

is a positively sloped, straight line. The *MPC* is equal to m, the slope; that is, given an added dollar of current income, the household will increase its current consumption by m dollars, the increase being less than 1.

The second hypothesis, that the rich save a higher fraction of current income than the poor, is also illustrated by the consumption function in Figure 4.7. Take two points on the consumption function, one representing a low-income consumer, E, and the other representing a high-income consumer, F. Draw straight lines from E and F to the origin. The slopes of $0E$ and $0F$, C_1^e / Y_1^e and C_1^f / Y_1^f respectively, represent the consumption/income ratios at these points.[3] Note that $0F$ has less slope than $0E$,

---

[3] Note that we discussed the ratios of aggregate consumption to aggregate income in the United States at the beginning of this chapter when we discussed Table 4.1. In Table 4.1 the sum of personal consumption expenditures plus interest paid by consumers and net transfers to rest of the world is analogous to current consumption as defined here. Thus, the consumption/income ratio in 1998 was 99.5 percent and the saving/income ratio was 0.5 percent.

indicating that the high-income family has a lower consumption/income ratio than the poor family. Since $S_1 = Y_1 - p_c C_1$, the saving/income ratio must be higher for the rich family at F than for the poor family at E.

The consumption function in Figure 4.7, then, captures the two features of the absolute income hypothesis:

(1) $0 < MPC < 1$ and
(2) S_1/Y_1 rises as current income rises.

Any straight-line consumption function with $0 < m < 1$ and a positive intercept, b, is consistent with the absolute income hypothesis. Finally, recall from Chapter 3 that linear Engel curves with positive intercepts on the quantity axis exhibit income elasticities of demand that are less than 1. Thus, the absolute income hypothesis also implies that

(3) the income elasticity of current consumption, η_c, is less than 1:

$$\eta_c < 1, \text{ where } \eta_c = (\Delta C_1/\Delta Y_1)(Y_1/C_1)$$

because $\Delta C_1/\Delta Y_1 < Y_1/C_1$ (see Figure 4.7).

Thus, Keynes expected that a 1 percent increase in current income would result in a less than 1 percent increase in current consumption.

Although consumption functions estimated on the basis of Keynes's absolute income hypothesis contribute importantly to the explanation of differences between families' consumption patterns at any point in time, they predict badly what happens to aggregate consumption when aggregate income changes through time. Studies of the saving/income ratio for the nation as a whole over a long stretch of time (from the 1870s to the 1940s), ignoring depressions and periods of high inflations, showed that saving as a fraction of income remained constant at about 0.1 (Goldsmith 1955; Kuznets 1942). Real family income, however, quadrupled over this period. Keynes's absolute income consumption function, in which people save a higher fraction of income as their income rises, would predict that the saving/income ratio for the nation would have risen in the face of this massive increase in income. Yet, it did not. Something was wrong with the hypothesis.

THE PERMANENT AND LIFE-CYCLE INCOME HYPOTHESES

Several alternative hypotheses have been put forward as replacements for the Keynesian absolute income consumption function. Two have become quite important: the permanent income and the life-cycle income consumption functions.[4] Both are special cases of the model of intertemporal satisfaction maximization already presented. We will treat them as if they are the same hypothesis but we will use the permanent income hypothesis terminology. Both differ from the Keynesian consumption function in that they measure income by total resources, R_1, rather than by current income, Y_1. Also, both take note of the long-run constancy of the saving/income ratio.

Implicit in the absolute income hypothesis is the view that the family bases its consumption and saving decisions solely on the size of its current income. However, the household and lending institutions expect a stream of earnings and other income to accrue to the household in future periods. Current consumption can be financed out of net assets and out of loans against future expected income as well as out of current income. Consequently, the relevant relationship is between total resources and consumption, not current income and consumption.

That people base their consumption and saving decisions on their views of their total resources and not just on their current income also accords well with one of the major motives for saving. Not only do people realistically expect a stream of income in future periods, they also realistically expect that stream to vary over their expected life. Young people expect low incomes because they have yet to complete their education or are just beginning their careers. They also expect their incomes to rise as they gain experience and responsibility. They expect their incomes to level off and, perhaps, to fall upon retirement too. Furthermore, people in occupations with unstable employment patterns expect some unemployment and, consequently, some variability in their earnings over their work life. In contrast, employees in secure occupations expect little unemployment-related income variation.

Although people expect their incomes to vary over their lifetimes, they expect less variation in their consumption patterns over time: they must continue to be fed, clothed, and housed. Consequently, there is a need to shift resources from periods of high income to periods of low income in order to provide for consumption. The way this is done is by borrowing

---

[4] When first offered, the permanent income and the life-cycle income hypotheses were viewed as quite different. In the interim, the essential similarities have been identified so that the two have become almost one. The permanent income hypothesis is due to Milton Friedman and is found in his *A Theory of the Consumption Function* (1957). The life-cycle income hypothesis was put forward by Franco Modigliani, and a version can be found in Ando and Modigliani (1963).

from the future in times of low income to provide for current consumption and by saving in times of high income to pay back past debts and to provide for future consumption. Not only are total resources important to the saving-consumption decision, therefore, but the expected pattern of income over time is also important.

Both the permanent income and the life-cycle income hypotheses emphasize this reason for saving and borrowing: to even out the variations in one's income stream over time so as to make it match a relatively constant demand for goods and services through time. Indeed, both hypothesize that in the absence of changes in prices and interest rates and if family size and composition are constant, households with the same total resources will demand the same quantities of goods and services each year and so demand a constant consumption stream through time. Households with different total resources will demand different consumption streams: those with few total resources will consume less and those with more total resources will consume more. But, regardless of the quantity of resources households possess, each will try to have a constant consumption stream over their life cycle.[5]

The total resources of the family can be measured in two ways: as a stock of wealth or as a flow of income. We are already familiar with measuring the household's total resources as a stock of wealth, for that is what R_1 is: the present value of the family's net assets, current income, and future expected income. In the context of our two-period model,

$$R_1 = A_1 + Y_1 + Y_2/(1 + r). \tag{4.11}$$

The permanent income consumption function, however, has been phrased in terms of a flow of income, called permanent income and denoted as Y_p rather than as a stock of wealth.

Definition: Permanent income is defined as the constant (i.e., equal in each time period) annual income the present value of which equals the

---

[5] Remember, these hypotheses do not take into account changing prices, interest rates, and family size through time. Certainly, as we saw at the end of Chapter 3, an increase in family size will alter the total demand for goods and services and, thus, can be expected to affect the fraction of income saved. This means that as families have children and as the children grow up, become independent, and leave home, one can expect the fraction of income saved first to fall and then to increase. Furthermore, in Chapter 5 we will see that the systematic changes in the price of people's time (i.e., their wage rates) over the life cycle affects the consumption pattern over the life cycle. But here we ignore these phenomena and concentrate on the relationship between total resources and consumption.

family's net wealth, R_1. That is, in our two-period model

$$R_1 = Y_p + Y_p/(1+r). \tag{4.12}$$

Solving for Y_p yields

$$Y_p = R_1(1+r)/(2+r). \tag{4.13}$$

This definition of Y_p is more in the spirit of Modigliani's life-cycle income hypothesis than of Friedman's permanent income hypothesis. Friedman defined permanent income as $Y_p = rR_1$, that is, the constant annual income that the family's net worth would yield if invested at the market rate of interest in perpetuity. Such a definition implies a bequest by the family to its heirs (valued in the current period) of R_1. Our diagrams of intertemporal resource allocation are based on a zero bequest. The first definition of Y_p is consistent with a zero bequest and, thus, with Modigliani's hypothesis that consumers act so as to leave no bequest to their heirs.

Having defined permanent income, what is its relationship with current income, Y_1? The relationship is depicted in Figure 4.8, where both permanent and current income are plotted. In both panels, net assets, A_1, are assumed to be 0 and $p_c = \$1.00$/unit for simplicity. Current income in year one, Y_1, is higher than permanent income in year one, Y_p, in panel A. Consequently, $Y_p < Y_1$. The reverse is the case in panel B.[6]

The difference between current income and permanent income is defined as *transitory income*, Y_t:

$$Y_t = Y_1 - Y_p. \tag{4.14}$$

Transitory income, then, is simply the excess or the deficit of current income over permanent income. Transitory income is positive if current income is greater than permanent income (i.e., year one, panel A). Transitory income is negative if current income falls below permanent income (i.e., year one, panel B).

Having defined permanent and transitory income, of what use are they in explaining consumption and saving patterns? Consider a consumer faced with the budget lines in Figure 4.9. In Figure 4.9 we have added an indifference curve to each budget line. It is the same consumer in each

[6] If the timing of income as well as total resources is important in people's consumption and saving decisions, then families with income patterns like that pictured in panel A of Figure 4.8 can be expected to save in year one. Families faced with income patterns like that pictured in panel B can be expected to be net borrowers in year one.

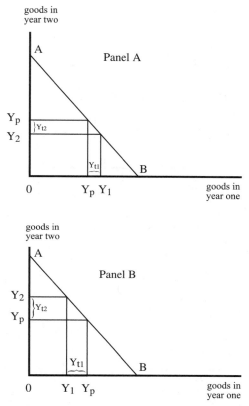

Figure 4.8. The relationship among current income, Y_1, permanent income, Y_p, and transitory income, Y_t.

panel and, thence, the same indifference curve. The only thing that differs between the two panels is the lifetime pattern of income. Total resources, prices, and interest rates are the same in the two panels. Because total resources are the same, permanent income, Y_p, remains the same. The time pattern of income differs from panel A to panel B: current income, Y_1, is higher than future income in panel A, and future income, Y_2, is higher than current income in panel B.

Now consider the consumer's consumption and saving behavior in the two circumstances. Despite the difference in the time pattern of income in the two panels, the consumer maximizes satisfaction at the same point on the budget line in each panel (at point E in panel A and E' in panel B) and, in consequence, has the same consumption, $C_1(C_1 = C_1')$. This is

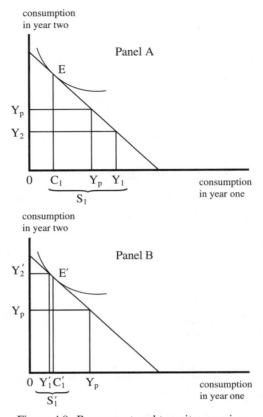

Figure 4.9. Permanent and transitory saving.

true because in each case he or she has the same total resources (i.e., the same permanent income) and faces the same prices and interest rate.

Although consumption is the same, saving is markedly different in the circumstances represented by the two panels. Faced with high current and low future income in panel A, the consumer saves $Y_1 - C_1 = S_1$. In contrast, when confronted with low current and high future income as in panel B, the consumer borrows $Y_1' - C_1' = S_1'$. The consumer has positive saving in panel A, but negative saving (i.e., he or she borrows) in panel B.

Now look more deeply into this behavior. In each case the consumer saves the same fraction of permanent income and in each case all of transitory income is saved! In panel A, total saving amounts to $S_1 = (Y_1 - Y_p) + (Y_p - C_1) = Y_1 - C_1$. Note that all of transitory income, $Y_t = Y_1 - Y_p$, and some of permanent income, $Y_p - C_1$, is saved. In panel B, total saving amounts to $S_1' = (Y_1' - Y_p) + (Y_p - C_1') = Y_1' - C_1'$. Again, the same amount is saved from permanent income, $Y_p - C_1'$, and again, all of transitory income, $Y_t = Y_1' - Y_p$, is saved (i.e., borrowed in this case).

We can draw the following conclusions from this example. Regardless of the time pattern of income, when faced with the same total resources, prices, and interest rate, the consumer (1) consumes the same fraction of permanent income, (2) saves the same fraction of permanent income, and (3) saves all of transitory income. If transitory income is positive, the saving is positive; if transitory income is negative, the saving is negative (i.e., borrowed). There are two components of saving: saving out of permanent income, which we can call permanent saving, and saving out of transitory income, which we can call transitory saving. Together, they equal current saving. Thus,

$$S_1 = S_p + S_t \qquad (4.15)$$

where S_1 = current saving, S_p = permanent saving, and S_t = transitory saving. In Figure 4.9, $S_p = Y_p - C_1$ and $S_t = Y_1 - Y_p = Y_t$.

The above conclusions constitute the permanent or life-cycle income hypothesis of consumption. Friedman's postulates are as follows.

1. In the absence of changes in prices and interest rates, consumers consume a constant fraction of their permanent income. If the constant fraction is k_p, then the permanent income consumption function[7] is

$$C_1 = k_p Y_p. \qquad (4.16)$$

The fraction k_p is termed the *marginal propensity to consume out of permanent income*. It is the added consumption resulting from an added dollar of permanent income.

2. Given that consumption is a constant fraction of permanent income, permanent saving is also a constant fraction of permanent income; the permanent saving function is

$$S_p = Y_p - C_1 = Y_p - k_p Y_p = (1 - k_p)Y_p. \qquad (4.17)$$

The fraction $(1 - k_p)$ is termed the *marginal propensity to save out of permanent income*; that is, the added saving resulting from an added dollar of permanent income.

---

[7] In Friedman's framework transitory consumption appears as a random disturbance term and not as part of the systematic model. Since we are dealing here with only the non-stochastic elements of the hypothesis, the distinction between permanent and transitory consumption is neglected: C_1 is permanent consumption.

3. All transitory income is saved:

$$S_t = Y_t. \tag{4.18}$$

Thus, the *marginal propensity to save out of transitory income* is hypothesized to be equal to 1.

Now return to the evidence that led economists to doubt the veracity of Keynes's absolute income hypothesis and to consider it in the light of Friedman's permanent income hypothesis. Recall that Kuznets (1942) found that the aggregate saving/income ratio, adjusted for the business cycle, remained constant from the 1870s to the 1940s. The depressions and expansions implicit in the business cycle, however, can be viewed as "transitory" phenomena when viewed in the long run. When the saving/income ratio was adjusted for the business cycle, the adjustments served to exclude transitory saving from the numerator of the ratio and transitory income from the denominator, leaving only the ratio of permanent saving to permanent income. This ratio measures the fraction $(1 - k_p)$. If, as the theory suggests, households really do base their consumption and saving decisions on their total resources (i.e., their permanent income) and not just on current income, and if the fraction they save of permanent income is constant, the saving/income ratio Kuznets constructed would be constant from the 1870s to the 1940s despite the fact that real income quadrupled (see mathematical note 4). Kuznets's findings, therefore, are more consistent with the permanent than with the absolute income hypothesis.

So much for the consistency of the long-run aggregate results with the permanent income hypothesis. What about the assertion that the rich save a higher fraction of their income than the poor? Is it consistent with the permanent income hypothesis? Yes, so long as the difference between current and permanent income is remembered. Those people who are rich at any point in time do save a higher fraction of their current income than those who are poor in the same period. The rich in any year are made up of the permanently rich, plus those who happen to be at their peak lifetime earnings, plus those who are receiving current incomes higher than they expected. Likewise, the poor in any year comprise the permanently poor, plus those who happen to be at the low point in their lifetime earnings, plus those who are receiving current incomes less than they expected. Those at the peak of their lifetime earnings, plus those who are having an unexpectedly "good" year with respect to earnings are temporarily rich because they are receiving positive transitory income. They can be expected to save their positive transitory income, thereby inflating the savings/current income ratio above what the permanent saving/permanent income ratio would be. Those who are at the low point in their lifetime earnings and those who are having an unexpectedly "bad" year with respect to earnings are the temporary poor because they are receiving negative transitory income. They can be expected to "save" this negative transitory income (i.e., borrow), thereby reducing their saving/ current income ratio below what their permanent saving/permanent income ratio would be. The permanent income hypothesis, then, explains why the rich do save a higher fraction of their current income than the poor.[8]

Friedman hypothesized that families consume a constant proportion of their permanent incomes (i.e., their total resources) and none of their transitory income. They save all of their transitory income, according to Friedman, in order to even out their consumption path through time. Subsequent empirical work has shown that families tend to save a constant proportion of their permanent incomes. But Friedman was wrong about families' behavior with respect to transitory income. Although the marginal propensity to save out of transitory income is more than the marginal propensity to save out of permanent income, it is not one as Friedman hypothesized (Mayer 1972).

While the permanent income hypothesis (life-cycle income hypothesis) does go some way to explaining the long-run constancy of the savings/ income ratio and why the rich save more than the poor, the framework does not explain other savings phenomena. The life-cycle income hypothesis implies that life-cycle consumption patterns (i.e., how much consumers consume as they grow older) will be much flatter than life-cycle income patterns; that is, consumers will save while young in order to finance their consumption in retirement. Retirees will, therefore, dissave and in the absence of any bequest motive will die penniless. In short, the pattern of consumption by consumers over their life cycles should not be highly correlated with the pattern of their income over their life cycles.

But, it turns out that consumption is more tightly related to income than the life-cycle income hypothesis implies. The pattern of consumption over the life cycle is in general humped just like the pattern of income over the life cycle. Both income and consumption are low when consumers are young. Both income and consumption rise as consumers move into middle age, and both tend to flatten out or fall as consumers become old. Indeed, the elderly, especially the oldest of the old, have quite low consumption

---

[8] See Duncan (1984) for data showing the remarkably large fraction of the poor in any year who are temporarily poor.

and consequently continue to save in violation of the life-cycle income hypothesis (Borsch-Supan and Stahl 1991).

Several factors are hypothesized to account for these discrepancies. The life-cycle income hypothesis presumes a perfect capital market. That assumption is the basis for assuming that consumers can borrow up to the maximum allowed by their future expected income (i.e., B_1^m) at a constant rate of interest, r. In reality, however, low-income consumers are "liquidity-constrained"; that is, either they do not have access to credit at all or do so only at increasingly high interest rates.[9] Not being able to finance consumption out of loans, consumers' consumption would be much more closely related to income than the life-cycle income hypothesis predicts. Work by Hayashi (1985) confirms that liquidity constraints play a role.

Another factor is that consumption is a function of the demographic composition of the household. As consumers marry, have children, and raise them, and as the children leave the household, the marginal utility of consumption will rise and fall with the resultant rise and fall in consumption over the consumers' life cycle. Because the consumers' income also displays the same humped pattern over the life cycle, consumption will appear to be closely related to income.[10]

Two other factors appear to play more important roles than the simple life-cycle income hypothesis assigns to them. The first is the bequest motive, which the life-cycle income hypothesis completely excludes. It is now clear that consumers do save in part to leave inheritances (Kotlikoff 1988). Second, in the face of uncertainty, there may be a demand by consumers for precautionary saving against the possibility of unexpected declines of income in the future. Precautionary saving may be important for the elderly who face very uncertain but expensive health care costs – this circumstance induces saving by the elderly. Neither of these two factors can be discussed in the context of the simple model presented here.[11]

---

[9] The inability to borrow at all would change Figure 4.4 such that the budget line would have a slope of $-(1+r)$ from point A to point $(Y_2/p_c, Y_1/p_c)$. Because the consumer cannot borrow, the budget line would then drop vertically at point $(Y_2/p_c, Y_1/p_c)$ to the horizontal axis. If faced with increasingly high interest rates as the sum borrowed increases, the budget line would become convex to the origin from point $(Y_2/p_c, Y_1/p_c)$ to the horizontal axis: the greater the convexity the more rapidly the interest rate increases, as the loan increases.

[10] See A. Deaton (1992, p. 5) for the inclusion of life-cycle demographic variables into the life-cycle income model.

[11] See A. Deaton (1992, Chapter 6) for an in-depth discussion of models that include the precautionary motive and liquidity constraints.

THE INTEREST RATE–CONSUMPTION–SAVING RELATION

To this point in the chapter we have held interest rates and prices constant while we have discussed how the household adjusts its consumption and saving behavior in the face of changes in income. It is now time to discuss how consumption and saving change as interest rates change, holding resources and prices constant. Out of this discussion will come a better understanding of how changes in interest rates affect the borrowing and lending behavior of families.

Suppose that the market rate of interest rises from, say, r_0 to r_1. The increase in the interest rate has two effects that are like the effects of any price change: (1) future consumption becomes cheaper relative to present consumption (this is essentially a change in relative prices) and (2) the consumption alternatives open to the family are changed. As with price changes, the former is called a substitution effect and the latter is termed an income effect. We deal with the substitution effect first.

The Substitution Effect of the Change in the Interest Rate

When the rate of interest rises (resources and market prices held constant), saving (i.e., future consumption) becomes cheaper relative to present consumption. Holding satisfaction constant, there is an incentive for the consumer to increase saving at the expense of current consumption; that is, to substitute future consumption for present consumption (hence, the term substitution effect). If the consumer was a net borrower prior to the rise in the interest rate, borrowing (i.e., using future income to pay for current consumption) becomes more expensive, and consequently, less is borrowed, holding satisfaction constant. The substitution effect of a rise in the interest rate, therefore, increases saving (or decreases borrowing) at the expense of current consumption.

The Income Effect of the Change in the Interest Rate

When the interest rate rises, the consumer's real income is also altered. Whether real income rises or falls depends on whether the consumer was a net borrower or a net saver prior to the rise in the interest rate. If the family was a net saver, then a rise in the interest rate means that the same dollars currently saved will yield more in the future. Thus, the family can consume more, both currently and in the future. The real income of net savers is increased by a rise in the rate of interest, therefore. The reverse is true for the net borrower. At a higher rate of interest, current loans cost more than before. Consequently, the consumption options open to the net borrower decline with an increase in the interest rate. The real income of net borrowers, therefore, declines in the face of a rise in the rate of interest.[12] Providing current consumption is a normal good (and we know it to be from the discussion in the preceding section), the real income effect of a rise in the interest rate will expand the current consumption of net savers and lower the current consumption of net borrowers (see mathematical note 5).

These effects are illustrated in Figure 4.10. Given resources Y_1 and Y_2, the market rate of interest at r_0, and the price level at p_c, the consumer faces budget line AB. Satisfaction is maximized at E_0, where the family purchases C_1^0 of current consumption and saves $Y_1 - C_1^0 = S_1^0$. The rise in the interest rate from r_0 to r_1 rotates the budget line around point P, the point at which the consumer neither borrows nor lends.[13] Since the slope of the budget line is $-(1 + r)$, the increase in r from r_0 to r_1 will increase the slope, rotating the budget line clockwise around P. The budget line when $r = r_1$ is DF. Given the new budget line, the consumer reestablishes equilibrium at E_1, where current consumption, C_1^1, is less than before and saving, $Y_1 - C_1^1 = S_1^1$, is more than before. The total interest rate effect on consumption is, therefore, $C_1^1 - C_1^0$.

The substitution and income effects of the interest rate increase are separated by drawing a straight line, GG', parallel to the new budget line,

---

[12] This analysis is correct in a market environment in which saving and borrowing are refinanced each year, that is, where there are no fixed-rate securities or loans. The relative price and real income effects of interest rate changes apply only to new saving and new loans if old saving and loans were made at fixed rates on long-term contracts. Examples are twenty-five-year mortgages at a fixed rate of interest, say at 6 percent, and five-year saving certificates at a fixed interest rate set at, say, 4 percent.

The situation is somewhat more complicated with fixed-rate bonds for which there is a market. Suppose a bond were bought at 10 percent and subsequently interest rates rose. If the consumer owning the bond were to sell it, the selling price would be lower than the price at which it was originally bought in order to compensate the buyer for the lower rate of interest it carries. Consequently, interest rate changes do, indirectly, have both relative price and real income effects in such markets. The change in the interest rate is reflected in an opposite change in bond prices with consequent capital gains or losses to the original bond holders.

Currently, money markets are characterized by adjustable-rate loan instruments and fixed-rate instruments with short terms. Thus, the current situation is much closer to the theory than conditions before 1980. Obviously, regardless of what the interest rate is, the family can always be at point P by neither borrowing nor lending. Consequently, point P is on both budget lines.

[13] See also A. Deaton (1992, Section 2.2).

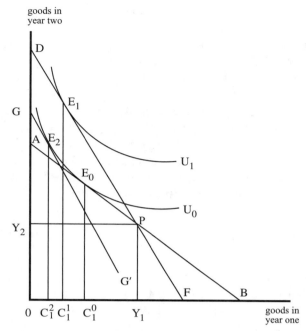

Figure 4.10. The effect of an increase in the interest rate on the consumption and saving behavior.

DF, and tangent to the old indifference curve, U_0 at E_2. The substitution effect of the interest rate increase is $C_1^0 - C_1^2$; that is, future consumption is substituted for current consumption by an increase in saving as future consumption becomes cheaper relative to current consumption.

The real income effect of the rise in the interest rate is $C_1^1 - C_1^2$. In response to the expansion of consumption alternatives (measured by distance GD) brought about by the rise in the interest rate, holding relative prices constant at the new level, $-(1 + r_1)p_c$ (as measured by the slopes of GG' and DF), the consumer increased current consumption and saving (i.e., future consumption) from C_1^2 to C_1^1.

Although not illustrated, the effect of a rise in the interest rate on a net borrower is also clear from Figure 4.10. The net borrower would have maximized satisfaction at a point between P and B on the original budget line AB. The rise in the interest rate would force such a family to the PF segment of the new budget line, DF, making that family less satisfied than before. While the substitution effect induces that family to decrease borrowing by decreasing current consumption, the decline in real income leads to a further decline in current consumption, provided current consumption is a normal good.

The empirical evidence on the interest rate effect on saving and consumption is restricted to evidence on the substitution effect. In a study of U.S. data from 1897 to 1949 and from 1929 to 1958 Wright (1969) found the compensated interest rate elasticity of saving to be very inelastic: 0.18 to 0.27. That is, consumers responded to a 10 percent increase in the interest rate by increasing their saving by 1.8 to 2.7 percent, holding satisfaction constant. More recently, Hall (1988) found the compensated interest rate elasticity of saving to be positive but close to 0. Both earlier and later data are consistent with the idea that the substitution effect of changes in interest rates, while consistent with economic theory, is quite small.

CHANGES IN THE PRICES OF CONSUMPTION GOODS THROUGH TIME

Prices have not entered the discussion up to this point because they were held constant through time; that is, it has been assumed that $p_{c1} = p_{c2} = p_c$. But what if the consumer expects inflation to occur? What are the effects of expected inflation on current consumption and saving likely to be? More correctly, what are the effects of changes in inflationary expectations; for instance, what if the family expects greater inflation than in the past?

Suppose the consumer initially expects prices to rise at a rate of $g_0 100$ percent per year, where $g_0 > 0$. Consequently, if the price level is currently p_c then it will be $(1 + g_0)p_c$ next year. Then suppose that the consumer changes his or her price expectations so that next year prices are expected to be $(1 + g_1)p_c$ where $g_1 100$ percent is the new expected rate of inflation. What effect will this change in price expectations have on the family's consumption and saving behavior?

In the model presented thus far in this chapter, prices of goods and services in the two periods have been assumed to be the same and equal to p_c. The slope of the household budget line was

$$-C_2^m / C_1^m = (R_2/p_c)/(R_1/p_c) = R_2/R_1 = -(1 + r)$$

where $C_2^m =$ maximum consumption in year two if the household consumed nothing in year one, $C_1^m =$ maximum consumption in year one if the household consumed nothing in year two, and R_1 and R_2 represent total resources evaluated in years one and two.

Now, suppose that the family expects prices in year two to be $p_{c2} = (1 + g)p_c$, where p_c is the price in year one and $g100$ percent is the expected inflation rate. As a result of this change in inflationary expectations, the slope of the budget line becomes

$$\text{slope} = C_2^{m\prime}/C_1^m = -\frac{[R_2/(1+g)p_c]}{R_1/p_c} = -\frac{(R_2/R_1)}{[1/(1+g)]} = -\frac{(1+r)}{(1+g)}$$
$$= -(1+r)/(1+g)$$

where $C_2^{m\prime}$ = maximum consumption in year two given the new price expectations and zero consumption in year one.

So long as $g > 0$ (i.e., prices are expected to rise next year),

$$(1+r)/(1+g) < (1+r)$$

and the larger the expected rate of inflation, g, the gentler the slope of the budget line; that is, the greater is g, the more expensive is future consumption relative to current consumption.

A change in consumer inflationary expectations therefore changes the intertemporal budget line facing the consumer. In consequence, not only are the consumption-saving options open to the consumer altered but the price of present consumption relative to the future is altered too. In short, changing expectations about inflation have both substitution and income effects.

As the expected inflation rate increases (the expected rate of inflation rises from 0 in our example to g, where $g > 0$), present consumption becomes cheaper than future consumption. The rise in the price of future consumption relative to present consumption creates an incentive for the consumer to substitute present consumption for future consumption by saving less, holding satisfaction constant. This is the substitution effect of expected increases in the inflation rate.

There is another, more common, way to formulate the argument underlying the substitution effect. When prices rise, loans become cheaper. They become cheaper because the loan is taken out today when "a dollar buys a lot" and paid off tomorrow when (given that prices are expected to rise) "a dollar will buy less." There is, in consequence, an incentive to borrow "dear" money today and pay the loan off with "cheap" money tomorrow. The loan increases consumption and reduces saving.

The income effect of increases in the expected rate of inflation concerns both the net saver and the net borrower alike. If future consumption is expected to become more expensive because of inflation, the net saver finds the real return on current savings smaller, reducing his real income. His savings will buy less in the future than it did before, and real income has declined. In consequence, his current consumption will fall so long as

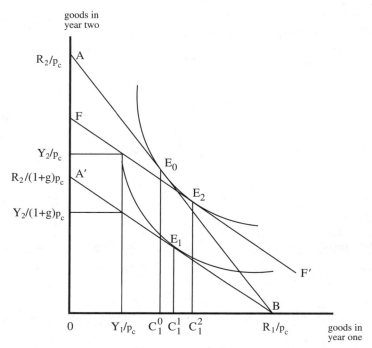

Figure 4.11. The effects of expectations of increasing inflation.

consumption is a normal good. For the net saver the income effect of rising inflationary expectations, therefore, tends to counteract the substitution effect.

The income effect on the net borrower is similar. Being a net borrower means that future consumption is reduced by the necessity of debt repayments. Rising prices mean that future consumption will be reduced even more because goods and services will be more expensive in the future than at present. Rising price expectations, therefore, reduce the net borrower's alternatives and, thus, real income in the same way they reduce those of the net saver and with the same results: a decline in current consumption so long as consumption is a normal good.

The net effect of rising inflationary expectations, then, depends on the relative sizes of the substitution effect and the income effect. If the substitution effect is the greater, saving falls and consumption increases. If the income effect is the larger of the two, rising price expectations will result in a decline in consumption and a rise in saving.

The effects of expecting price increases are illustrated in Figure 4.11. In Figure 4.11, *AB* is the initial household budget line prior to the increase in inflationary expectations, where point A represents $R_2/p_c = C_2^m$ and point B represents $R_1/p_c = C_1^m$. The consumer whose indifference curves are pictured maximizes satisfaction at E_o consuming C_1^0 and saving $S_1^0 = Y_1/p_c - C_1^0$.

Expecting the rate of inflation to increase from 0 to g moves the budget line to $A'B$, where A' represents the new maximum possible consumption in year two, $R_2/(1+g)p_c$. Maximum possible consumption in year two has fallen because the consumer expects prices to rise by $g100$ percent between years one and two. Maximum possible consumption in year one has not changed, because prices in year one have not changed. As a result of the expected increase in inflation, the pictured consumer reestablishes equilibrium at E_1 where he consumes C_1^1, more than C_1^0, and saves $S_1^1 = Y_1/p_c - C_1^1$, less than S_1^0. $C_1^1 - C_1^0$ is the total effect on consumption and $S_1^1 - S_1^0 = C_1^0 - C_1^1$ is the total effect on saving of the expected increase in inflation.

To reveal the income and substitution effects embedded in these total effects, draw line FF' parallel to the new budget line, $A'B$, and tangent to the old indifference curve, U_1. The point of tangency occurs at E_2. The substitution effect (that is, the effect of the expected increase in inflation on consumption, holding satisfaction constant) is $C_1^2 - C_1^0$. This represents a substitution of current consumption for future consumption because future consumption is expected to become more expensive. Saving falls to $S_1^2 = Y_1/p_c - C_1^0$ as current consumption rises due to the substitution effect.

The reduction in real income resulting from the rise in inflationary expectations is represented by FA' on the vertical axis. As real income falls, the consumer reduces consumption from C_1^2 to C_1^1. In consequence, the consumer increases saving to $S_1^1 = Y_1/p_c - C_1^1$.

Given that current consumption is a normal good, the income effect of an expected rise in inflation tends to offset the substitution effect. For the consumer pictured in Figure 4.11 the offset is not complete and the total effect is to increase consumption somewhat. Clearly, the more income elastic is current consumption, the more likely the income effect will more than offset the substitution effect, leading to a reduction, rather than an increase, in current consumption.

Expectations about inflation are hard to measure, and therefore, empirical evidence is somewhat difficult to obtain. Nonetheless, a number of studies have measured the effects of changing rates of inflation on consumption and saving. The conclusions of Weber's study (1975) of consumption expenditures in the United States from 1930 through 1970 were that changes in the rate of inflation had no effect on personal consumption expenditures and, thus, none on saving. Over this long stretch of time, therefore, the income and substitution effects of changing rates of inflation nearly canceled each other out. However, studies focusing on the period between World War II and the early 1970s indicated that increases in the rate of inflation resulted in increasing rates of saving. During this period, then, the income effect more than offset the substitution effect of rising future prices, leading to a net decline in consumption and an increase in saving. A part of this increase in saving was found to be linked to the increased uncertainty that rising rates of inflation bring (Wachtel 1977).

In their study, which included data from the late 1970s, Campbell and Lovati (1979) point out that whereas purchases of consumer durables are largely acts of saving, they are not counted as saving in the National Income Accounts data, the data source commonly used in saving studies. Campbell and Lovati show that rising rates of inflation depressed purchases of consumer durables at the same time saving rates increased. In the 1970s, then, it appears that consumers reacted to rising rates of inflation by making their total saving more liquid by reducing their saving in the form of consumer durables and increasing their saving in the form of bank accounts, stocks, bonds, and the like. Thus, recent changes in the rate of inflation have had greater effects on the manner in which families have saved than on how much they have saved.

SUMMARY

This chapter initiated an explanation of the consumption and saving behavior of the household. The household is pictured as allocating its present and future expected resources among time periods over its expected life so as to maximize its satisfaction. According to both the permanent and the life-cycle income hypotheses, the household engages in borrowing and lending activities to even out its income stream over its life cycle to better match its desired consumption plan over the life cycle. If the permanent income hypothesis were strictly correct, consumers could be expected to consume only the annual return on their resources, leaving their total resources to their heirs as bequests. If the life-cycle income hypothesis were strictly correct, consumers could be expected to live off their assets in their declining years and die leaving no bequests. As usual, reality is poised somewhere between these simple but extreme hypotheses. Nonetheless, these simple hypotheses capture much reality.

Besides income, both interest rates and price expectations are also determinants of household consumption and saving behavior. The former affect net savers and borrowers differently, whereas the latter affect the two in same manner. Much less is known empirically about interest rate and price expectation effects than about income effects.

This completes our introduction to the theory of the household as it relates to the demand and consumption activities of the household. Throughout Chapters 1 through 4 it has been presumed that the household has had no choice over the amount of income it receives, no choice over the number and spacing of children, and no choice over its form, that is, whether it is single, married, or divorced. And no recognition has been given to the household's role as a producer of goods and services. We will begin to rectify these deficiencies in the next chapter, which deals with the work activities of the household.

Mathematical Notes

1. $Y_2/(1+r)$ is the present value of Y_2 valued at the beginning of year one. This can be generalized to many periods quite easily. Suppose Y_3 is the expected income in year three. Then, the present value of Y_3, valued at the beginning of year one, is the sum that, if invested at an interest rate of r, would total Y_3 in year three. Call the sum PV_3; then

$$PV_3 + r PV_3 + r(PV_3 + r PV_3) = Y_3$$

or, when factored out,

$$PV_3(1+r)^2 = Y_3.$$

Dividing through by $(1+r)^2$ yields

$$PV_3 = Y_3/(1+r)^2.$$

Generalizing to the present value of income in year n, Y_n, yields

$$PV_n = Y_n/(1+r)^{n-1}.$$

Finally, the present value of an income stream beginning in year one and ending in year n is

$$PV = PV_1 + PV_2 + \cdots + PV_n$$

or

$$PV = Y_1 + [Y_2/(1+r)] + \cdots + [Y_n/(1+r)^{n-1}].$$

If income is constant through time and equal to Y, then

$$PV = Y\Sigma_{t=1}^{n}[1/(1+r)^{t-1}].$$

2. The rate of time preference can be represented algebraically quite simply. Suppose the intertemporally additive utility function

$$U = v(C_1) + (1 + \delta)^{-1} v(C_2) \tag{1}$$

where $v_i = \partial v / \partial C_i > 0 \, (i = 1, 2)$, $v_{ii} = \partial v_i / \partial C_i < 0$, and $\delta =$ rate of time preference. ∂ can also be seen as the subjective rate at which the consumer discounts future consumption to the present.

Now, the budget constraint under the assumptions that $r = 0$, $p_1 = p_2 = p_c$, $A_1 = 0$, and $Y_1 = Y_2$ is

$$p_c C_1 + p_c C_2 = 2Y_1. \tag{2}$$

To maximize intertemporal utility, (1), subject to the budget constraint, (2), form the Lagrangean expression

$$Lg = v(C_1) + (1 + \delta)^{-1} v(C_2) - \lambda [p_c C_1 + p_c C_2 - 2Y_1]. \tag{3}$$

The first-order conditions are

$$v_1 = \lambda p_c = 0 \tag{4}$$

$$(1 + \delta)^{-1} v_2 - \lambda p_c = 0. \tag{5}$$

Or, by substituting (4) into (5),

$$v_1 / v_2 = 1 / (1 + \delta). \tag{6}$$

Suppose $\delta = 0$. Then, $v_1 = v_2$, $C_2 = C_1$ and the budget constraint, (2), becomes $2C_1 = 2Y_1$. Thus, $C_1 = Y_1$ and $S_1 = 0$. This is the definition of *neutral time preference*. Now, suppose $\delta > 0$. Then, $v_2 > v_1$. Because of diminishing marginal utility (i.e., $v_{ii} < 0$), $C_2 < C_1$, which, with the budget constraint, implies that $C_1 > Y_1$ and $S_1 < 0$. Thus, when $\partial > 0$, the consumer is *present oriented*. Conversely, if $\delta < 0$, then $v_2 < v_1$. Because of diminishing marginal utility, $C_2 > C_1$, which, with the budget constraint, implies that $C_1 < Y_1$ and $S_1 > 0$. Thus, when $\delta < 0$, the consumer is *future oriented*.

3. The calculus solution to this maximization problem is as follows. To maximize the intertemporal utility function in mathematical note 2,

$$U = v(C_1) + (1 + \delta)^{-1} v(C_2) \tag{1}$$

subject to the intertemporal budget constraint

$$p_c C_1 + p_c C_2 / (1 + r) = A_1 + Y_1 + Y_2 / (1 + r) \tag{7}$$

form the Lagrangean expression

$$Lg = v(C_1) + \frac{v(C_2)}{(1 + \delta)} - \lambda \left[p_c C_1 + \frac{p_c C_2}{(1 + r)} - A_1 - Y_1 - \frac{Y_2}{(1 + r)} \right]. \tag{8}$$

Differentiate with respect to C_1, C_2, and λ, and set each partial derivative equal to 0. This yields the equilibrium conditions

$$v_1 - \lambda p_c = 0 \tag{9}$$

$$\frac{v_2}{(1 + \delta)} - \lambda \frac{p_c}{(1 + r)} = 0 \tag{10}$$

$$-p_c C_1 - \frac{p_c C_2}{(1+r)} + A_1 + Y_1 + \frac{Y_2}{(1+r)} = 0. \tag{11}$$

Solving (9) and (10) each for λ, equating, and rearranging yields

$$v_1/v_2 = (1+r)/(1+\delta) \tag{12}$$

where $(1+\delta)v_1/v_2 = $ the marginal rate of substitution of consumption in year one for consumption in year two; and $1 + r = $ the rate at which consumers can exchange a dollar in year two for a dollar in year one. $(1+\delta)v_1/v_2 = $ the slope of the indifference curve at E in Figure 4.4, whereas $(1+r) = $ the slope of the budget line, AB.

4. If the permanent consumption/permanent income ratio, C_p/Y_p, is constant over time despite large increases in income, then the marginal propensity to consume out of permanent income, $\Delta C_p/\Delta Y_p$, must be equal to C_p/Y_p. To see this, consider the contrary. If $\Delta C_p/\Delta Y_p > C_p/Y_p$, then as permanent income rises, C_p/Y_p must rise. C_p/Y_p must fall with increases in income if $\Delta C_p/\Delta Y_p < C_p/Y_p$. Consequently, a constant C_p/Y_p implies that $C_p/Y_p = \Delta C_p/Y_p$. Thus, $\eta_p = (C_p/Y_p)/(C_p/Y_p) = 1$.

5. If one takes the total differential of equations (9) to (11) and solves the resulting system of equations for dC_1, one obtains

$$dC_1 = \frac{\lambda D_{11}}{D} dp_c + \frac{\lambda D_{12}}{(1+r)D} dp_c - \frac{p_c \lambda D_{12}}{(1+r)^2 D} dr$$
$$+ \left\{ \frac{D_{1\lambda}}{D} \left[C_1 dp_c + \frac{C_2}{(1+r)} dp_c - \frac{p_c C_2}{(1+r)^2} dr - dR_1 + \frac{Y_2}{(1+r)^2} dr \right] \right\} \tag{13}$$

where $R_1 = A_1 + Y_1 + Y_2/(1+r)$, D is the determinant, and D_{ij} $(i, j = 1, 2, \lambda)$ is the cofactor of the ijth element of the bordered Hessian

$$\begin{bmatrix} v_{11} & v_{12} & -p_c \\ v_{21} & v_{22} & -p_c/(1+r) \\ -p_c & -p_c/(1+r) & 0 \end{bmatrix}.$$

Now set $dp_c = dr = 0$, divide by dR_1, and change the d notation to ∂ notation to reflect the fact that we are considering a partial derivative. This yields

$$\partial C_1/\partial R_1 = -D_{1\lambda}/D, \tag{14}$$

which is the net wealth effect on consumption. The net wealth effect is analogous to the income effect in a one-period model.

To find the interest rate effect, set $dp_c = dR_1 = 0$, divide through by dr, and change the d notation to ∂ notation to obtain

$$\partial C_1/\partial r = -\frac{p_c}{(1+r)^2} \frac{\lambda D_{12}}{D} - \frac{(p_c C_2 - Y_2)}{(1+r)^2} \frac{D_{1\lambda}}{D}. \tag{15}$$

Substituting (14) into (15) yields

$$\partial C_1/\partial r = -\frac{p_c}{(1+r)^2} \frac{\lambda D_{12}}{D} + \frac{(p_c C_2 - Y_2)}{(1+r)^2} \frac{\partial C}{\partial R_1}. \tag{16}$$

The first term on the right-hand side is the substitution effect of a change in the interest rate; the second term on the right-hand side is the income effect. Assume that $p_c = \$1.00$/unit for simplicity. If $C_2 > Y_2$, then saving in year one must be positive and the income effect of the interest rate change is positive. However, if $C_2 < Y_2$, saving in year one must be negative (i.e., the consumer is a borrower in year one) and the income effect of the interest rate change is negative.

FIVE

Work and Leisure

How the Household Spends Its Time

INTRODUCTION

During the first half of the twentieth century, American males in non-agricultural employment reduced the average annual weekly hours they worked from 60 hours per week to about 40. This change took the form of a reduced workweek, longer annual vacations, and more holidays (Costa 2000; Owen 1970). At the same time, men also reduced the fraction of their lives they spent working in the labor market from 0.23 in 1900 to 0.15 in 1960 (Owen 1970). During the second half of the twentieth century, males' weekly work hours have remained relatively stable, hovering between 40 and 42 hours per week (Herman 1999). But, the proportion of males who worked full-time year-round declined from 72 percent in 1969 to 57 percent by 1997 (Herman 1999). Although some of this reduction in male labor supply is the result of lengthened life expectancy, also important is the increased amount of time spent in school and in retirement. For instance, in 1950, the average age of retirement for American men was 70. By 1985, it had dropped to 63 and it has remained near 63 through 1999 (Burtless and Quinn 2000).

The work patterns of American females have also undergone revolutionary changes over the past 100 years. The labor force participation rate of married females was approximately 4.5 percent in 1900 (Lebergott 1968). By 1969, 46.8 percent of married women between the ages of 35 and 44 were in the labor force and by 2003, this number had risen to 73.3 (U.S. Bureau of the Census 2004–2005, Table 577). Perhaps more remarkable is the fact that those women with very young children increased their labor force participation rates even more dramatically. In 1969, only 23 percent of women between the ages of 25 and 54 with one or more children under age 3 were in the labor force. By 1998, the number had risen to 63 percent (Herman 1999). By 2003, 59.8 percent of married mothers and 70.2 percent of single mothers with children under age 6 were in the labor force (U.S. Bureau of the Census 2004–2005, Table 579).

How Americans spend their nonmarket time has seen similar transformations in the twentieth century. This is much better documented for women than for men. The average married woman's workday in the home in 1900 has been reported to be about 12 hours/day, too high to be believed on a 7-day-per-week basis but nevertheless indicating a very long workday. By 1929 it had been measured accurately at 7.6 hours. It had fallen to about 6 hours by 1967 (Bryant 1996). By the 1980s the average amount of time spent by married women in household work activities was somewhere between 4.5 and 5.0 hours per day (Bryant, Zick, and Kim 1992, Table 1.1; Hill 1985, Table 7.3; Robinson and Godbey 1997, Table 3). Although the time spent in household tasks by married men relative to married women has been consistently less throughout the past century, modest increases in men's housework time have been observed. For example, Zick and McCullough (1991) report that married men with two children spent approximately 1.67 hours per day in housework on average in 1977–1978. By 1987–1988, this average figure had increased to 2.18 hours per day.

The patterns of time use of single men and women are somewhat different from those of married people. In 1969, roughly 65 percent of single women between the ages of 25 and 54 were in the labor force (compared to only 43 percent of similarly aged married women) (Herman 1999). By 1998, this figure had risen to 80 percent. Over the same period, the labor force participation rates of single males between the ages of 15 and 54 remained between 92 and 95 percent. One of the few analyses on the housework time of single individuals reveals that in 1975 single females spent about 3.4 hours per day in household work while single males averaged 1.7 hours per day in household work (Hill 1985, Table 7.3).

New statistics from the 2003 American Time Use Survey suggest that as we enter the twenty-first century, adult males (regardless of marital status) typically average 4.57 hours per day in work and work-related activities while they average 1.67 hours per day in housework and family care activities. The corresponding averages for all adult women are 2.87 hours for work and work-related activities and 3.05 hours per day for housework and family care activities (U.S. Bureau of Labor Statistics 2004b).

The picture of time use that emerges is one in which women have dramatically shifted their productive time from the home to the market-place. Simultaneously, men have reduced their market work and moderately increased their housework time. What caused these changes? Did employers change the amount of work they have offered men and women or have the households exercised choice over how much they work, when, and where? In this chapter we argue that households do have considerable choice over the way time is spent, we develop a small economic model by which households' time use choices can be understood, and we discuss the major economic determinants of households' time use.

The analysis in Chapter 3 began with whatever income the household possessed and then asked how the household allocated that income across various expenditure categories given market prices. Chapter 4 was concerned with the pattern of consumption over the household's life cycle. That analysis began with a particular pattern of income receipts across the household's expected life. Then it asked how the household would, so to speak, rearrange its resources, via borrowing and lending, to create the family's desired pattern of consumption through time.

To this point, therefore, it has been presumed that the household has no control over how much income it receives or over when it receives it. But we know that this is incorrect. People do choose whether to look for work and which job offer to accept. Because earnings from employment are the most important source of a household's income, the household does, therefore, exert control over how much income it has and the timing of its receipt over the life cycle.

The decisions by which the household orders the size and timing of its income turn out to be about how family members spend their time: how much time will be spent in income-earning activities, how much in household production activities, and how much in recreation, or "leisure," activities. With the exception of the last section in the chapter, the discussion in this chapter will be restricted to one period. That is, the questions asked will be how the household allocates its time at any given point in time.[1]

---

[1] The one-period model of time allocation that we develop is consistent with the single-period approaches used in Chapters 2 and 3. But, as Chapter 4 made clear, people make decisions about their consumption of goods and services today in light of what they expect in the future. If this is true with respect to the consumption of goods and services, then it should be the case with respect to time allocation as well, since time is also a "good." Economic models of time allocation over the life cycle have been developed but for the most part the presentation of these models are beyond the scope of this book. For a detailed presentation of a general life-cycle model of time allocation, see Blundell and MaCurdy (1999).

Just as the household's work and leisure decisions were ignored in earlier chapters so we could focus on its demand, consumption, and saving decisions, we will de-emphasize these decisions in this chapter so as to focus on the family's time use decisions. Doing this does not deny that the decisions as to the allocation of income and the allocation of time interact. It merely simplifies things in the hope of making the time allocation decision process more clear. As in earlier chapters we begin by building a small model of the household within which the discussion can be cast. Despite the gross simplifications that are made in the model, it contains major insights about how families allocate their available time.

A WORK-LEISURE MODEL OF THE HOUSEHOLD

We will begin the discussion by supposing that we are observing a single-person family over a period of time, such as a week, a month, or a year. We could equally begin with a family in which only one family member has the opportunity of being employed in the labor market. The model will focus on the allocation decisions with respect to this person's time. As in earlier chapters our model of the household must have three components: a description of the family's preferences, a description of the household's resources and how they restrict the alternatives open to the family, and a behavioral relation describing the rule by which decisions are made. Let us describe the household's preferences first.

The Utility Function

Suppose that during any time period under analysis, say a week, the household derives satisfaction from three composite goods: goods and services purchased in the market, called "market goods" and denoted by C; goods and services produced and consumed by the household, called "home goods" and denoted by G; and the leisure time of the individual in the single-person family or the individual who has the opportunity of being employed in the multi-person family. The quantity of this person's leisure time will be denoted by L.

We can express the consumer's preferences with respect to these three goods algebraically with the following general utility function:

$$U = u(C, G, L). \tag{5.1}$$

These preferences could be represented geometrically on a three-dimensional graph with quantities of C, G, and L measured along the three axes. Thus, each point in the three-dimensional space would represent a particular combination of market goods, home goods, and leisure. Instead of using indifference curves to represent all the combinations of goods among which the consumer is indifferent, one would have to use *indifference dishes*. A good drafter could draw such diagrams, but they would be hard to understand. Because graphs are supposed to aid rather than hinder understanding, we must find some way to utilize two-dimensional graphs.

One useful simplification is to assume that the consumer regards market and home goods, C and G, as *perfect substitutes*. That is, the consumer derives as much satisfaction from a bakery cake as from a homemade cake, from a flute solo played by Jean-Pierre Rampal as played by himself or herself. Although this assumption is patently false, it will be made anyway because its falsity has little effect on the conclusions that can be drawn from the model. So long as we keep the assumption firmly in mind, we can adjust our conclusions by relaxing the assumption that C and G are perfect substitutes and considering the changes in the conclusions that result.

Assuming that home and market goods are perfect substitutes allows us to write the consumer's utility function as

$$U = u(C + G, L). \tag{5.2}$$

Thus, the three-dimensional diagram of the household's preferences collapses into two dimensions with this assumption: one dimension representing goods, $C + G$, and one representing leisure, L. The indifference dishes collapse into the more familiar and understandable indifference curves.

Figure 5.1 is an illustration of the consumer's preference map with respect to goods, $C + G$, and leisure time, L. U_0 and U_1 are two of the many indifference curves in the map. Point A, for instance, represents the combination of $0L_a$ hours per week of leisure and $(C + G)_a$ quantity of goods that yields the consumer U_0 amount of satisfaction where

$$U_o = u(C + G, L) \tag{5.3}$$

is the equation for the indifference curve U_o.

The Time Constraint

Figure 5.1 also contains a straight, vertical line, TT. Although the consumer may prefer to have more leisure per week than there are hours in the week, it is physically impossible. TT, therefore, is drawn at $7 \times 24 = 168$ hours and represents one aspect of the time constraint. Any point on TT or to the left of it represents a physically possible combination of

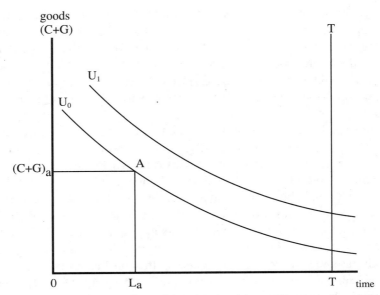

Figure 5.1. The household's preference map with respect to goods and time.

goods and leisure. Points to the right of *TT* represent physically impossible combinations simply because there cannot be more than 168 hours in any week.

Another aspect of the time constraint requires further specification of the way households use time. Suppose the various uses to which the individual in the single-person family (or the individual in the multi-person family whose time is the focus of study) devotes her time are classified into three categories: market work, household work, and leisure. Market work includes all the time the individual spends per week working for pay. It is denoted by M. Household work includes all the time the individual spends per week in household production activities like cooking; laundry; house, car, lawn, and garden maintenance; child care and the care of sick persons; and planning, shopping, and other family managerial activities. Household work time is denoted by H. We have already introduced the concept of leisure, L. We define it formally as the time not spent in market work or household work. Finally, we can denote the total time available (168 hours in the case of a week) as T.

The time constraint, then, simply makes the point that the sum of all the possible uses of time must equal the total time available:

$$T = M + H + L. \tag{5.4}$$

Note that the model of the household states that satisfaction is derived from the consumption of goods, $C + G$, and from leisure, L. No satisfaction arises directly from spending time either in market work or in household work. This, again, is a simplification of reality. Most employed people do get some satisfaction from their jobs in addition to income. And most of us do get some satisfaction from some aspects of household work. We may hate to cook but like to garden, for instance.

Our simple model of the household neglects these sources of satisfaction for two reasons. First, job (whether market or household work) satisfaction appears to have more to do with the type of job we have than it does with the time we spend on the job. Since our model is being built expressly to lead to a greater understanding of how much time we spend in market work, in household work, and in leisure pursuits, we can safely neglect these sources of utility. Second, experience has proved that models that include job satisfaction do not explain much more about work and leisure behavior than those that exclude job satisfaction from consideration. Consequently, we ignore it for simplicity, knowing that our model will be fairly accurate.[2]

The Household Production Function

Not only is the household physically bound by the time constraint, it is bound by the technology of household production. Household goods and services are produced by combining household members' labor in specific ways with other inputs (i.e., purchased goods and services that are used, in turn, as inputs into household processes) to produce cooked and served meals; cleaned and pressed clothes; clean and maintained houses, gardens, lawns, cars, and other durables; and clean, fed, healthy, and developing children. The household production function specifies the technological relationships (i.e., technological constraints) involved in these productive processes.

The household production function, as it appears in this simple model, emphasizes the relationship between the time spent by the individual in household work activities and the quantity of household goods produced. And it is conditioned by the quantity of goods and service inputs with which the individual's household work time is combined. Let the

---

[2] If we were interested in building a model to explain occupation choice, however, the job satisfaction each occupation renders becomes much more important and would have to be taken into account explicitly.

quantity of goods and service inputs that the family combines with the individual's labor to produce household goods be represented by X. Then, the household production function can be expressed algebraically as

$$G = g(H; X). \tag{5.5}$$

Equation (5.5) can be interpreted as follows: Given that the household has quantity of X of other inputs on hand, if H hours of household labor are used in household production per week, G quantity of household goods will be produced. The semicolon dividing H from X in the equation indicates that the household can alter the amount of time the individual spends in household work, H, but cannot alter the quantity of inputs with which the labor is combined. Thus, the focus is on the household's time use decision and not on its decisions about the quantity of inputs to demand.

The easiest way to think about the fixed quantity of X is to link it with the array of appliances, furniture, and housing characteristics that tend to be fixed for any household in the short run. This array of appliances and the like partially determine the technical relationship between the time spent in household work and the quantity of household goods and services that results. A much smaller quantity of clothes can be washed, dried, and pressed per hour, for instance, if the individual is working with a scrub board, a laundry tub, a bar of brown soap, a clothesline in the backyard, and sad irons[3] than if one performs the same functions with a modern complement of automatic clothes washer, detergents, dryer, and steam iron. Similarly, a microwave oven as opposed to a self-cleaning electric stove will alter household labor productivity.

A representative household production function is illustrated in Figure 5.2. The horizontal axis of Figure 5.2 represents hours per week. Measuring from left to right along the horizontal axis beginning at 0 are measured hours per week of leisure, L. Measuring from right to left along the horizontal axis beginning at T are hours per week spent in household work, H. To be clear and consistent throughout this chapter, we will measure time as the distance between two points on the horizontal axis and we will denote it by a line segment. Thus, in Figure 5.2, at point P, $H_p T$ represents the amount of time the individual spends in household production and $0H_p$ represents the amount of time the individual spends in leisure activities. The vertical line TT again represents the idea that no

---

[3] A sad iron was a very heavy iron (made of iron) that was heated on the top of a stove. Several were used and rotated from stove to ironing board and back as they cooled down and needed reheating.

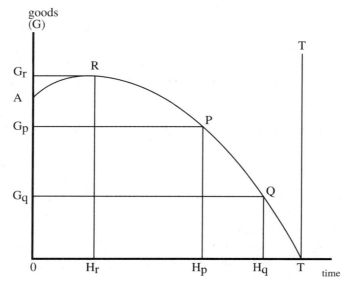

Figure 5.2. The household production function: $G = g(H; X)$.

more than 168 hours per week are available for any activity. The vertical axis represents increasing quantities of household goods produced by the household per week, G.

The curve TA represents the household production function. Thus, if $H_q T$ hours of the individual's time are devoted per week to household work, then G_q quantity of household goods and services is produced per week. If more time is spent, say $H_p T$ hours per week, then more households goods and services, G_p, are produced.

Note that the slope of TA is positive (reading the graph from right to left), being quite steep for few hours spent and shallower as more time is spent in household production per week. Past point R, the household production function becomes negatively sloped. The slope of the household production function represents the marginal product of labor in household production, which we will denote by g_h (see mathematical note 1).

Definition: The marginal product of labor in household production is the change in the quantity of household output due to a very small change in the quantity of labor used.

The fact that the household production function is drawn as a line concave to the hours axis represents the principle of diminishing marginal productivity. The principle says that when one input in a production process is increased, holding all other inputs constant, the marginal product of that input falls; that is, as more of the input is used, holding other input uses constant, the input's productivity falls. The productivity of the input may even turn negative, as is pictured in Figure 5.2. In the region to the left of point R, output actually falls as more than H_rT hours per week of the individual's time are devoted to household production. Thus, the more time that is spent in household production, the less productive yet another hour will be: g_h, therefore, falls as HT increases and beyond point R in Figure 5.2 it becomes negative.

The principle of diminishing marginal productivity is based on two common phenomena: tiredness and congestion. An individual can work continuously for so many hours and, consequently, become so tired that further labor destroys more than is produced. Students who study all night prior to an examination frequently experience this. During the first hour or two of studying, the student learns much. But as each hour wears on without a break, less additional material is learned until, past some point, forgetting takes place.

The classic folk injunction that "too many cooks spoil the broth" conjures up a scene in which many cooks fight for space at the stove and in the process ruin, or spill the soup. It exemplifies the problem of congestion. Increasing congestion also occurs when an individual spends more and more time with a given amount of other inputs. Added minutes spent ironing and folding clothes can increase quantity and quality of the ironing. Many more minutes spent ironing the same clothes, however, leads either to no more cleaned and pressed laundry or even to scorched and burned clothes. Too much time was spent with the same iron and the same clothes. Congestion reduces productivity and can even destroy output.

Equilibrium in a "Castaway" Household. Remember the Chuck Noland character played by Tom Hanks in the film *Castaway*? While Noland was stranded on the island, he had absolutely no access to paid employment or other sources of income and no access to consumer markets; thus, he was someone who had to home produce everything he consumed. For such an individual or castaway, TA in Figure 5.2 represents the budget line. This is so because purchased goods, C, and market work, M, do not exist, and whatever time is spent in household production, say H_qT, leaves $0H_q$ as leisure. Furthermore, the H_qT household work produces G_q quantity of household goods, which the castaway consumes. Implicit then is the notion that for a castaway there are simply two uses of time, H and L, and they must sum to the total time available, T. Therefore,

$$T = H + L. \tag{5.6}$$

By substituting the relation $H = T - L$ from equation (5.6) into the household production function, one obtains

$$G = g(T - L; X). \tag{5.7}$$

Equation (5.7) can be regarded as the budget line for such a household. Equation (5.7) is essentially the equation for AT in Figure 5.2.

One could, then, superimpose our hypothetical castaway's preference map on the diagram, assume that he allocates his time between household production and leisure so as to maximize satisfaction, and have a simple model of such households. Figure 5.3 illustrates such a case. Given his preferences for goods and leisure represented by indifference curves U_0, U_1, and U_2, our castaway maximizes satisfaction by spending $H_p T$ hours each week producing G_p goods, which he consumes, and $0H_p$ hours each week in leisure pursuits.

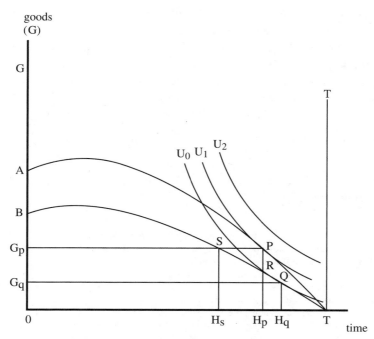

Figure 5.3. A castaway household.

Suppose, now, he injures himself – for example, he hurts his leg while body surfing in the waters off his island one day. As a result he must spend more time per week to produce a given quantity of goods. Thus, his household production function would shift down to, say, BT. Whereas before the injury H_pT hours per week are sufficient to produce G_p quantity of goods, after the injury it takes him H_sT per week to produce the same quantity. Thus, his labor productivity falls as a result of his injury.[4] After the injury he would maximize satisfaction at point Q, where he spends H_qT hours per week producing G_q goods, which he consumes, and $0H_q$ hours of leisure. As a result of his injury he spends less time working and more time in leisure pursuits (perhaps resting more) and consuming fewer goods than before. If his production function had been differently shaped or his preferences between goods and leisure different (as represented by the shapes of the indifference curves), the result might have been different.

Although Figure 5.3 has been explained in terms of a fictional castaway household, it still has much relevance in today's world because it captures important elements of the reality faced by rural families in third-world countries. Household models only slightly more complicated than Figure 5.3 are used by development economists to better understand the time allocation behavior of these rural families and to evaluate policies that would improve their lot.[5]

The typical American family, however, faces opportunities in the labor market as well as opportunities for home production. American families also are confronted with a myriad of consumer goods that they can purchase and consume if they have the money. In consequence, a model of the typical American family must incorporate the possibility of employment in the labor market and the purchase and consumption of market goods from the family's labor and nonlabor income. We proceed to specify these other relations.

---

[4] Note that the slope of the post-injury production function, BT, is less for any given amount of time spent than the slope of the pre-injury production function, AT, indicating that our castaway's marginal productivity has fallen as a result of the injury; that is $g'_h|_R < g_h|_P$ where $g'_h|_R$ is the post-injury marginal product of labor at R and $g_h|_P$ is the pre-injury marginal product of labor at P.

[5] In the peasant household case, the family uses its time either in leisure or on the land to produce a crop, say rice. It consumes some of the rice and sells the rest to obtain the money required to purchase other needed consumption goods and, perhaps, agricultural inputs like fertilizer. See mathematical note 2 for a simple peasant model. For a more general review of the economic modeling of household decisions in the context of developing countries, see Strauss and Thomas (1995).

The Market Work Budget Constraint

The family's weekly income of Y dollars is composed of earnings from employment, E, and nonlabor income, V. Thus,

$$Y = E + V. \tag{5.8}$$

Nonlabor income includes such things as rent from real property, dividends from stocks, interest on bonds and savings accounts, and gifts received; that is, income that does not result from employment and is not affected by the amount one works. Benefits from most welfare programs like the Temporary Assistance to Needy Families Program, the Supplemental Security Income Program, and the Food Stamp Program are affected by the amount one works and therefore are not included in nonlabor income.

The family's expenditures on market goods are pC, where p is the price index for market goods. Since expenditures exhaust income,

$$pC = Y = E + V. \tag{5.9}$$

Recognize that earnings depend on how much time is spent per week in market work. If the individual can command a wage rate per hour of $\$w$/hour, then weekly earnings must be

$$E = wM. \tag{5.10}$$

And, therefore, by substituting equation (5.10) into (5.9) the budget constraint can be expressed as

$$pC = wM + V. \tag{5.11}$$

Equilibrium in a Household with No Household Production. We can make use of this simple market work budget line to construct a model of a household that is the reverse of the castaway's. Whereas the castaway household could work only in household production and consumed only household-produced goods and services, its opposite can perform only market work, has no household production, and consumes only market goods. This implies that time can be spent only in market work, M, and leisure, L, and that they must sum to the total time available; that is,

$$T = M + L. \tag{5.12}$$

Substituting equation (5.12) into the equation for the budget line, equation (5.11), yields

$$pC = w(T - L) + V$$

or, after multiplying through and shifting wL to the left-hand side,

$$pC + wL = wT + V. \tag{5.13}$$

The expression on the right-hand side of equation (5.13) represents the total income the household could have if the individual worked every minute of every day in the labor market at the wage rate w. In consequence, $wT + V$ has been called *full income*. It represents the resources available to the household. The expression on the left-hand side of equation (5.13) shows how full income is spent: pC on purchased goods and services and wL on leisure.

The budget line, equation (5.13), is graphed in Figure 5.4. As before, quantities of goods (market goods in this case) are measured up the

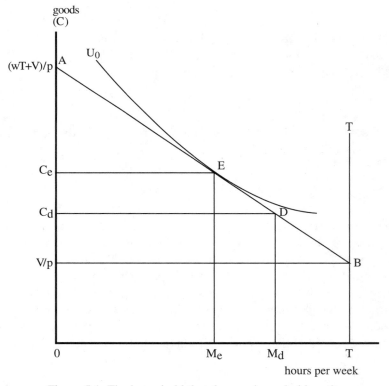

Figure 5.4. The household that does no household work.

vertical axis and time is measured along the horizontal axis. Time is measured from left to right beginning at 0 and ending at T. Point B represents the combination of market goods (V/p) and leisure ($0T$ hours) that the individual could have if he did no paid work and had only the market goods purchasable with his nonlabor income, V. In contrast, point A represents the quantity of market goods purchasable, $(wT + V)/p$, if the individual had no leisure and, therefore, worked $0T$ hours. Points on line AB represent other possible combinations of market goods and leisure and, therefore, work. Point D, for instance, represents a situation in which the individual works $M_d T$ hours per week and with the income so generated purchases and consumes $C_d V/p$ quantity of market goods and services over and above what was purchased with nonlabor income, V, and spends $0M_d$ hours per week in leisure.

The slope of the budget line has the same interpretation as the slope of any budget line. It represents the market rate of exchange between goods and leisure. This is seen by computing the slope:

$$\text{slope of } AB = -[(wT + V)/p - V/p]/T = -[(wT)/p]/T = -w/p.$$

w/p is the quantity of market goods and services that must be given up to gain an added hour of leisure. w/p is, therefore, the real *price of leisure*.

If the preference map of such a household is superimposed on the budget line in Figure 5.4, one can observe the household's equilibrium quantities of market goods, leisure, and market work. This occurs at point E, where the household's budget line is tangent to the highest attainable indifference curve, U_0. At point E the individual has $0M_e$ hours per week of leisure and spends $M_e T$ hours per week in the labor market earning $w(M_e T)$ earned income. Total income, $w(M_e T) + V$, is then spent on C_e market goods and services.

Such a model of the household is quite useful if one wishes to focus only on market work. The distinction between time spent in leisure and time spent in household production is lost in such applications.[6] Figure 5.4 or variants of it are often used by labor economists in analyzing the household's supply of time to the labor market.

Our focus, however, is on household time spent in the household and the labor market. The typical American household (indeed, the typical household in most countries in the world) faces a more complicated set of circumstances in which some household work is done, some market

---

[6] Leisure time and household work time can be aggregated because both ways of spending time have the same price, w, the wage rate. When aggregated, $H + L$ is called a Hicks' composite good (mathematical note 1, Chapter 3, and Hicks 1946, mathematical appendix).

work is done, and some time is spent in leisure activities. To understand how the household allocates its time among market work, household work, and leisure, a more complicated budget line must be built. It must include aspects of both the market work budget line, equation (5.13), and the household work budget line, equation (5.7). We proceed to build the total budget line.

The Total Household Budget Line

Definition: The total budget line is the locus of points representing the maximum quantity of goods (either market or household) obtainable from each number of hours spent in either market or household work and nonlabor income.

To derive this line a behavioral rule must be introduced. The behavioral rule derives from the assumption that more is better so long as more is free. The rule is that the household allocates time to market and to household work so as to maximize the quantity of goods derivable from each hour worked.

An example will help. Suppose the household production function is

$$G = 40H - 0.5H^2;$$

the price of market goods, p, is \$ 1.00/unit; and the wage rate the individual can command in the labor market is \$10.00/hour.

Now, compare the quantity of goods the individual can produce with one hour spent in household production with the quantity of goods that the individual can purchase with the earnings from one hour of market work. If $H = 1$, then $G_1 = 40(1) - 0.5(1)^2 = 39.5$ units. If $M = 1$, then earnings are \$10.00 and $C_1 = w/p = 10/1 = 10$ units of market goods can be purchased. The first hour spent in household work yields more goods than the first hour in market work. In consequence, if the individual were to spend one hour working, she or he would spend it in household production rather than working in the labor market.

The calculations for succeeding hours worked in household production are contained in Table 5.1. The leftmost column shows the hours worked in household production per week, H. The middle column displays the quantity of household goods, G, produced per week given the hours worked in the first column. The rightmost column displays the marginal product of labor in household production, g_h, given the hours worked in the first column; that is, the added household output produced given an added

Table 5.1. *Total Hours Worked, Total Product, and Marginal Product in Household Production*

Hours Worked (H)	Total Product (G)	Marginal Product (g_h)
0	0	0
1	39.5	39.5
2	78.0	38.5
3	115.5	37.5
4	152.0	36.5
•	•	•
•	•	•
•	•	•
29	739.5	11.5
30	750	10.5
31	759.5	9.5
•	•	•
•	•	•
•	•	•

Note: Figures based on household production function $G = 40H - 0.5H^2$.

hour of labor. Thus, if 4 hours are worked in household production per week, 152 units of household goods, G, are produced and the marginal product of the fourth hour is 36.5 units; working the fourth hour in the household yields $152 - 115.5 = 36.5$ additional units of household goods.

The thirtieth hour worked in the household per week yields $750 - 739.5 = 10.5$ added units of household goods. If the thirtieth hour were spent in market work instead, the earnings from it would buy $w/p = 10$ units of goods. Clearly, if 30 hours are to be spent working per week, they are better spent in household work than in market work. However, the thirty-first hour worked will yield more goods if spent in market work than in household work because the marginal product of the thirty-first hour in household work is only 9.5, whereas it is 10 in market work. If the individual were to work 31 hours/week, he or she would produce the maximum quantity of goods by spending 30 hours in household work and 1 hour in market work. If this were done, then 750 units of household goods would be produced and 10 units of market goods would be purchased for a total of 760 units. If the entire 31 hours had been spent in household production, 759.5 units would have been produced. If the 31 hours had been spent in market work, only 310 units of goods would have been purchased. Because any hours worked beyond 30 per week yield more goods if spent in market work than in household work, the individual possessing this production function and who can command \$10/hour in the labor market will spend no more than 30 hours/week in household work.

Notice that the individual ceases to do more household work when the marginal product of labor in household work, g_h, equals the real wage rate, w/p:

$$g_h = w/p. \tag{5.14}$$

This condition, then, determines the point at which an individual ceases to do household work and begins to do market work. For fewer hours worked, $g_h > w/p$, and the time is more productively spent in household work. For more hours worked, $g_h < w/p$, and the extra time is more productively spent in market work.

These relationships are illustrated in Figure 5.5. Point B represents the combination of goods and leisure available to the household if no work whatsoever is done and it has V dollars of nonlabor income per week to spend on market goods. Since we are assuming that $p = \$1.00$/unit,

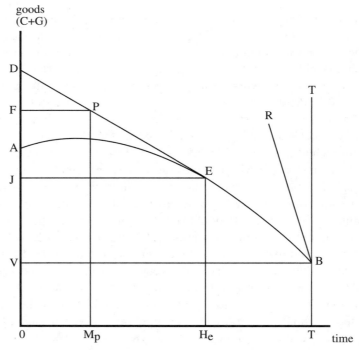

Figure 5.5. The total household budget line, $DEBT$.

then point B represents $0V$ market goods and $T = 168$ hours of leisure per week.

AB is the household production function; any point on it represents a quantity of hours per week spent in household work, say, H_e, and the output of household goods produced with that labor, say VJ ($0V$ quantity of goods are market purchased with the household's nonlabor income so that $H_e T$ hours of household work yield VJ units of *G-goods*). The slope of AB at any point represents the marginal product of labor in household work, g_h.

Line DE is the market work portion of the total household budget line. The slope of DE is $-w/p$; that is, the real wage rate. Since no market work is contemplated until enough household work is done to drive the marginal product of labor in the household down to the real wage rate ($g_h = w/p$), DE is not drawn from the T axis but rather begins at point E on AB, where DE is tangent to AB. At the point of tangency, E, the slopes of AB and DE are equal; that is, $g_h = w/p$ at E.

Any point on DE, say point P, represents the total quantity of goods (market purchased and household produced) available to the household if it works $H_e T$ hours per week in the household and $M_p H_e$ hours per week in the market and uses its nonlabor income, V, to purchase goods also. In particular, at P the household purchases $0V$ goods with its nonlabor income, produces VJ household goods by spending $H_e T$ in household work, and purchases JF market goods with the earnings from $M_p H_e$ hours of market work.

Line $DEBT$, then, is the total household budget line. It is made up of three parts. The TB part represents the quantity of market goods purchasable with the household's unearned income, V. The EB part is derived from the household production function and represents the region in which household work is efficiently done. The DE part represents the region in which both household and market work are done.

The household budget line, $DEBT$, implies that market work will never be done unless some household work is done. Put differently, so long as the marginal product of labor in household production is higher than the real wage rate commanded by the individual in the labor market, the individual will do no market work. The reason is simple but bears repeating: no market work will be done so long as more goods can be produced in an added hour worked at home than in the labor market.

Figure 5.5 is representative of all but a very few American families in that most adult members of most families do some household work (even if it is simply showering, dressing, and brushing their teeth each morning) and some family members also engage in market work. Only those individuals whose real wage rates are higher than the productivity of their first hour in household work will do no household work. In such a case, the market work portion of the budget line would be steeper than even the steepest part of the household production function. This is represented by the line RB in Figure 5.5, which is steeper than AB at zero hours. While such may be the case for the highest paid individuals in our society, it is unrealistic for most families.

To summarize: The household's total budget line is made up of pieces of the household production function and the market work budget line. The household will produce and/or purchase goods so as to maximize the total quantity of goods it can consume for the hours it spends working. Because the first few hours of work are most productively spent in household production, the household will be employed in the labor market only if its real wage rate, w/p, is at least equal to its marginal productivity in home production, g_h. Geometrically, this occurs when the slope of the household production function equals the slope of the market work budget line, that is, where DE is tangent to AB in Figure 5.5.

Equilibrium in the Household Work–Market Work–Leisure Model. With the total household budget line and the household's preferences described, we can now introduce satisfaction-maximizing behavior and use the model to discover the household's equilibrium allocations of time to household work, market work, and leisure activities. We illustrate this in Figure 5.6.

Figure 5.6 illustrates the preference maps of two households that happen to face the same total household budget line, $DEBT$. The S family's preferences are represented by indifference curves U_0^s and U_1^s and the R family's preferences are represented by indifference curves U_0^r to U_3^r. The preferences of these two families are between goods (whether market purchased or home produced) and leisure in accordance with the assumptions that C and G are perfect substitutes and that market work, M and household work, H, yield satisfaction only through the goods produced or purchased by the labor. Assume for the sake of discussion that both the S and the R families are single individuals.

Individual R maximizes satisfaction at point Q, where the total household budget line, $DEBT$, touches his highest attainable indifference curve, U_2^r. At Q, R's marginal rate of substitution of leisure for goods equals his productivity in home production, g_h. Thus, for R at Q

$$MRS_{lc} = u_l/u_g|_Q = g_h|_Q$$

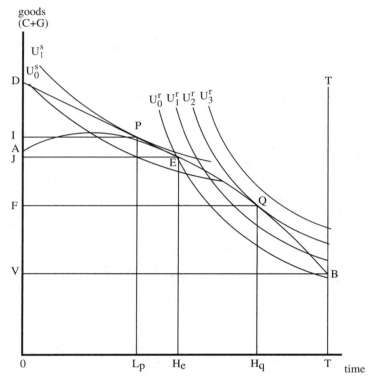

Figure 5.6. Two households' equilibrium positions.

where u_l = marginal utility of leisure, u_g = marginal utility of goods, and g_h = marginal product of labor in household production.[7] At Q the rate at which R is willing to exchange leisure for goods is exactly equal to the rate at which he can exchange leisure for goods by engaging in household production. R consumes $0H_q$ hours of leisure and $0F$ goods per week. He also spends $H_q T$ hours per week engaged in household production activities in which he produces VF units of household goods. In addition, he purchases $0V$ quantity of goods in the market with his weekly nonlabor income of V.

In equilibrium R is not employed. He is not employed because in equilibrium his marginal product of labor in household work exceeds the real wage rate he can command in the labor market, w/p; that is, $g_h|_Q > w/p$. The real wage rate he commands in the labor market is represented by

---

[7] The notation $|_Q$ reminds us that the equality occurs at point Q.

the slope of DE. The slope of EB at Q is $g_h|_Q$ and is greater than at E, where it equals the slope of DE (i.e., w/p).

R is not unemployed because he cannot find work. Work is available to him at a real wage rate of w/p. Rather, R is not employed because at a wage rate of w/p per hour, his time is worth more to him at home in household production or in leisure. R could be a retired individual, in which case V represents his weekly pension. R might also be sufficiently independently wealthy so that his nonlabor income and his household production provide him with enough material goods and services that he is happiest not working. R could also be a student whose time is worth more studying than if spent in the labor market. Or R has a great enough relative preference for leisure that he would rather make do with fewer goods and services than give up more of his leisure and do any more household work or any market work.

That R prefers to do no market work is evident from Figure 5.6. The slope of R's indifference curve, U_0^r, through point E (the point at which it would be efficient for him to cease further household work and work the first hour in the labor market instead) is greater than the slope of DE (i.e., w/p). That it has greater slope than w/p indicates that the price he is willing to pay for added leisure at E is greater than he must pay. Consequently, he "buys" more than $0H_e$ hours of leisure by sacrificing FJ units of goods and working H_qT hours rather than H_eT hours in household production per week. The real wage rate would have to be at least equal to the slope of his indifference curve at point Q to induce him to enter the labor market at all. The slope of U_2^r at Q, therefore, is R's *reservation wage rate* – the wage rate at which R would be indifferent between working in the labor market or not.

Now consider individual S. She maximizes satisfaction at point P, where she consumes $0I$ total goods (market purchased and home pro-duced) and $0L_p$ hours of leisure per week. S spends L_pT hours per week working: H_eT of them in household production and L_pH_e in market work. The $0I$ goods she consumes each week are made up of $0V$ goods pur-chased with her weekly nonlabor income, VJ home-produced goods and services, and JI goods and services purchased with her earnings from employment.

For individual S at point P

$$u_l/u_g|_P = w/p = g_h|_E;$$

that is, S's marginal rate of substitution of leisure for goods at point P (i.e., the slope of U_1^s at P) equals the real wage rate (i.e., the slope of DE), which also equals her marginal productivity in household production (i.e., the slope of BE at E) (see mathematical note 3). Thus, the rate at which S is willing to exchange leisure for goods (u_l/u_g) is equal to the rates at which she is able to exchange leisure for goods (w/p via the labor and purchased goods markets and g_h via household production).

Figure 5.6 is a remarkable diagram. It indicates the equilibrium allocation of time among market work, household work, and leisure for the person being analyzed. It also shows how the equilibrium total consumption of goods arises: from goods purchased with unearned income, from goods purchased with earned income, and from goods produced within the household.

Before we begin to use the model in Figure 5.6 to analyze the time use decisions in families, we need to point out that it is capable of being interpreted in a wider context than it has been thus far in the discussion. To this point it has been interpreted as a model of a single individual's time allocation or of the employed individual in a one-earner family. It can also represent the time allocation of either spouse in families in which both may be employed. In the latter interpretation of the model, nonlabor income includes the earnings of the spouse whose time allocation is not being analyzed.

Suppose, for example, we interpret Figure 5.6 as a model of the time allocation of a married woman in a typical family. The horizontal axis, then, refers to her time and the vertical axis refers to total goods, both purchased and home produced. Her husband's earnings (his labor income) are included in nonlabor income because the married woman does not earn it. When interpreted in this way, however, we will still consider a change in nonlabor income as a change only in that part of family income that is unearned by both spouses; the earned income of the spouse included in V will remain constant (see mathematical note 4). With these assumptions, we can now begin to use the model to analyze the time use decisions of family members.

INCOME EFFECTS ON THE WORK BEHAVIOR OF THE HOUSEHOLD

Family income has two sources: labor and nonlabor income. Since labor income is the product of the wage rate, w, and the hours employed in the labor market, M, a change in earned income can arise because either w or M changes. But w is the price of leisure and any change in w can be expected to affect the household's equilibrium in a manner similar to the way changes in the price of any other consumption good affects it.

However, if a change in M is the source of the change in earned income, then the work behavior of the household has changed and we are interested in explaining why it changed. Consequently, when we talk about the effects of income changes on the work behavior of family members, we are not referring to changes in earned income. Instead, we are referring to changes in nonlabor income, V.

An increase in nonlabor income, V, increases the resources available to the household and, thus, increases the available combinations of goods (purchased and produced) and leisure that are available. Such a change cannot be expected to change the wage rates family members command in the labor market, the price at which goods can be purchased in the goods market, or the basic parameters of the production function by which goods and services are produced in the home. An increase in nonlabor income, therefore, simply increases the resources available to the family but does not change the market rates of exchange between goods and leisure or conditions of household production. An increase in nonlabor income thus shifts the household's total budget line up in a parallel fashion. Consequently, the family's demand for goods and for the leisure of each family member will increase so long as they are normal goods.

The increase in the demand for leisure time will, of course, mean that the amount of time spent working by each family member will decrease. For individuals who are not employed, the reduction in work time must be a reduction in household work time. For individuals who are employed, how is the reduction in work time taken? Do such individuals reduce their market work time, their household work time, or both? So long as the increase in unearned income has no effect on the household production function, then all the reduction in work time will be in market work time, and household work time will be unaffected. This is so because the increase in nonlabor income does not affect the trade-off between market and household work.

Figure 5.7 illustrates these points. The total household budget line, $DEBT$, represents the initial alternatives open to the household. The households facing this total household budget line (i.e., our friends, the R and S families) have V nonlabor income per week (the units in which goods are measured being such that $p = \$1.00/\text{unit}$) and the family member whose time use is pictured can command a wage rate of $\$w/\text{hour}$ in the labor market (the slope of DE). Indifference curves U_0^r and U_1^r represent the preferences of household R, and U_0^s and U_1^s represent those of household S.

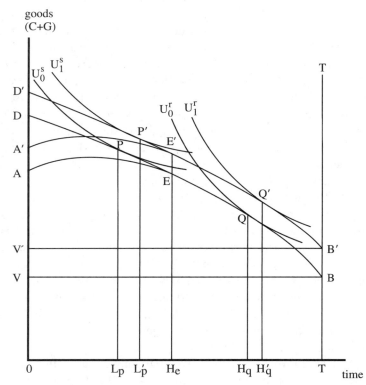

Figure 5.7. The effects of an increase in unearned income on household work behavior.

Initially, family S is in equilibrium at point P, and family R maximizes satisfaction at point Q. At P, the individual in family S spends $H_e T$ hours per week in household work, $L_p H_e$ hours employed in the labor market, and $0L_p$ hours in leisure activities. The individual under study in family R is not employed, spending $H_q T$ hours per week in household work and $0H_q$ hours in leisure pursuits.

Now presume that each household receives an added VV' dollars of unearned income per week. Recall that this additional income does not emanate from the labor earnings of any family member. It is additional nonlabor income, perhaps from an increase in the return to some of the family's assets.

The increase in nonlabor income shifts the new total household budget line to $D'E'B'T$, a shift that is simply a vertical and parallel translation of

DEBT. It is vertical and parallel because the increase in nonlabor income has no effect on the wage rate at which R and S can find employment; employers will not alter what they are willing to pay R and S simply because R and S are now wealthier. Nor has the increase in nonlabor income any effect on the household production function; if R and S could produce an added 10 units of goods in the twenty-first hour of household production before the receipt of the nonlabor income, then they can do no more and no less after its receipt. Consequently, the additional nonlabor income simply adds to the households' purchases of market goods by VV'.

Consider household S. With the receipt of VV' added nonlabor income, S reaches a new equilibrium at P', at which $H_e T$ hours are spent in household work (the same as before), $L'_p H_e$ hours per week are spent in market work (less than before), and $0L'_p$ hours are spent per week in leisure activities (more than before). Clearly, leisure is a normal good and, just as clearly, so are goods. The increase in nonlabor income has been used partly to buy more market goods and partly to "buy" more leisure. The added leisure is obtained by reducing the number of hours per week of market work. The amount of time devoted to household work is unchanged by such an increase. This is so because the number of hours of household work for which $g_h = w/p$ remains unchanged by the increment in nonlabor income.

The household work of an employed person would be affected by an increase in nonlabor income only if market- and home-produced goods are not perfect substitutes (see mathematical note 5 for the case in which C-goods and G-goods are not perfect substitutes) or if the increase was large enough to induce the individual to cease market work altogether. The latter frequently happens when the increase in nonlabor income is huge; for example, when someone wins $20 million in a lottery. Here, the desired increase in leisure is more than the total number of hours worked in the market per week. Consequently, the individual quits market work and also reduces somewhat his or her weekly household work.[8]

Now turn to household R. Household R is not employed before and after the increment in nonlabor income. After its receipt R spends $H'_q T$ hours per week working at household tasks (less than before) and $0H'_q$ hours per week in leisure activities (more than before). Leisure is a normal

---

[8] Imbens, Rubin, and Sacerdote (1999) used survey data from a sample of lottery winners to examine the impact of such nonwage income on labor supply. Their study revealed that when the lottery prize is modest (i.e., $15,000 per year for 20 years), labor supply is unaffected. But, if the lottery prize is larger (i.e., $80,000 per year for 20 years), then labor supply and labor force participation rates both decline.

good for R as well as for S but because R is not employed, the only way R can consume more leisure is to reduce the amount of household work she performs.

Do we have any evidence to support the hypotheses about the effects of nonlabor income? Yes. Consider first the effects of changes in nonlabor income on the market work behavior of individuals. There is wide agreement based on cross-section data that both males and females, married and single, devote less time to market work as nonlabor income rises.[9] Pencavel (1986, p. 70) hazards the opinion that the nonlabor income elasticity of men's market work is about −0.23. More recently, a summary of labor supply studies done by Blundell and MaCurdy (1999, Table 1) reports income elasticities for men in the range of −0.02 to −0.287. The studies of female labor supply summarized by Killingsworth and Heckman (1986, Table 2.26) and Blundell and MaCurdy (1999, Table 2) contain estimates of the income elasticity for women in the same neighborhood.

Turn now to the question of the effect of nonlabor income on the time spent on household work. Cross-section studies of the household work time of American married males and females are consistent with Figure 5.7. As nonwage income rises, the household work times of employed married men and women are unaffected but that of nonemployed married women falls. Gronau's results (1977) are the most evocative. He finds that an increase in nonlabor income of $1000/year leads to a decline of 44 hours in the annual time spent in household work by White nonemployed married women. No such decline is observed for White employed married women (1977, Table 3). Kooreman and Kapteyn (1987, pp. 242–243) find the household work time of employed married men, employed married women, and nonemployed married women in 1975 to be unresponsive to changes in nonlabor income. Solberg and Wong (1992) excluded nonemployed married women from their analyses, but they also find that the household work times of employed married men and employed married women are unresponsive to changes in nonlabor income. Hersch and Stratton (1997) generate estimates using a combined sample of employed and nonemployed married individuals between the ages of 20 and 64. They report small but statistically significant negative nonwage income effects on time spent in housework for both men and women if nonwage income is under $100,000 per year.

---

[9] See Pencavel (1986), Killingsworth and Heckman (1986), and Blundell and MaCurdy (1999) for extensive surveys of the empirical cross-section literature.

One must conclude, therefore, that the hypotheses contained in Figure 5.7 are founded in empirical fact. For both men and women leisure is a normal, income-inelastic good. The household work of nonemployed married females falls by a small amount as nonwage income rises, where that of employed men and women does not.

WAGE RATE EFFECTS ON TIME USE

The household production model depicted in Figure 5.6 assumes that an individual's wage rate affects the choices she makes about how much time to spend in the labor market, housework, and leisure. But, it is possible that the causation runs in the opposite direction. For example, Hersch and Stratton (1997) have provided empirical evidence that time spent in housework is inversely related to the wage rate women are able to command in the labor market.[10] In addition, Mroz (1987), Zabel (1993), and Wolf (1999) have provided evidence that wage rates offered to an individual are related to the hours she works in the labor market. Discussion of these more complex relationships between wages rates and time spent in the labor market, housework, and leisure are beyond the scope of this book. As a consequence, we focus on describing the wage predictions that can be generated from the household production model under the assumption that individuals view their market wage rates as being outside of their control – that is, under the assumption that individuals cannot alter their wage rates by changing their time allocations.[11]

As has been pointed out before, the wage rate an individual can command in the labor market is also the price of leisure, that is, the amount of money that has to be sacrificed for the household to consume an added hour of leisure. When wage rates change, therefore, the price of leisure changes and one can expect the family to respond by changing its demand for leisure.

The wage rate, however, is also an integral part of the individual's productivity in gaining purchased goods; that is, w/p represents the quantity of market goods that can be gained by doing an hour of market work and

---

[10] Hersch and Stratton (1997) speculate that this inverse relationship exists either because (1) women who spend more time in housework have less energy to devote to paid employment, thus reducing their marginal productivity in the labor market, or (2) employers discriminate against women employees who spend large amounts of time in housework.

[11] This assumption must hold in the short run but not in the long run. In the long run, an individual can alter his wage rate by increasing his education and/or work experience. We will discuss the returns to such long-term investments in oneself in Chapter 6.

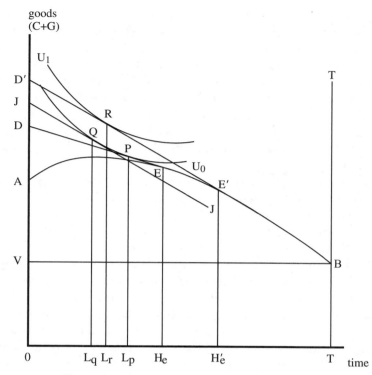

Figure 5.8. The own-wage-rate effect on time use.

using the earnings to purchase goods. Therefore, a change in the wage rate also changes the individual's "market productivity" relative to household productivity (i.e., g_h) and, thus, affects the trade-off between market and household work. The altered trade-off, in turn, affects the distribution of work time between market and household production.

Figure 5.8 disentangles these effects of an own-wage-rate change; that is, a change in the wage rate of the individual whose time allocation is under study. $DEBT$, as usual, is the total household budget line facing the household prior to the wage rate change. The initial wage rate facing the individual is w and, therefore, the slope of DE is w/p. The household maximizes satisfaction at point P, where the individual spends $0L_p$ hours per week in leisure activities, L_pH_e hours in the labor market, and H_eT hours in household work activities.

Now consider the change in the individual's behavior in response to an increase in his or her wage rate from w to w'. First, the relationship between the individual's market productivity, w/p, and household productivity, g_h, changes. With an increase in w, the quantity of goods the individual can purchase with the first hour of time spent in market work, w/p, becomes greater than the quantity of goods he or she can produce with the last hour spent in household work at point E; that is, $g_h|_E < w'/p$. Consequently, the household finds that it can have more goods with the same hours devoted to work if the amount of time the individual spends in household work is reduced and the amount of time spent in market work is increased. Thus, the rise in the real wage rate induces the individual to substitute market work for household work, holding the total amount of work time constant.

This substitution of market work for household work is illustrated by the shift in the total household budget line from $DEBT$ to $D'E'BT$, the decline in household work time of $H_e H'_e$, and the commensurate increase in market work. Prior to the rise in the wage rate, point E is the point of tangency between the household production function AB and the market work budget line, DE. At E, $w/p = g_h|_E$. When w rises to w', $w'/p > g_h|_E$ and the individual substitutes market for household work, finding a new equilibrium at point E', where $w'/p = g_h|_{E'}$. $D'E'$, then, has slope w'/p.

We can call this substitution of market work for household work as the own wage rate changes a *production substitution effect*. In the production substitution effect the individual does not change the total amount of time he or she spends working. Rather, one way of gaining access to goods is substituted for another way. In Figure 5.8, the production substitution effect is the substitution of $H_e H'_e$ hours of market work for $H_e H'_e$ hours of household work. Total hours of work, $L_p T$, remain constant.

The production substitution effect is, however, not the only substitution effect caused by a wage rate change. As the real wage rate rises from w/p to w'/p, the individual's leisure becomes more expensive relative to goods. Holding satisfaction constant, the household is induced by this relative price change to substitute the now-cheaper goods for the now relatively more expensive leisure. This is done by increasing the time the individual spends working and by using the extra earnings to increase the family's consumption of goods. This can be called the *consumption substitution effect* because the substitution occurs in consumption, not production.

The consumption substitution effect is illustrated geometrically in the same way as the substitution effect was illustrated in Chapter 3: by drawing a straight line parallel to the new budget line (i.e., $D'E'$) and tangent to the original indifference curve (U_0). JJ is such a line and is tangent to U_0 at Q. JD' is the amount of real income that must be hypothetically taken away from the household to make it as satisfied at the new wage rate as it was at the old wage rate. The consumption substitution effect of the wage rate increase, then, is the decline in the quantity of leisure consumed from $0L_p$ to $0L_q$, holding satisfaction constant.

The *total substitution effect* of the own-wage-rate increase on market work, then, is the sum of the production substitution effect and the consumption substitution effect. As the wage rate rises, the production substitution effect induces the individual to substitute market work for a like amount of household work, holding total hours of work constant. The consumption substitution effect induces the individual to work more to earn the income required to buy the added goods that the household substitutes for its now more expensive leisure, holding satisfaction constant.

Thus far, we have neglected the fact that a rise in the individual's wage rate increases the household's real income. With the increase in real income come increases in the household's demands for goods and leisure, so long as both are normal goods. This is the *income effect* of the rise in wage rate. It is illustrated by the parallel shift from *JJ* to *D′E′* in Figure 5.8 and the consequent increase in the demand for the individual's leisure from $0L_q$ to $0L_r$ as the household equilibrium moves from Q to R. The income effect of the wage rate increase, therefore, serves to increase the demand for leisure and decrease the individual's supply of labor. But the decrease in the supply of labor comes entirely out of market work; time spent in household work does not decline due to the income effect.

The *total own-wage-rate effect on market work* is the sum of the production and consumption substitution effects and the income effect. In Figure 5.8 the total own-wage-rate effect on market work is

$$L_r H'_e - L_p H_e = H_e H'_e + L_p L_q + L_q L_r.$$

Whereas the two substitution effects of a wage rate increase market work, the income effect reduces market work. The total own-wage-rate effect, therefore, is negative or positive depending on the ability of the income effect to offset the two substitution effects. Thus, the supply curve of labor to the labor market can be conventionally positive (the higher the wage rate, the more labor is supplied to the labor market), or "backward bending," and negative (the higher the wage rate, the less labor is supplied to the labor market).

The *total own-wage-rate effect on household work* is made up solely of the production substitution effect: as the wage rate rises, the time spent in household work declines as more and more labor is shifted from household to market production. In Figure 5.8, this is represented by $H_e H'_e$.

The *total own-wage-rate effect on leisure* is composed of the consumption substitution effect and the income effect. As the price of leisure rises relative to goods, the household substitutes goods for leisure. As the rise in the wage rate increases real income, more leisure is demanded. Since the two effects oppose each other, the total effect on leisure depends on which is the stronger. In terms of Figure 5.8,

$$L_r L_p = L_p L_q + L_q L_r.$$

What evidence do we have that these hypothesized effects occur in the real world? We have more evidence with respect to market work than with respect to household work or leisure. Early studies found that the supply of labor by American males is moderately "backward bending"; that is, as male wage rates rise, the amount of time American males spend in market work declines modestly. Pencavel (1986) summarizes the findings across numerous studies that have focused on men. The empirical evidence he presents suggests that the total own-wage-rate effect on males' labor supply is negative and quite inelastic – in the neighborhood of –0.09 to –0.29 (Pencavel 1986, p. 69). More recent empirical work, summarized in Blundell and MaCurdy (1999, Table 1), factors in more complicated budget constraints[12] than the one depicted in Figure 5.8. These studies all conclude that the uncompensated wage rate elasticity for men is either zero or positive. That is, the slope of the labor supply curve for men is positive. A change in the historical relationship between men's wages and their hours of market work is supported by Costa (2000), who finds negative wage elasticities for men in the 1890s and in 1973, but positive wage elasticities in 1991. This suggests that men's underlying preferences for leisure and/or commodities may have shifted during the past twenty years.[13]

[12] Over the past fifteen years, labor economists have developed and estimated models that allow for numerous nonlinearities in budget constraints. These more complicated budget constraints, reviewed in Blundell and MaCurdy (1999), recognize that certain types of transfer income (e.g., Temporary Assistance to Needy Families) vary with the hours someone works in the labor market and thus these programs can impact the shape of the budget constraint. They also recognize that changes in the marginal income tax rate can affect the shape of the budget constraint. We will discuss some of these complications in more detail later in this chapter.

[13] Pencavel (2002) argues that the reason for the observed differences in men's uncompensated wage elasticities is due to the fact that more recent studies have been estimating elasticities that show how an individual adjusts his work hours in response to changes in wages *as he ages*, holding other factors constant. In contrast, estimation of uncompensated wage elasticities hold age constant.

The compensated wage rate elasticity of labor supply is the sum of the consumption substitution effect and production substitution effect expressed in elasticity terms. As illustrated in Figure 5.8, both are expected to be positive, and so the total substitution effect is also expected to be positive. From estimates of the uncompensated wage rate elasticity (i.e., the sum of the production and consumption substitution effects and the income effect) and the nonlabor income elasticity, Pencavel (1986) deduces that the compensated wage rate elasticity (the sum of the production and consumption substitution effects on labor supply) for men is in the neighborhood of 0.11. Holding satisfaction constant, therefore, the average male can be expected to increase his labor supply by 1.1 percent in response to a 10 percent increase in his wage rate. Kimmel and Kniesner (1998) estimate the compensated wage elasticity for employed single and married men to be 0.4. The signs of these elasticities are consistent with the hypotheses in Figure 5.8: the total substitution effect is positive; holding satisfaction constant, American males increase their labor supply in the face of a rise in wage rates. The extent of their response depends on their demographic characteristics.

In contrast with males, both earlier and more recent empirical work affirm the conclusion that American married women have a positively sloped supply curve of labor to the market. Killingsworth and Heckman (1986) summarized thirty-three cross-section studies and found virtually all uncompensated and compensated wage rate elasticities for females to be positive. Blundell and MaCurdy (1999, Table 2) review eleven studies and with the exception of one, all report positive uncompensated wage elasticities. When taken in combination with the negative income elasticities, these findings suggest that as female wage rates rise, the production and substitution effects more than offset the income effects so that females increase the time they spend employed in the labor market.

The sizes of women's uncompensated wage elasticities depend somewhat on the characteristics of the women studied. For instance, Cogan (1980) estimates that the uncompensated wage rate elasticity for White married women aged thirty to forty-four is 0.65 and the compensated wage rate elasticity is 0.68. Estimates for Black married women have been calculated by Dooley (1982). He estimates that the uncompensated wage rate elasticity for Black married women aged thirty to thirty-four is 0.67 and the compensated wage rate elasticity is 1.01. Interestingly, his estimates of the wage rate elasticities for older Black married women become negative. Building on the idea that married women's wage elasticities may vary by age cohort is work done by Pencavel (1998). He estimates that the uncompensated wage rate elasticity for annual hours worked for married women age 25 to 30 is 0.60 while the corresponding estimate for married women age 56 to 60 is 0.19.

Much less is known about the effects of wage rate changes on the household work of individuals. Gronau (1977) has performed one of the few studies on total housework. For employed American married women he found that the annual hours of household work declined by 500 hours (about 1.4 hours/day) for each 1 percent increase in the wage rate. This is an estimate of the production substitution effect in Figure 5.8. These results are consistent with those of Gramm (1974), who studied Chicago high school teachers, and those of Cochrane and Logan (1975), who studied college graduates in South Carolina. More recently, Solberg and Wong (1992) estimate that a 1 percent increase in the wage rate of a married woman who is employed outside of the home translates into a 6.6 percent decline in her housework time. It is clear, therefore, that married women respond to wage rates as Figure 5.8 suggests.

Even less is known about the relationship between wages and married men's household work time. What little research has been done suggests that married men's household work time is very unresponsive to changes in their wage rates (or to anything else, for that matter!). Stafford and Duncan (1985) estimate the compensated wage rate effect on husband's household work time (i.e., the production substitution effect expressed in elasticity form) to be about −0.17. Bryant, Zick, and Kim's (1992) estimate of the compensated wage effect for husband's housework is also negative at −0.289. In contrast, Kooreman and Kapteyn (1987) and Solberg and Wong (1992) find a positive relationship between married, employed men's wage rates and housework time. Thus, the empirical evidence on this model prediction is mixed for married men. Moreover, the statistical confidence associated with the married men's estimates is low and thus not much weight should be placed on these conflicting estimates.

Since economists have typically defined leisure as the time not spent in market work, they have combined the time spent in household work and the time spent in leisure pursuits. In consequence, much less is known about leisure as we are defining it. Gronau, in his study of American married women's time use (1977), found that employed married women devoted less time to leisure activities as their wage rates rose. Cochrane and Logan (1975) found that married South Carolinian women who were college graduates also reduced the amount of time they devoted to leisure activities as their wage rates rose. Solberg and Wong (1992), using time diary data from 1977–1978, reported that as married, employed men's wage rates rise, so does the time they spend in leisure activities. They observed the same positive relationship for married, employed women although in the case of the women, the estimated relationship does not reach conventional levels of statistical significance. Using the 1975 national time use sample (see Juster et al. 1978), Kooreman and Kapteyn (1987) studied three categories of leisure: (1) organizational activities and sports; (2) entertainment and social activities; and (3) reading, watching TV, and listening to the radio. They found that married females spend more time in entertainment and social activities and less in both of the other two leisure time activities as their wage rates rise. Married men's behavior with respect to these three leisure time activities is similar.

SPECIALIZATION OF FUNCTION AND THE DIVISION OF LABOR

The results of the above research indicate that the effect of female wage rate changes on the household work of married women is larger than the effect of male wage rate changes on the household work of married men. How does one account for this difference? Why is the household work time of married women more responsive to wage rate changes than men's? One explanation is grounded in the specialization of function and division of labor between spouses that occur in two-spouse households. Therefore, we will now outline the economics of the specialization of function and division of labor in the household.

To the extent that the husband and wife are substitutes in household work – either can do it – there are powerful economic incentives for a division of labor between spouses. The reason is that the household can have more goods and services (i.e., the sum of market-purchased and home-produced goods in terms of our simple model) for any given amount of time spent working if each spouse specializes in market work or household work in accordance with their comparative advantage.

Define the wife's comparative advantage for market work over household work as w_f/g_f, where w_f is the wage rate she commands in the labor market and g_f is the marginal productivity of her time in household work. Likewise, define the husband's comparative advantage for market work over household work as w_m/g_m, where w_m is the wage rate he commands in the labor market and g_m is the marginal productivity of his time in household work.

If $w_f/g_f < w_m/g_m$, then the household will have more total goods and services for any given time they spend working if the wife specializes in household work and the husband specializes in market work. If, however,

$w_f/g_f > w_m/g_m$, then total goods and services are greater if he specializes in household work and she specializes in market work. (See mathematical note 4, equation [31].)

How so? To make things simple, suppose that both husband and wife are equally productive in household work ($g_f = g_m$) but that the wife commands a higher wage rate than the husband ($w_f > w_m$). Suppose that initially both spouses are employed and also do some household work. Now suppose that she works an hour longer at her job and he works an hour less in his. Further, suppose that he works an hour more in the household and she an hour less. Both work the same amount of time as before: she, an hour more in market work and an hour less in household work; he, the reverse.

Because their household productivities are equal, their output of home-produced goods remains the same: the household production lost because she worked an hour less is exactly made up by the added household output produced by his additional hour. Because her wage rate is higher than his, their output of market-purchased goods and services has increased. The household loses w_m/p units of market goods and services because he spends an hour less working in the labor market.[14] It gains w_f/p units of market goods and services because she spends an hour more at her job. Since $w_f > w_m$, the household gains more purchased goods and services than it loses and, thus, benefits from this relative specialization of function.

So long as their household productivities, g_f and g_m, are equal and so long as $w_f > w_m$, the incentive exists for her to substitute market work for household work while he substitutes household work for market work. This will continue until she ceases all household work and he ceases all market work. Complete specialization of function by both spouses occurs. Only if the couple has a great demand for goods and services will the husband increase his total work time and re-enter the labor market. His wife, however, will continue to do no household work.[15]

Current reality, of course, is the reverse of the simple example given above. While there is active debate as to whether female and male time are substitutes in household work,[16] women's wage rates are less than men's.

---

[14] Recall that since p is the price of purchased goods, an hour of his market work can buy w_m/p units of goods and services.

[15] See Becker (1991, Chapter 2) for an extensive discussion of this topic. See mathematical note 6 for an outline of a two-person model with specialization of function.

[16] Becker (1991, Chapter 2) argues that a division of labor by sex in which the wife is specialized in housework is more economically efficient. Owen (1987) presents the contrary view. See Bryant and Wang (1990b) for an empirical analysis confirming that in

It is equally clear that currently married women are more specialized in household work than married men even though over one half of all married women also work at paid jobs.

The presence of such specialization implies that the household work of those specialized in market work will be less responsive to wage rate changes than the household work of those specialized in household work. An increase in the wage rate of males will have a consumption substitution effect and an income effect on the times married men spend in leisure and in market work. But there will be little if any production substitution effect of the wage rate increase on their household work for the simple reason that they do little or no household work anyway. Only if their wage rates were less than their wives' would one expect much change. In contrast, an increase in female wage rates can be expected to affect the time married women spend in household work because they either specialize in household work or divide their work time between the labor market and the home. An increased wage rate will induce some of those married women who are totally specialized in household work into the labor market, substituting market for household work. The same wage rate increase will induce those married women working both in the market and in the home to shift more of their time away from household work and toward market work. Thus, the current and historical specialization of function and division of labor between married men and women partially explains the greater response by women than men to changes in their own wage rates.

In sum, although the sizes of the effects vary from study to study, the market work, household work, and leisure time of both men and women do, in general, respond to changes in their wage rates in the fashion hypothesized by our model as modified by specialization of function and division of labor.

CROSS-WAGE-RATE EFFECTS

Cross-wage-rate effects refer to the effect of changes in the wage rate of one spouse on the time use of the other spouse. As such they are similar to cross-price effects. Indeed, since wage rates are the prices of leisure, the analogy is exact.

Consider an increase in the wage rate of the husband. This constitutes an increase in the price of his leisure. The consumption substitution effect

---

two-parent, two-child families, the amounts of time males and females spend on household work and leisure activities together are perfect complements rather than the substitutes required for specialization of function.

of the increase will lead the family to substitute goods for his leisure given that his leisure has become more expensive. The income effect of the increase in his wage rate will increase the family's demand for his leisure, it being a normal good.

Now trace the impacts of his wage rate increase through to his wife's time use. Since neither her home productivity nor her market productivity is affected by the increase in his wage rate, the trade-off between her household production and her market work remains unchanged. Consequently, the amount of time she devotes to household work will not change if she was employed prior to the increase in his wage rate. The amount of time she spends in market work, however, will be affected. If the spouses' leisure times are complements and, therefore, tend to be consumed together by the family, her leisure will fall as his falls due to the consumption substitution effect of his wage rate increase. If, however, the spouses' leisure times are substitutes for each other, then the family will substitute her leisure for his leisure as the consumption substitution effect reduces his leisure time. Furthermore, regardless of the status of their leisure times as substitutes for or complements of each other, the income effect of the rise in his wage rate will increase the demand for her leisure. The net effects on her leisure and market work, therefore, depend on whether her leisure is a substitute for or complement of her husband's leisure and on the strength of the income effect.

If the wife was not employed prior to the increase in his wage rate, the substitution and income effects bear directly on the division of her time between household work and leisure. The cross-substitution effect (between his and her leisure) will increase (decrease) her leisure time and decrease (increase) her household work time if her leisure is a substitute for (complement of) her husband's. The income effect will increase the demand for her leisure time and, in consequence, lower the time she spends in household work.

Although the cross-wage-rate effect has been explained in terms of the effect of the husband's wage rate on the wife's time use, the effects are symmetric; that is, the effect of the wife's wage rate on the husband's time use can be expected to be the same. Indeed, the results are completely general. In principle, the effect of any family member's wage rate on the time use of any other family member can be expected to have the very same components.

We again turn to the work of Gronau, Cochrane and Logan, and Kooreman and Kapteyn, as well as others, for evidence of the cross-wage-rate effects. Gronau (1977) found that as the employed married female's market work time falls, her leisure time rises, and her household work time remains unchanged when her husband's wage rate increases. Among nonemployed married women, an increase in the husband's wage rate increases their leisure and reduces the time spent in household work. On the basis of this evidence, then, her leisure is a gross substitute of his. Cochrane and Logan (1975) and Solberg and Wong (1992) also found employed wives' household work time was unresponsive to the husband's wage rate while their leisure rose with the husband's wage rate.

Kooreman and Kapteyn's (1987) results are more complicated because they disaggregated household work into three categories of "household activities" (cooking, cleaning, laundry, etc.; child care; and shopping). Leisure is also broken down into the three categories (organizational activities and sports; entertainment and social activities; and reading, TV, and radio), and the time spent in personal care is classified separately. As the husband's wage rate rises, the time the wife spends in market work falls, indicating that in total the wife's time is a substitute for the husband's in household work and leisure activities. The distribution of the increased time she spends in household work and leisure activities is interesting. As his wage rate rises, she spends more time in all three of the household work activities. And although she spends more time in reading, TV, and radio and in entertainment and social activities, she spends less time in organizational activities and sports as his wage rate rises.[17]

---

[17] Note that Kooreman and Kapteyn (1987) find that the total time wives spend in household work changes as their husbands' wage rates change. But we argued above that her household work time would *not* change when his wage rate changes because his wage rate changes neither her household productivity nor her market wage rate and, consequently, the trade-off between market and household work would not change for her. Kooreman and Kapteyn's results do not support the simple model presented in this chapter.

Is the model too simple, then? Yes and no. The findings of Kooreman and Kapteyn suggest that one or the other of two simplifying assumptions that were made is incorrect. To be able to use two-dimensional diagrams we assumed that (1) market-purchased goods are perfect substitutes for homemade goods (see equation [5.2]) and (2) household production is a function of the time spent in household production of only one household member (see equation [5.5]). If, for instance, purchased goods and homemade goods are not perfect substitutes, then an increase in his wage rate changes the trade-off between his leisure and homemade goods and leads to a change in the time the wife spends making them. Alternatively, if homemade goods are produced by both spouses, a change in his wage rate alters the trade-off between his and her household work time and leads to a change in the time she spends in household work.

The model of household time allocation we are discussing, then, may be too simple if the behavior analyzed is disaggregated as in the Kooreman and Kapteyn study. It is quite adequate if the behavior is aggregate, as in the Gronau study (1977) (which distinguishes only among total leisure, total household work, and market work), or in the studies of

In contrast, Kooreman and Kapteyn (1987) found husbands' time use to be much less responsive to changes in wives' wage rates than wives' time use is to changes in husbands'. Although husbands do slightly reduce the amount of time they spend in market work in response to increases in their wives' wage rates, the increased nonmarket time is spread evenly across the several categories of household work and leisure. The overall reduction in husbands' market work time in response to changes in wives' wage rates is consistent with the results of other studies of the labor market behavior of males. Gerner and Zick (1983), for instance, in a study of husbands in two-parent, two-child families find that husbands do, in fact, reduce the time they spend in market work in response to increases in their wives' wage rates, but the reduction is quite small.

The smaller response of male time use to changes in female wage rates is consistent with the observed specialization of function and division of labor by spouses. Given that male wage rates are higher than females' and given that most husbands are specialized in market work and most wives in household work, changes in female wage rates should have little effect on the time use of married men except through the income effect and through any complementarities that may exist between husbands' and wives' leisure times. There will be little if any cross-substitution between husbands' and wives' household work time.

TECHNICAL CHANGE EFFECTS

As we noted earlier, the rules by which families combine market goods with their time to generate home-produced goods are represented by the household production function (i.e., AB in Figure 5.6). For instance, an individual may combine her time with the purchased ingredients needed to make a cake given that she has a bowl, a spoon with which to mix the ingredients, and a wood-burning oven. But, the time required to make a cake may be altered if she has an electric mixer rather than a spoon and a gas oven rather than a wood-burning one. In this section, we examine what happens to household time use when the technical rules that govern household production change.

Technical change has two distinct effects on time use in the household production model. Because technical change expands family choice,

labor market behavior (which distinguish only between market work and nonmarket time). Note that the same economic principles underlie both the simple model and the more complicated model. The model is simply adapted to suit the complexity of the problem.

it acts like an increase in income by increasing the demands for most market- and home-produced goods and services. The first effect, then, is to increase the family's demand for all normal goods including such items as household cleanliness, higher quality and greater variety of meals, and better kept yards. Because these increased demands increase the time spent in household work to produce the added goods and services, technical change can actually increase the time spent in household work.

The second effect of technical change is its influence on the efficient combination of labor and nonlabor inputs used to produce household goods and services, which will affect the substitution of nonlabor for labor inputs in household production. If the technical change increases the marginal productivity of all inputs equally, the technical change is deemed neutral and this second effect will be zero. If the technical change is labor saving then it increases the marginal productivity of capital (i.e., household equipment and market goods used in the production process) by a greater percentage than the marginal productivity of labor, and the household will increase its use of capital and decrease its use of labor. Similarly, if the technical change is capital saving, then it increases the marginal productivity of labor by a greater percentage than it increases the marginal productivity of capital and this leads the household to increase its use of labor. Examples include (1) the substitution of home permanents for permanents done in a hair salon in the early 1960s (capital saving) and (2) the substitution of convenience foods for the wife's cooking time after World War II (labor saving) (Bryant 1986; Cowan 1983).

On balance, how have these income and production substitution effects influenced household time use? Bryant (1996) assessed the role that changes in household production factors played in the modest decline in married women's housework time that was observed between the mid-1920s and the late 1960s. He estimates that over this forty-year period, married women's housework time declined by 9.9 percent because of rising household income and technical change. This suggests that during this era the substitution effect of improvements in household technology were generally labor saving and they outweighed the income effect so that on balance the time married women spent in household work declined.

PREFERENCE EFFECTS

In Chapter 3, we discussed how preference shifters can alter the household's demand for goods and services. Preference shifters were grouped into two general categories: (1) variables that measure attributes of the purchase situation, and (2) variables that measure relevant socio-demographic features of the household. In the context of our time allocation model, we must modify this distinction so that the focus is on attributes of the time allocation situation, and socio-demographic features of the household that are relevant to time use. Situational specific attributes that influence household preferences include such variables as season of the year and day of the week. For instance, Zick and McCullough (1991) report, not surprisingly, that both husbands and wives do significantly more housework on weekends compared to weekdays.

Relevant socio-demographic characteristics that measure preference differences across households include age, education, ethnicity, attitudes about gender specific work roles, household size, and household composition. The interpretation of the role that such socio-demographic characteristics play, however, is complicated in our time allocation model. In some instances, these variables may simply affect preferences. For example, a woman who believes in traditional gender roles within the family may have stronger preferences for home-produced goods and services than an otherwise comparable woman who does not hold such beliefs. In other instances, these variables may affect both preferences and the family's technical abilities as reflected in the home production function. Frequently used examples of household characteristics that may affect both the technical production relationships and preferences are household size and household composition.

Household Size, Household Composition, and Time Use

When we think of changes in family size and composition we typically think of changes brought about by the arrival of children, what happens to the family as children grow and mature, and what happens when they leave to form a new household. Consequently, we will deal with the effects of family size and composition by considering the effects children have upon parents' time use.

The relationships between children and parental time use are complicated. Not only does the presence of children of different ages affect parental time use differently, but the relationship is quite different in the short run from that in the long run. In the short run it is clear that the causation runs from children to time use. In the long run it is equally clear that neither parental time use nor children are the cause or effect of the other. Rather, they are both planned responses to an underlying set of forces. Over the long run, parental time use, especially that of the mother, and the number and timing of children are consequences of long-run planning the family executes on the basis of family goals in the light of resources and prices. This long-run view will be dealt with in Chapter 7. Here, we shall consider the short-run effects of the presence and development of children on parental time use.

The change in family size that is brought on by the arrival of a child has three effects on parents – two that are related to the increased household productivity (i.e., the technical change) and one that is related to the shift in household preferences. The birth of a child increases home productivity, g_h of each spouse, because it induces each to substitute the now marginally more productive time spent in housework for the now marginally less productive time spent in market work. The increase in home productivity also generates an income effect that leads to an increase in the demand for all normal goods including parental leisure. Finally, the birth of a child creates a shift in household preferences that increases the demand for market goods and services (more food, clothes, furniture, housing, etc.), inducing increases in the market work of each spouse to earn the income to buy them.

Why does the arrival of a child increase household productivity? The increase in household productivity arises out of increased opportunities for *joint* production and out of *economies of size* that the family can exploit given the larger family size. Joint production occurs when more than one good or service is produced with the same inputs, as when clothes are washed, a meal is cooked, and a child cared for all at the same time. The opportunities for joint production with the addition of a child occur because much child care allows other tasks to be carried out simultaneously.

Size economies are instances in which the average cost of a good or service falls as its output rises. The new infant increases the demand for all home-produced goods and services (meals, laundry, cleaning, shopping, etc., as well as child care). Given the increased demands, the family can enlarge its production of these goods and services and so exploit a number of cost-reducing (and, therefore, home productivity increasing) economies. Laundry equipment is a good example. Many childless couples find it more economical to do their washing at a nearby laundromat. The arrival of a child, however, often increases the demand for laundry services sufficiently to warrant the purchase of a washer and dryer. Food preparation is another example. Increasing family size reduces food loss and spoilage. Also, the increase in food preparation time is proportionately less than the increase in family size. As a final example, the arrival of a baby also creates a demand for child care, a service that is quite expensive when purchased and considerably cheaper when produced in the home. Given the large commitment to child care that one child entails, added children do not increase the commitment in proportion to the increase in family size. Efficiency in the home production of child care is high and it essentially becomes higher as more children are added.

Both joint production and economies of size effects increase household productivity, g_h. Their combined production substitution effect causes parents to spend more time in housework. In contrast, how parental time use is affected by the associated income effect is less clear. As we noted earlier, the income effect causes the household to increase its demand for all normal goods and services. We know that the demand for goods and services rises as family size increases for the simple reason that there are more members to be housed, clothed, transported, and fed. This should encourage parents to increase their paid work time so that they have the funds to cover these expenses. Yet, if parental leisure is also a normal good, the net impact of this income effect on paid employment time becomes ambiguous.

What about preferences? Do changes in family size alter the family's preferences for goods and services relative to leisure? Again the prediction is somewhat ambiguous. Certainly the birth of a child may led parents to have greater preferences for purchasing items like strollers, highchairs, car safety seats, cribs, and so on. At the same time, parents' preferences for their own leisure probably increase with the arrival of a child because of the satisfaction obtained from playing and interacting with a child. The arrival of a child, however, probably increases the demand for goods and services, purchased and homemade, relative to parental leisure, as any new parent lacking sleep can attest.

The increased demand for goods relative to leisure, of course, induces family members to work longer hours in the market or at household tasks, or both, in order to supply them. Given the sexual division of labor within the family, however, the pressure to work longer hours may induce the father to do more market work while it may induce the mother to do more household work. Indeed, the rise in the mother's household productivity, g_h, tilts the trade-off between market and household work toward the latter and typically induces her to increase household work at the expense of market work. And the increased demand for purchased goods induces fathers to spend more time in paid employment earning the money to buy them.

So much for an increase in family size via childbirth. What about the effects of changes in family composition as children grow and mature? One can classify activities as "goods-intensive" or "time-intensive" according to the ratio of goods to time used in the activity: the higher the ratio of goods to time, the more goods-intensive. Child rearing begins as a time-intensive activity and becomes more goods-intensive as they grow older and gain physical, emotional, and intellectual independence from their parents. Economic independence is not typically gained until the schooling process is complete and the child has formed an independent household.

A crucial point in the drift toward the goods-intensive period of the child-rearing process occurs when school begins. Once in school (or in purchased child care) the time burden of children becomes much less. One would expect, then, that the time spent in household work by mothers would decline as the age of the youngest child increases and that the time spent in market work or leisure or both would increase. The same cannot be said about the household's preferences for goods and services relative to leisure. As the child grows up, relative preferences are likely to shift even more toward purchased goods and services (e.g., summer camps, sports equipment, music lessons, automobiles). Thus, one would expect the father's market work to remain high or to grow until the child leaves home. Of course, the entry or reentry of the mother into the labor force also importantly meets the increased demands for purchased goods and services.

Gronau's work, again, offers empirical evidence with respect to the effects of children on the time use of married women. The household work of unemployed married women increased by 328 hours/year and their leisure fell by a like amount with the addition of a preschool child. Employed married women increased their household work by 276 hours annually and reduced their market work by 190 hours and their leisure by 89 hours with the addition of a preschool child (Gronau 1977). These are the effects of an increase in family size by one infant. Bryant, Zick, and Kim (1992) estimate that married women increase their housework time by 8.7 hours per week (452 hours per year) with the addition of each child under age three. Solberg and Wong (1992) report that employed, married women increase their housework by slightly more than 2 hours per day (730 hours per year) and decrease their market work by almost an equal amount when there is at least one preschool child in the home. Both Bryant, Zick, and Kim (1992) and Solberg and Wong (1992) find that the housework time of married men is unaffected by the addition of a young child.

The evidence of the effects of changes in family composition when children grow up is also clear. When the child becomes school-aged, Gronau (1977) found that the household work time of unemployed married women fell by 125 hours annually. If employed, the married woman's household work time declined by about 100 hours, her market work time increased by a like amount, and her leisure time was unaffected as the child reached school age.

The work of Zick and Bryant (1996) on two-parent, two-child families holds family size constant and allows the effects of children's ages on time spent specifically in child care to be isolated. They found that married mothers spent almost 3 hours more per day doing child care when the youngest child was under age one compared to when the youngest child was between the ages of 12 and 17. Married fathers likewise spent approximately 1 hour more per day in child care when the youngest child was under age one compared to when the youngest child was between the ages of 12 and 17. Clearly, the age distribution of the children in a household exercises considerable influence on parental time use.

PUBLIC POLICIES AND HOUSEHOLD TIME USE

There is probably no subject more infused with political rhetoric than the long-standing debate over the impact that income taxes and welfare payments have on the incentive to work. Political conservatives take it as a matter of faith that the high marginal income tax rates faced by affluent people induce them to work less and, thus, rob society of their productivity. Likewise, they fervently believe that the welfare payments targeted for the poor blunt their incentive to work and impede their progress toward economic independence. Political liberals have argued equally passionately that income taxes do not penalize ambition and welfare payments do not reward laziness and sloth.

Our model of household time use activities is ideally suited to analyze the effects of how public policies may alter individual time use. Here we will analyze simple versions of both an income tax and a welfare program to show how the model can be used to shed light on such controversies. In both cases, the public policies in question change the nature of the budget constraint faced by the household. This shift in the budget constraint will translate into a new optimization point for the household, which will in turn lead to a change in time allocation.

An Analysis of an Income Tax

The federal income tax, even as simplified in the 1986 Tax Reform Act, is much too complex to analyze completely. Instead, a simple proportional income tax similar in spirit to the Social Security tax will be investigated.

Suppose that a simple proportional income tax of $t100$ percent (where $0 < t < 1$) is levied on all earned income. The total tax paid by an individual, Tx, is, therefore,

$$Tx = tE = twM \tag{5.15a}$$

and after-tax income, AY, is

$$AY = E + V - Tx = wM - twM + V = (1 - t)wM + V. \tag{5.15b}$$

The time constraint $M = T - H - L$ can be substituted into (5.15b) and expenditures on purchased goods, pC, can be equated with after-tax income to yield the market work portion of the household's budget constraint:

$$pC + (1 - t)wL + (1 - t)wH = (1 - t)wT + V. \tag{5.16}$$

What equation (5.16) makes clear is that the proportional income tax alters the price of time. In the absence of any income tax, the price of time is the wage rate, w, for employed individuals. In the presence of the income tax, however, the price of time is $(1 - t)w$. Since t is a fraction like 0.10 or 0.20, the price of time is lower in the presence of the income tax than in its absence. That being said, we can analyze the imposition of an income tax in exactly the same way as a drop in the wage rate would be analyzed. This is done with the help of Figure 5.9.

In Figure 5.9, the income tax lowers the real wage rate and, therefore, the individual's market productivity from w/p to $(1 - t)w/p$. This changes the slope of the budget constraint from $DEBT$ to $D'E'BT$. This reduction induces the individual to substitute household work for market work as market productivity falls below household productivity, $g_h|_E$. In consequence, through the vehicle of the production substitution effect, the income tax relocates some of the individual's work time from the labor market to the home. This is represented by the increase in housework from H_eT to H'_eT. Since market work is readily observable and recorded in national statistics whereas household work is not, political conservatives mistakenly believe that work effort has been reduced when, in fact, it simply has been relocated from the office, factory, and field to the home.

The incentives for substitution are not completely encompassed by the production substitution effect, however. The reduction in the price of time due to the income tax rate also lowers the price of leisure relative to goods, inducing a consumption substitution effect. As leisure is made cheaper than goods as a result of the imposition of the income tax, individuals are induced to increase their consumption of leisure and reduce

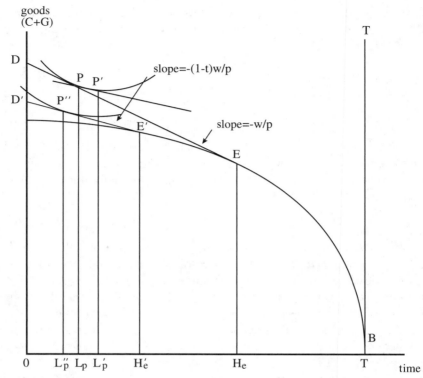

Figure 5.9. The effects of an increase in income tax rates on time allocation.

their consumption of purchased goods, holding satisfaction constant. In Figure 5.9 this is reflected in the $L_p L'_p$ reduction in paid employment time. Here, via the consumption substitution effect of the income tax rate, is the reduction in work focused on by political conservatives and ignored by political liberals.

But the effects of the income tax have not yet been exhausted. The reduction in the after-tax wage rate also lowers the individual's real income and induces an income effect. Since we know that leisure is a normal good, we know that the income effect of the imposition of the income tax is to lower the individual's consumption of leisure, thereby increasing his or her work effort. This is represented in Figure 5.9 by the movement from L'_p to L''_p. This effect is ignored by political conservatives and liberals alike.

In reality, of course, the beliefs of both conservatives and liberals are about the total effect of the income tax. Most are unaware of the complexities of substitution and income effects. What is clear, however, is that individuals' responses to income taxes will depend on their marital status, age, and gender if the own-wage-rate elasticities discussed earlier in the chapter are applicable to cases in which wage rates are changed by taxes. If so (and most economists believe they are applicable) then we would expect (1) people's work effort to be quite inelastic with respect to changes in income tax rates and (2) married men and women to decrease their paid work effort. In the case of married men, these predictions are confirmed by the empirical work of MaCurdy, Green, and Paarsch (1990) and Triest (1990). Triest, however, finds that the estimated effects of taxation on married women's labor supply are somewhat larger, suggesting that the empirical findings on this issue are somewhat mixed. What is clear is that political rhetoric from the Left and from the Right both overstate reality: labor supply responses to income taxes are likely smaller than conservative ideology states and likely larger than liberal ideology maintains.

Welfare Programs: The Case of the Earned Income Tax Credit

Programs like Supplemental Security Income (SSI), Temporary Assistance to Needy Families (TANF), and the Earned Income Tax Credit (EITC) are all examples of welfare programs that provide cash income to families and individuals temporarily destitute and to those with no possibility of supporting themselves completely. Historically, many welfare programs have come under political fire because their benefits structures are perceived to discourage market work. In this section we will use an economic model of time allocation to examine how the structure of the EITC is likely to affect low-income adults' time allocation.

We choose to focus on the EITC because it is one of the largest cash-transfer programs targeted at low-income families (Almanac of Policy Issues 2002). Advocates of the program argue that the structure of the EITC creates work incentives for nonemployed single parents while critics contend that the program reduces the work hours of low-income parents already in the labor market.

A family is eligible for the EITC if one or more family members has earned income, their adjusted gross income is below a specified threshold, and there is a qualifying child present in the household. If an eligible family's EITC is larger than its federal tax liability, then the excess EITC comes to the family in the form of a cash refund. Hence, it can be viewed as a type of negative income tax.

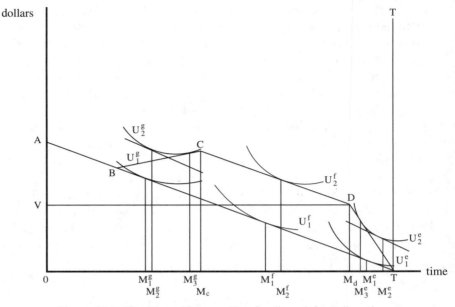

Figure 5.10. The Earned Income Tax Credit and time allocation.

The EITC has three distinct ranges depending on the income of the household: the subsidy range, the flat range, and the phase-out range. Households with very low levels of income receive a wage subsidy through their refundable federal income tax credit. Households with somewhat higher incomes receive the maximum tax credit amount and increases in earnings do not alter the credit amount in this range. Finally, in the phase-out range, the credit is gradually reduced as the household's earnings increase to the point at which the household is no longer eligible for the EITC.

The precise structure of the EITC is complicated because the credit varies by household size and total earnings. We present a simplified EITC model that abstracts from these complexities while retaining the essential features of the program. In this simple model represented in Figure 5.10, we focus exclusively on the market work of a single parent who has no nonlabor income. He can allocate his time to leisure activities (measured from left to right) or productive activities in the labor market (measured from right to left on the horizontal axis). Household work is subsumed under the heading of leisure in this model and thus it will not be considered separately. Also for simplicity, the units of purchased goods are defined so that $p = \$1.00$/unit and we can measure dollars of income on the vertical axis.

Line AT represents the household's budget line in the absence of the EITC. The slope of AT equals the negative of the individual's real wage rate, $-w$. The shape of this household's budget constraint is changed with the introduction of the EITC. Let's begin by examining the EITC subsidy range, $M_d T$. In this range, it provides the single parent with a refundable tax credit, the amount of which is determined by the subsidy rate, s_i, (where $0 < s_i < 1.0$) and his labor earnings. In this range, his hourly wage rate effectively increases to $w(1 + s_i)$. Thus, compared to the situation where the EITC does not exist, the slope of the market work constraint $-w(1 + s_i)$ is steeper in this phase-in range where the single parent works between one and $M_d T$ hours in the labor market.

At $M_d T$ hours of work, the EITC reaches its maximum amount, V. The credit remains at this maximum amount as the single parent continues to increase his work hours up to $M_c T$. In this flat range of work hours, the wage rate faced by this single parent is again w and the household receives nonlabor income, V, in the form of the refundable tax credit.

At $M_c T$ hours of market work, the EITC begins to phase out. In this region, the EITC has two distinct effects. The refundable tax credit, V, operates like an increase in unearned income, shifting the whole budget upward. The benefit reduction rate in this range serves to reduce the price of time from w to $w(1 - s_p)$ where $0 < s_p < 1$. This flattens the budget line to the left of point C.

In the presence of the EITC program, the household's full budget constraint becomes $ABCDT$. What does the model predict will happen to the single parent's time allocation in the presence of the EITC program? The answer to that question depends on household preferences. In Figure 5.10, we have added the indifference curves for three different single parents to the diagram. Each single parent faces the same wage and the same parameters of the EITC program. They only differ in terms of their preferences.

In the absence of the EITC, the single parent represented by indifference curve U_1^e spends $M_1^e T$ hours in market work. With the EITC in place, her wage increase from w to $w(1 + s_i)$ creates both an income and a substitution effect. Assuming that leisure is a normal good, the income effect will encourage her to do less market work and spend more time in leisure. The reduction in market work in Figure 5.10 is $M_1^e M_2^e$. In contrast, the substitution effect will lead her to cut back on the now more expensive leisure time and increase her market work time (i.e., increasing market work by $M_2^e M_3^e$). On balance, then, the impact of the EITC on the market work time of a single parent in the subsidy range is generally ambiguous (although for the single parent represented by U^e it increases her labor supply by $M_1^e M_3^e$).

Now turn to the single parent represented by the U^f indifference curves. In the absence of the EITC, he spends $M_1^f T$ hours in market work. With the introduction of the EITC, this single parent moves to the portion of the ABCDT budget constraint where the refundable credit is constant and at its maximum amount (i.e., between C and D). In this range the single parent's wage rate is unchanged and the EITC exerts only an income effect. Again, assuming that the parent's leisure is a normal good, this will lead him to reduce his market work by $M_1^f M_2^f$ and increase his leisure time by a commensurate amount.

Now turn to the single parent whose preferences are represented by the indifference curves labeled U^g. In the absence of the EITC, this individual works $M_1^g T$. For individuals whose preferences put them in the BC portion of the EITC budget constraint, the impact of the program is twofold. First, the credit operates like an increase in unearned income, shifting the whole budget line upward. Second, the tax credit reduction rate serves to reduce the price of time from w to $(1 - s_p) w$ and, thus, flattens the budget line to the left of point C.

Focus first on the effect of the refundable tax credit reduction. The tax credit reduction serves to lower the price of time for the eligible parent to $w(1 - s_p)$ similar to the way an income tax lowers one's wage rate. As the price of time is lowered, the recipient is induced to substitute leisure time for market work time, holding satisfaction constant. In Figure 5.10 the amount of this increase in leisure time is $M_2^g M_3^g$.

Additionally, since the real wage rate is reduced, the recipient's real income falls as a result of the credit reduction rate, s_p, and the single parent is induced to consume less leisure time and work more. The credit reduction rate will increase or decrease a single parent's work effort, therefore depending on whether the income effect offsets the substitution effect; that is, whether the uncompensated wage rate elasticity of labor supply is positive or negative. Consequently, we can expect single mothers (by far the majority of the recipients of the EITC) to reduce the time they spend in the labor market as a result of the credit reduction rate.

The effect of the credit guarantee, V, has not been discussed. For recipients, V is simply the same as an increase in nonlabor income. We can expect that the larger the guarantee level built into the EITC, the less market work recipients will do because of its income effect.

Since the program increases rather than decreases recipients' total income, Y, the income effect due to the guarantee must be larger than the income effect due to the credit reduction rate. This is shown in the move of $M_1^g M_2^g$, which contains the two income effects: the increase in work due to the decline in income brought about by the credit reduction rate and the decline in work due to the increase in real income brought about by the guarantee. Consequently, the total effect of the EITC in the BC range will be to reduce the time spent by recipients in market work.

Finally, we need to examine how the EITC budget constraint affects two other groups: (1) single parents who, in the absence of the EITC, are not employed and (2) single parents who are employed but whose income is high enough that they are ineligible to receive the EITC. Let's begin with the single parent who is not employed. That is, his preferences, depicted by indifference curves U_1^e, are such that he maximizes utility at T in Figure 5.11. Given that the EITC benefit is only available if one is employed, it will serve to increase the probability of employment for those parents whose preferences are such that they otherwise would allocate their time solely to nonmarket activities. This occurs because at zero hours of work, the wage subsidy, s_i, exerts only a substitution effect. This effect

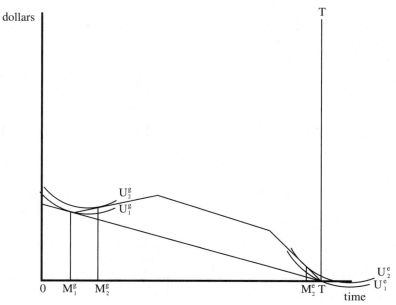

Figure 5.11. The impact of the Earned Income Tax Credit on the time allocation of individuals initially out of the credit's range.

is shown in Figure 5.11 as the movement to working $M_2^e T$ hours in the labor market.

Now turn to the case of the single parent whose earnings are sufficiently high that she in ineligible for the EITC. Her preferences are represented by U^g in Figure 5.11. Like the individual on the BC segment of the budget constraint in Figure 5.10, the EITC encourages this individual to cut back on her labor supply through both the benefit reduction rate and the guarantee. This is shown graphically in Figure 5.11 by the $M_1^g M_2^g$ reduction in work hours.

In sum, the economic model of time allocation suggests that the impact of the EITC on single parents' labor supply is dependent on the segment of the budget constraint on which they find themselves. In the case of the nonemployed single parent, the model predicts that the EITC will increase the probability of work. For a single parent whose preferences place him on the subsidy range, the effect of the EITC is ambiguous with work hours either increasing or decreasing depending on the relative magnitudes of the income and substitution effects. Finally, for single parents in the flat range, the phase-out range, or in the range just above the eligibility threshold (i.e., those working just a few too many hours to qualify), the model predicts that the EITC will induce a reduction in work hours.

Does the empirical literature confirm the predictions of the time allocation model? There is considerable evidence that the EITC increases single mothers' labor force participation rates, albeit modestly. Eissa and Liebman (1996) estimate the marginal increase in labor force participation to be 2.8 percent while Dickert, Houser, and Scholz (1995) estimate the increase to be 3.3 percent and Meyer and Rosenbaum (2000) calculate the increase to be 1.9 percent. These positive labor force participation effects are consistent with what the model predicts.

In contrast, the evidence of the EITC's impact on the work hours of single mothers who are already in the labor force is less consistent with the model's predictions. Eissa and Liebman (1996) report that the labor supply of single mothers already in the labor force is virtually unaltered by an increase in EITC benefits. Liebman (1997) also finds no evidence of negative effects on hours worked for those already in the labor market. If most of the single mothers who are already employed are on the subsidy portion of the budget constraint, then the finding of no labor supply effect could be consistent with the theory. But, if most mothers are on the flat or phase-out portions of the budget constraint, then these empirical results would not be consistent with the model's prediction.

Policy makers have identified the high implicit tax rates of various welfare programs as problematic because they discourage market work. It would appear that advocates of the EITC are correct in arguing that its structure encourages single mothers to enter the labor market but these positive effects are modest. In contrast, there is little evidence to support detractors' claims that the EITC reduces the labor supply of single mothers who are already employed.[18] This may be because it is only one of many welfare programs that alter the after-tax wage rate of low-income workers.[19]

As with their ideological positions on income taxes, the positions of both conservatives and liberals overstate the work disincentive effects of welfare programs. Welfare programs do, indeed, induce recipients to work less than they would in the absence of such programs, to the dismay of doctrinaire liberals, but the effect is far less than doctrinaire conservatives would like to believe (Danziger, Haveman, and Plotnick 1981).

UNEMPLOYMENT, THE RESERVATION WAGE, AND THE
VALUE OF TIME

Voluntary Unemployment and the Reservation Wage

The only kind of unemployment that has been recognized up to this point is voluntary unemployment. A person is voluntarily unemployed when the wage rate the person is offered is lower than the person's reservation wage. A person's reservation wage rate is that wage rate at which the individual

---

[18] Our discussion of the EITC has focused exclusively on the labor supply predictions for single-parent households. Yet, approximately one-third of all EITC recipients are married couples with one or more minor children. Eissa and Hoynes (1998) argue that since eligibility of the EITC is based on family earnings, its impact on labor supply is likely to vary across husbands and wives. If family labor supply decisions are made sequentially and husbands are the primary earners and wives are the secondary earners, then wives may often find themselves on the phase-out section of the EITC budget constraint. This suggests that the structure of the EITC creates a work disincentive for married mothers in EITC-eligible households. Eissa and Hoynes's (1998) empirical work reveals that the EITC does indeed reduce the labor force participation rates of married women in EITC-eligible households by about 1 percent.

[19] Walden (1996) demonstrates how the benefits of Aid to Families with Dependent Children (now called Temporary Assistance to Needy Families), food stamps, housing assistance, Medicaid, and the Earned Income Tax Credit all change simultaneously with the household's earned income. He finds that over the earnings range where a single parent with two children is eligible for the EITC, the *overall* implicit marginal tax rate varies from −13.2 percent to 69.2 percent. (When the rate is negative, it is actually a subsidy rather than a tax.)

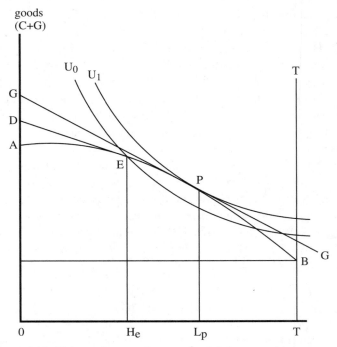

Figure 5.12. Voluntary unemployment and the reservation wage rate.

is indifferent between being employed and not. Another way of saying this is that a person is voluntarily unemployed when his or her leisure and household production activities are worth more to the individual than the goods that could be purchased if he or she were employed.

These concepts are illustrated in Figure 5.12. As usual *DEBT* is the individual's total household budget line. The person is in equilibrium at point *P*, at which he spends L_pT hours per week in household work and $0L_p$ hours in leisure activities. Clearly, he would be less satisfied if he did any work at the wage rate employers offer (i.e., the slope of *DE*): U_0, the indifference curve through point *E*, where market work would begin if he did any, is well below U_1. The individual is, therefore, voluntarily unemployed. Work is available to him at a wage rate of w/p, but the wage rate is not sufficiently high to draw him into the labor force.

At point *P* the individual's marginal rate of substitution of leisure for goods (the slope of U_1 at *P*) is equal to his household productivity (the slope of *DEBT* at *P*). And both are much higher than the wage rate he can command in the labor market (the slope of DE). That is,

$$u_l/u_g|_P = g_h|_P > w/p.$$

To emphasize this difference in Figure 5.12, line GG has been drawn through point P and tangent to both $DEBT$ at P and U_1 at P so that the slope of GG can be compared with that of DE: GG is steeper than DE.

What is also clear from Figure 5.12 is that the wage rate the individual is offered in the labor market must be greater than the slope of GG if the individual is to be induced into any market work. Indeed, a real wage rate equal to the slope of GG is the wage rate at which the individual would be indifferent between working an added hour in the household, having an additional hour of leisure, and working the first hour in the labor market. The slope of GG, therefore, is the reservation wage rate.

The Value of Time and the Reservation Wage. As a practical matter, empirical measures of the value of time are some of the most sought numbers in economics. The values of the time of voluntarily unemployed people are especially sought.

Economists are quite interested in the value of the work done in the household. If the goods and services produced in the household could be valued, they could be added to the nation's gross national product and we would have a much better idea of the true wealth and productivity of the nation.[20] Since much of the value of home-produced goods and services is contributed by household work time, an accurate measure of the value of time spent in the household would greatly improve our national economic accounts.

Measures of the value of time are also of great importance in political and legal arenas. The benefits in accident, product liability, and divorce cases all hinge on estimates of the value of time. If, for instance, a housewife or house-husband is permanently disabled and no longer can perform household tasks, insurance benefits will depend on the lost value of the individual's time in household work. Likewise, divorce settlements may depend on the relative contributions of the two spouses and their contributions depend on their respective values of time and on how much each worked in the home and in the labor market. In the political arena it is argued that the Social Security benefits of married women who have never been employed should be linked to the value of their household

---

[20] See for example, Ironmonger (1997) and Ironmonger and Soupourmas (2003).

production. Again, this argument hinges on the value of the individual's time.

What, then, is the value of an individual's time? The answer is the individual's opportunity cost of time.

Definition: The opportunity cost of time is the value of what was forgone in order for the individual to spend his or her time in the manner he or she did.

For the employed person, the opportunity cost of time is his or her wage rate. Recall that in equilibrium

$$u_l/u_g = g_h = w/p$$

for the employed person; that is, the marginal rate of substitution of leisure for goods equals the individual's productivity in household work and also the individual's real wage rate. The employed person, therefore, gives up consuming w/p quantity of goods for each hour spent in leisure activities or in household work. The individual must judge that this sacrifice is worth it, else he or she would alter behavior to reduce the sacrifice. The real wage rate, then, must equal the opportunity cost of time and, thus, be the value of the individual's time either in household work or in leisure activities.

The wage rate the voluntarily unemployed individual can command in the labor market is lower than the value of his or her time. Recall that for voluntarily unemployed individuals in equilibrium,

$$u_l/u_g = g_h > w/p$$

as is shown in Figure 5.12. If this were not true, then the individual would increase satisfaction by spending some time in market work. To use the wage rate voluntarily unemployed individuals command in the labor market as the measure of the value of their time, then, is to underestimate it.

For the voluntarily unemployed individual the opportunity cost of time spent in household work is the value of the forgone leisure the individual could have had. Likewise, the opportunity cost of the time the individual spends in leisure pursuits is the value of the forgone goods and services that could have been produced and consumed had the individual chosen to spend the time in household work instead. What is this value per hour? It is the reservation wage rate. This is clearly seen in Figure 5.12, where the slope of GG (i.e., the real reservation wage rate, w_r/p, where w_r is the reservation wage rate) equals the marginal rate of substitution of leisure for goods (i.e., $u_l/u_g|_P$) and also equals the marginal product of labor in household work (i.e., $g_h|_P$).

The techniques by which reservation wage rates are estimated have become firmly established in the past two decades. For example, Bryant, Zick, and Kim (1992) have estimated the median after-tax reservation wage rates in 1988 for a sample of White, married men and women between the ages of 25 and 65. They report that the males have a median reservation wage of $8.33/hour and a median market wage of $9.93/hour while the median reservation wage for the females is $8.41/hour and their median market wage is $5.67/hour (all measured in 1988 dollars). The fact that, on average, the men's market wage rate is greater than their reservation wage is consistent with the observation that most married men between the ages of 25 and 65 are employed. In contrast, for married women, their reservation wage rate is greater, on average, than their market wage rate. This would lead one to predict that a sizable fraction of married women (i.e., those whose reservation wage rates are greater than the wage they could possibly earn in the labor market) would elect to be full-time homemakers rather than enter the labor market. This is also consistent with the fact that only 56.7 percent of married women were employed in 1988 (U.S. Bureau of the Census 2003, Table 569).

Involuntary Unemployment

To argue that all unemployment is voluntary is to misrepresent reality; involuntary unemployment does exist. Involuntary unemployment occurs when a person is willing to work more hours than she is allowed to work at the wage rate offered by employers. What is the behavior of the family in the face of involuntary unemployment?

Not being able to work as many hours as would be preferred at the offered wage rate implies that the individual would prefer to reduce the amount of time spent in leisure and household work in order to do more market work. Put another way, the individual has more leisure and does more household work than she would prefer. The individual's marginal rate of substitution of leisure for goods, u_l/u_g, and the individual's household productivity, g_h, must therefore be lower than the individual's real wage rate, w/p. Economic conditions in the labor market, not in the household, prevent the person from shifting hours from the household to the labor market and so equate the value of her time in household activities (leisure and household work) with her real wage rate. Nothing prevents the individual, however, from allocating her time within the household

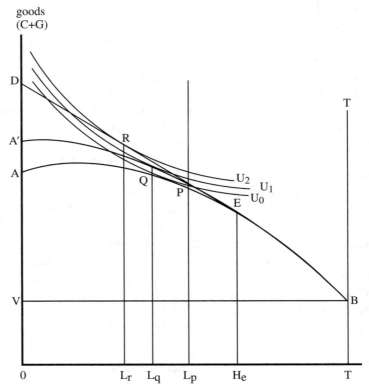

Figure 5.13. Time use during involuntary unemployment.

so as to be as satisfied as possible given the unemployment situation. Thus, she will arrange her household activities so as to equate the value of time in leisure activities with the value of time in household work. Consequently, for the involuntarily unemployed person it will be the case that

$$u_l/u_g = g_h < w/p.$$

This is illustrated in Figure 5.13. The total household budget line facing the individual is $DEBT$. In the absence of any constraints on hours worked, the pictured individual would maximize satisfaction at point R on U_2, at which she would spend H_eT hours per week doing household work, L_rH_e hours per week in market work, and $0L_r$ hours per week in leisure activities.

What she prefers cannot be realized, however. Given conditions in the labor market, she can work only L_pH_e hours in the labor market; more hours are not available. At point P the slope of U_0 is less than the slope of DE; that is,

$$u_l/u_g|_P < w/p = g_h|_E.$$

Clearly, she would give up additional leisure (a maximum of $L_r L_p$ hours) if she could work more hours per week. Although she cannot work more hours in the labor market, she can do more household work and will, since her marginal rate of substitution of leisure for goods ($u_l/u_g|_P$) is less than the marginal product of her time in household work ($g_h|_E$). She will continue to exchange leisure for household work until her marginal rate of substitution of leisure for goods equals her household productivity; that is, until

$$u_l/u_g = g_h < w/p.$$

Geometrically, this occurs at point Q. How is point Q determined? Since involuntary unemployment induces the individual to do more household work than she would prefer had she a choice, she must do more household work than TH_e. How much more depends on the relationship between the marginal productivity of her time in household work (i.e., the slope of the household production function) and her relative preference for leisure (i.e., the slopes of her indifference curves).

To find out how much more household work (and how much less leisure) she will do, one must take the AE portion of the household production function and shift it up to point P, where it becomes $A'P$. Any additional household work performed, then, is measured along $A'P$ beginning at P. The individual will maximize satisfaction, given the restrictions in the labor market, at point Q where she is more satisfied than at point P ($U_1 > U_0$) but less satisfied than at point R ($U_1 < U_2$). At Q she will work $H_e L_p$ hours per week in the labor market, work $TH_e + L_p L_q$ hours per week in household production, and have $0L_q$ hours of leisure.

Is such behavior reasonable? Certainly. Faced with involuntary unemployment, people do not simply lie around the house "doing nothing" with the excess time ($L_p L_r$) at their disposal. Instead, they will spend some of it ($L_p L_q$) in various productive activities: gardening, painting and fixing up, lawn and car maintenance, and so on. The rest ($L_q L_r$) will be spent in added leisure activities.

TIME AND CONSUMPTION ALLOCATION OVER THE LIFE CYCLE

Up to this point, time allocation in the chapter has been discussed within the context of a single period: how individuals allocate the 24 hours they

Table 5.2. *Percent of the Civilian Population Employed by Age and Sex,* [1] *and Total Consumer Expenditures per Household by Age of Householder,* [2] *2002*

Age Group	Percent Civilian Population Employed		Consumer Expenditures per Household (Dollars)
	Male	Female	
16–19 years	38.9	40.3	
20–24 years	72.5	65.5	24,229
25–34 years	87.7	71.2	40,318
35–44 years	87.4	72.4	48,330
45–54 years	84.8	73.2	48,748
55–64 years	66.6	53.2	44,330
65+ years	17.3	9.4	28,105

Sources: [1] U.S. Bureau of the Census (2003, Tables 587 and 621). [2] U.S. Bureau of the Census (2004–2005, Table 660).

have during a day, for instance, or the 168 hours they have during a week. Similarly in Chapters 2 and 3, we presented models that focus on how consumers allocate their income for a particular period among consumer goods and purchases. But, as Chapter 4 made clear, people also make decisions about their consumption in the light of their past actions and expectations about future incomes and prices. Explicit was the idea that people have expectations about their resources over their entire lifetime and they plan how these are to be spent over their lifetime. If such plans are made and roughly carried out with respect to people's financial resources (i.e., their lifetime incomes and assets), then people can be expected to make similar plans as to how they will spend the time they have over their lifetime. Furthermore, to the extent that people's expectations about future prices and interest rates influence these actions, then the pattern of consumption over the life cycle will be related to the pattern of time use over the life cycle. These interrelationships are the subject of this section.

First, however, consider the empirical record. Table 5.2 contains measures of market work behavior and of consumption by age for the United States for 2002, percentage of the civilian population employed by age and sex, and total consumer expenditures per household by age of the householder. Notice that the pattern of both market work behavior and consumer expenditures by age have the same general shape: lower at younger ages, rising and then leveling off in middle age, and declining past age

65 years. While such factors as the timing of education, marriage, having and rearing children, and the departure of children to form their own households all play their roles in shaping this pattern, the pattern of real wage rates commanded by individuals also plays a role. Because real wage rates reflect the price of time, w, relative to the price of consumption goods and services, p, that is, w/p, the expected pattern of real wage rates over individuals' life cycles can be expected to influence both individuals' patterns of market work and the timing of their consumption of goods and services over the life cycle.

It is a common expectation of people that the wage rates they command will increase as they grow older. They also expect that their earning power will level out as they reach and pass middle age and approach retirement. These expectations are with respect to their real wage rates, w/p, not simply their money wage rates, w. In fact, such expectations are realistic, for this is exactly how real wage rates move as individuals grow older. Figure 5.14 illustrates the typical relationship between age and the real wage rate or earning power; the curve rises with age and then levels out as middle age and beyond are reached. For some people it may also fall as they pass middle age. Indeed, the more education one has the more

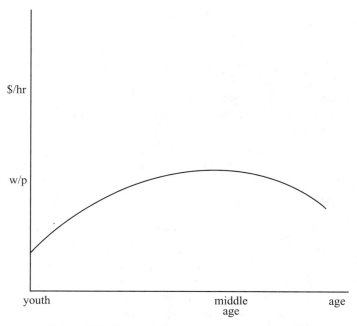

Figure 5.14. The typical age–real wage rate profile.

rapidly real wage rates rise with age and the less they will level out or fall past middle age. (See Chapter 6 for an in depth discussion of the reasons for this pattern.)

Faced with such expectations, how would a satisfaction-maximizing person plan his or her pattern of consumption and home time $(H + L)$ over the life cycle? At each age an individual would seek to equate his or her marginal rate of substitution of home time for consumption with the market rate of exchange of home time for consumption at that age; that is,

$$(u_l/u_c)_a = (w/p)_a \qquad (5.17)$$

where $(u_l/u_c)_a$ is the individual's marginal rate of substitution of home time for consumption at age a, u_l being the marginal utility of home time and u_c being the marginal utility of consumption, and $(w/p)_a$ is the individual's expected real wage rate at age a.

As the individual's age increases, his/her earning power, w/p rises, making home time more expensive relative to consumption. In response, the individual will substitute consumption for home time and, in so doing, reduce u_c and increase u_l to equate his/her marginal rate of substitution with the market rate of exchange. As a result, the individual's demand for consumption expenditures rises and the demand for home time will fall (i.e., the extent of paid employment will increase).

The process of increasing consumption expenditures and reducing home time (increasing the extent of market work) as w/p rises will continue until middle age or beyond when the individual's real wage rate flattens out and perhaps begins to fall. At that point, the process of substitution will slow and reverse itself: the individual will begin to demand more home time, to work less, and consumption expenditures will fall. On either side of middle age, the individual will substitute the good becoming cheaper with age for the good becoming more expensive. From youth to middle age, home time gets more expensive relative to consumption, whereas after middle age home time becomes less expensive relative to consumption.

In other words, the satisfaction-maximizing individual will emphasize household activities (household work and leisure activities) when time is relatively cheap and emphasize the consumption of purchased goods and services when time is expensive. Such an individual's youth is devoted to education, which is preeminently a time-intensive activity. The prime of such a person's life is devoted to paid employment and goods-intensive activities. Old age is spent in time-intensive, household activities.

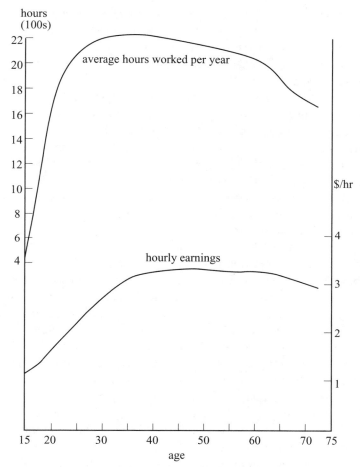

Figure 5.15. Five-year moving averages of hourly earnings and average hours worked per year for employed White males in the United States in 1960 [*Source:* Reprinted, by permission, from Ghez and Becker (1975, Figure 3.1, p. 85)].

The evidence for this intertemporal substitution of time for consumption is clear. Ghez and Becker (1975) used 1960 census data to test the intertemporal substitution hypothesis. Figure 5.15 is taken from their study and shows five-year moving averages of hourly earnings and hours worked per year by age for employed White males. Clearly evident is the rise in hours worked per year with age, as age and the real wage rate both increase and the ultimate fall in hours worked as wage rates level out and ultimately fall.

Ghez and Becker (1975) estimate that the wage rate elasticity of annual home time across the life cycle for White males is −0.12; that is, a 10 percent increase (decrease) in the real wage rate induces a 1.2 percent fall (rise) in annual home time (household work plus leisure). Thus, as White males' real wage rates rise as they grow older, they reduce the amount of home time they consume annually. Conversely, as real wage rates fall when they are in middle to late middle age, they begin to increase the time they spend in household production and leisure activities. Over their life cycle it does appear that White men work when their wage rates are high and spend their time in other activities when their time is cheap. Ghez and Becker estimate the analogous wage rate elasticity for Black males to be −0.05. The same tendency is present among Black males but the responsiveness to real wage rate changes is much less. The reasons for the smaller responsiveness is unclear.

Turn now to the evidence about consumption over the life cycle. Consumer expenditures per household by age of householder are displayed in Table 5.2. As with the percentage of the civilian population employed, consumer expenditures rise with age to middle age, level out and then fall for the 65+ age group. To what extent is this pattern a result of householders' responses to the pattern of real wage rates over the life cycle? Are we observing in these figures householders substituting the consumption of market-purchased goods and services for home time as their real wage rates rise to middle age followed by the substitution of home time for market-purchased goods and services as their real wage rates level out in middle age and decline in old age?

Consumer expenditures per household are highly correlated with household size. Furthermore, household size is highly correlated with age of householder as individuals marry, children are born and reared, and finally leave to form their own households. Thus the pattern of consumer expenditures with age displayed in Table 5.2 could be merely the result of the relationship between family size and age of householder and have nothing to do with the life-cycle pattern of real wage rates. After removing the influence of family size from a sample of families from the 1960–1961 Survey of Consumer Expenditures, Ghez and Becker (1975, Chapter 2) find the hump-shaped pattern of consumer expenditures by age is strongly related to the hump-shaped pattern of real wage rates by age. As the real wage rate rises with age by 10 percent, consumption expenditures rise by 0.55 percent. The relationship is very similar within educational groups: for households with only a grade school education, the elasticity of consumption with respect to real wage rates is 0.49; for households with nine to twelve years of schooling the real wage rate elasticity is 0.54; and for those with greater than twelve years of schooling the real wage rate elasticity is 0.60.

There is persuasive evidence from the 1960s, therefore, that families do allocate their time and consumption over the life cycle, increasing their consumption of market goods and services and decreasing their home time as real wage rates rise with age, and increasing their consumption of home time and decreasing their consumption of market goods and services as real wage rates level out and fall past middle age. There has been no published research on this subject since the Ghez and Becker work. It remains to be seen whether, at the beginning of the twenty-first century, the hypothesis of time and consumption over the life cycle continues to be confirmed. The gross data contained in Table 5.2 are consistent with the hypothesis but by no means confirm it.

SUMMARY

In contrast to the preceding chapters, which focused on the demand for goods and services and assumed that household income was fixed, this chapter has demonstrated that the household does have some control over its income by deciding when, where, and how much to work. Depending on individuals' market and household productivities, their nonwage income, and their preferences for consumption and leisure, individuals allocate their available time among market work, household work, and leisure pursuits. If one of these factors change, then we would forecast that household time use would shift as well. More specifically, economists argue that the historical shifts in market work time and household work time described at the beginning of this chapter are the result of changes in market wages, household technology, nonwage income, and preferences.

Throughout this chapter we have assumed that wage rates are set by employers and that employees have no control over them. Likewise, we have assumed household productivities are totally determined by the state of technology and are not affected by individuals' behavior other than the amount of time devoted to household production. Neither assumption is very realistic, however, because we can and do have great influence over what we are paid for our market work and over how productive we are in household work activities. In Chapter 6 we discuss these issues.

Mathematical Notes

1. The slope of the household production function is the first derivative of the household production function with respect to H; that is,

$$\partial G/\partial H = g_h > 0.$$

It is positive, indicating that more is produced if additional time is used. Under conditions discussed in the text, it can become negative. That the slope of the production function becomes shallower as more time is used refers to the second derivative:

$$\partial(\partial G/\partial H)/\partial H = g_{hh} < 0.$$

It is assumed to be negative in accordance with the principle of diminishing marginal productivity; that is, each added unit of an input yields less added output than the one before when other inputs in the production process are held constant.

2. A simple peasant model is as follows. Let

$$u = u(C, G_c, L) \tag{1}$$

be the peasant's utility function where C = purchased consumption goods, G_c = that portion of farm output (say, rice) that the peasant consumes, and L = the peasant's leisure. The peasant divides his time between farm production, H, and leisure, L, so that

$$T = H + L. \tag{2}$$

The production function representing the peasant's rice production is

$$G = g(H; X) \tag{3}$$

where X is the quantity of land on which the rice is planted. Rice output is divided between the quantity he consumes, G_c, and the quantity he sells, G_s. Therefore,

$$G = G_s + G_c. \tag{4}$$

The peasant sells G_s of his rice crop at a price of p_g for a total income, Y, of

$$Y = p_g G_s. \tag{5}$$

The receipts from selling G_s of his rice are used to purchase consumption goods, C. Thus,

$$p_c C = Y = p_g G_s. \tag{6}$$

The equilibrium conditions governing the time the peasant spends in rice production, the time left over for leisure, total rice output, the portion sold, and purchased goods consumed are found by substituting equation (2) into (3), and (3) and (4) into (6), and forming the expression

$$Lg = u(C, G_c, L) - \lambda_y[p_c C + p_g G_c - p_g g(T - L; X)] \tag{7}$$

where λ_y is the Lagrangean multiplier and equals the marginal utility of income. Differentiating (7) with respect to C, G_c, and L and setting each equal to 0 yields

$$u_c - \lambda_y p_c = 0 \tag{8}$$

$$u_g - \lambda_y p_g = 0 \tag{9}$$

$$u_l - \lambda_y p_g g_h = 0. \tag{10}$$

Solving (9) for λ_y and substituting into (10) yields

$$u_l/u_g = g_h. \tag{11}$$

Interpreted, this means that when the peasant is maximizing satisfaction, his marginal rate of substitution of time for rice in consumption equals his marginal product of time spent producing rice. This is analogous to point P in Figure 5.3.

Solving (8) and (9) for λ_y, equating, and rearranging yields

$$u_c/u_g = p_c/p_g. \tag{12}$$

Interpreted, this means that in equilibrium the peasant's marginal rate of substitution of rice for purchased consumption goods must equal the rate at which rice can be exchanged for purchased goods in the market. This is the same equilibrium condition discussed so extensively in Chapter 2.

The peasant agricultural model, therefore, combines elements of both the castaway model and the conventional demand model.

3. These conditions are found in the following way. Form the Lagrangean expression

$$Lg = u[C + g(H; X), L] - \lambda(pC + wH + wL - wT - V) \tag{13}$$

by substituting the household production function into the utility function for G and by substituting the time constraint for M in the budget constraint, $p_cC = wM + V$. λ is the Lagrangean multiplier, a positive number.

The equilibrium conditions are found by differentiating the Lagrangean expression by H, C, L, and λ in turn and equating each first derivative to 0. These are

$$\partial Lg/\partial H = u_g g_h - \lambda w = 0 \tag{14}$$

$$\partial Lg/\partial C = u_g - \lambda p = 0 \tag{15}$$

$$\partial Lg/\partial L = u_l - \lambda w = 0 \tag{16}$$

$$\partial Lg/\partial \lambda = -pC - wH - wL + wT + V = 0 \tag{17}$$

where u_g = marginal utility of goods (either C-goods or G-goods), u_l = marginal utility of leisure, g_h = marginal product of labor in household production, and λ = Lagrangean multiplier, which equals the marginal utility of income. Solving (14) and (16) each for λw and equating yields

$$u_l/u_g = g_h; \tag{18}$$

that is, the marginal rate of substitution of leisure for goods equals the marginal product of labor in household production in equilibrium. Solving (14) and (15) each for λ and equating yields

$$g_h = w/p; \tag{19}$$

that is, the marginal product of labor in household production equals the real wage rate in equilibrium. And, from (18) and (19) comes

$$u_l/u_g = g_h = w/p \tag{20}$$

which is the equilibrium condition for individual S.

Since individual R does no market work,

$$u_l/u_g = g_h > w/p \tag{21}$$

in equilibrium.

4. In a more complete model, the household is seen as deriving satisfaction from goods, from the wife's leisure, and from the husband's leisure. Thus, the utility function would be

$$u = u(C + G, L_f, L_m) \tag{22}$$

where L_f is the wife's leisure hours and L_m is the husband's. The household production function would be specified as

$$G = g(H_f, H_m; X) \tag{23}$$

where H_f and H_m, are the times spent in household work by the wife and husband, respectively. The budget constraint would be

$$pC + w_f H_f + w_f L_f + w_m H_m + w_m L_m = w_f T_f + w_m T_m + V \tag{24}$$

where T_f and T_m are the total times available for each spouse.

In this larger model the household decides how much time each spouse has for leisure activities and how much each spouse devotes to household work and to market work. Thus, the equilibrium conditions derivable by maximizing the Lagrangean expression,

$$Lg = u[C + g(H_f, H_m; X), L_f, L_m]$$
$$- \lambda[pC + w_f H_f + w_f L_f + w_m H_m + w_m L_m - w_f T_f - w_m T_m - V] \tag{25}$$

are

$$u_c - \lambda_p = 0 \tag{26}$$

$$u_g g_f - \lambda w_f = 0 \tag{27}$$

$$u_g g_m - \lambda w_m = 0 \tag{28}$$

$$u_f - \lambda w_f = 0 \tag{29}$$

$$u_m - \lambda w_m = 0 \tag{30}$$

where u_i ($i = f, m$) is the marginal utility of spouse i's leisure, g_i is the marginal product of spouse i's time in household production, and w_i is the market wage rate commanded by spouse i. From (27) and (28), for instance, one obtains

$$g_f/g_m = w_f/w_m; \tag{31}$$

that is, in equilibrium, the marginal rate of technical substitution of spouse f's time for spouse m's time in household production will equal the ratio of their wage rates. This implies that the proportion in which the two spouses combine their time in household production activities depends on the opportunity costs of time and not on their preferences.

The effect of change in one spouse's wage rate on the other's time allocation appears as a cross-wage effect in such models and will be discussed later in the chapter.

5. The conclusions about the effect of nonlabor income on the household work time of those who are also employed in market work are altered if market goods and home-produced goods are not perfect substitutes. In this case the household's utility function is

$$U = u(C, G, L). \tag{32}$$

Maximizing this utility function subject to

$$pC + wH + wL = wT + V \tag{33}$$

yields the following first-order conditions:

$$u_c - \lambda p = 0 \tag{34}$$

$$u_g g_h - \lambda w = 0 \tag{35}$$

$$u_l - \lambda w = 0 \tag{36}$$

where u_c is the marginal utility of market goods and u_g is the marginal utility of home-produced goods. These marginal utilities will not be the same, because C-goods and G-goods in this model are not perfect substitutes. From equations (34) to (36) it is seen that

$$u_l/u_c = w/p = (u_g/u_c)g_h \tag{37}$$

rather than the simpler version,

$$u_l/u_g = w/p = g_h \tag{38}$$

that results from assuming that C-goods and G-goods are perfect substitutes.

When an increase in nonlabor income increases the options open to the household, the demands for C, G, and L will each increase so long as each is a normal good. In order to obtain the increase in G-goods demanded, the household must increase the time spent in their production. Put differently, the increase in nonlabor income will alter the marginal rate of substitution of *G*-goods for *C*-goods, (u_g/u_c) in (37), and the household will adjust its household productivity, g_h, by changing *H* to compensate.

6. The two-person model outlined in mathematical note 4 can be altered to illustrate the specialization of function and division of labor between spouses. In contrast to mathematical note 4, assume that the wife's and husband's household work times, H_f, and H_m, are perfect substitutes. That is, the wife and the husband can do household work equally well. Thus, the household production function becomes

$$G = g(H_f + H_m; X). \tag{23a}$$

This implies that the marginal products of his and her household work times are equal: $g_f = g_m = g_h$. As in the text, assume also that $w_m < w_f$.

The couple has the incentive to produce any given level of household-produced goods as cheaply as possible. The marginal cost of producing *G* using H_f is w_f/g_h and the marginal cost of *G* using H_m is $w_m, /g_h$. Since $w_f > w_m$, it is cheaper to use the husband's time in household production and none of the wife's. Consequently, there are two possible situations in which the couple maximizes satisfaction. One is expressed by the Lagrangean

$$Lg = u(C + G, L_f, L_m) - \lambda(pC + w_f L_f + w_m L_m$$
$$+ w_m H_m - w_f T_f - w_m T_m - V) \tag{39}$$

which, when maximized, yields

$$u_c - \lambda_p = 0 \tag{40}$$

$$u_g g_h - \lambda w_m = 0 \tag{41}$$

$$u_f - \lambda w_f = 0 \tag{42}$$

$$u_m - \lambda w_m = 0. \tag{43}$$

Recognizing that $u_c = u_g$ (because *C* and *G* are perfect substitutes) and solving for λ yields

$$u_m/u_c = w_m/p = g_h \tag{44}$$

$$u_f/u_c = w_f/p > g_h. \tag{45}$$

The marginal rate of substitution of his leisure for goods equals his real wage rate and his household productivity in equilibrium. Her marginal rate of substitution of leisure for goods equals her real wage rate and both exceed her household productivity. In this situation the couple has a large enough demand for goods and services relative to his leisure that she specializes completely in market work and he does both market and household work.

The other possible situation is expressed by the Lagrangean

$$Lg = u(C + G, L_f, L_m) - \lambda_y(pC + w_f L_f - w_f T_f - V)$$
$$- \lambda_m(H_m - L_m - T_m) \tag{46}$$

which, when maximized, yields

$$u_c - \lambda_y p = 0 \tag{47}$$

$$u_g g_h - \lambda_m = 0 \tag{48}$$

$$u_m - \lambda_m = 0 \tag{49}$$

$$u_f - \lambda_y w_f = 0. \tag{50}$$

Thus,

$$u_f/u_c = w_f/p \tag{51}$$

and since $g_h > w_m/p$, because the husband is specialized in household work,

$$u_m/u_c = g_h > w_m/p. \tag{52}$$

Here, the wife is completely specialized in market work and her husband is completely specialized in household work. The marginal rate of substitution of her leisure for goods equals her real wage rate. The marginal rate of substitution of his leisure for goods equals his household productivity, and both exceed his real wage rate. In this situation, the couple's demand for goods and services relative to his leisure is low enough that he is not induced to work both at home and in the labor market.

SIX

Human Capital

Investing in Oneself and One's Family

Fully 25 percent of the U.S. population, 72.7 million people, were enrolled in school in 1999. Of those in school, 6.3 percent were in nursery school, 52.7 percent were enrolled in kindergarten or elementary schools, 20.5 percent were enrolled in high schools, and 20.5 percent were enrolled in institutions of higher education (U.S. Bureau of the Census 2000b, Table 239, p. 151, and Table 259, p. 162). These numbers exclude the millions of people who took private lessons in everything from sewing to music, from religion to skiing and hang gliding. The United States devoted 6.7 percent of its gross national product, $601 billion, to schools and schooling in 1999. Of this sum, $372 billion was spent on elementary and secondary schools, and $239 billion was spent on colleges and universities (U.S. Bureau of the Census 2000b, Table 240, p. 151). These figures ignore the billions of dollars of potential income students chose not to earn by virtue of their being in schools and colleges.

Turning to the nation's investment in and maintenance of their health stock, Americans spent $1113.7 billion on health services and medical facility construction in 1998 and $19.3 billion on medical research in 1998, an amount totaling 13.5 percent of GDP (U.S. Bureau of the Census 2000b, Table 151, p. 108). This excludes all of the expenditures on recreation equipment and lessons that build and maintain healthy bodies. Also excluded is the value of the time Americans spent in maintaining their health. The facts show that Americans spend great amounts of time and money investing in themselves.

What goes on under one's nose is frequently noticed and dealt with long after things more remote. So it is with human capital. Although people (and even economists) have been investing in themselves and their children for as long as there have been people (or economists), economists have paid serious attention to the fact only in the past forty years. Although economists have striven to understand households' saving behavior, they neglected until lately the process by which people invest in themselves, one of the most important ways of saving.

We do not yet have a full grasp of the magnitude of the nation's capital stock held in human form. Nor are the implications of saving by investing in oneself or one's family fully understood. It is clear, however, that the concept of human capital has been and is central to the understanding of the economic organization of the household. Consequently, this chapter is devoted to an introduction of the concept and to some of the ways that it has shed light on family behavior.

Most introductory treatments of human capital focus on the demand for education and the roles that schooling and experience play in influencing the labor market behavior of individuals. Because of the focus of this text on the household and the recognition that its behavior in the labor market is only one of its many activities, some of the nonlabor market implications of human capital will also be addressed.

HUMAN CAPITAL AS SAVING

In Chapter 4 we dealt with a two-period model (today and tomorrow) in which the household balances the demands for consumption today against the demands for future consumption. Depending on the household's time preference (i.e., the marginal rate of substitution of today's consumption for tomorrow's), the market rate of interest, and expected changes in prices (i.e., the expected rate of inflation or deflation), the household puts aside a fraction of its current income for use in the future. The equilibrium condition expressing this decision is that the household equates the rate at which it is willing to exchange present for future consumption with the rate at which it can do so in the marketplace. This is expressed concisely by the equilibrium condition

$$u_1/u_2 = (1+r)/(1+g) \tag{6.1}$$

where u_t ($t = 1, 2$) denotes the marginal utility of consumption in period t, and therefore u_1/u_2 represents the household's marginal rate of substitution of present consumption for future consumption; r is the rate of interest, g is the expected rate of inflation (deflation), and therefore $(1+r)/(1+g)$ is the market rate of exchange of present consumption for future consumption. You will recall that u_1/u_2 is the slope of the highest indifference curve attainable by the family with the resources it has available, and $-(1 + r)/(1 + g)$ is the slope of the household's intertemporal budget line (see Figure 4.4).

The process just summarized determines the total amount that the household plans to save but it leaves unanswered the question of what forms the saving will take. Will the household augment its savings account, buy added stocks and bonds, buy a house or improve one it owns, pay off some of its debts, or invest in family members?

Investing in family members – that is, investing in human capital – can take many different forms. The most recognized way to invest in human capital is through formal schooling. Additional education usually means additional study for a degree or for a high school diploma, but there are, in fact, a bewildering array of ways to augment one's formal schooling and an equally bewildering array of purposes for which formal schooling is relevant. These range from added schooling to complete requirements for a degree to a two-week class in word processing, knitting, painting, or ways of saying no.

One can also invest in human capital through *on-the-job training and experience* either in one's market job or in a household activity. Here, one takes time out from one's job or from a household activity (or does it more slowly, deliberately, and reflectively) in order to learn how to do it better. In so doing, one may have to accept a somewhat lower current income or accept lower current output from the household activity in order to increase one's productivity in the long run. In the case of market work, the difference between the income earned while receiving on-the-job training and what would have been received if one had not engaged in the training is the amount saved or invested in human capital via experience. In the case of a household activity, the forgone output from the household activity constitutes the investment in human capital in the form of experience. None of these expenditures are reflected in the expenditures on education noted above.

Another way of investing in human capital is by spending time and money in maintaining and augmenting one's health. Just as one invests in a car or a house by repairing it and making improvements on it, one invests in health by maintaining and augmenting one's physical and mental health. Thus, aerobics classes, jogging, physician visits, annual dental checkups, and good nutrition are all means to invest in our health. The results are fewer days of sickness per year, longer life expectancy, and higher productivity on the job and in household activities.

Formal education, experience, and health are only the three most obvious types of human capital investments. Another is migration from one city, state, or country to another in search of a better job or a different life style. In such instances, one forsakes the opportunities in one location to exploit those in another. The millions of people – our parents, grandparents, and great-grandparents – who left home and families in other countries to carve out new lives in North America all were making large investments in human capital by migrating. So too were the millions of people who have migrated from farms to cities in search of better lives and livelihoods during the twentieth century.

But there are yet more subtle ways of investing in human capital. Having children and raising them in particular ways may, in part, be ways by which a couple can provide for economic security in old age. This motive is very minor or absent in developed countries, which have other ways of providing economic security for elderly people, but it cannot be dismissed if one is to understand fertility behavior in less developed countries. Fertility behavior – the demand for children – is discussed more fully in Chapter 7. Marriage has been described by a wag as one of the few gambles fainthearted people take. It is also one of the few ways by which very poor people can invest: one gives up the advantages of remaining single for the future benefits of being married. Marriage and divorce are analyzed in this fashion in Chapter 8.

Having surveyed the types of investments in human capital, we can return to the question of the form in which the household will save: will it save in the form of physical capital (a new car, a house), financial capital (bank accounts, stocks and bonds, or lowering of debts), or human capital? As usual, this decision is most easily understood through simplification. We simplify by assuming that the household can save only in the form of financial or human capital and the motive for saving is to maximize total wealth.[1] We will begin our discussion of human capital by examining it in the context of the labor market, and we will first consider only one type of human capital: formal schooling.

HUMAN CAPITAL AND THE LABOR MARKET

A major reason individuals invest in human capital through formal schooling is to augment their income in the future and so to increase their total

---

[1] Total wealth really represents the total amount of resources available to the household. Total wealth in this chapter is the analogue to the full income concept used in Chapter 5.

wealth. Recognize, initially, that additional schooling increases an individual's productivity in the labor market, and employers, recognizing this, pay higher wage rates to individuals with more formal schooling. Consider an individual concerned only with the monetary payoff to formal schooling. Such an individual will invest in added schooling only if the payoff to added schooling is higher than or, at the margin, is equal to the payoff in alternative investments. In the simple case being analyzed, the only alternative to formal schooling is financial investments (stocks, bonds, savings accounts, etc.) at the going market rate of interest, r. The individual will, then, compare the "rate of return" from added schooling with the market rate of interest, r, and invest in the opportunity with the higher rate of return. If formal schooling initially has the higher rate of return, the individual will maximize his or her wealth by continuing to invest in schooling until the rate of return on schooling has been driven down to the market rate of interest.

The Rate of Return on Education

What is the rate of return on schooling? Formally, it is the interest rate that equates the cost of the investment with the present value of the stream of future benefits from the investment. We can define the rate of return to the investment (the so-called internal rate of return) more precisely through an example.

Suppose that Bob is contemplating a final year of high school at age eighteen and expects to retire at sixty-five. Let Bob's annual earnings in year t without the added year of school be E_t, and his annual earnings in year t with the added year of schooling be E_t', where $E_t' > E_t$.

The cost of the added year of school for Bob has two components: the earnings Bob forgoes while he is in school for the final year rather than working at a paid job, E_0, and the out-of-pocket costs of the final year of school (such as tuition, fees, and books), C. Denote the cost of the added year of school by MC, standing for marginal cost. Then,

$$MC = E_0 + C \tag{6.2}$$

where $t = 0$ is Bob's eighteenth year.

The benefit to Bob from the added year of school is the difference between (1) the future stream of annual earnings Bob expects given he has the added year of schooling and (2) the future stream of annual earnings Bob expects if he does not have the added year of schooling. The stream of differences is

Year	1		t		n
Bob's age	19		$18 + t$		65
Difference	$(E_1' - E_1),$	$\ldots,$	$(E_t' - E_t),$	$\ldots,$	$(E_n' - E_n)$

where n = the expected number of years until retirement.

Now find the interest rate, i, that equates the present value of the expected stream of benefits from the added year of schooling with the cost of the added year of school:

$$\sum_{t=1}^{n}(E_t' - E_t)/(1 + i)^t = MC = E_o + C. \qquad (6.3)$$

Then i is the rate of return on the investment in the added year of school. If i is greater than the market rate of interest on financial investments, r, Bob will increase his net wealth by getting the added year of formal schooling. If $i = r$, Bob will be indifferent between investing in financial capital or human capital.

Here, then, is the answer to the question concerning which form saving will take: it will take the form of the investment with the higher rate of return. In equilibrium, when the household is maximizing its total wealth, the rates of return on competing types of investment – financial, physical, and human – will all be equal.[2]

One can calculate the rate of return for each possible year of schooling Bob may take beginning with kindergarten. There are three prominent reasons why the rate of return to schooling, i, will decline with each added year of school. One raises the marginal costs, and the other two lower the marginal benefits of added schooling (see mathematical note 1).

First, each additional year of schooling increases the opportunity cost of any succeeding years of schooling, E_0, in the marginal cost formula, because the wage rates employers are prepared to pay employees rise with education. Suppose, for instance, that people with grade 11 are paid $7.00/hour and high school graduates earn $8.00/hour. On the basis of a 2000-hour work year, these translate into annual earnings of $14,000 and $16,000, respectively. Consequently, the individual who completes grade 12 forgoes $14,000 whereas the individual who completes the first year of college forgoes $16,000 for the added year of school. Clearly, then, the

---

[2] The rate of return is the only investment criterion for a wealth-maximizing household with perfect foresight, the case under discussion. There are other criteria, like the certainty of the rate of return if, in the more realistic case, the future is not foreseen perfectly. These added criteria are a major focus in standard finance theory texts.

marginal cost of schooling rises with additional schooling as E_0 rises, and this will depress the rate of return, i.[3]

Second, each additional year of schooling reduces the remaining years during which an individual works, shortening the expected stream of benefits of added schooling and reducing the marginal benefit. This can easily be seen in equation (6.3). With added years of schooling, the sum,

$$\sum_{t-1}^{n}(E'_t - E_t)/(1 + i)^t$$

becomes smaller because the remaining working life becomes shorter. The smaller the marginal benefit, of course, the lower the interest rate must be that equates the present value of the benefits with the marginal cost.

Third, the principle of diminishing marginal productivity also operates to reduce the marginal benefits. Recall that the principle of diminishing marginal productivity states that, holding other inputs in a production process constant, the marginal product of a particular input will fall as more of the input is used. The particular application of this principle here is that additional years of education are applied to an individual who is in a real sense fixed. Consequently, an individual's productivity per hour in the labor market will rise with additional education but at a declining rate. If, as in the previous example, the twelfth year of schooling raises Bob's annual labor productivity from $14,000 to $16,000 (an increase of $2000), the thirteenth year may increase it by only $1500, to $17,500. Thus, the more schooling an individual already has, the lower the marginal benefit of an additional year. Therefore, this, too, means that as the number of years of schooling rises, the rate of return to additional education falls.

The Demand Curve for Formal Education

The fact that the rate of return to schooling falls as the number of years of schooling rises allows one to plot an individual's demand for formal schooling as in Figure 6.1. The number of years of schooling demanded by the individual is plotted along the horizontal axis, and the rate of return to

---

[3] That is, as MC in equation (6.3) becomes larger, holding the stream of benefits, $E'_t - E_t$, constant, the rate of return, i, must fall in order to maintain the equality between marginal benefits and marginal costs.

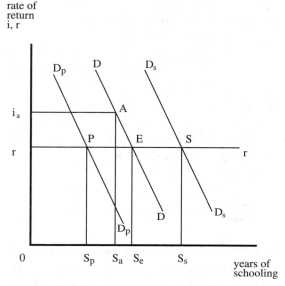

Figure 6.1. An individual's demand curve for formal schooling.

schooling, i, as well as the market rate of interest on financial investments, r, are plotted on the vertical axis.

Line DD shows the rate of return yielded for each year of schooling obtained by the individual. For instance, the rate of return to S_a years of schooling is i_a. Line DD slopes downward to the right, indicating that the rate of return to education falls as the number of years of schooling rises.

Also in Figure 6.1 is a horizontal line, rr. It represents the market rate of return on financial investments. Line rr is horizontal because the market rate of return on financial investments does not depend on how many years of schooling are being "purchased." The wealth-maximizing individual will invest in formal schooling until the rate of return to education is driven down to the rate of return on alternative investments. Consequently, the wealth-maximizing individual possessing DD in Figure 6.1 will "demand" S_e years of schooling when the rate of return on financial investments is r. He would demand more education only if the market rate of interest were lower. Line DD, then, is the individual's demand curve for formal education.

DD is the demand curve for formal schooling for the wealth-maximizing individual, the individual who goes to school only for the increase in future income more education promises. There are, however, few such people. Most people either like or dislike school. What are their demand curves for education like?

Consider an individual who likes school (a student[4]) and, therefore, derives satisfaction as well as future income from schooling. Such an individual also will attend school until the marginal benefit of additional schooling equals the marginal cost. But, compared with the wealth-maximizing individual, the marginal benefit of the added education to the "student" is more because she derives satisfaction from school as well as increased future income. Therefore, her rate of return for any given number of school years will be higher. That is,

$$\sum_{t=1}^{n} (E'_t - E_t)/(1+i)^t + V_s = E_0 + C \qquad (6.4)$$

where V_s is the dollar value of the added satisfaction from an additional year of school (mathematical note 2). The larger the V_s, the greater the marginal benefit and the higher must i be for the left-hand side (MB) to equal the right-hand side (MC). Consequently, the demand curve for a student will lie above that for a wealth maximizer. The demand curve for such a person is represented in Figure 6.1 by $D_s D_s$. Faced with the same array of alternative financial investments and, hence, the same r, the student will invest in more schooling (S_s rather than S_e) than the wealth maximizer.[5]

In contrast, the individual who dislikes school (a pupil[6]) derives not only added wealth from an additional year of school but also the added disutility from disliking the experience. In this case the dollar value of the reduction in satisfaction from the added schooling, V_s, is negative and reduces the marginal benefit. Therefore, i must be lower in order to equate MB with MC. For any given number of years of schooling, therefore, the rate of return to education for a pupil will be lower than that for a wealth maximizer. Consequently, the pupil's demand curve for schooling will be lower than that for the wealth maximizer; see $D_p D_p$ in

---

[4] The term student comes from the Latin verb *studere*, "to be zealous."

[5] Demand curve $D_s D_s$ can also represent the demand curve for education in the case in which education not only raises market productivity, w/p, but also household productivity, g_h. This will be discussed in detail later.

[6] Pupil comes from Latin *pupillus* (feminine, *pupilla*), "orphan" or "ward." The pupil is, then, the ward of the teacher and, like most orphans in fiction, an unwilling one!

Figure 6.1. Faced with the same market rate of interest, r, the pupil will demand fewer years of school, S_p, than either the wealth maximizer or the student.

Experience as a Form of Human Capital

If formal schooling were the only way by which human capital was augmented, then the earnings of full-time employees would not rise with age after adjusting for prices. Yet one of the most common expectations people possess, and one of the best documented facts about earnings, is that they rise with age to late middle age or beyond and then level out or decline to retirement. Why?

According to neoclassical economic theory, employers pay employees a real wage rate equal to their marginal productivity to the employer; that is,

$$w/p = MP \qquad (6:5)$$

where MP is the marginal product of the employee's labor in the employer's production process.[7] Now, education will raise the employee's marginal product in market employment, resulting in higher real wages. This explains why highly educated people earn more than the less educated. But once formal education has been completed, why would a forty-year-old high school graduate earn more than a twenty-year-old high school graduate? A good answer is "experience." Either through on-the-job training or learning by doing, the individual's marginal productivity, MP, continues to grow, and as it grows, real wage rates and, hence, earnings continue to rise.

There are two kinds of experience, *general* and *specific*. General experience raises the MP of an individual in all firms, whereas specific experience increases the individual's MP only in the firm where the experience is gained. Examples of general experience are work habits, personnel skills, problem-solving skills, and general skills of the trade or occupation that increase an individual's productivity for any employer. Examples of specific experience are knowledge of one company's administrative and

---

[7] This statement ignores monopsonistic labor markets, discriminatory wage differentials, and wage differentials that compensate workers for working in unsafe or distasteful occupations and for working at unpleasant locations and times. See Chapters 5 and 8 in Ehrenberg and Smith (1982) for a treatment of these issues.

accounting structures and personnel policies and experience with equipment that is used only by one particular firm.[8]

Employers have no incentive to pay the costs of general experience gained by employees, because they can leave after gaining the experience, taking the investment in human capital with them. Not reaping the benefits of general experience, employers visit the costs of general experience on their employees in the form of lower wage rates during the periods general experience is gained.

Because the investment in specific experience raises employees' labor productivity only in the firm in which the specific experience is gained, other employers will not pay them higher wages because of it. Consequently, even though a company's employees' *MP* is higher by virtue of the specific experience, the company has no incentive to pay them more for their specific experience. Employers reap the gains, therefore, from the investments in specific experience gained by their employees. On their part, employees will not accept lower wages while they are gaining specific experience, because they will reap no benefits from it in the future. And if employers did try to pay them less during the period in which they gain specific experience, the employees could respond by finding work elsewhere at a higher wage rate.[9]

In general, however, the human capital model predicts that the individual reaps the benefits and pays the cost of any general experience gained on the job. How much experience will the individual choose to gain? The answer is the same as for formal schooling: more experience on the job will be gained until the marginal benefits of added experience are driven down to the level of the marginal costs of the added experience. Put differently, the individual will gain more experience until the rate of return on added experience is driven down to the rate of return on alternative investments.

So long as the individual continues to gain experience on the job, therefore, the individual's market productivity, w/p, will increase and, with it, annual earnings. Since human capital via experience accumulates with the passage of time, earnings will increase with age. At the point at which the rate of return to experience is driven down to the rate of return on

---

[8] In reality, there is a continuum from general experience to specific experience rather than two discrete and mutually exclusive categories. The student who learns to use the university's computer, for instance, learns how to program and use any computer as well as the idiosyncrasies of the university's computer system.

[9] See Chapter 2 in Becker (1975) for a more detailed discussion of general and specific human capital.

Table 6.1. *Mean Earnings of Male Full-Time Workers, 1999*

Age	< High School	High School	Some College	Assoc. Degree	Bach. Degree
30	22,251	31,945	36,707	37,057	51,097
40	26,233	37,155	46,193	48,407	65,469
50	27,103	39,493	49,483	49,634	73,820
60	28,188	40,124	49,517	51,012	67,686
65+	24,274	46,628	31,562	–	61,285

Source: U.S. Bureau of the Census, "Educational Attainment in the United States, March 2000a," *Current Population Survey*, P20–536, Table 9: Washington, D.C.; http://www.census.gov/population/socdemo/education/p20-536/tab09.pdf.

alternative investments, further learning will cease. Past that point the individual will cease to learn more about his job and his earnings will no longer increase with age. If human capital obsolescence and depreciation become important, then the individual's *MP* will begin to fall and with it earnings.[10]

Formal schooling and experience, then, explain an important part of the age-earnings profiles of individuals. Tables 6.1 and 6.2 illustrate age-earnings profiles by education for males (Table 6.1) and females (Table 6.2) for the year 1999. The tables chart the mean annual earnings of full-time, full-year workers. Consequently, the differences must be due to differences in wage rates and not differences in annual hours worked. Clearly, education increases earnings. These age-earnings profiles are typical: the higher the level of education, the steeper the rise in earnings with age at least initially. The differences among people in their earnings, therefore, are importantly explained by education and experience. A caution should be sounded with respect to these age-earnings profiles. They also include important "cohort" effects in that, for instance, women age 55 to 64 in 1999 have lived very different lives than women who were age 25 to 34 in 1999 will lead by the time they reach age 55 to 64. Their lifetime path of earnings will likely, therefore, be somewhat different that those of earlier generations.

Much of the difference between the male and female age-earnings profiles is explained by differences in the labor force participation behavior and its consequences by age between males and females. Males tend to

---

[10] Another reason annual earnings begin to fall past middle age is that as the wage rate rises, individuals faced with the work-leisure trade-off discussed in Chapter 5 will increase their demand for leisure, reducing the number of hours they work annually. With the reduction in annual work time comes a decline in annual earnings. This partially explains why annual vacations tend to increase with job seniority.

Table 6.2. *Mean Annual Earnings of Full-Time Working Females, 1999*

Age	< High School	High School	Some College	Assoc. Degree	Bach. Degree
30	16,821	21,633	26,859	28,002	37,562
40	17,356	24,258	31,258	33,185	43,471
50	17,757	25,756	31,330	33,559	43,337
60	25,143	25,935	31,341	35,012	42,649
65+	16,634	20,469	34,530	–	28,207

Source: See Table 6.1.

enter the labor force upon completing school and not leave until retirement. The labor market experience of men, therefore, is highly correlated
with age. Not so for females. Some females tend to drop out of the labor
market when they marry and do not return unless they are divorced or
widowed. More drop out to give birth to children and return to the labor
market when adequate child day care is found or when their children enter
school. Consequently, the labor market experience of females is not as
highly correlated with age. This generalization, however, is becoming less
clear as more females enter and remain in the labor force despite marriage and child bearing. Sex discrimination in the labor market, of course,
also explains some of the differences.[11]

Many analysts have estimated rates of return to education and experience. Willis (1986, Table 10.2, p. 537) surveyed the literature and reports
estimates of the rate of return to higher education (four years of college)
of 8 to 9 percent in the late 1970s and early 1980s and estimates of the
rate of return to secondary education of 11 percent for the mid-1970s. In
his classic work on the returns to education, Mincer (1974) obtained estimates of the rate of return to education for nonfarm White males in 1960
of 17.4 percent for 8 years of school, 15.1 percent for 12 years of schooling,
and 12.8 percent for 16 years.[12] Based on the data for 1999 in Tables 6.1
and 6.2, the rates of return are 15.5 percent for 8 years, 14.9 percent for
12 years, and 14.2 percent for 16 years of schooling for males. For females,
the rate of return to education appears to be flat at 13.5 percent.[13]

---

[11] See Blau and Kahn (2000) for a review of the literature on gender differences in pay.

[12] These rates of return assume eight years of experience.

[13] These rates were computed from the following regression equations fitted by the authors
to the data displayed in Tables 6.1 and 6.2 on mean earnings by age and education classes:

$$\log(\text{male mean annual earnings in 1999})$$
$$= 8.322 + .1688Ed - .0008446Ed^2 + .007762Exp$$
$$+ .4345Prof \quad (adjR^2 = .9119)$$

The estimated rates of return to experience appear to be much more modest. For nonfarm White male high school graduates in 1960, the rate of return to experience is 5.3 percent initially and declines to zero after 15 years. The data for 1999 in Tables 6.1 and 6.2 yield estimates of the returns to experience of 0.27 percent per year for females and 0.78 percent for males.[14]

Rates of return to education have varied substantially over time. Earnings of college graduates relative to those with high school increased substantially during the 1960s, fell during the 1970s, and rose again in the 1980s and 1990s. For instance, between 1989 and 1993 the ratio of mean, real, hourly earnings of male college graduates to that of high school graduates rose by 4.1 percent; for females the same ratio rose by 2.1 percent (Frazis and Stewart 1999).

These increases in the return to college education relative to high school reflect widening wage inequalities that have been the subject of much political and scholarly debate as to the causes. Underlying the changes are changes in the demand for and supply of labor with different stocks of human capital reflected by their education and experience levels. The rise in the return to college relative to high school graduates and those without high school during the 1980s and 1990s is partially explained by the slower rate of growth of the supply of college-educated individuals in the 1980s and 1990s after the influx of baby boomers into the labor force ceased in the early 1980s. Factors on the demand side appear to have been the increase in manufactured imports, which lowered the demand for the less educated individuals, and technical change that emphasized pay-offs to a college education. Those who have completed college more recently and, hence, have less experience seem to have benefitted the most.[15]

Part of the evidence on the returns to education is that possessing a graduation diploma raises the return to education. That is, comparing

log(female annual earnings in 1999)

$$= 8.3744 + .1345Ed + .002701Exp + .3375Prof \quad (adjR^2 = .9162)$$

where Ed = years of school completed; $Exp = Age - Ed - 6$; $Prof = 1$ if a professional degree was completed. All coefficients are significantly different from zero. These results imply that the completion of a professional degree (e.g., MBA) increases male earnings by 54.4 percent and female earnings by 40.1 percent.

[14] The evidence from 1960 is from Mincer (1974). The estimates of the rates of return to experience calculated from the data in Tables 6.1 and 6.2 may be low because they are based on regressions on cell means and midpoints that do not allow a more sophisticated model to be estimated. Regressions on the underlying data on individuals would yield more sophisticated and more reliable estimates.

[15] See Katz and Murphy (1992), Murphy and Welch (1992), and Macunovich (1999) for analyses.

two individuals with, say, two years of college, the individual with an "associate's" degree will earn more than the one without. Compare the age-earnings profiles in Table 6.1 and 6.2 for "some college" and "associate's degree." More dramatic differences were calculated by Leigh and Gill (1997). After controlling for many other factors, they found that male holders of associate degrees had annual earnings about 11 percent higher than those with two years of college but with no degree. The analogous differential for females was 21.6 percent.[16] Human capital theory may not predict this result.

Signaling: An Alternative Explanation

The fact of the returns to a completed degree (i.e., the diploma) suggests that there may be more going on here than just getting more education to raise one's productivity and, hence, one's wage rate. Why should a person with a diploma in hand earn more than a person with the equivalent number of years of schooling but without a diploma? One answer is that diploma holders have had to complete a specific program of course work with grades that meet minimum criteria. Individuals with the same number of years of schooling completed but who haven't undergone the rigor of a program meriting a diploma have not learned as much, are thereby less productive, and consequently earn less in the labor market. Hence, there is a diploma effect. This hypothesis argues that education is not well measured by the number of years of schooling completed and is not inconsistent with human capital theory.

Another hypothesis is that the diploma is a "signal" acquired by a job applicant and taken by employers as evidence that the diploma holder will likely be more productive than otherwise identical job applicants who do not have a diploma. Postulated here is an environment in which employers do not know with certainty the productivity of the people they hire until after they have been on the job for some time. This means that when employers hire employees, they have an incentive to reduce this uncertainty. Employers do so by choosing to hire those individuals with observable attributes they believe to be positively correlated with worker productivity. Observable attributes that individuals may possess are of two types: some are alterable by the individuals, others are not alterable. Education is an example of an attribute alterable by the individual. Race and sex are examples of unalterable characteristics. Of the alterable

---

[16] See also the study by Jaeger and Page (1996).

attributes, it is reasonable to suppose that individuals will manipulate them to make themselves appear more productive to potential employers if (1) they perceive that possessing those attributes acts as a signal of productivity to employers and (2) if it is cost effective.

If manipulating these alterable attributes is costless, then everyone will do so, employers will not be able to distinguish among applicants, and the value of possessing the attribute will be zero and will be a useless signal. Only if the cost of acquiring an attribute is negatively correlated with the productivity for which the employer is searching will the attribute have any worth as a signal. Thus, if a high school diploma is equally costly to unproductive and productive individuals, then employers will, through experience, learn that hiring individuals with high school diplomas does not better their chances of hiring more productive individuals. Employers will then cease regarding high school diplomas as signals of productivity and the value of a high school diploma will be zero. If, however, productive individuals find it easier (i.e., less costly) to qualify for a high school diploma than less productive individuals, then more productive individuals will earn high school diplomas and less productive individuals will not. Under these circumstances, employers' beliefs that high school diplomas signal higher productivity will be affirmed by the experience they gain from hiring individuals possessing them. Provided employers respond by paying individuals with high school diplomas a premium warranted by their higher productivity, then more productive individuals will find that the extra time, expense, and effort of earning a high school diploma will be worth it. In contrast, it will not be worthwhile for less productive people to do so. An equilibrium in the jobs market exists when the probabilistic beliefs employers have about the link between the signal and employee productivity, how these translate into premium wage offers for those possessing the signal, and the investments in the signal that more productive individuals make are confirmed.[17]

Notice two important aspects of the signaling hypothesis. The first is that education is not hypothesized to be a means by which productivity is enhanced. Rather, the causation goes the other way: more productive people are hypothesized to become more educated for the purpose of signaling their already high productivity. And, more productive individuals will complete programs and possess diplomas whereas individuals

---

[17] See Spence (1974) and Arrow (1973) for discussions of market signaling with applications to the job market, college admissions processes, product guarantees, the credit market, and the car market.

with lower productivity will not. In this context, then, the diploma effect is hypothesized to be evidence of higher productivity separate from and over and above any pay-off to mere years of school completed. In reality, it is difficult to think of an empirical means by which the two hypotheses can be distinguished.

The second noteworthy aspect of the signaling hypothesis is that obtaining an education or additional diplomas, as signals of one's productivity, is no less an investment than obtaining them for the purpose of enhancing productivity. The former is an investment in signals; the latter is an investment in human capital. The logic determining how much of each to invest in is identical: one invests in productivity enhancing education or in education as a signal up to the point at which the marginal benefits equal the marginal costs.

THE TIMING OF FORMAL SCHOOLING AND EXPERIENCE

Even though more older people than in the past attend schools and colleges, it remains the case that most people complete their formal education when young. Why is this? More generally, why do people tend to invest in human capital, in the form of schooling or experience, when young and to reduce their investments in human capital as they grow older?

The marginal benefit equals marginal cost condition,

$$MB = \sum_{t=1}^{n}(E'_t - E_t)/(1+i)^t = E_0 + C = MC \qquad (6.6)$$

that directs human capital investments reveals three reasons.

First, the older the individual, the fewer remaining years left (i.e., the smaller is n in equation [6.6]) for the investment in human capital to pay off in terms of either higher labor market earnings or greater household production of goods and services. Thus, the later in life the investment in human capital is made, the lower the marginal returns and, *ceteris paribus*, the less likely it will be made.

Second, the farther into the future any investment in human capital is postponed, the lower the present value of the returns on the investment and, therefore, the lower the marginal benefits. The lower the marginal benefits from the postponed investment, the less likely it will be postponed. When human capital formation is postponed, say five years, the index, t, begins at $t = 6$ rather than $t = 1$ in equation (6.6). Consequently, the returns to future investments are discounted more than present ones.

A simple example will clarify this point. Suppose a given investment in human capital, such as an added year of school, would increase annual earnings by $500/year whether the investment is made immediately or five years hence. At a market rate of interest equal to 10 percent, the present value of the first year's return on the investment when made immediately is $500/(1.10)^2 = $413.22 because the investment takes a year to make plus a year to receive the first annual return of $500. If the investment were to be postponed for five years, the present value of the first year's return on the investment would be $500/ (1.10)^6 = $282.24. Postponing human capital formation lowers the marginal benefits.

Third, the farther into the future an investment in human capital is postponed, the more experience will have been gained in the interim, and the higher the opportunity cost of the investment when it is made. Consequently, the marginal costs of postponed human capital investments rise the more they are postponed, and therefore, the less likely it will be that they will be postponed. In terms of equation (6.6), the farther into the future any human capital investment is postponed, the higher E_0 becomes through experience, raising the marginal cost of the investment.

For these reasons, then, we can expect most people to obtain their formal schooling when young and to accumulate experience at a declining rate as they grow older. For some people past a certain age, depreciation and obsolescence exceed their investments in human capital through experience and, in consequence, their total human capital stock declines with each passing year. This phenomenon is most easily observed in the relationship between age and physical health. Although more difficult to observe, it is present nonetheless with respect to mental acuity.

It is very clear that the results of human capital formation activities – formal schooling and experience – are important and explain many of the differences among people in their real wage rates. But the impacts of human capital are not restricted to their effects on the market productivities of men and women. There are two other areas where human capital accumulation and maintenance is very important: health and child rearing. We discuss each of these in turn.

HEALTH AS A HUMAN CAPITAL INVESTMENT

The common view of health has been that one went to a doctor if one was sick or injured. Beyond some simple rules of public health and good nutrition, the rest of the time one's attention was on other things. In a remarkably short period of years, however, this view of health has been radically altered. What was a minor concern over public health has blossomed into an intense concern for the public health implications of the environment and for what humans are doing to it. Much more attention is now paid to nutrition witnessed by increased attention to weight and diets, the requirements for nutritional labeling of food products, and by the rise of nutritional advertising. And, issues such as food safety and genetically modified foods have become major public policy foci. Sports and exercise are no longer viewed as idle pursuits for some adults but as crucial for the improvement and maintenance of health. In short, nowadays most people view health as an investment and consciously invest in it.

Theoretically, health is no different from other aspects of human capital in that one will invest in it until the marginal benefits of the added investment equal the marginal cost. However, health capital is different from education capital in several respects. While education capital raises an individual's market work productivity and, thus, her wage rate, health capital lowers the number of days in any period during which an individual is sick and cannot engage in either household activities or market work. Additionally, investments in health capital promote a longer life. And, being healthy is a consumption good in and of itself. The marginal benefits of health, therefore, may be more complicated than for education.

The concept of household production developed in Chapter 5 is helpful in analyzing investments in health capital because such investments are, fundamentally, produced in the household. Doctors, dentists, health clinics, hospital services, laboratory tests, and pharmaceuticals are just some of the purchased inputs used to maintain and augment one's health. Diet, jogging shoes, exercise clothing, whether and the extent to which one smokes, drinks alcohol, or consumes other drugs are important too. The individual's time is also important: for instance, the time one spends meeting doctor and dental appointments, exercising, learning about various health conditions and possible remedies, and the like. Thus, maintaining and augmenting one's health capital is a productive process in which the individual combines many purchased inputs with the individual's time.

As with education and experience, investing in health capital takes place, and the benefits are reaped, throughout one's life. To fully analyze the process and its effects, therefore, a multi-period, life-cycle model is required. But, such models are complex. The first and best known multi-period analysis of health capital and its effects is that of Grossman (1972, 2000). Rather than attempt to present it in detail, we will, instead, develop a much simpler one-period model that will ignore the life-lengthening effect of health capital and concentrate on health as a consumption good as well as a means to reduce the time during one's lifetime that one is sick.

A Simple One-Period Health Model

In this model, the individual derives satisfaction from the time during her life she is healthy, D, and a composite home-produced commodity denoted by Z. Her utility function, therefore, is

$$U = u(D, Z). \tag{6.7}$$

By producing health capital, H, the individual determines the number of days, D, during her lifetime, T, that she is healthy. For simplicity, the relationship between D and H is written as

$$D = \phi H \tag{6.8}$$

where $\phi = $ a positive constant. Such healthy days are spent in market work, N, in maintaining and augmenting health capital, Q, and in the days, L, spent producing and consuming Z. The days she is sick, S, are wasted and not available for productive or pleasurable pursuits. Thus, the individual's time constraint is

$$T = N + Q + L + S. \tag{6.9}$$

Since D equals the number of healthy days during the individual's life,

$$T - S = D = \phi H = N + Q + L. \tag{6.10}$$

The individual is pictured as making decisions about the amount of health capital, H, she will produce, her lifetime consumption of the composite commodity, Z, and the time she will spend employed, N. By making the decision as to the optimal amount of health capital to produce and consume, the individual implicitly makes a decision as to the number of healthy days she has during her life.

Underlying her decisions about the desired quantity of health capital are decisions as to how to produce it at least cost. That is, decisions are made about the quantity of purchased health inputs, M, to combine with the time, Q, spent in the production of health capital. Similarly, underlying the optimum quantity of Z to consume during her life are decisions as to the optimal quantities of purchased inputs, X, and time, L, which are combined to produce Z.

A household health production function describes how purchased health inputs, M, and time, Q, are combined to produce H:

$$H = h(M, Q; E) \tag{6.11}$$

where $h(.)$ increases as M, Q, or E increase, and $E =$ the stock of education capital. Note that the amount of health capital is made a function of educational capital, E. This reflects the hypothesis that more educated people are healthier perhaps because they know more about what it takes to be healthy. Thus, $\partial H / \partial E > 0$. Similarly, the composite commodity, Z, is produced by combining purchased inputs, X, and time, L,

$$Z = z(X, L; E) \tag{6.12}$$

where $z(.)$ increases as X or L increase (see mathematical note 3).

To maximize satisfaction over her lifetime, T, the individual will invest in health capital until the "price" of health capital (i.e., the marginal cost) equals the dollar value of the utility gained from an added unit of health capital plus the dollar value of the added number of healthy days produced by the added unit of health capital (i.e., the marginal benefit):

$$\pi_h = \phi u_d / \lambda + \phi w \tag{6.13}$$

where $\pi_h =$ the price of a unit of health capital, $u_d =$ marginal utility of a healthy day, $\phi u_d / \lambda =$ marginal utility of a unit of health capital, and $\lambda =$ marginal utility of income (see mathematical note 4).

The first term on the right-hand side of equation (6.13) (i.e., the first component of the marginal benefit) is the dollar value of the additional satisfaction due to the added health capital. The second term or component of the marginal benefit is the dollar value of the additional healthy days brought about by the added health capital. Thus, investing in health capital has two effects. The first represents the "consumption" attribute of health capital: being healthy is preferred to being sick. The second represents the resource augmenting or "investment" aspect of health capital: it increases the number of healthy days at the disposal of the individual and, hence, the monetary return to being healthy. Greater health capital means being sick fewer days during one's life and, therefore, possessing more time for production or consumption pursuits.

To invest in health capital at least cost, the marginal cost of health capital produced by an added unit of purchased health inputs, M, must equal the marginal cost of health capital produced by an added unit of time, Q, spent investing in health capital; that is,

$$\pi_h = p_m/(g - g't) = wg' \tag{6.14}$$

where $g = g(t; E)$, $g' = \partial g/\partial t$, $t = Q/M$, p_m = the market price of purchased health inputs, w = daily wage rate, $p_m/(g - g't)$ = marginal resource cost of H due to a one-unit increase in M, and w/g' = the marginal resource cost of H due to a one-unit increase in Q. Because the health production function is assumed to be linear homogeneous, these two marginal resource costs each equal the marginal cost of H as well as the price of health capital, π_h[18] (see mathematical note 3).

The one-period model is silent with respect to the timing of health capital investments over the life course and silent as well with respect to trade-offs with other types of investments, human capital or financial. Moving to multi-period considerations, the equilibrium conditions for period i become

$$\phi u_{id}/\lambda(1 + r)^i + \phi w_i = \pi_{i-1}(r - \pi^*_{i-1} + \delta_i) \tag{6.15}$$

where: r = the market interest rate, π^*_{i-1} = the percentage change in the marginal cost (i.e., price) of health capital investments in period i between period $(i - 1)$ and i, and δ_i = the rate of depreciation in one's health capital in period i (the natural effects of aging, if you will).

The left-hand side of equation (6.15) is simply the undiscounted marginal benefit from an added unit of investment in health capital in period i. With the exception of the term $(1 + r)$, which introduces the notion of discounting (see Chapter 4), it is identical to the right-hand side of equation (6.13) with subscripts, i, added to denote the period in which it applies.

The right-hand side of equation (6.15) is referred to as the "rental price" or "user cost" of health capital. The user cost takes into account the opportunity cost of investing in health capital rather than in other forms of capital (i.e., r, the market rate of interest), whether there are health capital gains or capital losses from period $(i - 1)$ to i caused by variations in the price of purchased health inputs or in the wage rate over the period (i.e., π^*_{i-1}) and the rate of health capital depreciation (i.e., δ_i). These are all elements absent in the marginal cost in the one-period model.

As r, π^*_{i-1}, and δ_i change over an individual's life course, the marginal costs of further investments in health capital change. These changes lead to alterations in the rate individuals invest in health capital as they seek to

---

[18] Equation (6.14) is the same as equation (15) in mathematical note 3.

equate the marginal benefits of further investments, $\phi u_{id}/\lambda(1 + r)^i + \phi w$, to the changes in marginal cost. In particular, if an individual's health capital depreciates more rapidly with age as is likely, then the marginal cost of further investments rise. Unless some element entering the marginal benefits of health also rises with age, individuals will invest in health less as they grow older. For instance, if as death approaches as we age, life becomes sweeter (i.e., the marginal utility of healthy days increase as one grows older), then the increase in the marginal benefit might offset the marginal cost and added investments in health would be made.

Empirical Work

Empirical work on health has emphasized either the "consumption" or the "investment" motive for investing in health. To emphasize the difference in these two approaches, consider the predictions the two different approaches yield with respect to the effects of changes in the wage rate on the demands for health and for purchased medical care. Consider the investment approach first.

If individuals invest in health capital solely as an investment (i.e., solely for the monetary return it will yield), then $\phi u_{id}/\lambda(1 + r)^i = 0$ in the equilibrium conditions depicted by equation (6.15). If so, consider the effect of a rise in the individual's wage rate in period i on both the demand for health (i.e., investments in health capital) and the demand for medical care (i.e., as a major component of purchased health inputs) (Grossman 1972, pp. 22–24; Grossman 2000, pp. 371–372).

Think about the demand for health first. The benefits of additional health capital will increase because the monetary value of healthy days increases $(\partial \phi w/\partial w = \phi > 0)$. But, since investments in health capital take the individual's time because they are home produced, the cost of an additional investment in health capital rises also. Only if the rise in the wage rate increases marginal benefits more than marginal costs will health capital, and therefore a person's health, be positively related to the wage rate. Indeed, so long as the ratio of the time costs to the total costs (i.e., wQ/C_h) is less than one, the demand for health capital and a person's health will be positively related with her wage rate.

Turn now to the effect of an increase in w on the demand for medical care under the investment-only approach. An increase in the demand for health (brought about via an increase in w) implies that the individual will produce more of it to meet the demand. If purchased inputs and the person's time input into health must be used in fixed proportions to produce more health capital, then a rise in her wage rate will increase the demand for medical care. But, given some substitutability between purchased inputs and her time input, she will substitute some purchased medical care for some of her now more expensive time as her wage rate increases. Consequently, the relationship between the wage rate and medical care should be even more positive.

Instead, if one considers only the consumption motive, then $\phi w = 0$ in the equilibrium conditions for equation (6.15). Then, an increase in the individual's wage rate, holding real wealth constant, will increase the marginal cost of health capital, the individual's time being an input into the production of health capital. But, since her time is also an input into the production of Z-commodities, the marginal cost of Z will also increase with an increase in w. The demand for health will increase (decrease) as w rises if the rise in w induces the marginal cost of H to rise less (more) than the marginal cost of Z because the individual will, therefore, be induced to substitute H for Z (Z for H). It turns out that with an increase in w, the demand for health will increase (decrease) as

$$w Q / C_h \lessgtr w L / C_z. \tag{6.16}$$

That is, the demand for health will increase with an increase in w only if the production of health is less "time intensive" than the production of Z (see mathematical note 5). If consumption is the only motive, therefore, the effect of w on H is ambiguous. The effect of change in w on purchased medical care is similarly ambiguous.

Empirical studies of the demand for health and for medical care are many, quite complicated, and utilize data sets drawn from other countries as well as the United States. Grossman (2000) summarizes his own work as well as that of others. The main findings are that the demand for health, where an individual's state of health is measured by a variety of variables (such as mortality, work loss days, restricted activity days, etc.), rises with the individual's level of schooling, rises with the individual's wage rate and falls with one's age and with income. The demand for medical care (i.e., expenditures on doctors, dentists, hospital visits, drugs and the like, excluding health insurance premiums) rises with age, falls with the wage rate (but the effect is statistically insignificant), and rises with income and family size.

Some of the more interesting empirical work is on unhealthy or potentially unhealthy behavior like smoking, heavy drinking, and illicit drug use. Kenkel (1996), for instance, has studied heavy drinking (i.e., the number of days with five or more drinks per day in 1984). He finds income elasticities of 0.03 for males and 0.0 for females and price elasticities of demand for heavy drinking of −0.522 for males and −1.29 for females. Harris and Chan (1999) studied cigarette smoking among young people, age 15 to 29 years, with data from the early 1990s. They found that the likelihood of cigarette smoking falls as family income rises. The price elasticity of the likelihood of smoking among young people falls as they grow older from −0.83 for 15 to 17 year olds to −0.10 for 27 to 29 year olds. DeCicca, Kenkel and Mathios (2002), however, cast doubt on whether the price elasticities for young people are as high as reported by others. Saffer and Chaloupka (1995) studied the demands for marijuana, cocaine and heroin with the National Household Survey of Drug Abuse. They find cocaine and heroin demands (whether consumed in past year) both fall as their own prices rise: for example, the own-price elasticities of demand for cocaine is between −0.55 and −0.56 and for heroin is between −0.90 and −0.80. Decriminalizing marijuana would increase the number of marijuana users by 4 to 6 percent.

The finding that health is an inferior good is based on data from the early 1960s. That one's state of health was negatively related to income while the demand for medical care is a positive function of income is puzzling. One possible explanation is that as one's income rose (holding wage rates, education, and other factors constant), individuals might have demanded more unhealthy purchased health inputs like tobacco, alcohol, cholesterol-rich foods, and the like, all of which may have reduced one's health and stimulated the demand for medical care. More recent evidence, however, is that goods such as tobacco and alcohol have income elasticities that are negative or, if positive, very small. It may be that the public health campaigns of recent decades (e.g., removing tobacco advertisements from television, adding health warning labels to alcohol and tobacco products) have made people more aware of the adverse health consequences associated with consuming these products and thus shifted people's preferences.

The link between health capital and education capital is profound and complex. The hypothesis that education positively affects investments in health capital is built into the model presented in the previous section and studies confirm the effect. For instance, Grossman (1976, Table 11, p. 189) estimates that an added year of school completed increases the likelihood of a White male being in excellent health by 0.011. However, it also appears true that the direction of causation runs the other way too: better health promotes more education.

Edwards and Grossman (1979) have shown that health positively affects the intellectual development of children. They studied a national sample of children aged six to eleven in 1963–1965. Relating a set of health-related variables as well as other variables to measures of the children's IQs and to their scores on an achievement test, they found that whether the child was breast-fed, whether it was lighter than 4.4 pounds at birth, whether it was short for its age and sex, whether it had more tooth decay given its age and sex, and whether it had significant abnormalities all affected the child's measured IQ. Holding IQ constant, whether the child was breast-fed, whether it was lighter than 4.4 pounds at birth, whether it had hearing deficiencies or significant abnormalities, and whether the child was short for its age and sex all affected its score on the achievement test (Edwards and Grossman, 1979, Table 2, p. 287). Whether children are breast-fed, whether they are light at birth, and whether they are shorter than average for their age and sex are all known to be related to nutritional status. These variables may also measure other things.

Human capital in the form of health and in the form of education and intellectual development interact with each other: the more of one increases the stock of the other. Healthy children accomplish more in school. Better educated people are healthier.

CHILDREN AS A HUMAN CAPITAL INVESTMENT

Children as an investment can be seen most clearly through a simple model of fertility developed by Becker and Lewis (1974). They argue that couples demand "child services," C, rather than numbers of children *per se*. "Child services" are the product of the number of children, N, and per child "child quality," Q. In the present context, child quality can be interpreted as the human capital embodied in children per child; that is, the investment per child. Hence,

$$C = NQ. \tag{6.17}$$

In their framework, investment per child in children, Q, involves both parental time and parental expenditures: T_q representing parental time and X_q representing purchased investment goods and services spent on children, that is,

$$Q = q(T_q, X_q). \tag{6.18}$$

Purchased investment goods and services consumed by children are such things as child health care; healthy food; education; music lessons;

car seats for children; children's safety clothes worn while skateboarding, in-line skating, skiing, bicycling, and other activities; fees for summer camp; and the like. Parental time involves not only primary child care like feeding, bathing, clothing, and chauffeuring children as well as reading to them, helping them with their homework, and playing with them. It also includes secondary child care and shared time with children in other activities. Secondary child care is time looking after children while doing something else. Hence, a parent can help a child with their homework while watching TV or reading. Shared time is time parents and children spend together in the host of other household activities. Much of secondary time directly or indirectly is involved with teaching children a particular skill, whether it is, for instance, cooking if the child helps in the kitchen or lawn and garden care if parent and child garden and maintain the lawn together.

Studies by Olson (1983), Espenshade (1984), Lazear and Michael (1988), and Lino (2001) report the investment by parents in goods and services on children. Olson's estimate of the cost of raising a child born in 1980 to age 18 by an average couple in 2001 dollars amounts to $160,680. Based on Espenshade's study, Haveman and Wolfe (1995) estimate that parents annually spent $7579 per child between the ages of 0 and 18 in 1992 dollars on food, housing, transportation, and other goods and services. Changed into 2001 dollars and multiplied by 18 yields $172,281 dollars. Based on Lazear and Michael's work, the direct cost to a couple with average income of raising a child to age 18 would be about $102,541 in 2001 dollars. Finally, Lino estimates the direct costs of raising one child in a two-child household in 2001 to be $170,460 for a middle-income family. Each of these estimates are based on different models embodying different assumptions about how total family expenditures are split between children and parents, the income and other socioeconomic characteristics of the parents, and assumptions about the calculation of present value. Regardless of the methods used, the estimates show that the out-of-pocket cost of raising children is high. Note also that these costs do not include the cost of college. If they did, the cost would skyrocket.

Parental investment of time in raising children is also substantial. It is considerably less studied but a nonetheless crucial aspect of investing in children. The data we present on parental time spent on children come from a variety of time use studies beginning in the mid-1920s and running through the mid-1980s. The detailed analyses are reported in Bryant and

Zick (1996a, 1996b, and 1996–1997) and Zick and Bryant (1996). Despite the conventional wisdom that parents engage in less parental child care now than in the early years of the twentieth century, the time spent in primary child care by married men and women actually increased per child: from 1.20 hours per day for women in 1924–1931 to 1.26 hours per day in 1985. For men the figures are 0.35 hours per day in 1975 and 0.43 hours per day in 1985. The reason for the contrary belief is that total primary child care by parents has decreased because children per family has fallen over the century: family size in the United States fell from 4.16 persons in 1925 to 3.42 persons in 1985.

We have far less information about secondary child care and shared time with children. The information we have comes from two-parent, two-child families in 1977–1978 in which data existed on the ages of the two children (Bryant and Zick 1996b; Zick and Bryant 1996). Using these data, one can calculate the total time taken to raise two children to age 18 years. Moms spent 9511 hours in primary care, 4218 hours in secondary child care, 4851 hours sharing household work time with their children, 10,008 hours sharing leisure time with their children, and 7961 hours sharing meal times with their children. In total 36,549 hours were spent by moms with the two children over the 18 years they were growing up. Dads in such families spent 2893, 1257, 2475, 8169, and 6318 hours in primary, secondary, shared household, shared leisure, and shared meal times respectively for a total of 21,112 hours. In total, parents in two-parent, two-child families spent 57,661 hours or 7.52 hours per day raising their two children. On a per child basis, parents in two-parent, two-child families spent 28,830 hours raising each child. A person who works 2000 hours per year is reckoned to be fully employed during the year. Measured this way, between them, parents spend 14.4 fully employed years raising a child from birth through age 18.

However, having children is some combination of consumption and investment. Certainly some of the money and time spent on children by parents is consumption by the parents. As parents we like to see our children healthy, well dressed, and engaged in activities they enjoy. Nonetheless, a large part of the parental time and money spent on children is investment because parents also want their children to become happy, healthy, productive adults and accordingly expend money and time for this purpose. No good way has yet been devised to accurately divide the total money and time spent on children by parents between parental consumption and parental investment in their children.

Expectations and the Sex Typing of Human Capital Investments

Parents and society at large see to it that children invest in themselves to augment their productivity in the labor market, in the household, and in leisure activities. As children attain a degree of social and economic independence, parental and societal pressures to invest in human capital recede, and individuals take over more of the responsibility for making their own human capital investment decisions.

The process is well known. Society enforces school attendance, currently until the age of sixteen. Parents make sure the children engage in certain household and leisure activities in which experience is accumulated. Common examples of learning-by-doing household tasks are making beds, drying dishes, mowing the lawn, looking after pets, and washing the family car. Music, swimming, dancing, and skiing lessons, as well as participation in organized (soccer, baseball, basketball, hockey, etc.) and unorganized sports, are all ways by which investments in leisure activity–specific human capital are made by and on behalf of children.

Expectations about future activities are extremely important in governing how much and what kind of human capital investments individuals make or are made by parents on their behalf. An individual (or a parent on the child's behalf) will invest in human capital that raises his or her labor market productivity, w/p, only if he or she expects to spend much time in the labor market in the future. The more time individuals expect to spend in the labor market over their lifetimes, the higher the marginal benefits to labor market–specific human capital and the greater the investment that will be made. Likewise, the more time one expects to spend over one's lifetime in household or leisure activities, the greater the rate of return to household- or leisure-specific human capital formation and the greater the investments in these kinds of human capital that will be made.

These points are summarized in a somewhat generalized marginal-benefits-equal-to-marginal-costs condition for investment in human capital on the assumption that any investment in human capital has the possibility of increasing the individual's productivity in the labor market, $\hat{w}$, his or her household productivity, $\hat{g}_h$, or productivity in leisure activities, $\hat{r}_l$.[19] Given this perspective, the equilibrium condition for investment in

---

[19] Suppose the output of leisure activities is denoted by R, where R stands for recreation. The output, R, can be viewed as an index of the music made or listened to, vacations taken, books read, TV programs watched, chess games played, and so on. Suppose, further, that the output of recreation activities increases with the time, L, spent in leisure activities and with the amount of other inputs that are used with the leisure time, X (e.g., books,

human capital becomes

$$\sum_{t=1}^{n} w_t(\hat{g}_h H_t + \hat{w} M_t + \hat{r}_l L_t)/(1+r)^t = MC \tag{6.19}$$

where w_t = the individual's wage rate in year t in the future; $\hat{g}_h$, $\hat{w}$, and $\hat{r}_l$ are the percentage increases in household productivity, labor market productivity, and leisure activity productivity, respectively, due to a one-unit investment in human capital; and H_t, M_t, and L_t are the times the individual expects to spend in household production, labor market employment, and leisure activity in year t in the future, respectively.[20]

The left-hand side of equation (6.19) is the marginal benefit of an added unit of human capital. The larger the H_t (M_t, L_t), the more time the individual expects to spend in household production (market work, leisure activity) in year t in the future and the greater the marginal benefit from the investment. If $H_t = 0$ ($M_t = 0$, $L_t = 0$), however, the individual expects to spend no time in household production (market work, leisure), and the marginal benefit of the human capital investment will be lower. Alternatively, if $\hat{g}_h = 0$ ($\hat{w} = 0$, $\hat{r}_l = 0$) then the contemplated investment in human capital does not augment household productivity (labor market productivity, leisure productivity), and again, the marginal benefit from the contemplated human capital investment is lower.

Sex typing of human capital investments can occur when individuals' expectations, or those of their parents, about their future activities depend on gender. Historically, females were expected to spend the majority of their lives in household and leisure activities. Consequently, the marginal benefits to labor market–specific human capital investments by or on behalf of females were lower than those for males, reducing the amount of such investments made by females or by society and parents on their behalf.

Although being literate was important for household management and child rearing, higher education for females had a low rate of return because of these expectations and, consequently, few females entered college or graduated. If females entered college, their motives (or those of their parents) were not to amass labor market–specific human capital

beer, TVs, musical instruments, theater tickets, chess sets, skiing equipment). Then the recreation activity can be written as $R = r(L, X)$, where $r_l = \partial R/\partial L$ = the marginal product of time in leisure activities; that is, the added amount of recreation output obtainable by increasing the amount of time spent in leisure activities by one hour.

[20] This expression is a generalization of expression (1.25) in Becker (1981, pp. 9–12). We have assumed that $\partial H_t/\partial Q_{t-1} = 1$ in Becker's expression (1.25).

except as insurance against the possibility of being widowed. Rather, their motives were to invest further in household- and leisure-specific human capital or in some cases to participate in the college "marriage market." As expectations about the future roles of females changed through time, however, rates of return to education of females rose and their high school and college completion rates rose.

In the forty years from 1960 to 2000, the fraction of those, age 25 or older, who were college graduates rose from 9.7 percent to 27.8 percent for males and from 5.8 percent to 23.6 percent for females (U.S. Bureau of the Census 2000b, Table 209). What is important is that the female percentage increased by 307 percent whereas that for males increased only 187 percent. The almost double rate of increase by females over males (307 percent compared with 187 percent) reflects in part the rising labor market expectations of and on behalf of females, increasing the rate of return to education for females and inducing an increasing number to go to college. Not only did females increasingly attend and complete college, they increasingly have entered fields with high labor market pay-offs. In 1959–1960, 0.8 percent of the DDS degrees, 5.5 percent of the MD degrees, and 2.5 percent of the law degrees conferred went to females. In 1999–2000, these percentages had increased to 40.0 percent, 42.7 percent, and 45.9 percent respectively (U.S. National Center for Education Statistics 2003).

Another place where altered expectations change investments in human capital is in activities that increase human capital specific to household production activities. These changes can be observed by comparing the time use patterns of children in two-parent, two-child families in Syracuse, New York, in 1967 and 1977 (O'Neill 1978). In 1967 82.1 percent of all girls aged 16 to 17 participated in household production tasks, compared with 78.9 percent of boys. For 1977 the comparable participation rates were 87.7 percent for girls and 88.6 percent for boys. Although the participation in household production activities of both boys and girls increased over the ten-year period, the rate of increase for boys was almost double that for girls. Part of this differential increase stems from changed parental expectations about how their children will spend their time in the future. Using national data, Hofferth and Sandberg (1999) looked at changes in children's activities from 1981 to 1997. Boys under 12 years of age increased the housework they did by an average of 21.3 minutes per day whereas the time spent by girls in housework increased by 28.1 minutes per day. While the absolute increase by girls was larger than by boys, the percentage increase by boys was somewhat larger reflecting, perhaps, the larger fraction of housework males are expected to do in today's households.

Human Capital and Household Type

Human capital formation is an important household activity in both its explicit and implicit forms: explicitly when the activity is primarily motivated as a device to build human capital, as in formal instruction, preventive medicine, exercise, and nutrition; and implicitly when human capital formation accumulates as experience in doing the activity, regardless of whether the activity is market work, household production, or leisure. Because the human capital formation, especially that gained through experience in household activities, takes place in the context of a household, the type of household affects the returns to investments in human capital and, therefore, the amounts and types of human capital formation. In particular, the sex of the individual, marital status, and household composition (i.e., the number of children) are important.

Because single people can exploit neither the advantages of specialization of function nor economies of size in household production activities, and because their demands for household-produced goods and services are less than that of a multi-person household, single people do less household work than multi-person households and, therefore, accumulate less household production–related experience than people in multi-person households. Slowly changing social norms, household production skills learned as a child, and continuing lower wages for women lead women, single or married, to do more household work than males. The experience of doing more household work results in females having more household production–specific human capital than men.

The concepts of general and specific human capital apply to the human capital amassed as experience in households as well as to the labor market. Some of the human relations, child-rearing, management, shopping, and household maintenance skills one learns in a marriage are general to any marriage and, perhaps, to firms as well.[21] The returns to such general human capital are difficult for other family members to capture in the same way the returns to general human capital cannot be easily captured by employers. The reasons are the same. If other family members seek to

---

[21] There appear to be labor market implications for women of spending time in housework. Hersch and Stratton (1997) find that, *ceteris paribus*, employed women who do more housework have lower wage rates. The same seems not to be true for men.

capture these returns or seek to capture an inordinate share of them, the family member possessing them can remove the human capital from the family, depriving it of the benefits or at least reserving a higher fraction of the benefits for himself or herself.

There are several implications of this fact. Some of the general human capital accumulated through experience in the family is applicable in the labor market and serves to raise the individual's market productivity. One way of removing this general human capital from the family is to increase the proportion of time one spends in paid employment. Here, the returns to the general human capital accrue to the individual through his or her earnings. Depending on the financial organization of the household, individual family members' labor earnings may not be fully shared with other family members. If not, then the substitution of market for household work may have the effect of reserving for the possessor the returns to general experience gained within the household. This could partly explain the traditional resistance on the part of husbands to the entry of their wives into the labor force. And it could equally be part of the explanation for the rapid increase in the labor force participation rate of married women after 1940.

Another part of the human capital gained within a marriage is general in the sense that it is as productive in any household. Faced with the threat of having to share an inordinate fraction of the returns to such general human capital with other family members, an individual may leave the family and form another household, single or married. Such is the stuff of divorce discussed more fully in Chapter 8.

Marriage-specific human capital yields returns in the context of the household within which it is accumulated but in no other household or context. The particular knowledge of and skills in handling the personality, capabilities, and failings of one's mate that are gained over time in a marriage are examples of marriage-specific human capital. So, too, are children of the marriage: however charming, likable, and smart, children are "worth" less to others than to their parents (see, for instance, Weiss and Willis [1985]). Such capital (i.e., children from a previous marriage) is carried into another marriage with difficulty and either is not productive or is much less productive than in the marriage in which it was accumulated. This explains, in part, why the remarriage rate of divorced persons with children is lower than the remarriage rate of divorced persons without children. It may also partially explain why the divorce rate among those once divorced and remarried is higher than the divorce rate of people in their first marriage. See Chapter 8 for an elaboration of these points.

Human capital formed during a marriage has important implications for divorce settlements. This is most easily and commonly seen in the archetypical case in which one spouse "puts the other spouse through school," and subsequently, there is a divorce. It is argued that the mate putting the spouse through school invested in the spouse's schooling and the returns to that investment (i.e., that part of the spouse's higher income due to the mate's efforts) should go to the mate in the divorce settlement (Borenstein and Courant 1989). Again, these issues are more fully discussed in Chapter 8.

SUMMARY

The model of the household has been broadened in this chapter to include the investment in human capital activities that are properly construed as a special type of household production in which the output is received and consumed in the future. Human capital investment augments not only one's market productivity but one's household productivity as well, thus altering the trade-offs individuals make among household work, market work, and leisure.

Mathematical Notes

1. While multi-period models reveal much, the added mathematics they entail can also obscure. Here is a one-period analogue to the model underlying equation (6.3) that may aid intuition. What it cannot do that multi-period models can is to explain the trade-off between investing in education versus financial instruments or when during one's life investments in education are made. The period is the individual's lifetime the length of which is T years. Suppose the individual derives satisfaction from market goods, X, and leisure time, L. Thus,

$$U = u(X, L). \tag{1}$$

Suppose the annual wage rate (i.e., full-time earnings) at which the individual may work is w and that it depends on the years of schooling, S, the individual undergoes. Thus,

$$w = w(S), \quad \partial w/\partial S = w_s > 0, \quad \text{and} \quad \partial w_s/\partial S < 0 \tag{2}$$

where w_s is the increase in the annual wage rate due to an added year of school. Diminishing marginal productivity of schooling is assumed in that

$\partial w_s/\partial S < 0$. The lifetime time constraint faced by the individual is:

$$T = M + L + S \qquad (3)$$

where $M =$ number of years the individual spends working. The individual's lifetime income is

$$Y = wM + V \qquad (4)$$

where $V =$ nonlabor income. The individual's lifetime expenditures are $pX + CS$, where p is the price of market goods and C is the out-of-pocket costs of a year of school. Thus, the combined budget constraint is

$$pX + wL + (w + C)S = wT + V. \qquad (5)$$

The individual maximizes (1) subject to (5). Form the Lagrangean expression

$$Lg = u(X, L) - \lambda[pX + wL + (w + C)S - wT - V]. \qquad (6)$$

The first order condition for S is:

$$\partial Lg/\partial S = \lambda w_s(T - L - S) - \lambda(w + C) = 0$$

or, since $T - L - S = M$ and the λ can be eliminated,

$$w_s M - (w + C) = 0. \qquad (7)$$

Equation (7) is the lifetime analogue to equation (6.3). $w_s M$ is the marginal benefit from an added year of school whereas $w + C$ is the marginal cost. w_s is the analogue to $(E'_t - E_t)$; that is, the increase in annual earnings due to an added year of school. M is the number of years over the lifetime the individual earns the extra annual income from an added year of school. w is the analogue to E_0, the foregone earnings of the added year of school and C is the out-of-pocket cost of the added year of school. While one cannot speak of the rate of return to schooling and, hence, its decline with added schooling in the context of this model, analogous comments can be made. The marginal benefit of added schooling falls and the marginal cost rises with added schooling. First, because of diminishing marginal productivity, w_s declines as S rises, lowering the marginal benefit as S rises. Second, as S rises, there is less time left for the individual to work during his/her life, reducing M and with it the marginal benefit. Third, the marginal cost of schooling rises with schooling because with more schooling, w, the foregone earnings, rises.

2. If the individual derives satisfaction (positive if school is enjoyed, negative is school is disliked) from schooling, then instead of equation (1) the utility function in the one-period lifetime model analogue is

$$U = u(X, L, S). \qquad (8)$$

The utility (disutility) of additional schooling is $\partial U/\partial S = u_s$. The first order condition for a maximum in this case is, then,

$$u_s/\lambda + w_s M - (w + C) = 0 \qquad (9)$$

where $u_s/\lambda = V_s$ is the dollar value of the added schooling (positive if schooling is liked, negative if schooling is disliked) and λ is the marginal utility of money.

3. In order to simplify the model further by having a linear budget constraint, both the $h(.)$ and the $z(.)$ functions are assumed to be linearly homogeneous. Thus, the health capital production function can be written as

$$H = Mg(t; E) \tag{10}$$

where $t = Q/M$ and $g(.)$ is formed by multiplying $h(.)$ through by $1/M$; that is,

$$g(.) = h(1, Q/M; E).$$

Similarly, the production function for Z can be written as

$$Z = Xf(b; E) \tag{11}$$

where $b = L/X$ and $f(.)$ is formed by multiplying $z(.)$ through by $1/X$; that is,

$$f(.) = z(1, L/X; E).$$

The assumption of linear homogeneity (Chiang 1967, pp. 404–407) is a simplifying assumption that ensures that the average costs of producing, say, H, equals the marginal cost and both are constant with changes in H. This is shown as follows. With p_m being the price of M and the price of time being the wage rate, w, the least cost way of producing any given quantity of health capital, H^*, is found by minimizing

$$Lg = p_m M + wQ - \lambda[Mg(t; E) - H^*] \tag{12}$$

by differentiating (12) with respect to M and Q and by setting the derivatives to zero; that is,

$$p_m = \lambda(g - g't) \tag{13}$$

$$w = \lambda g' \tag{14}$$

where $p_m M + wQ = C_h$, $g = g(.)$, $g' = \partial g/\partial t$, and $\lambda = \partial C_h/\partial H =$ marginal cost. Least cost equilibrium conditions (13) and (14) can be rephrased as

$$MC_h = \lambda = p_m/(g - g't) = w/g'. \tag{15}$$

Note that in equilibrium (13) and (14) can be substituted into C_h to form

$$C_h = \lambda(g - g't)M + \lambda g'Q.$$

Dividing C_h by H yields average cost; that is,

$$AC_h = [\lambda(g - g't)M + \lambda g'Q]/Mg = \lambda = MC_h \tag{16}$$

showing that average cost does, indeed, equal marginal cost.

Finally, note that MC_h is a function only of the ratio, $t = Q/M$ because both g and g' are functions only of t. Thus, changes in H will affect neither

AC_h nor MC_h. Note also since as the prices of M and Q do not change, the optimum ratio of Q to M, t, will not change and neither will either the average or marginal cost of producing H.

4. Several more equations are needed to complete the model. Given her daily wage of w, her total life's income is

$$Y = wN + V \tag{17}$$

where $V =$ nonlabor income. Total life's income is exhausted by purchases of M and X and prices p_m and p_x respectively; that is,

$$p_m M + p_x X = wN + V. \tag{18}$$

The total budget constraint can be found by substituting equations (6.9) and (6.10) into (18):

$$p_m M + wQ + p_x X + wL = w\phi H + V. \tag{19}$$

We can rephrase (19) totally in terms of H and Z by defining the total costs of H and Z, respectively, as

$$C_h = p_m M + wQ \tag{20}$$
$$C_z = p_x X + wL.$$

And, therefore,

$$C_h + C_z = w\phi H + V \tag{21}$$

The satisfaction-maximizing conditions are derived by forming the Lagrangean expression

$$Lg = u(\phi H, Z) - \lambda[C_h + C_z - w\phi H - V]. \tag{22}$$

Differentiating Lg by H and Z, in turn, and setting each to zero yields

$$\partial U/\partial H - \lambda \partial C_h/\partial H + \lambda w\phi = 0 \tag{23}$$
$$\partial U/\partial Z - \lambda \partial C_z/\partial Z = 0. \tag{24}$$

Letting $\partial U/\partial H = u_d\phi$, $u_d = \partial U/\partial D$, $\partial C_h/\partial H = \pi_h$, and $\partial C_z/\partial Z = \pi_z$, then equation (23) becomes equation (6.13) in the text.

5. The issue is the sign of $\partial(\pi_h/\pi_z)\partial w$, holding real wealth, that is, utility, constant. If this is positive, health capital becomes more expensive than Z as w increases, lowering the demand for H relative to Z. If negative, health capital becomes less expensive than Z, increasing the demand for H relative to Z. Since real wealth (i.e., utility) is held constant, this amounts to a substitution of H for Z or the reverse.

$$\partial(\pi_h/\pi_z)/\partial w = [\pi_z \partial(C_h/H)/\partial w - \pi_h \partial(C_z/Z)/\partial w]/\pi_z^2$$
$$= [\pi_z Q/H - \pi_h L/Z]/\pi_z^2. \tag{25}$$

The sign of equation (25) depends on the numerator since the deonominator is positive. Thus,

$$\partial(\pi_z/\pi_h)/\partial w \gtrless 0$$

as

$$\pi_z Q/H \gtrless \pi_h L/Z. \tag{26}$$

Multiply through (26) by $w/\pi_h\pi_z$ to get

$$w Q/C_h \gtrless w L/C_z \tag{27}$$

where $w Q/C_h$ is the time cost fraction of the total cost of H and $w L/C_z$ is the time cost fraction of the total cost of Z. These are called the "time intensities" of H and Z respectively.

SEVEN

The Economics of Fertility

INTRODUCTION

In the United States the birthrate has fallen over the past 185 years from about 55.2 births per 1000 population in 1820 to 32.2 in 1900, and 13.9 in 2002.[1] Over the long run and with the exception of the post–World War II baby boom, Americans have been having fewer children.

The post–World War II baby boom followed by the baby bust of the 1960s and 1970s is the major exception to the long-run trend. Total fertility rates from 1940 to the present tell this tale. The total fertility rate is a better measure of the fertility experience of women than the birthrate because "the total fertility rate is the number of births that 1000 women would have in their lifetime if at each year of age, they experienced the birth rates occurring in the specified year" (U.S. Bureau of the Census 1999). In 1940–1944 the total fertility rate was 2523 per 1000 women. It peaked in the 1955–1959 period with 3690 births per 1000 women, after which total fertility rates started to fall. In the 1975–1979 period the total fertility rate was 1810 per 1000 women. After reaching a low of 1738 births per 1000 women in 1976, it has increased to 2115 in 2001.[2]

---

[1] U.S. Bureau of the Census. *Statistical Abstract of the United States*, various volumes. The White birthrate declined from 55 per 1000 population in 1800 to 17.6 in 1933, increased to 24 in 1956 (the peak year of the baby boom), and decreased to 14.1 in 2000. The non-White birthrate declined from 35 in 1920 (the first year for which data exist) to 25.5 in 1933, rose to 35.4 in 1956, and declined to 17.6 in 2000.

[2] U.S. Bureau of the Census. *Statistical Abstract of the United States*, various volumes. After falling to a low of 1652 in 1976, the total White fertility rate has risen again to 2110 by 2001. The total Black and other fertility rate continued to fall until 1984 when it was 2071. By 2001 it had risen again to 2124 (U.S. Bureau of the Census 2002, Table 88).

Over this period the replacement rate (i.e., the birthrate necessary to sustain a constant population in the absence of net immigration) has been 2110 births per 1000 women. Since 1972 the total fertility rate has been above the replacement rate in only two years: 2000 and 2001.

The fertility experience of women has varied widely not only over both the long and the short run but also among women at any point in time. Fertility is negatively related to family income, for instance. Consider the number of women who gave birth in 2000. The birth rate was 86.8 per 1000 women in families with incomes less than $10,000, falling to 60.1 births per 1000 women in families with incomes $75,000 or more (U.S. Bureau of the Census 2003, Table 99). Fertility is also negatively related to women's educational levels. The total fertility rate of women by education in 2000 was: 3.2 births per woman with 0 to 8 years of school completed; 2.3 births per woman with 9 to 11 years of schooling; 2.7 births per woman with 12 years of completed schooling; 1.4 births per woman with 13 to 15 years of completed schooling; and 1.7 births per woman for those with 16 or more years of schooling.[3] Although these figures reflect much more than merely the relationships among fertility, family income, and women's education, they do illustrate that the wide variation is related to their socioeconomic characteristics and is not simply a matter of biology.

Besides the decline in total fertility over the past two centuries, a dramatic rise in out-of-wedlock births has occurred beginning in the early 1960s and continuing to the present. The number of nonmarital births per 1000 unmarried women, age 15 to 44 years, rose from 23 in 1963 to 45 in 1992. Over the same period, the number of births to married women per 1000 married women fell from 146 in 1963 to 90 in 1992 (Hotz, Klerman, and Willis 1997). From 1963 to 2000, the percent of births to unmarried mothers to total births rose from 6.0 to 33.2 (Hotz, Klerman, and Willis 1997 and U.S. Bureau of the Census 2000b, Table 74, p. 63). Most of this rise occurred among unmarried White women: while the percent of births to unmarried White mothers to total White births rose from 16.9 in 1990 to 27.1 in 2000, the analogous percent for unmarried Black mothers hovered between 66.7 and 69.9. And, despite the focus in the press on teenage pregnancy and births, the percent of births to

---

[3] U.S. National Center for Health Statistics (1997). The total fertility rate in this instance is calculated for women who have completed the years of schooling at the time of the survey. Clearly women less than 25 years old may not have completed their schooling and, therefore, the total fertility rate for 0 to 8 and 9 to 11 years of completed schooling calculated in this fashion is less reliable than the rates for higher levels of education.

teenage mothers to total births has declined modestly in recent years. In 1990, births to teenagers accounted for 12.8 percent of all births while in 2001, the number had dropped to 11.3 percent of all births (U.S. Bureau of the Census 2003, Table 91).

This brief recital of facts about American fertility indicates that over both the short and the long run Americans have varied their fertility behavior dramatically. What are the determinants of fertility behavior and how have they changed? Can economics join biology, sociology, and psychology in contributing to the explanation of fertility?

For economics to contribute anything at all to the understanding of fertility behavior, three conditions must be present: (1) Children must yield satisfaction to their parents. (2) Parents must be able to choose whether to have children, how many to have, when to have them, and, perhaps, their genders. (3) Children must be costly; that is, bearing and rearing children must use scarce resources. We discuss each of these points in turn.

Currently and historically children have given satisfaction in at least one of four major ways.

1. Parents love their children and children return that love. Thus, children yield satisfaction directly to their parents.

2. Children are themselves a resource in the production of goods and services either for home consumption or for sale. Wresting America from the wilderness would have taken much longer and would have been harder had it not been for the labor of generations of children on their parents' frontier farms and in their businesses. Likewise, few suburban parents want to face the summer's lawns or the winter's snows without the assistance of their children. Thus, children also yield satisfaction to their parents indirectly through the goods and services they produce for family consumption or sale.

3. Children provide social, psychological, and economic security in their parents' old age. Security for the parents when they are elderly is another indirect way in which children increase their parents' satisfaction. Economic security for their parents was a more cogent reason for couples to have children earlier in our history when Social Security, Medicare, and pensions were not as prevalent. It continues to be quite important for couples in less developed countries.

4. Sociobiologists remind us that from an evolutionary perspective ensuring that one's gene pool survives and continues into future generations is a powerful drive, whether for iguanas or for humans. Success and happiness, therefore, derive from the number of progeny and their likelihood of survival.

Despite the fact that having children remains a probabilistic, biological process, people have always had choice over whether to have children and when to have them. In earlier times choice was controlled by devices like infanticide, sale into slavery,[4] primitive contraception and abortion techniques, delaying marriage, and social and religious sanctions surrounding marriage. Today, we have much more sophisticated contraception and abortion techniques and we attempt to control decisions as to whether and when to have children by religious, social, and public policy sanctions. Moreover, modern medicine and adoption practices allow those who are infertile to have children.

Children certainly are costly in time and money. Bearing and raising a child to age 18 costs in excess of $100,000 and 28,000 hours of parents time (see Chapter 6).

It is clear, then, that the three conditions are present that make economics relevant to the explanation of fertility phenomena. However, children have special attributes that prohibit the easy application of the economics of the household to the explanation of fertility behavior. These attributes need to be discussed.

Children have been likened to durable goods because they yield satisfaction and command resources over a long period of time. With a child, as with other durable goods, the economic focus is on the flow of services to the family through time. Likewise, both durables and children require maintenance through time. In the case of durables the goal is to maintain them in good working order, whereas with children the goal is to encourage their growth, development, and their eventual social and economic independence. Thus, the decision to have children takes on the character of an investment-saving decision. The implication of the durable-like attributes of children is that an intertemporal model is probably the most accurate way to clarify parents' fertility choices. Failing this, one must still come to terms with the fact that children yield satisfaction and entail expenditures of resources over long periods.

Children also differ from durables in important ways. The patterns of the money and time costs for durables are very different from those for children. In the case of most durables, the ratio of money-to-time cost initially is quite high. As durables age, more time is spent maintaining them, leading to a decline in the ratio of money-to-time cost. In contrast,

---

[4] Among the ancient Romans, "infanticide remained an accepted practice, widespread among the poor, occasional among their betters. Roman Law also sanctioned ... the custom of selling surplus children" (Gies and Gies 1987, p. 27).

children have modest initial money costs compared with their initial time costs. As children grow up and attain first physical, then sociological, and finally economic independence, the ratio of money-to-time costs rises up to the point of economic independence.

The high initial time-to-money costs of children, when combined with the division of labor by sex in most couples, means that the decisions to have children and their number and spacing are very intertwined with decisions concerning the amount and timing of the mother's market work. The blending of the mother's work life with the birthing and rearing of children, as well as the fact that children typically come one at a time after a nine-month gestation period, means that achieving the desired family size can be a lengthy process. This implies that the characteristics of each child affect the timing and number of subsequent children.

A SIMPLE MODEL OF FERTILITY

There are many important questions that could be asked about the fertility choices of people. They include questions about family size (why, for instance, has family size decreased in the United States except for the post–World War II baby boom?), the nonmarital birthrate, the spacing of children, the timing of children with respect to the age of the mother, the sex of children, the effects of modern contraceptives, the influence (if any) of tax and welfare programs, and on and on. No single model of family behavior can address all of these questions: family size questions and timing and spacing questions require different models as does nonmarital fertility. Here, the goal is to introduce the student to how the tools of economics can shed light on a few of these questions. Initially, then, a simple model of marital fertility choice will be built concentrating on the question of family size. The timing and spacing of births, a subject for which there is a large literature, will be ignored both because of space limitations and because of model complexities. Nonmarital fertility will be postponed until Chapter 8 because the current explanations have as much or more to do with marriage as they do with fertility.[5]

To address the question of family size with the aid of a simple model, we will focus on a few attributes of children and choices involving them and

---

[5] See Hotz, Klerman, and Willis (1997) for a survey of multi-period models that focus on timing and spacing of children as well as with the hypotheses dealing with the rise in out-of-wedlock births.

neglect the myriad other attributes that surely impinge on other questions. We will focus initially on three.

First, since we wish the model to address the question of family size, it makes sense to focus on completed family size. By completed family size is meant the number of children a couple has and rears to adulthood. The number of children a family has by the time the mother is, say, 25 years old is irrelevant because she may desire and have several more children during the remaining years she is fecund. The consequence of focusing on completed family size is that the period of analysis is the period of fecundity of the woman. Choosing this as the period of analysis allows us to avoid the complexities of multi-period models like the ones developed in Chapters 4 and 6 and to benefit from the simplicities of one-period models.

Second, children are a home-produced good requiring combinations of parental time and purchased goods. The parental time involved includes the time spent on prenatal and postnatal child care and nurturing plus the added time required to perform household tasks when children are present. The purchased goods include the food, clothing, housing, toys, transportation, education, and so on that all must be produced by the family or purchased for children as they grow and develop.

Third, given the historic and current specialization of function within the family, it is the married woman's time rather than the husband's that makes up the majority of the time used in having and rearing children. Consequently, we will focus on the mother's time input and ignore the father's. Furthermore, the model will focus on the woman and neglect the man. This is done not only to focus on the woman's time input but also because most data on fertility are collected relative to women rather than men.

As a first approximation it is probably the case that most parents prefer to treat each child equally: that is, to ensure that each of their children is as happy, skilled, healthy, and educated as their other children. Thus, we can avoid having to assume that children within a family differ with regard to the attributes they possess.[6]

We formalize these ideas simply by supposing that a couple derives satisfaction from the number of children they have and raise, N, and all other services consumed by the couple, S, called adult services. The

---

[6] For a discussion of family models in which our assumption of equality of treatment among children is dropped, see Pollak (1988).

couple's utility function is, therefore,

$$U = u(N, S; Z) \tag{7.1}$$

where the utility function, $u\,(.)$, is defined over the period stretching from the couple's marriage to the end of the wife's fecundity somewhere in the neighborhood of 45 years of age, and Z is a vector of preference shifters. The couple is visualized, then, as being poised at marriage and planning the number of children and adult services they would like to consume over the period.

Bearing and raising children is a production process involving the combination of goods, X_n, specifically devoted to children and the wife's time spent bearing and raising children, T_n. X_n and T_n are defined over the planning period. The child-bearing and raising process can be represented by the production process characterized as

$$T_n = t_n N$$
$$X_n = b_n N \tag{7.2}$$

where t_n = the time required by the mother to bear and raise each child, T_n/N, and b_n = the quantity of goods required to bear and raise each child, X_n/N. The coefficients t_n and b_n are to be regarded as technical in nature and represent the household production process involved.

Similarly, adult services, S, take T_s hours over the planning period and X_s quantity of goods. The adult services production process involved is represented by

$$T_s = t_s S$$
$$X_s = b_x S \tag{7.3}$$

where $t_s = T_s/S$ and $b_s = X_s/S$ are technical parameters of the adult services household production process (see mathematical note 1).

The wife spends the planning period, T, in bearing and raising children, in the production and consumption of adult services, and in paid employment, M; that is,

$$T = T_n + T_s + M. \tag{7.4}$$

Of course, T_n is zero in the case in which a couple demands no children.

The couple spends the income, Y, it receives over the planning period on child goods, X_n, and adult goods, X_s which can be purchased at prices p_n and p_s, respectively. The budget constraint the couple faces, then, is

$$p_n X_n + p_s X_s = Y. \tag{7.5}$$

The couple's income is the sum of the wife's earnings, wM, where w is her wage rate,[7] and other income, V, which includes the husband's earnings and nonlabor income.[8] Hence,

$$Y = wM + V. \qquad (7.6)$$

Substituting (7.4) and (7.6) into (7.5) results in the total budget constraint facing the couple in its planning

$$p_n X_n + w T_n + p_s X_s + w T_s = wT + V. \qquad (7.7)$$

The budget constraint as represented by (7.7) is expressed in terms of time and goods rather than in terms of the number of children and adult services. As such it cannot be used with the utility function, (7.1), to determine the number of children and quantity of adult services the couple demands given its resources and the prices of goods and the wife's time. To make (7.7) commensurate with (7.1), substitute (7.2) and (7.3) into (7.7) to yield

$$\pi_n N + \pi_s S = wT + V \qquad (7.8)$$

where

$$\pi_n = p_n b_n + w t_n$$
$$\pi_s = p_s b_s + w t_s. \qquad (7.9)$$

The utility function (7.1) and the budget constraint (7.8) are illustrated in Figure 7.1 The couple's preferences for children and parental services are represented by $U_1, U_2,$ and so on while the budget constraint facing the couple over its planning period is represented by AB.[9] Given its resources, $wT + V$, the prices of child and adult goods, p_n and p_s, and the price of the wife's time, w, the couple maximizes satisfaction at point E, demanding $0N_e$ numbers of children and $0S_e$ quantity of adult services.

---

[7] The woman's wage rate, w, comes very close to being the woman's permanent wage rate over the couple's expected life. The term permanent is used in the same sense as in permanent income in Chapter 4. This is because, by necessity, it ignores the year-to-year variations in her wage rate throughout the period. These year-to-year variations can be interpreted as transitory variations around a permanent level.

[8] Including the husband's earnings in V implies that variations in the price of his time over the couple's planning period play no role in their decisions as to how many children they demand. His earnings, however, do have income effects. Likewise, the model presumes that the husband spends no time or a fixed amount of time in child care.

[9] AB is shown as linear because $t_n, b_n, t_s,$ and b_s are initially assumed to be constants. Instead, if they depend on the amounts of time and goods used to produce N and S, then AB is nonlinear and becomes concave to the origin.

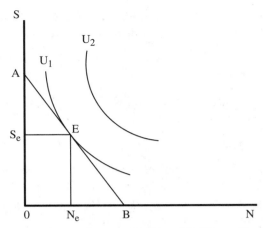

Figure 7.1. The couple's preferences for N and S, (U), and budget line AB.

The equilibrium conditions are

$$u_n - \lambda \pi_n = 0$$
$$u_s - \lambda \pi_s = 0 \tag{7.10}$$

or

$$u_n/u_s = \pi_n/\pi_s. \tag{7.11}$$

These are the familiar equilibrium conditions from Chapter 3. That is, the marginal rate of substitution between children and parental services must equal the ratio of their prices.

The demands for children and adult services are to be construed as demands that are realized only in a world in which the couple knows their own biology (and that conception is certain and not probabilistic), the resources they will have, and the prices of goods and the wife's time over the time period. It also assumes that the arrival of a child does not change their preferences for subsequent children. In reality, such perfect certainty is a myth. Instead, one can more realistically interpret these as expected demands.

Given the model, the couple's demand for children (i.e., completed number of births) is a function of the prices of children and adult services, the couple's "full income," $wT + V$, and the preference shifters, Z, that alter the couple's preferences as represented by their utility function; that is,

$$N^d = n^d \left(\pi_n, \pi_s, wT + V, Z \right). \tag{7.12}$$

Alternatively, given (7.9) the demand for children can be expressed as a function of the price of the wife's time, w, the prices of child and adult goods, p_n and p_x, full income, $wT + V$, and preference shifters, Z; that is,

$$N^d = n^d (p_n, p_s, w, wT + V, Z).\qquad(7.13)$$

Z, the vector of preference shifters, includes factors like the couple's race and ethnicity, the couple's education, and biological characteristics of the couple that influence the couple's fertility including age at marriage. Both expressions are useful. Because the technical properties of the child and parental services production functions are not yet fully understood, the prices of children and parental services are not known and equation (7.12) cannot be empirically estimated directly. Thus, the demand for children in the form of equation (7.13) is more useful. However, equation (7.12) is very useful for deriving hypotheses.

Given this model, we can then use it to create hypothesized explanations of trends in family size as well as differences in the number of children couples have depending on couples' socioeconomic characteristics. We begin with a discussion of the effects of changes in the price of the wife's time, w. Because the wife's time is such an important input into bearing and raising children and because women's wage rates (i.e., the price of their time) have risen throughout the twentieth century, the effect of rising female wage rates can be expected to have been an important determinant of twentieth century trends in fertility.

The Effect of Wage Rate Changes

Suppose the wife's wage rate rises. Differentiating the demand for children, (7.12) by w, yields (see mathematical note 2)

$$\partial N^d/\partial w = (t_n - \pi_n t_s/\pi_s)(\partial n^d/\partial \pi_n)|_{u=c} + M \partial n^d/\partial FY.\qquad(7.14)$$

The first term of (7.14) is the substitution effect while the second term is the income effect of a change in the wage rate. Since $(\partial n^d/\partial \pi_n)|_{u=c}$ is the substitution effect of a change in the price of children, it is negative. The sign of the first term, then, depends on the sign of $(t_n - \pi_n t_s/\pi_s)$. Since both π_n and π_s increase when w increases, this term determines which increases more. Multiplying $(t_n - \pi_n t_s/\pi_s)$ by w/π_n doesn't change its sign but transforms it into $(wt_n/\pi_n - wt/\pi_s)$. wt_n/π_n is the wife's time's share of the per child cost; that is, it is the "time intensity" of children. Likewise, wt_s/π_s is the time intensity of adult services. The entire term,

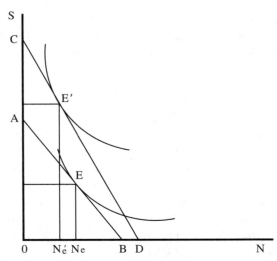

Figure 7.2. The effect of an increase of the wife's wage rate on the demand for children.

therefore, measures the *relative* time intensity of children. If children are more time intensive than adult services, then a rise in the wife's wage rate increases the price of children relative to the price of adult services inducing a substitution of adult services for children, holding satisfaction constant. If adult services are more time intensive than children, then the reverse occurs.

The second term of equation (7.14) is the income effect. An increase in the wife's wage rate increases family income and, thereby, increases (decreases) the demand for children should they be normal (inferior) goods.

The effect of an increase in the wife's wage rate is illustrated in Figure 7.2. Initially, the couple maximizes satisfaction at point E demanding N_e children. A rise in the wife's wage rate shifts the budget line facing the couple from AB to CD. CD has been drawn to illustrate the case in which children are more time intensive than adult services and, thus, the price of children rises more than the price of adult services with an increase in her wage rate, making CD steeper than AB. Given the child care required at least early in a child's life, it is believed that children are more time intensive than adult services. CD is, however, farther to the right than AB illustrating the point that a rise in w also increases full income, $wT + V$, by the amount $\Delta wT = (w' - w)T$. In the case illustrated, the wage rate increase reduces the demand for children from N_e to N_e'. Because the increase in the wage rate increased the price of children relative to adult services, the substitution effect unambiguously induces the couple to substitute adult services for children. The income effect of the wage rate increase was insufficient to offset this decline in the demand for children, if children are normal goods. Or, it augmented the decline in demand if children are inferior.

The empirical evidence on the effect of female wage rates on the demand for children is clear. Mincer (1963) was first to examine the issue. He used a sample of urban, White, husband-wife families in 1950 in which both spouses were employed and the wife was between 35 and 45 years old. The age restriction was an attempt to ensure that the couples had ceased child bearing. Completed family size was regressed on husbands' full-time income, wives' full-time earnings, and husbands' years of schooling. Completed family size was negatively and significantly related to wives' full-time earnings confirming the hypothesis that a rise in the price of wives' time leads to a decline in the demand for children. Other cross-section and panel studies (Dooley 1982; Fleisher and Rhodes 1979; Moffitt 1984) support this conclusion. While Whittington (1992) and Whittington, Alm, and Peters (1990) find female wage rates have a negative effect on fertility (birthrate per 1000 women, aged 15 to 44 in the case of the latter study and the probability of giving birth in the former), in neither study are the effects uniformly statistically significant.

The general conclusion is that rising female wage rates continue to depress fertility among married couples. This wage rate effect, however, may have been weakening. The costs of post-secondary education and, perhaps also, the costs of purchased child day care have increased over the past two decades. If the demands for child care and post-secondary education are price inelastic as they are predicted to be, then the money costs of children will have increased, reducing the time-intensity of children, wt_n/π_n, relative to adult services, thereby weakening the negative wage effect on the demand for children.[10] Despite this potential weakening of the female wage effect, it is undoubtedly the case that rising female wage rates throughout the twentieth century are part of the explanation for the downward trend in fertility.

---

[10] A study of completed family size by Ermisch (1989) using British data shows that purchased child care is used by mothers with higher wage rates and that the effect of the mother's wage rate becomes less negative as wage rates rise. While not definitive, these results are consistent with the lessening negative wage rate effect in the United States.

The Effect of Changes in the Price of Children

Changes in female wage rates are complicated because they simultaneously change the prices of children and of adult services, as well as affecting full income. Changes in the cost of such items as post-secondary education or child day care, for instance, impact only the price of children and, hence, are more simply analyzed.

Suppose, initially, that the price of child goods, π_n, rises. For instance, suppose the cost of education rises. Education is regarded as a child good because most education expenses are made for children's education and not for parents' education. What effect might this have on the demand for children? This will lead to an unambiguous increase in the price of children, π_n, relative to adult services. The price effect is

$$\partial N^d / \partial \pi_n = (\partial n^d / \partial \pi_n)|_{u=c} - N(\partial n^d / \partial FY). \tag{7.15}$$

The effect of an increase in π_n is made up of conventional substitution and income effects as described in Chapter 3. The substitution effect of a rise in π_n will induce couples to substitute parental services for children, holding satisfaction constant, causing a decline in the demand for children. The income effect depends on whether children are a normal or an inferior good. So long as children are a normal good, the income effect will augment the substitution effect leading to a greater decline in the demand for children. If children are inferior goods, the income effect will dampen the negative substitution effect.

There are no empirical studies of the effect of changes in the price of children on fertility. Powerful indirect evidence, however, is available in the form of the effects of tax policy on fertility. The particular facet of tax policy at issue is the personal exemption for dependents that has been built into the federal income tax since 1917 (Whittington, Alm, and Peters 1990; Whittington 1992) and the much more recently enacted deduction for child day care expenses. A small change in the basic fertility model to incorporate a simplified version of the federal income tax makes the price-changing effect of exemptions quite clear.

Incorporating federal income taxes into the budget constraint represented by equation (7.5) involves recognizing that besides spending on child goods and parental goods, a couple must also pay federal income taxes, Tx; that is,

$$p_n X_n + p_s X_s + Tx = Y \tag{7.5a}$$

where

$$Tx = r(Y - EN) \tag{7.16}$$

and E = the exemption per dependent and r = federal income tax rate $(0 < r < 1)$. Substituting equations (7.2), (7.3), (7.4), (7.6), and (7.16) into (7.5a) and collecting terms results in

$$(\pi_n - rE)N + \pi_s S = (1 - r)wT + (1 - r)V \tag{7.5b}$$

where

$$\pi_n = p_n b_n + w^* t_n$$
$$\pi_s = p_s b_s + w^* t_s \tag{7.17}$$

and $w^* = (1 - r)w$.

Equation (7.5b) makes clear that the real or after-tax price of children is

$$\pi_n^* = \pi_n - rE \tag{7.18}$$

where π_n^* = the real or after-tax price of children. Equation (7.18) shows that the tax value of exemptions is the product of the tax rate and the size of the exemption per dependent.

Whittington et al. (1990) demonstrate that the tax value of exemptions has varied between 4 percent and 9 percent of the estimated monetary cost of raising a child from 1917 through 1984. Variations in r and E from time to time importantly affect the real price of children, therefore. The time-series analysis by Whittington et al. found that increases in the exemption for dependents, holding other factors constant, had a statistically significant positive impact on fertility (births per 1000 women, aged 15 to 44 years) over the 1913 to 1984 period in the United States, the elasticity of fertility with respect to the tax value of exemptions being between 0.13 and 0.25. This is strong indirect evidence of a negative own-price effect on fertility.

Deductions for child day care expenditures similarly affect the real price of children. If D represents per-child day care expenditures and π_n includes such expenditures, then modifying the budget constraint to include child day care deductibility results in

$$(\pi_n - rE - rD)N + \pi_s S = (1 - r)wT + (1 - r)V. \tag{7.5c}$$

Now

$$\pi_n^* = p_n - rE - rD \tag{7.19}$$

is the after-tax or real price of children. Again, equation (7.19) makes clear that deducting child day care costs constitutes a child subsidy and reduces the real price of children by $r\,D$. In a national longitudinal panel study of data from 1979 and 1983, Whittington (1992) found that an increase in the tax value of child day care deductions served to increase the probability that couples would give birth to an additional child. Again, this constitutes strong evidence of a negative own-price effect on fertility as well as the effect tax policies have on fertility.

Income Effects on Fertility

One of the most puzzling relationships with respect to fertility is that between fertility and family income. Regardless of the data set employed, there is a strong negative relationship between fertility or the number of children per family and family income. Does this mean that children are regarded by couples as inferior goods? This question has been given much attention by economists.

First, it is important to point out that a negative simple correlation between income and fertility (however, these two concepts are measured) is not evidence that children are inferior goods. Many other variables that also affect fertility are also correlated with income and these must be held constant if the income effect is to be uncovered. For instance and most important, family income includes wife's earnings. Thus, family income rises as the wife becomes employed and as her wage rate rises. The simple correlation between family income and fertility, therefore, includes a wage rate effect that, given the evidence of a negative wage effect, will make the income effect less positive if children are normal goods, and more negative if children are indeed inferior. In consequence, in most economic analyses of fertility, income is measured by asset income or as asset income plus husband's earnings and wife's wage rate is included as a separate variable. Note, here the inclusion of husband's earnings and wife's full-time earnings as separate variables in the Mincer (1963) study that first examined this issue empirically.

Second, it is well known that as family income rises, expenditures on children rise even if the number of children remains unchanged. For instance, the Olson (1983) study found that money expenditures on children rose $0.21 for each $1.00 increase in family income. This implies that couples derive satisfaction from more than just the number of children as our simple model specifies. Becker and Lewis (1974) postulate, instead, that couples derive satisfaction from "child services" which they argue includes not only the number of children but also the human capital invested in them. If so, then as family income rises, parents will demand more child services either by increasing the number of children they have or by increasing the human capital they invest in each. While "child services" may be a normal good, therefore, the number of children need not be.

Becker and Lewis formalized this hypothesis by defining child services, C, as the product of the number of children, N, and the human capital invested per child, Q; that is,

$$C = NQ. \tag{7.20}$$

This formulation assumes that couples practice equity in the amounts they invest in each of their children. Letting the price of child services be π_c, then the budget constraint of this more complex model of fertility is

$$\pi_c C + \pi_s S = Y \tag{7.21}$$

where the respective prices recognize the home production processes underlying C and S and are

$$\begin{aligned}\pi_c &= p_c b_c + wt_c \\ \pi_s &= p_s b_s + wt_s\end{aligned} \tag{7.22}$$

where p_c and p_s, respectively, represent the market prices of child and parental goods and services. b_c and t_c are, respectively, the amounts of purchased goods and services and female time required to produce one unit of child services. The purchased child goods and services include both the goods and services required to produce children, N, and the goods and services that constitute investments in child human capital, Q.

The couple's resources are represented by

$$FY = wT + V. \tag{7.23}$$

When combined with the altered utility function,

$$U = u(C, S, Z) \tag{7.1a}$$

the demands for child services and adult services become

$$\begin{aligned}C &= c^d \left(\pi_c, \pi_s, wT + V, Z\right) \\ S &= s^d \left(\pi_c, \pi_s, wT + V, Z\right).\end{aligned} \tag{7.24}$$

Now, consider the income effect on child services as represented by the income elasticity of demand. Based on equation (7.20), the income effect on child services is

$$\partial C / \partial V = Q \partial N / \partial V + N \partial Q / \partial V.$$

We differentiate by V instead of FY because FY includes the wage rate, which we need to hold constant. Converting the income effect into the income elasticity by multiplying by $V/C = V/NQ$ yields

$$\eta_c = \eta_n + \eta_q; \tag{7.25}$$

that is, the income elasticity of demand for child services is the sum of the income elasticities of demand for the number of children and the human capital investment in each.

The empirical evidence we have for the signs and sizes of these three income elasticities is quite inadequate but it suggests that children, N, are normal goods, but very weakly so, or are independent of income and that investments in children, Q, are also normal goods with an income elasticity larger than the income elasticity of demand for children (i.e., $\eta_q > \eta_n \geq 0$).[11] If so, then investments in human capital per child will rise with income, *ceteris paribus*, and do so more rapidly than the demand for children. Interestingly, this buttresses the negative correlation between family income and the number of children per family. The reason is that as investments per child rise more rapidly than the number of children as income rises, the price per child rises relative to the price of child human capital and so depresses further the demand for children.

To see this, consider the marginal conditions for an optimum when couples have preferences for both the number of children and for investment per child:

$$\begin{aligned} MU_n &= \lambda \pi_c Q \\ MU_q &= \lambda \pi_c N \end{aligned} \tag{7.26}$$

where MU_n and MU_q are, respectively, the marginal utilities of N and Q; $\pi_c Q = p_n$, the marginal price of child numbers; and, $\pi_c N = p_q$, the marginal price of investment per child. The marginal price of N relative to the marginal price of Q is, then, the ratio

$$p_n / p_q = \pi_c Q / \pi_c N = Q / N. \tag{7.27}$$

---

[11] Economists have assumed that $\eta_c > 0$ and that $\eta_q > \eta_n \geq 0$. See the first edition (Bryant 1990) for a lengthy manipulation of the extant empirical literature of the time that produces estimates of η_c, η_n, and η_q that accord with these assumptions.

Clearly, the relative price of children depends on the demands for children and for investments per child and, therefore, on income. Because both Q and N are normal and $\eta_q > \eta_n$, children become more expensive as income rises because parents will invest more in each. This induces couples to substitute investments in children for the number of children they bear and raise. High income couples, therefore, have fewer children than poor couples but invest more in each, yielding a negative correlation between family income and children per family. (See mathematical note 3.)

The fact that family income is positively correlated with female wage rates as well as the fact that the price of children rises with family income are two important reasons, then, why family income and numbers of children per family are negatively correlated. And, this arises despite the fact that the demand for children is normal or independent of income.

The Effect of Preference Shifters, Z

When we talk of preference shifters – the vector of Z variables in the utility function – we mean factors that change the shape of the indifference curves between children or child services and adult services and between the number of children and the investment per child. Of the host of factors that affect preferences with respect to fertility, two are chosen for brief discussion: education and religion. While age is a very important determinant of childbearing, it has more to do with the timing and spacing of children than it does with family size. Rindfuss, Morgan, and Offutt (1996) point out that despite the dramatic change in the age pattern of fertility in the past forty years (women, especially highly educated ones, have shifted from having their children in their early twenties to having them in their late twenties), the total fertility rate remained essentially constant at about 1.8 from 1973 through 1989.

Education. Education has at least three effects on fertility, one of them purely a preference effect. The other two are indirect effects of education that operate through female wage rates and because of marriage behavior, through family income.

We will deal with the preference effect first. It is hypothesized that highly educated women have a relative preference for highly educated children versus numbers of children in comparison with less-educated women. Presumably, more highly educated women have a better understanding of the benefits that being highly educated bestows and want the same or more for their children. Given any price of children relative to investments in children, p_n/p_q, then, in equilibrium more-educated women will opt to invest more per child and to have fewer children than less-educated ones. Thus, holding income and prices constant, completed family size will fall and the investment per child will increase as the education of the female rises.

The first of the indirect effects of education takes note of the high positive correlation between female education and female wage rates. Hence, the price of time of highly educated women is higher than that of the less educated. The time cost of children, therefore, is higher for more-educated women and, to the extent children are time intensive, more-educated women will substitute away from child services toward adult services. One of the important ways this substitution occurs is that highly educated women opt to spend more time in the labor market advancing their careers and delay childbearing until a later age than do less-educated women (Rindfuss, Morgan, and Offutt 1996). Delaying childbirth until a later age ensures that family income is higher and the couple is more able to afford the greater desired investment in children. Delaying childbirth until a later age also ensures that there is a shorter window during which the female is fecund, which in and of itself depresses fertility. This substitution away from children as female education rises will occur even if education did not affect preferences. It is not a preference effect, therefore.

The second of the indirect education effects on fertility arises because there is positive assortative mating with respect to education; that is, highly educated women tend to marry highly educated men and vice versa (see Chapter 8). Since highly educated men tend to have high incomes, women's education is positively correlated with family income independent of its effect on female wage rates. The effect of this is that women's education will have an indirect income effect independent of its preference effect or its wage effect. This income effect is identical to the income effect discussed in the previous section. As family income rises with women's education, the demand for investments per child will increase relative to the demand for child numbers, increasing the marginal price of children relative to child investments. This depresses the demand for completed family size even further.

Both the direct and indirect effects of rising female education work to depress fertility, therefore. Since female education rose throughout the twentieth century, the effects on fertility have been profound. The time series study of American fertility from 1913 through 1984 by Whittington et al. (1990) confirms this view: with male and asset income as well as other variables held constant, female education had a strong negative effect on fertility. Likewise, Lehrer (1996b), in her cross-section study of the effects of religion on fertility, controls for education. While not the focus of her study, she notes that higher levels of both wife's and husband's education at marriage depress fertility. Since she does not control for either wage rates or income, her education effects include all three effects discussed in a previous section.

Religion. In sociological terms, religions provide ideologies that determine the norms followed by adherents. Within Christianity, some denominations are more pro-natalist than others. Both Mormon and Roman Catholic ideologies contain strong pro-natalist positions. The proscription against the use of contraceptives by Catholic doctrine is well known. Some Protestant denominations are more pro-natalist than others. And, those ascribing to no religion have no given ideology with respect to family size. These norms with respect to family size are termed preference shifters by economists. More precisely, for any given price of children relative to other goods (i.e., child investments and parental services), couples who are members of denominations with more pro-natalist ideologies will choose to have more children than others.

So much for couples in which both spouses are of the same denomination (i.e., "homogamous" couples). If the spouses are of different denominations (i.e., "heterogamous"), the potential for conflict over desired family size is present. In a bargaining context, one would expect that compromise, if reached, would tend to be for a family size between the desires of the two spouses (see Thomson 1997 for a study of spouses' fertility desires and fertility). Homogamous couples, with no need for compromise, would likely, therefore, have more children than heterogamous couples except when the spouses belong to different yet pro-natalist denominations.

But there is more. Such conflict within heterogamous couples makes for increased marital instability and a heightened probability of divorce. Indeed, higher divorce rates among mixed-denomination couples relative to homogamous spouses are well documented (see Chapter 8). Given the greater likelihood of marital instability, a mixed-denomination couple may not wish to invest strongly in "spouse-specific" human capital. In such marriages, it is expected that spouses would be more likely to invest in their own human capital; human capital that can be taken from a marriage with fewer entanglements in the case of divorce. This strengthens the hypothesis that homogamous couples will have more children than heterogamous couples.

Lehrer (1996b) has studied the effects of religion extensively. She studied cross-section data from 1987–1988 of non-Hispanic, White couples who were married in 1960 or later. She classified families by whether both spouses were of the same denomination or were of different faiths. Holding other variables constant, she found mean family sizes to be

Both Spouses Mormon	3.29
Both Spouses Catholic	2.46
Both Spouses Exclusivist Protestant	2.20
Both Spouses Ecumenical Protestant	2.13
Both Spouses No Religion	2.11

In heterogamous couples for which one spouse was Mormon or Catholic and the other was not, mean family size was smaller than in homogamous Mormon or Catholic families, respectively. These results are consistent with the hypotheses. Clearly, religion is a powerful determinant of completed family size.

Contraceptive Knowledge, Use, and Cost

Knowledge of contraceptive techniques is viewed as an important determinant of fertility. In the absence of data on the extent of contraceptive knowledge and its effect on birth rates, women's education has been used as a proxy. The hypothesis is that along with education comes knowledge about the reproductive process and the varieties and characteristics of contraceptive methods. Hence, more-educated women will be more successful in matching their actual family size with their desires. Ryder and Westoff (1971, Table II-1) found that the difference between "expected" and "intended" family size narrowed with increased education of the woman. They hypothesized that "intended" family size indicates the plans women have made and, thus represents their demands for children and that "expected" family size represents a woman's realistic prediction as to what will happen and includes her estimate of unwanted children. Presumably, more highly educated women have more knowledge about the reproductive process and contraceptive options, use the knowledge, and so have fewer unwanted children than less-educated women.

But knowledge of contraceptive options is not the only issue. Contraception entails costs that are monetary, physical, psychological, and moral. These costs vary by type of contraceptive: some have high money prices, some are more inconvenient than others, some dampen sexual pleasure more than others, some have higher health risks than others, and some techniques, like abstinence and the rhythm method, are not proscribed by some religions. The moral issues raised by religion have already been discussed.

Contraceptives are used only when conception is not demanded. Hence, the costs incurred by contraceptive use are not incurred when conception is desired. That they are not incurred when conception is desired can be viewed as a *subsidy* for wanting children that reduces the cost per child. That is, the price of children can be phrased as

$$p_n = p_g - b(p_w u_o/u_w - p_o) \tag{7.28}$$

where p_g is the price of a child from conception to adulthood, $1/b$ the probability of conception without contraception, $p_i (i = w, o)$ the prices of intercourse with and without contraception, respectively, and $u_i (i = w, o)$ the marginal utilities of intercourse with and without intercourse respectively (see mathematical note 4).

The "subsidy" received by the couple from having unprotected intercourse when children are wanted is

$$b(p_w u_o/u_w - p_o). \tag{7.29}$$

The less fertile the couple (i.e., the larger the b), the more expensive the contraceptives (i.e., the higher the p_w), the more they enjoy unprotected intercourse relative to intercourse with contraception (i.e., the greater the marginal rate of substitution of unprotected sex relative to protected sex, u_o/u_w), and the cheaper the market price of the goods that are consumed with unprotected intercourse (i.e., the lower the p_o), the greater the subsidy and the lower the price of children.

Increased access to information about contraceptives and reductions in the price of contraceptives lower p_w, lower the subsidy, raise the price of children, and lead to a decline in demand for children. A reduction in moral sanctions against contraception and better knowledge of the health risks attached to contraceptive use increase u_o/u_w, raise the subsidy, lower the net price of children, and dampen the demand for children. Inconvenient or unpleasant features of contraceptive use increase u_o/u_w, increase the subsidy, lower the price of children, and increase the demand for children.

Whereas the subsidy for not using contraceptives discussed above is derived from a model of a married couple that may want children, most studies of contraception have targeted young, typically, single women. The factors the model highlights affecting the decision to have protected or unprotected sex, of course, are as relevant for single as for married females. The research shows that more than two thirds of young, single, pregnant women report their pregnancies to be unwanted or badly timed (Williams and Pratt 1990). Hypothesized factors affecting whether teens and young women use contraceptives include family background, mother's education, their anticipated levels of education, their desired occupations, and their labor market experiences. Kahn, Rindfuss, and Guilkey (1990) studied contraceptive choice among 15- to 24-year-old females who had premarital sex as teenagers. Nonuse of contraception at first sex fell as mother's education rose, was smaller for females from intact families, was largest for women who were fundamentalist Christians, and was larger for Black than White women. The probability of using condoms versus other contraceptive techniques rose with mother's education, was higher among females from intact families, and lowest among fundamentalist Christians. Kraft and Coverdill (1994) studied conceptive use among never-married, sexually active, 18- to 25-year-old females in 1983 who were not pregnant at time of interview between 1983 and 1985. They focused on the education and employment characteristics of the women in the belief that they help form the women's views of their life options. Contraceptive use was higher among females enrolled in school, those who were more highly educated, and who were employed longer in the past twenty-four months. Of those employed, the higher their wages, the higher the probability of contraceptive use, especially among Hispanic women.[12]

SUMMARY

The purpose of the chapter was to serve as an introduction to the economics of fertility. Three static models were developed and analyzed to exemplify economic thinking about fertility. The simplest focused on the decision as to the number of children, or completed family size, and the trade-offs couples make between children and the wife's employment. A second distinguished between desired child numbers and the desired investment per child. A third focused on the development of an expression for the price of children that highlighted the role that contraceptives play. Where possible, empirical work was discussed that related to the hypotheses developed from the models. The roles that female wage rates,

---

[12] The research on contraceptive use has been stimulated by the rise in nonmarital births from the 1960s to the 1990s noted at the beginning of the chapter. See Chapter 8 for a discussion of the other part of the puzzle; that is, why unmarried mothers have not married.

family income, and female education played in the trend toward smaller family size in the twentieth century were also discussed.

More economic and demographic literature on fertility was ignored than treated in this chapter. Among the important topics not treated were the timing and spacing of children, out-of-wedlock fertility, and abortion. The student interested in these topics would do well to start with the *Handbook of Population and Family Economics* (1997) edited by M. Rosenzweig and O. Stark.

Mathematical Notes

1. The type of household production function used in this chapter and exemplified by equations (7.2) and (7.3) is called the fixed coefficient or Leontief production function. Note that the marginal products of children with respect to child care time and child goods are $\partial N/\partial T_n = 1/t_n$ and $\partial N/\partial X_n = 1/b_n$, respectively. Since t_n and b_n are fixed coefficients, the marginal products do not change as input use changes. Thus, the marginal products equal the average products. Furthermore, the fixed coefficient nature of the production function implies that T_n and X_n are perfect complements and must be used in the same ratio; that is, $T_n/X_n = t_n/b_n$.

2. Differentiating equation (7.12) by w yields

$$\partial N^d/\partial w = (\partial n^d/\partial \pi_n)t_n + (\partial n^d/\partial \pi_s)t_s + (\partial n^d/\partial FY)T \tag{1}$$

where $FY = wT + V$, $\partial \pi_n/\partial w = t_n$, and $\partial \pi_s/\partial w = t_s$. Decomposing the price effects into substitution and income effects yields

$$\partial N^d/\partial w = [(\partial n^d/\partial \pi_n)|_{u=c} - N\partial n^d/\partial FY]t_n + [(\partial n^d/\partial \pi_s)|_{u=c}$$
$$- S\partial n^d/\partial FY]t_s + (\partial n^d/\partial FY)T. \tag{2}$$

Substituting in $N = T_n/t_n$, $S = T_s/t_s$, recognizing that $T = T_s + T_n + M$, and collecting terms yields

$$\partial n^d/\partial w = (\partial n^d/\partial \pi)|_{u=c} t_n + (\partial n^d/\partial \pi_s)|_{u=c}t_s + M\partial n^d/\partial FY.$$

But in a two-good model such as is posited,

$$\pi_n(\partial n^d/\partial \pi_n)|_{u=c} = -\pi_s(\partial n^d/\partial \pi_s)|_{u=c} \tag{3}$$

by Hicksian homogeneity. Therefore,

$$\partial N^d/\partial w = (t_n - \pi_n t_s/\pi_s)(\partial n^d/\partial \pi_n)|_{u=c} + M\partial n^d/\partial FY. \tag{4}$$

3. Form the Lagrangean expression from the preference function including child and parental services, equation (7.1a) and its analogous budget constraint (7.23):

$$Lg = u(C, S; Z) - \lambda[\pi_c NQ + \pi_s S - FY]. \tag{5}$$

Differentiating with respect to N and Q and setting the derivatives to zero yields

$$(\partial U/\partial C)(\partial C/\partial N) - \lambda \pi_c Q = 0$$

$$(\partial U/\partial C)(\partial C/\partial Q) - \lambda \pi_c N = 0.$$

Now, $(\partial U/\partial C)(\partial C/\partial N) = MU_n$ and $(\partial U/\partial C)(\partial C/\partial Q) = MU_q$, the marginal utilities of N and Q, respectively. $\pi_c Q = p_n$ and $\pi_c N = p_q$, the marginal prices of N and Q, respectively. Hence, equation (7.26). The price of child numbers relative to the price of investment per child is

$$p_n/p_q = \pi Q/\pi_c N = Q/N. \tag{6}$$

Clearly the relative price of child numbers depends solely on the demands for Q and N. Consider how the relative price of child numbers changes as income rises:

$$\partial(p_n/p_q)/\partial V = ((N\partial Q/\partial V) - (Q\partial N/\partial V))/N^2. \tag{7}$$

Multiplying equation (7) through by VN/Q expresses it in income elasticity terms; that is,

$$\eta_{(q/n)} = \eta_q - \eta_n. \tag{8}$$

Since $\eta_q > \eta_n \geq 0$, the price of children rises relative to the price of child investments as income increases.

4. The real price per child including the subsidy is derived as follows. Focusing on the expected number of children the couple want to have, let the couple derive satisfaction from intercourse without contraception, I_o, intercourse with contraception, I_w, children, N, and all other goods, A; that is,

$$U = u(I_w, I_o, N, A). \tag{9}$$

Suppose that the probability of conception without contraception is $1/b$. Then,

$$I_o/b = N \tag{10}$$

is the expected number of children resulting from unprotected intercourse. Contraception is assumed to be perfect for simplicity and, therefore, there is a zero probability of conception with protected intercourse. The budget constraint couples face is

$$p_o I_o + p_w I_w + p_g N + p_a A = Y \tag{11}$$

where p_o, p_w, p_g, and p_a are, respectively, the prices of intercourse without contraception, intercourse with contraception, children from conception to adulthood, and of all other goods. By the price of intercourse without contraception is meant the market prices of the goods required for intercourse without conception. By the price of intercourse with conception is meant the market price of the contraceptive plus the other goods required for intercourse. Clearly, $p_o < p_w$. The couple maximizes satisfaction as described in equation (9) subject to the budget constraint presented in equation (11). Substituting equation (10) into equations (9) and (11), and differentiating the Lagrangean expression,

$$Lg = u(I_w, bN, N, A) - \lambda[p_w I_w + (p_o b + p_g)N + p_a A - Y] \qquad (12)$$

with respect to N and A, and setting each derivative to zero, yields the equilibrium conditions:

$$u_w - \lambda p_w = 0 \qquad (13)$$

$$u_o b + u_n - \lambda(p_o b + p_g) = 0 \qquad (14)$$

$$u_a - \lambda p_a = 0 \qquad (15)$$

where $u_i (i = o, w, n, a)$ denotes the marginal utility of unprotected intercourse, protected intercourse, children, and all other goods, respectively, and λ = marginal utility of income. Solving equation (14) for u_n, substituting equation (13) into the right-hand side, and rearranging yields

$$u_n/\lambda = p_g - b(p_w u_o/u_w - p_o). \qquad (16)$$

Equation (7.37) says that when the couple is in equilibrium, the satisfaction they receive from an additional dollar spent "purchasing" a child, u_n/λ, must equal the price of an added child, where the price per child is

$$p_n = p_g - b(p_w u_o/u_w - p_o). \qquad (17)$$

The price of a child is made up of two components: p_g, the cost of a child from conception to adulthood, and

$$b(p_w u_o/u_w - p_o) \qquad (18)$$

the "subsidy" received by the couple from having unprotected intercourse when children are wanted.

EIGHT

The Economics of Marriage and Divorce

INTRODUCTION

Similar to the changes in fertility and household time allocation, demographers have noted significant shifts in marriage and divorce patterns over the past fifty years. In 1950, the marriage rate per 1000 population was 11.1 and the divorce rate per 1000 population was 2.6. The median age at first marriage was 22.8 for males and 20.3 for females. Sixty-eight percent (66%) of all adult males (females) were married in 1950 and only 2.0 percent (2.4%) were divorced. By 2001, the marriage rate per 1000 population had declined to 8.4 and the divorce rate had risen to 4.0. The median age at first marriage had climbed to 26.9 for males and 25.1 for females. Only 60.8 percent (57%) of all adult males (females) were married in 2002 while 8.6 percent (11.2%) were divorced (U.S. Bureau of the Census 2000b; 2003). Clearly, over the past fifty years marriage rates have declined and both age at first marriage and divorce rates have risen significantly.

Can economic theory help us understand why people marry and divorce and why patterns of marriage and divorce have changed over time? Economic theory is relevant as a (partial) explanation of marriage and divorce only if marriage and divorce can be viewed as economic activities over which the individuals involved have choice. As with fertility, if individuals have no choice over whether they are married or divorced, then economics is irrelevant. Individuals in most countries do have a choice over whether they marry, when and whom they marry, and whether they divorce. Thus, rational decision making with respect to marriage and divorce is possible.

For economics to be relevant, marriage and divorce must also affect individuals' satisfaction or well-being. Since marriage and divorce are preeminently affairs of the heart in this country today, saying that they affect individuals' well-being is almost tautological.

Finally, marriage and divorce must be costly for economics to be helpful in explaining these phenomena. We argue that marriage and divorce entail two kinds of costs: transaction costs and forgone costs. Transaction costs are the costs of marriage licenses, wedding ceremonies, lawyers' fees, court costs, and so on; that is, the costs of transacting the agreement to marry or divorce. Forgone costs are the benefits of the state that one gives up in order to reach another state. That is, the forgone costs of marriage are the benefits of being single that one forsakes in order to become married. Likewise, the forgone costs of divorce are the benefits of continuing the marriage. Although transaction costs can be substantial, it is likely that the forgone costs of marriage and divorce are greater.[1] Either way, marriage and divorce are costly.

Having established that economics may have relevance in the explanation of marriage and divorce, a simple model of the decision to marry will be built. The model will be built on the assumption that individuals act on the basis of their expectations about the future benefits and costs of marriage. Once built, the model will be used to draw inferences about the roles played by such factors as sex ratios, male and female wage rates, and tax policies in shaping marriage rates. Several empirical studies of marriage rates will be examined to see if the inferences are correct. Then a model of divorce will be discussed in which divorce is viewed as the reaction to failed marital expectations. Some empirical work that sheds light on the model of divorce is, then, discussed. The chapter ends with a discussion of the research that seeks to understand the puzzling rise in out-of-wedlock births because the prominent hypotheses focus on why single mothers do not marry prior to giving birth.

A MODEL OF MARRIAGE

There are two contending theoretical frameworks within economics that can be used to examine marriage. One, proposed by Becker (1973–1974), conceives of households as entities in which a single aggregate good is

[1] Furthermore, at least for marriage, it is frequently the parents of the principals that pay for much, if not all, of the monetary transaction costs. In the case of divorce, however, the couple pays the transaction costs.

home produced and consumed and which yields utility to its members. Two individuals (i.e., two single households) come together to form a married household if the income (broadly defined) of each when married is greater than the income of each when single. The other model, proposed principally by Manser and Brown (1980) and McElroy and Horney (1981), views marriage as the result of cooperative bargaining between the two partners.[2]

Empirically, there is little disagreement as to the major factors associated with marriage and divorce. At issue in the two models is the particular way the empirical associations between factors affecting marriage and divorce, on the one hand, and marriage and divorce rates or the likelihoods of marriage and divorce, on the other, are to be interpreted. The two theoretical perspectives allow somewhat different interpretations to be placed on some of the associations and stress different associations. In both frameworks, however, marriage is the result of rational decision making on the part of individuals who are seeking to make the best of their lives within the confines of the alternatives open to them. Seen in this light, the two contending theoretical perspectives reduce to variations on the same theme.[3]

It is the case that the theoretical perspective developed by Becker has been more articulated, its implications have been traced further, and more empirical work has been done based on it than upon the models developed by Manser and Brown and McElroy and Horney. Consequently, this chapter will use Becker's framework and, for the most part, neglect the other. Becker's framework has the additional advantage for us of employing many of the concepts already developed in this book.

A model of marriage begins with the idea that individuals will marry if they believe that they will be better off married than single. What is meant by this is that the individuals would be happier (i.e., have greater utility) married than single. Those individuals who remain single are those for whom marriage would not make them any better off. Most individuals would be better off married to any of several possible mates. Consequently, the individual must choose which of these people to marry. The

---

[2] In the bargaining model, two individuals "cooperatively bargain" to form a marriage when they maximize the product $U_f U_m$ of their respective utilities (where U_f = the female's utility when married and U_m = the male's) subject to the budget and time constraints and subject to the proviso that the marriage provides each mate at least as much satisfaction as each would have had by remaining single.

[3] Indeed, it can be shown that Becker's model is a special case "nested" within the more general cooperative bargaining model. See McElroy and Horney (1981) for details.

principle of satisfaction maximization implies that the individual confronted with several possible mates will marry the one who will make him or her "happiest" or "best off." The model formalizes these ideas by focusing on an individual's gain from marriage.

Let us focus on two individuals, denoted by M and F, and consider the gains each would obtain by remaining single and by marrying the other. These two individuals use their time along with purchased goods and services in a myriad of activities that yield satisfaction. These activities are household activities, possess all the characteristics of production, and range from preparing a meal, doing the laundry, and cleaning house to going to the theater, skiing, or sleeping. That is, they are engaged in household production (see Chapter 5). More significantly, when done with another person, the concept of household production also encompasses such activities as having, loving, and rearing children, and the host of other activities that require the time inputs of two people, typically of the opposite sex.

For the purposes of analysis we can aggregate the myriad of activities into one aggregate household activity. Denote the output of this single aggregate household activity over the individual's planning period as Z. We can write the relationship between time and purchased inputs, on the one hand, and the quantity of the aggregate household output, on the other, as

$$Z = z(H_m, H_f, X) \tag{8.1}$$

where $H_m =$ the time input over the planning period of individual M; $H_f =$ the time input over the planning period of individual F; and $X =$ the quantity of purchased inputs used in the single aggregate household activity. X includes both capital equipment like stoves, beds, and dishes and one-use goods and services like food, electricity, theater tickets, and baby-sitters' time.

Now, equation (8.1) has been specified as including the time inputs of both M and F. Clearly, this is correct only if M and F are married to each other. If each is single, then the time input of the other is zero. That is, the output of the household activity of F's single household would be

$$Z_f = z(H_m = 0, H_f, X). \tag{8.2}$$

And the output of M's single household would be what M could produce without F's time input; that is,

$$Z_m = z(H_m, H_f = 0, X). \tag{8.3}$$

Finally, the output of the household they would form if they married would be

$$Z_{mf} = z(H_m, H_f, X).\tag{8.4}$$

In this model, M and F each spend their time in two ways: in household activities, H_i ($i = m, f$), and in market work (i.e., "labor"), N_i ($i = f, m$), where H_i and N_i denote the times spent in household activities and in market work over the planning period, respectively. Thus, if T_i ($i = f, m$) denotes the length of the planning period, each individual's time use is bound by the constraint

$$T_i = H_i + N_i \qquad (i = f, m).\tag{8.5}$$

Each individual is assumed to work in the market some time during the planning period and to have some amount of unearned income, denoted by V_i ($i = f, m$). The individual's total income when single, then, is

$$Y_i = w_i N_i + V_i \qquad (i = f, m).\tag{8.6}$$

Of course, each individual seeks to maximize his or her own satisfaction over the planning period. Let the individual's utility be denoted as $U_i (i = m, f)$. It will be dependent on the output of household activities, Z_i, that is,

$$U_i = u_i(Z_i) \qquad (i = f, m)\tag{8.7}$$

where the greater the Z_i, the larger the U_i, that is, the happier the individual.

Thus, as a single household the individual seeks to maximize U_i over the planning horizon by allocating his or her time between household activity and market work and by using his or her income to buy inputs into household activities. This is no more and no less than the simple model of time use we developed in Chapter 5 and can be written mathematically as follows:

$$\begin{aligned}
&\text{Maximize } U_i = u_i(Z_i)\\
&\quad \text{subject to } T_i = H_i + N_i \quad \text{and} \quad pX + w_i H_i = w_i T_i + V_i\\
&\qquad \text{for } i = f, m.
\end{aligned}\tag{8.8}$$

However, in this case the individual is also faced with deciding whether to marry or to remain single.

Notice that the utility (i.e., the satisfaction) of each individual is a positive function of the quantity of output produced by the aggregate household production activity; the greater the quantity of Z, the more satisfied each individual. Recall that we are concerned only with whether an individual is more or less satisfied in any circumstance compared with any other and not by how much. Consequently, we know that if one situation results in more aggregate household output than another situation, the individual is more satisfied with the former situation. This means that we can neglect completely the individuals' utility functions from this point onward and concentrate on their respective outputs from household activity in married and single states.[4]

The Gains from Marriage

Given that we can neglect each individual's utility, the issue of whether any individual will marry depends on the answer to the following question: does the individual's output of Z when single exceed the individual's *share* of the output of Z when married? If the individual's single output, Z_i, exceeds the individual's share, call it S_i, of household output when married, then there is no incentive for individual i to marry. Why? Because, if $S_i < Z_i$, then the satisfaction i obtains from Z_i will exceed the satisfaction i obtains from S_i, i's share of marital output being smaller than i's single output.

Under what conditions will $Z_i > S_i$ and, therefore, marriage be preferred by individual i? First, marital output, Z_{mf}, must be at least equal to the sum of the two individuals' outputs when single:

$$Z_{mf} \geq Z_f + Z_m. \tag{8.9}$$

Why? Consider the case in which $Z_{mf} < Z_m + Z_f$. Now suppose that F's share of marital output with M exceeded her single output ($S_f > Z_f$), indicating that it would be in F's best interest to marry M. Since $Z_{mf} < Z_m + Z_f$, however, and $S_f > Z_f$, M's share of marital output with F would be less than his single output ($S_m < Z_m$) and M would have no incentive to

---

[4] Notice that this amounts to a lot of hand waving. By aggregating all household activities into one global activity on which individuals' well-being depends, the problem of making interpersonal utility comparisons is finessed. But every finesse comes at a cost. The cost in this case is the stringent conditions that must be met in order to aggregate all household activities into one global activity. Indeed, some economists count the cost too high and opt for alternative formulations (Manser and Brown 1979; McElroy and Horney 1981).

marry *F*. *F*'s love for *M* will go unrequited! Consequently, marital output must at least equal the sum of the couple's single outputs for marriage to be in the interest of both individuals.

Under what conditions, then, will marital output be at least equal to the sum of the individuals' single outputs and, thus, constitute a reason for marriage? Economists argue that there are a number of reasons why individuals might experience economic gains from marriage. For example, in some instances, spouses can provide an alternative source of credit or insurance when credit and/or insurance markets are imperfect.[5] But, the most commonly cited economic reasons for marital gains are (1) the sharing of household public goods, (2) specialization of function, and (3) economies of scale. These phenomena are experienced by virtually all couples who marry and thus we describe each in some detail.

Sharing Household Public Goods. A public good is any good the consumption of which by one person does not reduce the consumption of the same good by other people. The classic example of a public good is national defense: each person in society consumes it without altering the amount of national defense that is consumed by other people in society. Household public goods have the same nature but are restricted to the household. Two examples are children and housing. In each case, the utility derived by one spouse from children and housing does not reduce the utility derived from the same children and the same housing by the other spouse. That is, the mother's love of their children does not diminish the father's love of their children. Similarly, that a wife derives satisfaction from her living room does not diminish the satisfaction that her husband might derive from it.

Because household public goods are shared by spouses, each individual can be better off than s/he would be as single individuals. If single, each would be solely responsible for the purchase and use of these goods. It

---

[5] If credit markets are perfect, allowing individuals to borrow or lend at a fixed interest rate, each individual can invest in the optimal amount of human capital whether or not they are married. Similarly, if insurance markets are perfect, individuals can purchase policies at actuarially fair rates that would allow them to avoid the risk of lost labor income due to the onset of a disability or a spell of unemployment. In reality, both credit and insurance markets fall short on these counts. Spouses provide an alternative source of credit or insurance when these markets fail. That is, one spouse can increase his/her hours of paid employment to cover the income lost when the other spouse is temporarily unemployed, disabled, or going to school.

is certainly possible, for instance, for single individuals to have and rear children. No one denies, however, that child rearing is a more difficult endeavor for an individual than for a couple.

This can be illustrated as follows. Consider two individuals, $i = m, f$. Each derives utility from the consumption of a private good, c_i, and a public good, q. Thus, each has a utility function:

$$U_i = u_i(c_i, q) \qquad (i = m, f).^6 \qquad (8.10)$$

Suppose, too, that as singles each faces the budget constraint

$$c_i + q_i = y_i \qquad (i = m, f).^7 \qquad (8.11)$$

Suppose in equilibrium as singles they consume c_m^*, c_f^*, q_m^*, and q_f^* and in so doing attain u_m^* and u_f^* levels of satisfaction. Suppose, also, that $q_f^* \geq q_m^*.^8$

Now consider the two as a couple and assume that as a couple they face the joint budget constraint

$$c_f + c_m + q \leq y_f + y_m. \qquad (8.12)$$

Suppose further that as a couple they make decisions such that one spouse is made better off than as a single individual while the other is at least as well off married than as a single.[9] Thus, as a couple they can be conceived as maximizing

$$U_m = u_m(c_m, q) \qquad (8.13)$$

subject to budget constraint (8.12) and, also, subject to

$$U_f = u_f(c_f, q) \geq U_f^*. \qquad (8.14)$$

Because q is a household public good, q appears in the utility functions of both partners. Since c_m and c_f are private goods, each must be indexed by the spouse consuming them.

---

[6] q is not indexed by i because it is a household public good and, thus, capable of being shared.

[7] Prices can be ignored in this example. Thus, c_i and q are expenditures on the private and household public good, respectively.

[8] Note that the argument would not change if m consumed a greater amount of the public good as a single than f.

[9] When decisions are made such that one person is made better off while others are no worse off, the decisions are called Pareto efficient. The concept of Pareto efficiency lies at the base of most economic theories of marriage for it is difficult to conceive of a voluntary marriage occurring in which one of the partners is made worse off by the marriage. Such marriages very quickly end in divorce.

Now consider a particular allocation as a couple in which each consumes the same quantity of private goods they did as singles and they consume the quantity of the public good that f did as a single (i.e., $c_m = c_m^*$, $c_f = c_f^*$, and $q = q_f^*$). This makes f as well off married as single (i.e., equation [8.14] becomes an equality). Because $q_f^* \geq q_m^*$, by assumption, such an allocation makes m better off married than single. Finally, since $c_f^* + q_f^* = y_f$, then this allocation makes equation (8.12) an inequality; that is, this particular allocation does not exhaust their resources. With some resources not spent, the couple can consume more of some combination of c_m, c_f, and q, making them even better off. Thus,

$$U_{mf}^* \geq U_m^* + U_f^* \tag{8.15}$$

where U_{mf}^* is their utility as a couple. Household public goods, therefore, provide gains to marriage (see mathematical note 1).

Specialization of Function. An historically important benefit of the formation of families derives from the fact that spouses had different comparative advantages between household work and market work. In particular, females had a comparative advantage in household work relative to males while males had a comparative advantage in market work relative to females. Under these circumstances, a man and a woman could combine their efforts through marriage, each would specialize – he in market work, she in home work – and they would be better off than each could be single. Better off in terms of the total quantity of goods and services they could consume; better off, the greater the differences in the comparative advantages the two possessed. An example and a diagram illustrate the principle.

Suppose Bob can earn $5/hour in the labor market while he can produce $2 worth of goods per hour while working in the home. Suppose Sue can earn $3/hour in the labor market but she could also produce $6 worth of goods per hour working in the home. Thus, Bob's comparative advantage in market work relative to household work is $5/2 = 2.5/1$. In contrast, Sue's comparative advantage in market work is $3/6 = 0.5/1$. While Sue has a comparative advantage in household work relative to Bob, Bob has a comparative advantage in market work relative to Sue. It is her relative comparative advantage in household work that predisposes her to specialize in household work and his relative comparative advantage in market work that predisposes him to specialize in market work.

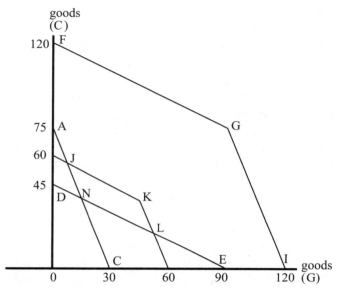

Figure 8.1. Married and single production possibility frontiers for two individuals.

Assume 9 hours per day are spent sleeping, leaving 15 hours for work – market and household. What are the possible ways in which Bob and Sue can each allocate their 15 hours of work time per day between the labor market and the home? How will these different allocations of time affect the quantities of home and market goods they can consume? How will this differ depending on whether they are singles or a couple? The table below gives what each could do per day if they specialized in market or home work:

	Bob	Sue	Total
Maximum Market Goods	15 × $5 = $75	15 × $3 = $45	$120
Maximum Home Goods	15 × $2 = $30	15 × $6 = $90	$120

These alternatives along with alternatives in which they each do some market work and some household work are illustrated in Figure 8.1.[10] Dollars per day of market goods are plotted on the vertical axis while dollars per day of home goods are plotted to the right along the horizontal axis. If Bob were to specialize completely in market work (i.e., 15 hours

[10] Figure 8.1 is an adaptation of Figure 3.1 in Blau, Ferber, and Winkler (2002).

per day), he could buy $5 \times 15 = \$75$ of market goods with his earnings (i.e., point A). Instead, if he were to spend all 15 hours per day specialized in home work, he could produce $2 \times 15 = \$30$ worth of home goods (i.e., point C). Line AC, then, represents all the possible combinations of market goods and home goods that Bob could have as a single by allocating his available 15 hours per day between market and home work. Likewise, line DE represents all the possible combinations of market and home goods Sue could have as a single by allocating her available 15 hours per day between market and home work. These lines are called production possibility curves. In particular, they are the production possibility curves for Bob and Sue should they remain single.

But what would the production possibility curve look like should they decide to become a couple? If Bob and Sue became a couple and both specialized in market work, they could have $\$75 + \$45 = \$120$ worth of market goods (i.e., point F). If both specialized in home work, they could have $\$30 + \$90 = \$120$ worth of home goods per day (i.e., point I). Should Bob specialize in market work and Sue in home work according to their respective relative comparative advantages, then they could have $75 of market goods and $90 worth of home goods (i.e., point G). Line segment FG represents the possible combinations of market and home goods should Bob specialize in market work and Sue does some market and some home work. Line segment GI represents the possible combinations of market and home goods if Sue specializes in home work and Bob does some market and some home work. FGI represents all the combinations of market and home goods possible if Bob and Sue become a couple and specialize either completely or incompletely in accordance with their relative comparative advantages. FGI, then, is the production possibility curve for the couple.

To see the benefits derived from becoming a couple and exploiting their respective relative comparative advantages – she for home work and he for market work – put the couple's production possibility curve on a per person basis by dividing by 2. This is represented by line $60K60$. Recall that AC represents Bob's production possibility curve while DE is Sue's. Note that if the couple behaves somewhere on the line segment JKL, which lies to the northwest of both AC and DE, they will have more market and home goods per person than if they each remained single. This is the benefit derived from specialization of function and division of labor in the household. Historically, it represented a powerful reason underlying family formation.

By experimenting with Figure 8.1 it will become clear that the benefits from specialization depend on the fact that Bob and Sue have different comparative advantages; the greater the differences in their comparative advantages, the greater the benefit. To see this, suppose the opposite: suppose that Bob's comparative advantage is identical to Sue's – 0.5:1. Both of their production possibility curves as singles would be represented by DE. The production possibility curve if they were a couple and put on a per-person basis would also be DE. If their comparative advantages were identical, then, there would be no benefits to be derived from the specialization as a couple.

While specialization has been historically potent in the United States, it has lessened considerably in recent years. How so? Historically, social norms dictated that girls were educated in the domestic arts and sciences while boys were prepared for market production. In part, social norms were in turn dictated by technology and the innate characteristics of males and females. Men were physically stronger and could expend the physical energy necessary to do the hard, physical work required in the labor market; women were able to bear and nurse children. The skills and other human capital each attained by adulthood, then, ensured that women were more productive in "housewifery" while men were more productive in market pursuits. Second, discrimination in the labor market restricted women to a few occupations and paid them less if they did find work in a male-dominated occupation. Occupational segregation and wage discrimination resulted in lower market wage rates for women than for men. Both forces – societal norms that led to sex-differentiated upbringing and sex-differentiated stocks of human capital as well as discrimination in the labor market – resulted in men possessing a relative comparative advantage for market work and women possessing a relative comparative advantage for home pursuits.

Throughout the twentieth century in the United States (and most other developed countries), occupational segregation and wage discrimination have lessened, the education of men and women have become more alike in type and quantity, and the upbringing of boys and girls has become more similar (see Chapter 6). Furthermore, the technical changes brought about by the industrial revolution made both market work and household work increasingly physically less demanding and more mentally demanding (Bryant 1986). All of these forces, therefore, have tended to equalize both the market and home productivities of men and women. With this equalization, then, came a lessening of gender-based comparative advantage and a corresponding decline in the marital benefits derived from it.[11,12]

Economies of Scale. Another reason for the formation of multiple person households, and families in particular, is economies of scale. This is the idea that two can live together cheaper than each can apart. Examples abound. Meals take about the same time to prepare and clean up whether for two people or one. Furthermore, food loss is less as family size rises. Laundry for two does not take double the time, soap, water, and electricity taken by laundry for one. Per person housing costs are reduced by doubling up – as any college student knows. Marriage, or any multiple person household for that matter, exploits economies of scale.

Economies of scale refers to a situation where output more than doubles when all the inputs that go into its production double. Thus, take the general production function

$$Z = z(X, t) \tag{8.16}$$

where $Z =$ output, $X =$ purchased inputs, and $t =$ householder time used in the production of Z. When both X and t are increased by a factor of k, economies of scale occur if output increases by more than k. Thus, if

$$z(kX, kt) > kZ \quad \text{for } k > 0 \tag{8.17}$$

then $z(kX, kt)$ exhibits economies of scale. For example, take the simple production function

$$Z = Xt. \tag{8.18}$$

Doubling X and t quadruples Z.

---

[11] Despite the lessening of the gender-based comparative advantage in household and labor market activities, Becker argues that women will continue to maintain some comparative advantage in household activities. He argues that because females, not males, carry and bear children and most mothers have an interest in nurturing them (and, remember, children are an important part of marital output, Z_{mf}), females have a biologically based comparative advantage for household activities.

[12] Our model illustrating comparative advantage and its benefits for marriage was a simple one in which there were only two activities: market and home work. In reality, there are a myriad of household activities ranging from child care and meal preparation through laundry, housecleaning, gardening, house, yard and car repair and maintenance, to shopping and family finance. Reality also suggests that spouses have different relative comparative advantages in these activities. As a result, there will be specialization among the household activities with the wife performing some of the activities and the husband others.

Let us use equation (8.18) to illustrate the gains to marriage (i.e., when two singles become a couple).[13] Suppose that equation (8.18) represents the household production function that either singles or couples use to transform purchased goods and their time into consumption commodities. For ease of exposition, t is expressed as a fraction of the time an individual has available to devote to home production. Thus, for any individual i, $0 \leq t_i \leq 1$. Individuals spend their time either working in the labor market or in home production. Thus,

$$t_i + n_i = 1 \tag{8.19}$$

where n_i = the fraction of time individual i spends in market work. Individual i's income, Y_i, arises from her labor earnings, $w_i n_i$, where $w_i =$ her hourly real wage rate.[14] Thus,

$$Y_i = w_i n_i. \tag{8.20}$$

Next, suppose that individual i spends all her income on purchased inputs, X. We ignore saving and debt, therefore. Thus,

$$X = w_i n_i = w_i (1 - t_i). \tag{8.21}$$

Finally suppose that the individual's utility is an increasing function of Z. If so, then utility can be ignored and we can concentrate only on maximizing Z subject to the time and budget constraint. Under such circumstances, individual i's production and consumption of commodities, Z_i^*, is

$$Z^* = w_i / 4. \tag{8.22}$$

In this example, each individual as a single spends half his/her time in home production, half in market work, earns $\$w_i/2$ of income and spends it all on X. As a result, each will consume $Z_i^* = \$w_i/4$ worth of commodities per period (see mathematical note 2).

What would be the case if these two individuals married? Suppose that they are perfect substitutes in home production; that is, they are equally productive in home activities. Then, the couple's home production function is

$$Z = X(t_m + t_f). \tag{8.23}$$

---

[13] What follows is an elaboration of an example used in Weiss (1997).
[14] By real wage rate is meant the wage rate deflated by the price of purchased goods, in this case X. Thus $w_i = w_i'/p$, where $p =$ price of X and $w_i' =$ nominal wage rate.

If each spouse's utility is simply his/her share of the couple's output of commodities, then the couple will seek to maximize Z. Family income is

$$Y = w_m(1 - t_m) + w_f(1 - t_f) \tag{8.24}$$

where $i = m$, f (m = male, f = female). As in each of the single households, the couple spends all of its income on purchased inputs. Thus,

$$X = w_m(1 - t_m) + w_f(1 - t_f). \tag{8.25}$$

Since they are perfect substitutes in home production, each individual will specialize either in market or home work: the one with the higher real wage rate in market work; the one with the lower real wage rate in home work. If $w_i > w_j$ ($ij = m$, f and $i \neq j$), then $t_i = 0$ and $t_j = 1$. The couple's optimal spending on X will be $w_i(1 - 0) + w_j(1 - 1)$, or

$$X^{**} = w_i \tag{8.26}$$

and the couple's optimal production of Z will be $Xt_j = w_i 1$, or

$$Z^{**} = w_i.{}^{15} \tag{8.27}$$

What, then, are the gains from becoming a couple in terms of economies of scale? Suppose, that the two individuals each command the same real wage rate (i.e., $w_i = w_j$). In this case the gains from marriage attributable to economies of scale, G, are

$$G = Z^{**} - Z_i^* - Z_j^* = .5w_i.{}^{16,\,17} \tag{8.28}$$

The Decision to Marry

The decision process to marry as conceived in Becker's theory of marriage, then, is as follows. Each individual identifies possible mates. Possible mates are those with whom the individual would be happier married than single. That is, they are the individuals with whom marital output,

---

[15] Compare X^{**}, t_j^{**} and Z^{**} with X^*, t_i^*, and Z^*. Note that X^{**} is double X^*, t_j^{**} is double t_i^*, and Z^{**} is quadruple Z_i^*.

[16] The gains, G, are measured as the couple's output, Z^{**}, minus each individual's output as a single, Z_i^*. Thus, $G = w_i - w_i/4 - w_j/4$. Since $w_i = w_j$, then $G = w_i(1 - .25 - .25) = 0.5w_i$.

[17] If $w_i > w_j$, then the gains from marriage are $G = (w_i - w_i/4) = (0.75w_i - 0.25w_j)$. These gains are the sum of the gains due to economies of scale and the gains from specialization. Since the gains from economies of scale are $0.5w_{i,}$, the gains from specialization must be $G_s = 0.25(w_i - w_j)$. The gains from specialization clearly increase as the difference between the individuals' real wage rates increase.

Z_{mf}, is at least equal to, if not greater than, the sum of their single outputs, $Z_m + Z_f$ and the individual's share of marital output, S_i, would in each case exceed his or her single output, Z_i. From this set of possible mates, the individual selects that mate to marry with whom his or her share of marital output would be the greatest.

This is an elaborate way of saying the following. Ken has Sally, Abby, Beth, Cathy, and Danielle as friends. Through the many social occasions in which he interacts with them he finds he likes Sally, Abby, and Beth much more than either Cathy or Danielle. The former three share his interests and are as romantically interested in him as he is in them. He is not romantically interested in either Cathy or Danielle. They are just good friends. In other words marriage with Sally, Abby, or Beth would produce marital outputs greater than the sums of his single output with each of theirs. The marital outputs if married to either Cathy or Danielle would not equal the sum of his single output with each of theirs. Furthermore, he would be happier married to any of the three women than if he remained single. That is, he estimates that his share of marital output if married to Sally, Abby, or Beth would exceed his single output. Sally, Abby, and Beth, then, are possible mates of Ken and he is a possible mate for each of them.

Through further interaction with the three women, Ken and Abby "fall in love" and decide to marry. In terms of Becker's model of marriage, Ken gets to know the three women well enough (and they him) that Ken determines that he would be happier with Abby than with either Sally or Beth. Happier here means that he estimates that his share of marital output with Abby would be higher than if he married either of the other two women. Thus, marriage with Abby would maximize his satisfaction.

Now each of the women goes through the same process. Each has a set of possible mates and within that set a particular mate with whom she would be happiest if they were married. In Abby's case, this is Ken. Thus, through marriage Abby's and Ken's shares of total marital output are greater than in any other marriage.

To summarize: according to the economic model of marriage, an individual will marry if three conditions are met. First, total output from the marriage must equal or exceed the sum of the single outputs of the two partners. That is, $Z_{mf} \geq Z_m + Z_f$. This will occur when the couple shares household public goods, engages in specialization of function, and/or capitalizes on economies of scale. Second, each individual's share of marital output must equal or exceed his or her single output, which in turn implies that

$$S_m + S_f \le Z_{mf}.^{18} \qquad (8.29)$$

Finally, since individuals are assumed to maximize satisfaction, each individual enters into that marriage in which his or her share of marital output is greatest compared with the shares from other possible marriages.

IMPLICATIONS OF THE MODEL

There are a number of implications of Becker's theory of marriage. We will pursue only two of them, leaving the other implications to your own reading. The implications we will pursue will be those that help explain variations in marriage rates through time and within local populations.

The Ratio of Males to Females

In the discussion of Becker's marriage model, it was implicitly assumed that there were equal numbers of males and females and that the gain from marriage was positive for each person. Therefore, everyone was married and no one was single. But this is not a very accurate picture of the world as we know it. Women outnumber men[19] and there are individuals for whom marriage is inferior to remaining single. Thus, the percentage of males or females married will never be 100 percent and it will vary through time and geographically. Can we use the theory to begin to understand why? We do this by deriving what amounts to supply and demand curves for mates.

Recall that the shares of marital output, S_m and S_f, must sum to total marital output, Z_{mf}. Recall also that an individual will not marry unless his or her share of marital output is at least equal to his or her single output. That is, an individual will not marry unless he or she is at least as happy married as single. We can regard an individual's single output, Z_i, as the individual's *reservation price of marriage*, therefore. That is, Z_i is the minimum share of marital output individual i will accept in order to

---

[18] The marital shares will sum to marital output in the absence of any transaction costs of marriage. Otherwise, the marital shares will sum to marital output net of transaction costs.

[19] Women outnumber men primarily because of the higher mortality rate among men. For instance, the U.S. Bureau of the Census (2003) projects that in 2005, there will be 97,164,000 women age 16 to 64 as compared with 96,475,000 men age 16 to 64 in the United States.

be married rather than single. If

$$S_i = Z_i \quad \text{for } i = m, f \tag{8.30}$$

individual i will be indifferent between being married and single. So long as

$$S_i > Z_i \quad \text{for } i = m, f \tag{8.31}$$

individual i will be married. Thus, Z_i is individual i's reservation price of marriage.

Now suppose we know the single outputs, Z_{mi}, for each male in the country or geographic region at time t, where there are $i = 1, \ldots, N_m$ males. Now rank the males by their single outputs so that Z_{m1} is the single output of the male with the lowest single output and Z_{mN} is the single output of the male with the highest single output. Prepare a diagram with single output and marital share measured on the vertical axis. The number of males is measured on the horizontal axis ranked so that the males closest to the vertical axis are those with the lowest Z_i's while those farthest to the right from the vertical axis are those with the highest Z_i's. Finally, plot the Z_i for each individual so ranked along the horizontal axis.

Such a diagram is illustrated in Figure 8.2. In Figure 8.2 the vertical line $N_m N_m$ represents the total number, N_m, of males in the country. Z_{m1} is the single output of the male in the country with the lowest single output. Z_{mN} is the single output of the male in the country with the highest single output. The line $Z_{m1} A$ represents the cumulative distribution of males with respect to their single outputs, Z_{mi}. At any point, X, on line $Z_{m1} A$, N_{mx} males have single outputs equal to or less than Z_{mx}. Put differently, at point X, N_{mx} males would marry if each could have a marital share from their respective marriages at least equal to Z_{mx}.[20] N_{mx}, therefore, is the "supply of male mates" at the "price" of Z_{mx}. Likewise, there is a zero supply of male mates at a price of Z_{m1}, and there is a supply of N_m male mates (i.e., all the males in the country) if females "paid" a price of at least Z_{mN}. The curve $Z_{m1} A$, therefore, is the supply curve of male mates. This can also be thought of as the minimum share asked for by males if they are to marry.

---

[20] Actually the N_{m-1} males with single outputs below Z_{mx} would marry because each of them would receive Z_{mx} as his marital share, which would exceed his single output. The N_{mx}^{th} male would be indifferent between marriage and remaining single because Z_{mx} would equal his single output.

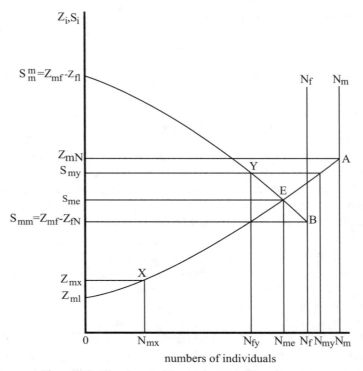

Figure 8.2. The demand for and supply of male mates.

What about the females' demand curve for male mates? As with males, females will not marry unless their shares of marital outputs are at least as large as their single outputs. Thus, the supply of female mates to the marriage market can be derived in exactly the same fashion as the supply of male mates. That is, if women are ranked from the woman with the lowest single output to the woman with the highest, then Z_{f1} is the single output of the woman with the lowest single output and Z_{fN} is the single output of the woman with the highest single output. A curve similar to $Z_{m1}A$ in Figure 8.2 representing the supply curve of female mates could, thus, be drawn.

However, we are interested in the demand curve for male mates on the part of females, not their supply curve. It happens that we can derive the demand for male mates from the supply of female mates. Recall that the sum of the marital shares equal marital output:

$$Z_{mf} = S_m + S_f. \tag{8.32}$$

Alternatively, we can say that the male's share of marital output is equal to marital output minus the female's share; that is,

$$S_m = Z_{mf} - S_f. \tag{8.33}$$

Now assume for geometric simplicity that marital output is constant across marriages.[21] Then by subtracting the minimum single output for females, Z_{f1}, from marital output, Z_{mf}, one obtains the maximum marital share, S_m^m, a male could obtain if married to the woman with the lowest marital share; that is, her single output. Thus,

$$S_m^m = Z_{mf} - Z_{f1}. \tag{8.34}$$

In other words, no woman could be found who would consent to marry if her husband's marital share was larger than S_m^m. Since in such a marriage she would receive Z_{f1} or lower, she would prefer to remain single and have Z_{f1}. S_m^m, therefore, is the highest price any woman will pay for a male mate. This point is plotted on the vertical axis in Figure 8.2 and constitutes the vertical intercept of the demand for male mates.

Similarly, we can subtract the single output of the woman with the greatest single output, Z_{fn}, from marital output, Z_{mf}, to obtain the minimum marital share any male could obtain; that is,

$$S_{mm} = Z_{mf} - Z_{fN}. \tag{8.35}$$

Recall that Z_{fN} is the minimum marital share that the woman with the maximum single output would accept if she were to marry: all other women would accept less than Z_{fN}. Consequently, all women would marry if each of their marital shares equaled Z_{fN}. S_{mm}, therefore, can be viewed as the price of male mates that would induce all women to marry. If a vertical line, $N_f N_f$, is erected in Figure 8.2 indicating the number of females in the country or region, then point B on $N_f N_f$ represents S_{mm}. Note that the number of females, N_f, need not equal the number of males, N_m. In the case pictured in Figure 8.2, $N_f < N_m$.

Since females have been ranked from the woman with the lowest Z_f to the woman with the highest Z_f, other points in Figure 8.2 can be found by plotting

$$S_m = Z_{mf} - Z_{fi} \quad \text{for } i = 1, \ldots, N_f$$

---

[21] The qualitative conclusions from the demand curve derived using this simplification are the same if Z_{mf} varies among marriages.

against the number of women, N_{fi}, with single output equal to or less than Z_{fi}. The line formed by these points is $S_m^m B$ in Figure 8.2. It represents the demand curve of male mates in the marriage market. It can also be thought of as the maximum marital share females are willing to offer if they are to marry.

Point Y on the demand curve for male mates by women is interpreted as follows: N_{fy} females are willing and able to pay S_{my} in order to have mates. N_{fy}, then, is the number of male mates demanded by females in the marriage market at the price of S_{my}. Recall that N_{fy} females are willing to pay S_{my} for mates in the sense that each of these females requires a marital share at least equal to Z_{fy} in order to be willing to marry. With given marital output, at most S_{my} would remain for the marital share of each of their mates.

Figure 8.2, then, is a diagram of the supply and demand curves for male mates. Their intersection notes the equilibrium where the supply of male mates (i.e., the minimum marital share asked by males) equals the demand for male mates (i.e., the maximum marital share offered by females). We could have drawn the supply and demand curves for female mates but the diagram would be symmetrical with Figure 8.2 since one is but a reflection of the other.

Now, consider again point Y. At a price of S_{my}, females demand N_{fy} male mates (i.e., N_{fy} females are willing to marry). But, at $S_{my} = Z_{my}$, N_{my} males are willing to marry. In other words, at a price of S_{my} there is an excess of willing males over willing females. If all the N_{my} willing males are to be married, they must accept lower marital shares than S_{my}. Only some will, however, and they will be the ones with single outputs lower than S_{my} and, thus, require lower marital shares than S_{my}. They will marry women willing to pay lower prices for male mates (i.e., women who have higher single outputs and, hence, require higher marital shares in order to marry).

The willingness of some men to accept a marital share of less than S_{my} will induce more women than N_{fy} to marry. The lower marital share offered by women will reduce the number of men willing to marry. Marriage market "equilibrium" will occur at point E in Figure 8.2. Point E represents the price at which the number of females demanding males equals the number of males willing to marry. N_{me}, therefore, will be the number of married couples. N_{me}/N_m is the fraction of males who are married, and N_{me}/N_f is the fraction of females who are married.

Figure 8.2 shows the marriage market when the number of females is less than the number of males, $N_f < N_m$. What would happen if the

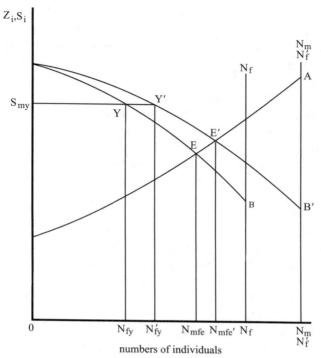

Figure 8.3. The effect of an increase in females on the demand for male mates and the number married.

number of females increased for some reason so that males equaled females?[22] This is shown in Figure 8.3. Supply curve A and demand curve B and their intersection at E represent the situation in the marriage market in which males exceed females.

Now suppose there is an exogenous increase in the number of females in the country or region so that after the increase $N_m = N_f$. What effects will there be on the demand curve of male mates? So long as the added females are similar to the females previously in the market (i.e., so long

---

[22] This would happen, for instance, if medical research reduced female-specific diseases by more than male-specific diseases; say, if breast and uterine cancers were reduced but prostate cancer was not. An exogenous increase in the number of women did occur in colonial French Canada when, in response to the dearth of women in the colony, the French authorities recruited French women willing to emigrate to Canada and marry there (McInnis 1959, p. 54). Today, advertising and publicity achieve the same end. Currently, there is an excess of men in Alaska, and a magazine published in Anchorage and entitled *Alaska Men* advertises the marriage virtues of men in Alaska (see www.alaskamen.com).

as the cumulative distribution of additional females with respect to Z_f is similar to that for the original females), then the demand curve for male mates will shift upward from curve B to curve B'. In other words, at any price, S_{my}, more females will be willing to marry and, hence, demand more males than before the increase in the number of females ($N'_{fy} > N_{fy}$). Likewise, given the increased demand for male mates as a result of the increase in females, the demand curve will intersect the (unchanged) supply curve at E' rather than at E and there will be more married couples, $N'_{mfe} > N_{mfe}$. Finally, notice that as the number of females in the population increases relative to men, the fraction of men married increases from N_{mfe}/N_m to N'_{mfe}/N_m and the fraction of married females falls from N_{mfe}/N_f to N'_{mfe}/N'_f.[23]

The sex ratio of the population (N_m/N_f or its inverse), then, is an important determinant of marital status. The more men there are relative to women, the higher the probability any women has of finding a mate and, therefore, the higher the fraction of females who will be married. Likewise, the more women there are relative to men, the more likely it will be that any man will find a mate and the higher the fraction of men who will be married.

The relationship between the sex ratio and the proportion married has long been observed by demographers and economists. Early work by Fredricka Santos (1972) used interstate data on females aged 15 to 44 years for 1950 and 1960, and found that a *ceteris paribus* increase in the sex ratio N_f/N_m by 1 percent induced an increase in the fraction of single females by about 0.05 in both 1950 and 1960. More recently, Michael Brien (1997) estimates that among White women, ages 20 to 34, an increase in the state-specific male-to-female sex ratio from 1.0 to 1.05 translates into a 4.1 percent increase in the odds of marrying in that state, holding other factors constant. A number of other studies have found similar positive effects (Lichter, LeClere, and McLaughlin 1991; Lichter, McLaughlin, Kephart, and Landry 1992; Lichter, Anderson, and Hayward 1995; Loughran 2002).

Analysis of sex ratio effects has also been useful in helping us to understand the growing differences in Black and White marriage rates in the United States. In 1940, 61.8 percent of all Black women and 69.8 percent

---

[23] The fall in the fraction of females married as the number of females in the population increases occurs so long as the supply curve of male mates is positively sloped. When the supply curve is positively sloped, $N'_{mfe} - N_{mfe} < N'_f - N_f$ and, in consequence, the fraction of females married will fall.

of all White women between the ages of 24 and 29 were married. By 1985 to 1987, these percentages were 31.8 percent and 61.5 percent, respectively (Mare and Winship, 1991). This represents a 12 percent decline in the fraction of White women who were married and a 48.5 percent decline in the fraction of Black women who were married in the 24 to 29 age range. William Julius Wilson and Kathryn Neckerman (1986) proposed that this widening racial gap in marriage rates is a direct result of the decline in "marriageable" Black males in this country. That is, they hypothesized that it is not the sex ratio *per se* that matters. Rather, it is the ratio of the number of Black (White) men who are employed (or who have annual incomes above the poverty threshold) to the number of Black (White) women that impacts the marriage rates (i.e., the ratio of marriageable men to women). Tests of Wilson and Nekerman's hypothesis have been moderately supported (Brien 1997; Lichter, LeClere, and McLaughlin 1991; Wood 1995). For example, Robert Wood (1995) finds that the decline in the number of higher-earning Black males relative to the number of Black females between 1970 and 1980 explains between 7 percent and 10 percent of the drop in Black female marriage rates during that decade.

Changes in Wage Rates

To investigate the implications of changes in wage rates for marriage markets, we must revisit the concept of comparative advantage and gains from specialization of function within the family. In Figure 8.4 we again depict the situation of Bob and Sue. Recall that AC denotes the production possibilities for Bob should he remain single while DE denotes the production possibilities for Sue should she remain single. As before, Bob's comparative advantage is in market work while Sue's comparative advantage is in home production. FGI reflects the production possibility frontier should Sue and Bob marry. The area within $JKLN$ represents the range of per capita gains in output that can occur if Sue and Bob marry.

Now suppose Bob's market wage rate increases from \$5.00/hour to \$7.00/hour. Holding everything else constant, this wage increase will shift Bob's production possibility frontier from AC to $A'C$ if he remains single. If Bob and Sue marry, their joint production possibility frontier becomes $F'G'I$ and the range of per capita gains in output are now represented by $J'K'L'N'$. The gain in per capita output is clearly positive suggesting that the benefits attributable to the specialization of function within marriage have grown, thus making marriage more attractive. On an aggregate level, if men have a comparative advantage in market work, then this graph

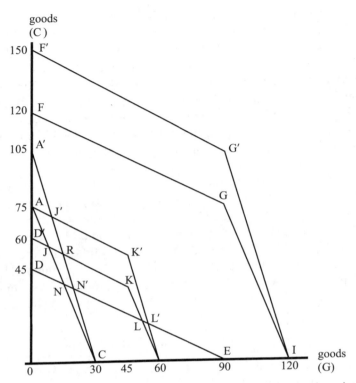

Figure 8.4. The effects of an increase in the male's market wage on the gains from marriage.

suggests that as the average male wage rate rises, with average female wage rates constant, the gains from marriage will increase. In turn, this will precipitate an outward shift in the females' demand curve for male mates and an increase in the fractions of men and women who marry, *ceteris paribus*.

What happens if there's an increase in the market wage rate paid to women? Turn again to the example of Bob and Sue. Figure 8.5 is identical to the production possibility frontiers drawn in Figure 8.4 except now Sue's market wage rate has increased from $3.00/hour to $4.00/hour, *ceteris paribus*. This wage rate increase is represented by the shift of ED to ED: With a wage of $3.00/hour, the range of potential per capita gains from Sue and Bob marrying are represented again by *JKLN*. But, if Sue's wage increases to $4.00/hour, the range of per capita gains from marriage will be *JKL'N'*. Since *JKLN > JKL'N'*, the per capita benefits of

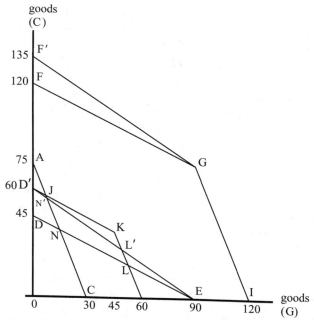

Figure 8.5. The effects of an increase in the female's market wage on the gains from marriage.

marriage attributable to specialization of function have fallen with this wage increase. This happens because a rise in Sue's wage rate increases her output as a single individual and it reduces her comparative advantage in household production. In the extreme case, if Sue's market wage rose to $5.00/hour – making it the same as Bob's market wage – then the gains from marriage attributable to specialization of function would fall to zero. Thus, in the aggregate, a rise in female wages will shift the demand for male mates inward and reduce the fractions of men and women who marry, *ceteris paribus*.

Do the data support the theory? Researchers have typically found statistically significant positive relationships between male wage rates in a local labor market and the proportion of women who are married (Blau, Kahn, and Waldfogel 2000; Lichter, LeClere, and McLaughlin 1991; Schultz 1994). Similarly, they have found statistically significant negative relationships between female wage rates in a local labor market and the proportion of women who are married (Lichter, LeClere, and McLaughlin 1991; Loughran 2002; Schultz 1994; Wood 1995). Some researchers have expanded their tests of the marriage model by examining how average wages *and* the distribution of wages in an area affect the propensity to marry. For instance, David Loughran (2002) estimates that between 1970 and 1990, between 7 percent and 18 percent of the overall decline in marriage rates for White females is attributable to rising male wage inequality in the United States. His results, consistent with the theory, suggest that both the level and the variation in male wages affect the proportion of women who are married in a local area.

The relationship between wage rates and marriage probabilities has also been examined in the context of federal income tax policy. Alm and Whittington (1996) estimate that in the 1990s, approximately 60 percent of married couples paid more in federal income taxes than they would have paid if they had remained single.[24] The increase in the marginal federal income tax rate faced by the majority of married couples has two effects that work in opposition to one another. First, the marriage tax penalty lowers the after-tax wage rate of the secondary (i.e., marginal) earner – typically the wife. The wage effect induced by this change in the after-tax wage increases the potential gains from specialization of function within the marriage and thus raises the expected benefits of marrying. Second, the marriage tax creates an income effect by increasing the total taxes paid by the couple which in turn reduces their after-tax income and lowers the benefits of marrying. Whittington and Alm (2003) provide an extensive review of the relevant empirical literature and conclude that, on balance, the income effect modestly outweighs the wage effect. That is, the average marriage tax has a small, negative effect on the marriage rate. For instance, Alm and Whittington (1995) estimate that a 1 percent increase in the marriage tax translates into a 0.05 percent decline in the married population.

The arguments made here with respect to changes in relative male and female wage rates are predicated on the assumption that males have a comparative advantage in market work and females have a comparative advantage in household activities, that is $w_f/g_f < w_m/g_m$. If the reverse were the case, then the predicted wage rate effects would be reversed.

---

[24] The couples facing a marriage tax penalty are typically those in which both spouses work outside of the home. Alm and Whittington (1996) also report that another 30 percent of married couples paid less in federal income taxes than they would have paid if they had remained single. These are typically couples where one spouse works outside of the home and the other does not. The remaining 10 percent paid approximately the same amount in federal taxes whether they filed as a married couple or as single individuals.

Costs of Marriage

In Becker's theory the most prominent cost of being married is the forgone benefit to be gained from remaining single. But this is not the only cost. Other costs impinge on the decision to be married also. We will consider the extent to which marriage is revocable; that is, the ease of getting a divorce once married.

Included in the calculation that rational individuals make in deciding whether to marry is the cost of dissolving a marriage should it turn out to be less than desired. Such a cost was not included in the gain from marriage discussed earlier because the model assumed that the decision was made in the presence of perfect certainty. That is, the individuals knew with certainty how the marriage was going to turn out. Of course, that is a caricature of reality. In truth, people can never be certain how marriage will turn out. Consequently, the ease or difficulty of dissolving a marriage once made does moderate the gains from marriage: the more difficult is divorce, the lower the gains from marriage and the more likely the individual will remain single.

As an example, consider the role of religious faith. It is well known that different religious faiths hold different views on whether marriage is revocable. Although it is fair to say that no religious faith common in the United States holds that divorce is an insignificant matter, there is great variance in beliefs regarding divorce. They range from the Roman Catholic belief that regards marriage as well-nigh irrevocable to the belief of some other faiths and the posture taken by most states that divorce is a necessary institution that dissolves bad and destructive marriages. Roman Catholics, therefore, in comparison with people of other faiths would be somewhat less likely to marry, because the extremely high cost of divorce would discourage some from becoming married in the first place. Early work by Santos (1972) and Freidan (1974) found that the higher the percentage of Roman Catholics in the state, the lower the proportion of married females. Recently, Lehrer (2004) used data from the 1995 National Survey of Family Growth to examine the relationship between religious affiliation and marital timing. Again, consistent with the theory, she found that being a member of the Catholic faith led to a statistically significant delay in first marriage for women, *ceteris paribus*. Catholic women had a 5 percent probability of being married by age 20 in her study. This is in sharp contrast to the 9 percent probability of being married by age 20 for mainline Protestant women and the 17 percent predicted probability for conservative Protestant women.

A MODEL OF DIVORCE

The model of marriage presented earlier in this chapter was phrased as if there were perfect certainty. People knew with certainty what it was going to be like married to each of their potential partners, knew with certainty what it was going to be like remaining single, and could calculate the gain from marriage based on this knowledge.

Of course, reality is not like that. People must make forecasts of what marriage with potential partners and remaining single will be like and these forecasts will be made with considerable uncertainty and so, consequently, will people's estimates of the net gain from marriage. Since divorce dissolves marriages that have not worked, the discrepancy between the actual and the expected gain from any marriage is an important part of the explanation for divorce.

The model of marriage laid out in the first part of this chapter also assumed that people identify and get to know potential mates costlessly and without effort, when, in fact, searching for a mate is a costly business (in terms of time, money, and emotional energy). Costly search reduces the net gain from marriage, inducing some people to remain single and others to enter less attractive marriages than they would have, had search costs been zero. Given that the net gain from marriage will be smaller the higher the search costs, there will be a smaller margin for error in choosing a mate. With large expected (i.e., forecasted prior to marriage) gains from marriage, actual gains can be much lower before becoming negative. Search costs reduce this cushion by reducing expected net gains. Search costs, therefore, also figure prominently in any explanation of divorce.

Marriage can thus be likened to an implicit contractual agreement between spouses based on each spouse's expectations as to how the marriage will turn out. To the extent that the expectations are not met, the implicit contract is broken. If the reality departs from expectations sufficiently, then divorce ensues.

What constitutes departing from expectations "sufficiently"? If the actual output from a marriage falls below the sum of the outputs of the two partners if they become divorced or, alternatively, falls below the sum of the expected marital shares of the two partners if married to other people, then the marriage fails and divorce ensues.

There are circumstances, however, where this condition is not present yet the marital share of one of the partners is below his or her single output or is below his or her expected marital share if married to someone else.

Such an individual wants a divorce whereas his or her partner does not. This implies that the other partner has captured most of the benefits of marriage, leaving too little for the other one. In these circumstances the marriage contract can be renegotiated so as to increase the marital share of the partner with too little and reduce the marital share of the one with too much, and divorce can be forestalled. Such bargaining must be more frequent than one might think given that the profession of marriage counseling has arisen to facilitate negotiations between partners. While negotiation is possible, it can be defeated if negotiation costs are high or if one of the partners is obdurate.[25]

Clearly, divorce is more likely the smaller the initial net expected gain from marriage. Given the uncertainty surrounding marriage, actual gains can depart widely (larger or smaller) from what is expected. The lower the expected gain from marriage, the more likely the actual gain will be less than zero, and the higher the probability of divorce. Furthermore, the greater the uncertainty, the wider the distribution of actual net gains around the expected net gains (i.e., the larger the variance in actual net gains), the more likely the actual net gain will fall below zero, and, again, the higher the probability of divorce.

These hypotheses can be illustrated diagrammatically. Consider the panels in Figure 8.6. Panels A and B picture the distribution of possible gains from different kinds of marriage. Along the horizontal axis of each panel is plotted the possible gains from the two types of marriage: A and B. Marriage A could be, for instance, between two people with equal amounts of education whereas marriage B might be between two people with differing amounts of education. In each case, the marriages could be "made in heaven," and the gains from the marriages would be infinitely large, or they might be "made in hell," with the gains not just negative but infinitely negative. Up the vertical axis is plotted the frequency with which the gains occur in each type of marriage.

The location and spread of the bell-shaped curve in each panel describes the frequency with which marriages with each of the possible net gains occur. In both cases, marriages made in heaven and in hell are most infrequent, and consequently, the bell-shaped curves rest on or very near the horizontal axis at these extremes. In both cases marriages with positive net gains are most frequent, and thus, the bell-shaped curves

---

[25] See Peters (1986) for an elaboration of this argument and empirical evidence bearing on it.

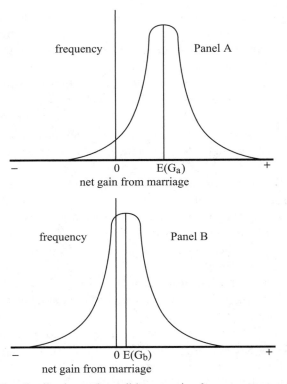

Figure 8.6. The distributions of possible net gains from two types of marriages, each with the same variance but with different expected net gains.

peak in the positive quadrant. But marriages between partners with equal education more frequently have positive net gains than marriages with wide divergences in the partners' educations, and in consequence, the bell-shaped curve in panel A peaks farther to the right than the one in panel B. The average marriage between equally educated partners has a net gain of $E(G_a)$. $E(G_a)$ is the "expected net gain" from marriages of type A. Likewise, $E(G_b)$ is the "expected net gain" from marriages of type B. The locations of the distribution peaks describe the expected net gains from the two types of marriages.

Now, we have argued that an important determinant of whether two people marry is whether they expect the net gain from marriage to be positive. Thus, the higher the expected net gain from marriage, the more likely it is two people marry. Given that they marry, however, the net gain they actually experience is unlikely to be $E(G)$ but something else,

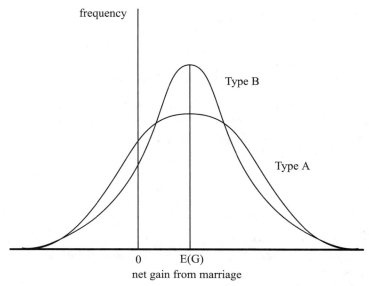

Figure 8.7. The distributions of possible net gains from two types of marriages, each with the same expected net gains but with different variances.

either higher or lower. The bell-shaped curves show only the likelihoods of different outcomes not the actual outcome. What is clear from the diagrams is that the smaller the expected net gains, the more likely it is that the actual net gain from the marriage will be negative. This is shown by the area under the bell-shaped curve lying to the left of zero; the greater the area under the curve to the left of zero, the more likely the actual gain from the marriage will be negative. Thus, Figure 8.6 illustrates the hypothesis that it is more likely that marriage between partners with widely disparate levels of education will end in divorce than ones between partners with equal educations because the expected net gain of the latter is greater than the former.

Figure 8.7 illustrates the point that the greater the uncertainty about the net gain from marriage, the higher the probability of divorce. In Figure 8.7 the shape of the distribution of net gains from marriage represents the extent of the uncertainty. Here, the distributions of possible outcomes for two types of marriage are plotted on the same graph. Both types of marriage, type A and type B, have the same expected net gain, $E(G)$. But the dispersion of possible outcomes (i.e., the variance) is far wider in the case of type A than for type B. Again, the area under the curve to the left of zero represents the likelihood of divorce. Here, type A

has the greater variance in net gains and, therefore, the greater likelihood of divorce.

We can formalize these hypotheses algebraically as follows:

$$P\{D\} = d[E(G), Var(G)] \tag{8.36}$$

where $P\{D\} = $ the probability of divorce, $E(G) = $ initial expected net gain from marriage, and $Var(G) = $ variance of actual net gains around the expected net gain from marriage. As $E(G)$ increases or $Var(G)$ decreases, the probability of divorce will decrease:

$$\partial P\{D\}/\partial E(G) < 0 \tag{8.37}$$

$$\partial P\{D\}/\partial Var(G) > 0. \tag{8.38}$$

Search costs play a role by depressing the net gain from marriage. In consequence, the higher the search costs, the lower the expected gain from marriage:

$$\partial E(G)/\partial C_s < 0 \tag{8.39}$$

where C_s search costs.

Search costs also increase the variance in actual net gains from marriage around the expected net gain. The greater the search costs, the less search will be undertaken: fewer potential mates will be identified and less will be known about each. Greater search costs increase uncertainty, therefore, and increase the variance of actual net gains from marriage around the expected net gains. Thus,

$$\partial Var(G)/\partial C_s > 0. \tag{8.40}$$

One of the strongest correlates of divorce is age at first marriage: the younger the age, the higher the probability of divorce (Lehrer 1996a; Michael 1988; Ressler and Waters 2000). People who marry young have not searched much, perhaps because they have a very high preference for marriage or because they face high search costs. For whatever reason, their search has not been extensive, the uncertainty about the gains from marriage is high, and the probability of divorce is likewise high.

More generally, under what circumstances will the expected gains from marriage be low and/or the variance in actual gains high, thus raising the probability of divorce? To find out we have to return to the theory of marriage and discuss positive and negative assortative mating.

Positive and Negative Assortative Mating and Divorce

Positive assortative mating is the tendency of people with similar traits to marry. Negative assortative mating is the tendency of people with opposite traits to marry.

Without saying so, we have already discussed negative assortative mating when we discussed the implications of comparative advantage for marriage. That is, the greatest gains from marriage occur when, holding other things constant, individuals with a great comparative advantage in market activities marry individuals with a great comparative advantage in household activities. Thus, the gains from marriage are greater when individuals with high market productivities (i.e., wage rates) marry individuals with low market productivities.

In general, negative assortative mating increases the gains from marriage in productive activities because the principle of comparative advantage will induce specialization of function and make married output larger than otherwise. This means we would expect negative assortative mating to occur with respect to traits that affect people's productivities in market and household activities; for instance, wage rates, labor market experience, and child-rearing abilities.

Given that men's wage rates are typically higher than women's wage rates, if negative assortative mating occurs with regard to production traits, we would expect that an increase in the husband's wage would be associated with a lower probability of divorce because it translates into increased gains from production specialization in marriage holding the level of uncertainty constant (i.e., the $\mathrm{Var}(G)$ in equation [8.36]). In contrast, a *ceteris paribus* increase in the wife's wage would reduce the gains from specialization of function within marriage and thus it would be associated with a higher probability of divorce. These hypotheses are generally confirmed in the empirical literature. That is, researchers consistently find a negative relationship between men's earning capacity and the likelihood of divorce (Hoffman and Duncan 1995; Michael 1988; Ressler and Waters 2000; Weiss and Willis 1997) and a positive relationship between women's earning capacity and the likelihood of divorce (Michael 1988; Ressler and Waters 2000; Weiss and Willis 1997).

Positive assortative mating increases the gains from marriage in consumption activities. Married couples tend to engage in consumption activities together rather than separately. People with similar educational levels, religious preferences, intelligence, and ages will tend to have similar outlooks on life, and thus similar consumption preferences. They will

tend to like the same consumption activities (including the same public goods) and their shared participation in these activities will increase
their total enjoyment by creating positive externalities in consumption.[26]
For instance, spouses may gain greater enjoyment from going out to eat
together rather than eating out alone. In short, people with similar traits
are *complements* of each other in consumption activities, and thus, positive assortative mating with respect to these traits will increase the gains
from marriage.

It is thus more likely that people with similar educational backgrounds,
religious preferences, ages, and so on will marry, because such marriages
will tend to maximize marital gains. Furthermore, because of the great
expected gains from marriage, such marriages will be less likely to dissolve
in divorce due to subsequent divergences between actual and expected
gains. In contrast, marriages between people with unlike consumption
traits will tend to have smaller expected gains from marriage and a greater
likelihood that the actual gains will be zero for any given amount of
uncertainty. For this reason, marriages between people with dissimilar
consumption traits will be more likely to dissolve than those between
people with similar traits.

Empirical work supports the hypothesis that people with similar consumption traits will tend to marry and be less likely to divorce once married. Weiss and Willis (1997) use data from the National Longitudinal
Study of the High School Class of 1972 to examine how complementarity in consumption traits affects the likelihood of divorce. Their analysis
reveals that couples who have similar education levels, religions, or ethnic-
ities have significantly lower probabilities of divorce. Taking the opposite
approach, Lehrer (1996a) looks at dissimilarities in religion and finds that
White couples in a first marriage have a 2.06 greater risk of divorcing during the first five years of marriage if the husband and wife are of different
religions than do couples where the husband and wife are of the same
religion, *ceteris paribus*.

Marriage-Specific Human Capital and Divorce

The final influence affecting the gains from marriage and their uncertainty that we will discuss has to do with marriage-specific human capital. Marriage-specific human capital refers to human capital investments

---

[26] For an analysis of the extent to which spouses share household activities see Bryant and
Wang (1990b).

made by individuals after they are married that increase the net gains from marriage. Two types of such investments are discussed: duration of the marriage and children.

As marriages are lived, couples gain experience in the marriage and the experience augments the net gains from marriage. When a couple is first married, the partners know relatively little about each other and how to work and play together in ways that make the marriage more meaningful. As time goes on, however, couples learn a great deal about how to make the marriage work. In the language of economics, experience in the marriage augments the human capital of the partners, raising their productivities in the marriage.

This human capital is marriage specific in two senses. First, it can be specific to marriage as opposed to single status in that couples learn ways to behave that make being married more fulfilling than being single. Second, it can be specific to "this" marriage in that the partners learn more and more about how to live with and enjoy marriage to their particular partner. The first kind of experience leads people to benefit more from being married than from being single. The second type of experience leads people to benefit more from their current marriage than either from being single or from being married to someone else.

Given that experience in the marriage adds to the human capital of the partners, the likelihood of becoming divorced, therefore, can be expected to fall the longer the duration of marriage. This relationship is a common one found in divorce studies. Becker and colleagues (1977) estimate that other things held constant, the likelihood of becoming divorced fell from 0.04 for White men or women married less than 5 years to 0.02 for those married 15 to 20 years in 1967.

Children are also very important types of marriage-specific human capital. As public goods within the household, children increase the net gain to the marriage and thus the probability of divorce should fall as the number of children born into a family rises.

The above point, however, refers to *desired* children and not to *unanticipated* children. Unanticipated children, like any other unanticipated occurrence in a marriage, tend to break the marriage contract that was based on a set of expectations. Thus, unanticipated children reduce the net gain from marriage and lead to higher divorce rates. It is well to remember, however, that unanticipated children can be "positive" or "negative" in the sense that a couple may desire two children and have either fewer than or more than two. Consequently, having fewer children than desired may be just as destabilizing to the marriage as having too many children.

The timing of children is crucial to the relationship, however. Couples not only want a certain number of children but also plan when to have them. Having more children than planned early in the marriage may not be very destabilizing because planned family size may have been achieved, just faster than anticipated. Similarly, too few children early in the marriage can always be rectified later in the marriage provided the couple is fertile.[27] Having unplanned children late in the marriage will be more destabilizing simply because the mistake cannot be rectified.

The relationship between the number of children in the marriage and the likelihood of divorce, therefore, should be somewhat U- or J-shaped: the probability of divorce should first fall and then rise as the number of children in the family increases. Furthermore, the number of children at which the probability of divorce begins to rise should be lower the longer the marriage.

Becker and colleagues (1977) present evidence confirming these hypotheses. They find, for instance, that the probability of divorce in the second five years of marriage among White women falls from 6 percent if there were no children born in the first five years to 2.8 percent if there were two children and to 2.4 percent if there were three children born. If there were four children in the first five years of marriage, however, the divorce probability rises again to 2.8 percent. Furthermore, a fourth child born in the second five years of marriage is somewhat more destabilizing to the marriage than a fourth child born in the first five years of marriage.

Children are also an excellent example of marriage-specific human capital that is specific to the marriage into which they are born. That is, the marriage-specific human capital embodied in children does not transfer well to subsequent marriages. This point is demonstrated by Weiss and Willis (1997) who find that the presence of a child from a prior relationship significantly increases the risk of divorce in comparison to those unions for which there are no children from a prior relationship present in the home.

In general, couples whose expected gains from marriage are low and/or who have greater uncertainty about their expected gains are predicted to make fewer marriage-specific human capital investments. That is, they are less likely to learn about their spouse's preferences and habits, they may see fewer benefits to be gained from working through conflicts, and,

---

[27] Of course, other strategies, like adoption, surrogate mothers, or artificial insemination, can also be utilized to rectify too few children early in the marriage if it is caused by the infertility of either or both of the partners.

most important, they may be less inclined to have children. This latter contention is supported by Becker and colleagues' (1977) empirical work. They show that couples who differ in race or education (traits that when shared by both spouses are generally believed to enhance consumption complementarity), generally have fewer children than do couples who are of the same race or who have similar educations. In some sense, then, one can argue that this becomes a self-fulfilling prophecy. That is, couples who have low expected gains from marriage or who have greater uncertainty about their gains invest less in post-marriage human capital. In turn, their lower marriage-specific human capital investments exacerbate their risk of divorce.

MARRIAGE AND OUT-OF-WEDLOCK BIRTHS

The trends in out-of-wedlock births have been reviewed in Chapter 7. They include a dramatic rise in the out-of-wedlock birth rate during the 1960s through to the mid-1990s after which they leveled off. This rise has become an important social problem. Because the majority (about 80 percent in 2001) of these births are to teenage mothers, much of the concern over out-of-wedlock births has focused on the teenage birth rate. Scholars have sought to explain the rise in the out-of wedlock birth rate from the 1960s to the mid-1990s and the teenage birth rate, especially its fall during the 1990s. Since out-of-wedlock births are as much a marriage matter as they are a fertility matter, the scholarly as well as the policy focus has been on marriage as well as on sexual activity, contraception, pregnancy, and abortion. The literature on each is extensive and, if justice were done to it, the discussion would fill an entire book. Consequently, this section will survey only the major hypotheses that attempt to account for the trends and do so only briefly. The hypotheses deal either with out-of-wedlock birth rates or teenage birth rates in particular and deal with demographic factors, economic including policy factors, and socio-cultural change factors.

The demographic facts of out-of-wedlock births are well known. Out-of-wedlock births are demographically driven by birth rates and the number of unmarried women. Teenage birth rates and out-of-wedlock birth rates vary systematically by age, race/ethnicity, and education. Black and Hispanic women have higher birth rates and out-of-wedlock birth rates than White women. By age, birth rates rise with age through about age 29 and decline thereafter. Birth rates fall with women's education and marriage is delayed by women with more education. Out-of-wedlock birth rates are much more concentrated at younger ages. Fewer Blacks and Hispanics marry than White women and marriage rates increase with age. Changes in the marital, age, education, and race/ethnicity composition in the population from the 1960s to the present could account for the observed trends. Studies of teenage fertility from 1980 to date show that while changes in the demographic composition of women have occurred, they account for only a very small proportion of the changes in the teenage birth rate over the period (Manlove, Gitelson, Papillo, and Russel 2000; Lopoo, McLanahan, and Garfinkel 2004).

There are several economic hypotheses that have been put forward. The first is that welfare and child support policies have been important in influencing out-of-wedlock birth rates. Welfare benefits (Aid to Families with Dependent Children [AFDC] and its replacement, Temporary Assistance to Needy Families [TANF]) provide financial support to poor, unmarried women who have children and, therefore, lower the cost of having children to unmarried women, especially teenagers. It is hypothesized that the lowered cost acts as an incentive for unmarried women either to be more sexually active, fail to use contraceptives, fail to resort to abortion if pregnant, or not to become married once pregnant. This hypothesis was first raised by Murray (1984). It also may reduce the responsibility felt by fathers either to marry the mothers of their children or to provide child support in lieu of marriage. This aspect of the hypothesis was formalized by Akerlof, Yellen, and Katz (1996). AFDC benefit levels rose through the 1960s to the mid-1970s and fell thereafter until the program was replaced by TANF in 1996. Lopoo, McLanahan, and Garfinkel (2004) quote Congress to the effect that a motivating force for replacing AFDC with TANF was to reduce out-of-wedlock births.

On the basis of a statistical analysis of longitudinal panel data from 1968 through 1985, Duncan and Hoffman (1990) find the effect of AFDC benefit levels on Black teenage out-of-wedlock birth rates to be positive but statistically insignificant. Similarly, in a study of Black nonmarital fertility in large cities in 1980, South and Lloyd (1992) find the effect of AFDC benefit levels to be weak and inconsistent across age categories. These results are typical of studies utilizing data before the 1990s when out-of-wedlock births began to stabilize and decline. These studies are uniform in finding weak evidence that welfare benefit levels had much if any effect out-of-wedlock and teenage birth rates. Studies of the question utilizing data since 1990, however, conclude that AFDC/TANF benefits, which fell throughout the 1990s were responsible for an important fraction of the decline in teenage birth rates. Lopoo, McLanahan, and Garfinkel (2004) summarize the literature on this question and analyze state-level panel data from 1990 to 1999. Holding other factors constant, they conclude that declines in AFDC/TANF benefits are responsible for an important fraction of the decline in teenage birth rates from 1990 to 1999. Clearly, the more recent studies contradict the earlier studies. More research needs to be done to resolve the question. But, it is entirely possible that both are correct. In the social environment prior to 1990, welfare benefit levels may not have been important. But, in the face of the large declines in benefits levels during the 1990s and the replacement of AFDC with the less forgiving TANF program, welfare benefit levels and restrictions may have become more important.

Child support enforcement policies put in place in the 1990s, through which the paternity of out-of-wedlock births is established and the fathers are required to pay child support, are also hypothesized to influence out-of-wedlock birth rates. The hypothesis here is that such policies act as a disincentive to males to be sexually active. Whether fathers of children conceived out of wedlock marry the mothers, they are still responsible for child support under the new child support enforcement legislation. This raises the cost to males of being sexually active and lowers the cost to men of marriage to the mothers of their children. The same policies, however, can be seen by females as lowering the cost of children and, hence, increasing out-of-wedlock birth rates. Lopoo, McLanahan, and Garfinkel (2004) have investigated this hypothesis with the 1900 to 1999 state-level data panel and have found strong support for the hypothesis that child support enforcement regulations put in place in the 1990s are responsible for some of the decline in teenage birth rates.

A third economic hypothesis is that women faced with a marriage market replete with men with poor economic prospects will refuse to marry and opt to bear children out of wedlock. This hypothesis was first put forward to explain the lower marriage rates and higher unmarried birth rates among Blacks (Wilson 1987; Wilson and Neckerman 1986). Faced with severe discrimination in the labor market and with lower education levels, Black men's unemployment rates are high and, in consequence, they make less attractive marriage partners. Furthermore, the far higher incarceration rate of young Black males removes many from the marriage pool. The analogue to this hypothesis is that improving labor markets for women, in which female wage rates increased and jobs not previously open to females became available, lowered the cost to women of remaining unmarried and having children out-of-wedlock. Presumably, this set of forces would be felt more by White women than Black or Hispanic women for whom labor market conditions have improved more slowly.

While there is some empirical support for the Wilson hypothesis, it is believed that it has played a more minor role in explaining nonmarital birth rates. For instance, Duncan and Hoffman (1990) find that the higher were Black teenage women's economic prospects in the absence of bearing children, the lower was the Black teenage birth rate, *ceteris paribus*. In contrast, South and Lloyd's cross-sectional study of nonmarital birth rates by city in 1980 finds contrary results. Finally, Lopoo, McLanahan, and Garfinkel (2004) find that unemployment rates above 6.2 percent induce higher teenage birth rates, a finding consistent with the Wilson hypothesis. Unemployment rates below 6.2 percent, however, induce lower teenage birth rates. Neither of the measures of income opportunities for males and females used by Lopoo, McLanahan, and Garfinkel were related to teen birth rates. Each of these studies use different variables to measure the attractiveness of marriage (the supply of marriageable men and the income opportunities of women) and study different data sets. The results are inconclusive at best. Clearly research needs to be done using a common set of definitions and data sets.

Akerlof, Yellen, and Katz (1996) note that neither Murray's welfare benefits argument nor Wilson's supply of marriageable males argument can fully explain the rise in the out-of-wedlock birth rate from the 1960s to the end of the 1980s. They postulate bargaining models in which easy and legal access to female contraception beginning in the early 1960s and the legalization and increased access to abortion in the early 1970s caused an increase in nonmarital sexual activity (some of it unprotected), an increase in the incidence of pregnancy, a less than one-for-one increase in the incidence of abortion, and a sharp decline in the incidence of shotgun marriages. They argue that these factors, along with a lessening of the stigma attached to bearing out-of-wedlock children, fed the dramatic increases in nonmarital birth and teenage birthrates.

Akerlof, Yellen, and Katz liken easy, effective female contraception and the legalization of abortion to technical change because they have "shifted out the frontier of available choices" open to women (Akerlof, Yellen, and Katz 1996, p. 279). While female contraception and abortion have expanded the choices open to women, they are also similar to technical change in that there are winners and losers. The argument is as follows.

Those women who do not want children and will reliably contracept (or will abort if pregnancy occurs) have no need to exact an implicit or explicit promise of marriage from their partners should pregnancy occur. Those women who want children and will not contracept or abort for moral reasons, and those who are only sporadic users of contraceptives, will find it difficult to extract an implicit or explicit promise to marry from their partners if they become pregnant. The reason is that they compete in the same market for partners as those who have no need to elicit implicit or explicit marriage promises and because of the new "technology" this drastically reduces their ability to bargain. In a market in which males wishing to have sexual relations now have alternatives that do not require a promise of marriage, they no longer need to agree implicitly or explicitly to marriage if pregnancy results or they can, without cost, break the promise. Women, who in the past were protected by the promise of marriage, hence will be pressured to have sexual relations without such guarantees. In the language of the market, they have been put at a competitive disadvantage. Women who agree to sexual relations and contracept sporadically or do not contracept on moral or religious grounds and who also refuse to abort, lose. They bear out-of-wedlock children and bear the financial and social responsibility for their rearing. Because they are primarily very young and poorly educated, out-of-wedlock motherhood lowers their income opportunities even further.

It is also the case while female contraception and legalized abortion have given to women the physical choice of having children, they have also led to making the decision to marry the choice of men (Akerlof, Yellen, and Katz 1996, p. 281). That is, the decision that women make whether to contracept or to terminate a pregnancy affects her partner's decision whether to marry in the event of pregnancy and whether to shoulder any financial or social responsibility in the rearing of such children.

Finally, they argue that the legalization and easy access to female contraception and abortion has reduced the stigma of out-of-wedlock births. This is a preference shifting effect whereas the previous effects were price effects or competitive market effects.[28] Akerlof, Yellen, and Katz (1996, p. 310) note that the high school completion rates of pregnant girls was 19 percent in 1958 and at 56 percent in 1986, and that a 1972 federal law made it illegal for schools to expel pregnant girls.

---

[28] See Bryant (1986) for an analysis of technical change and the family that decomposes technical change effects into income and price effects.

In such an environment, Akerlof, Yellen, and Katz (1996) argue that shotgun marriages will decline and out-of-wedlock birth rates will rise so long as the incidence of abortion does not increase one for one with the increase in nonmarital pregnancies. They present evidence that the timing of the legalization and easy access to female contraception and the legalization of abortion roughly coincides with the dramatic up-turn in out-of-wedlock births and the decline in shotgun marriages (i.e., marriages that occur within seven months prior to the birth of the baby).

The indifferent success in confirming the variety of extant hypotheses as to the cause(s) of out-of-wedlock births as powerful forces over the entire approximately forty-five-year period from the late 1950s onward means that much more research needs to be done. What is likely is that no single set of causes operated both to greatly increase the out-of-wedlock birth rate from the late 1950s to the early 1990s and then to stabilize it or make it fall. Entirely likely, in our view, is that the effects of the legalization and easy access of female contraception and abortion along with the accompanying reduction in the stigma of out-of-wedlock pregnancy benefitted most women but may have made losers out of a sufficient minority of women, most of them young and poorly educated with few alternatives, to cause the out-of-wedlock birth rate to sky rocket. In such an environment, welfare programs and weak or absent child support policies may have been relatively passive facilitators to the increase. The continual decline in AFDC benefits after the mid-1970s, the institution of the much more penurious TANF program in 1996, and the institution of much more severe child support regulations in the 1990s may have exerted enough pressure to cause the out-of wedlock birth rate to level off and begin to decline beginning in the early 1990s. The merits of such a hypothesis can only be determined with much more research.

SUMMARY

Marriage and divorce are economic events in the sense that economics provides insights into their trends as well as the probabilities of marriage and divorce that individuals of given characteristics face. Economic variables play important roles in determining marriage and divorce. Furthermore, interpretations of the well-known relationships between marriage and divorce, on the one hand, and variables commonly not thought of as economic variables, on the other, like number of children, religious preference, and education, have great economic content.

Mathematical Notes

1. As an example (taken from Weiss [1997]), consider the utility function

$$u_i = c_i q \quad (i = m, f). \tag{1}$$

As a single, individual i ($i = m, f$) maximizes equation (1) subject to

$$c_i + q_i = y_i \tag{2}$$

and the resulting equilibrium values of c_i, q_i, and U_i are $c_i^* = y_i/2$, $q_i^* = y_i/2$, and $U_i^* = y_i^2/4$. As a couple, consider them maximizing

$$U_m = c_m q \tag{3}$$

subject to

$$c_m + c_f + q \leq y_m + y_f \tag{4}$$

and

$$U_f^* = c_f q \geq y_f^2/4. \tag{5}$$

Setting equation (5) as an equality and substituting equation (5) into equation (4), one can form the Lagrangean

$$Lg = c_m q + \lambda \left[y_m + y_f - c_m - \left(y_f^2/4q \right) - q \right]. \tag{6}$$

The first order conditions are

$$q - \lambda = 0 \tag{7}$$

$$c_m - \lambda + \lambda 4 y_f^2/(4q)^2 = 0. \tag{8}$$

Solving equations (7), (8), and (4) for q^{**} yields

$$q^{**} = y/2 \tag{9}$$

where $y = y_m + y_f$,

$$c_m^{**} = \left(y^2 - y_f^2 \right)/2y \tag{10}$$

and

$$U_m^{**} = \left(y^2 - y_f^2 \right)/4 = y_m^2/4 + 2y_m y_f/4 > y_m^2/4 = U_m^*. \tag{11}$$

Thus, the presence of household public good, q, yields a gain from marriage equal to $y_m y_f/2$ in this case.

2. Form the Lagrangean expression from equations (8.18) and (8.21):

$$Lg = X t_i + \lambda[w(1 - t_i) - X]. \tag{12}$$

The first order conditions for a maximum of equation (12) are

$$t_i - \lambda = 0 \tag{13}$$

$$X - \lambda w_i = 0. \tag{14}$$

Eliminating λ from equations (13) and (14) yields

$$X = t_i w_i \tag{15}$$

which is the least cost combination of X and t_i in the production of Z. Substituting equation (15) into equation (8.21) yields

$$t_i^* = 1/2 \tag{16}$$

which is the demand function for time spent in home production. Substituting (16) back into equation (8.21) yields

$$X^* = w_i/2 \tag{17}$$

which is the demand function for purchased inputs into home production. Finally, substituting equations (16) and (17) into the home production function yields optimum production (and consumption) of commodities

$$Z_i^* = w_i/4. \tag{18}$$

References

Adrian, J., and R. Daniel. 1976. Impact of Socioeconomics Factors on Consumption of Selected Food Nutrients in the United States. *American Journal of Agricultural Economics, 58*, 31–38.

Akerlof, G. A., J. Yellen, and M. L. Katz. 1996. An Analysis of Out-of-Wedlock Childbearing in the United States. *Quarterly Journal of Economics, 111*, 277–317.

Alm, J., and L. A. Whittington. 1995. Income Taxes and the Marriage Decision. *Applied Economics, 27*(1), 25–31.

Alm, J., and L. A. Whittington. 1996. The Rise and Fall and Rise . . . of the Marriage Tax. *National Tax Journal, 49*(4), 571–589.

Almanac of Policy Issues. 2002. *The Earned Income Tax Credit*, from http://www.policyalmanac.org/social_welfare/eitc.shtml.

Ando, A., and F. Modigliani. 1963. The Life-Cycle Hypothesis of Saving: Aggregate Implications and Tests. *American Economic Review, 53*, 55–84.

Arrow, K. 1973. Higher Education as a Filter. *Journal of Public Economics, 2*, 193–216.

Becker, G. S. 1965. A Theory of the Allocation of Time. *Economic Journal, 75*(299), 493–517.

Becker, G. S. 1973–1974. A Theory of Marriage: Parts I and II. *Journal of Political Economy, 81*(4), 813–846, and *81*(2), S811–S826.

Becker, G. S. 1975. *Human Capital*. Second edition. New York: Columbia University Press for the NBER.

Becker, G. S. 1981. *A Treatise on the Family*. Cambridge, MA: Harvard University Press.

Becker, G. S. 1991. *A Treatise on the Family, enlarged edition*. Cambridge, MA: Harvard University Press.

Becker, G. S., and G. Lewis. 1974. Interaction between Quantity and Quality of Children. In T. W. Schultz (Ed.), *Economics of the Family: Marriage, Children and Human Capital*, pp. 81–90. Chicago: University of Chicago Press for the National Bureau of Economic Research.

307

Becker, G. S., R. T. Michael, and E. M. Landes. 1977. An Economic Analysis of Marital Instability. *Journal of Political Economy, 85*(6), 1153–1189.

Beierlein, J. G., J. W. Dunn, and J. C. McCornon, Jr. 1981. The Demand for Electricity in the Northeastern United States. *Review of Economics and Statistics, 58*(3), 403–408.

Blau, F. D., and L. M. Kahn. 2000. Gender Differences in Pay. *Journal of Economic Perspectives, 14*(4), 75–100.

Blau, F. D., L. M. Kahn, and J. Waldfogel. 2000. Understanding Young Women's Marriage Decisions: The Role of Labor and Marriage Market Conditions. *Industrial and Labor Relations Review, 53*(4), 624–647.

Blau, F. D., M. A. Ferber., and A. E. Winkler. 2002. *The Economics of Women, Men and Work*. Fourth edition. Upper Saddle River, NJ: Prentice Hall.

Blundell, R., and T. MaCurdy. 1999. *Labor Supply*: A Review of Alternative Approaches in O. Ashenfelter and D. Card (Eds.) *Handbook of Labor Economics Volume 3A*, pp. 1559–1696. New York: Elsevier.

Borenstein, S., and P. N. Courant. 1989. How to Carve a Medical Degree: Human Capital Assets in Divorce Settlements. *American Economic Review, 79*(5), 992–1009.

Borsch-Supan, A. and Stahl, K. 1991. Life-Cycle Savings and Consumption Constraints: Theory, Empirical Evidence, and Fiscal Implications. *Journal of Population Economics, 4*, 233–255.

Branch, E. R. 1993. Short Run Income Elasticity of Demand for Residential Electricity Using Consumer Expenditure Survey Data. *Energy Journal, 14*(4), 111–122.

Brien, M. J. 1997. Racial Differences in Marriage and the Role of Marriage Markets. *The Journal of Human Resources, 32*(4), 741–778.

Bryant, W. K. 1986. Technology and the Family: An Initial Foray. In R. E. Deacon. W. E. Huffman (Eds.), *Human Resources Research, 1887–1987: Proceedings*, pp. 117–26. Ames: College of Home Economics, Iowa State University.

Bryant, W. K. 1990. *The Economic Organization of the Household*. First edition. New York: Cambridge University Press.

Bryant, W. K. 1996. A Comparison of the Household Work of Married Females: The Mid-1920s and the Late 1960s. *Family and Consumer Sciences Research Journal, 24*(4), 358–384.

Bryant, W. K. and Y. Wang. 1990a. American Consumption Patterns and the Prices of Time: A Time Series Analysis. *Journal of Consumer Affairs, 24*(2), 280–306.

Bryant, W. K., and Y. Wang. 1990b. Time Together, Time Apart: An Economic Analysis of Wives' Solitary Time and Time Shared with Spouses. *Lifestyles: Journal of Family and Economic Issues, 11*(1), 87–117.

Bryant, W. K., and C. D. Zick. 1996a. Are We Investing Less in the Next Generation? Historical Trends in Time Spent Caring for Children. *Journal of Family and Economic Issues, 17*(3–4), 365–392.

Bryant, W. K., and C. D. Zick. 1996b. An Examination of Parent-Child Shared Time. *Journal of Marriage and the Family, 58*, 227–237.

Bryant, W. K., and C. D. Zick, 1996–1997. Child Rearing Time by Parents: A Report of Research in Progress, *Consumer Close-ups*, 3. Department of Consumer Economics and Housing, Cornell University.

Bryant, W. K., C. D. Zick, and H. Kim. 1992. *The Dollar Value of Household Work*. Ithaca, NY: College of Human Ecology, Cornell University.

Burtless, G. and J. F. Quinn. 2000. Retirement Trends and Policies to Encourage Work among Older Americans. *Brookings Institution Economic Studies Papers*, from http:/www.brook.edu/es/commentary/papers/2000.htm.

Campbell, C. R., and J. M. Lovati. 1979. Inflation and Personal Saving: An Update. *Federal Reserve Bank of St. Louis Review, 61*(8), 3–9.

Capps, O., Jr., and J. Havlicek, Jr. 1987. Analysis of Household Demand for Meat, Poultry, and Seafood using the S1-Branch System. In R. Rauniker and C. L. Huang (Eds.), *Food Demand Analysis: Problems, Issues, and Empirical Evidence*, pp. 128–142. Ames: Iowa State University.

Chiang, A. 1967. *Fundamental Methods of Mathematical Economics*. Second edition. New York: McGraw-Hill.

Cochrane, S. H., and S. P. Logan. 1975. The Demand for Wife's Nonmarket Time: A Comparison of Results from Surveys of Chicago School Teachers and South Carolina College Graduates. *Southern Economic Journal, 42*, 285–293.

Cogan, J. 1980. Labor Supply with Fixed Costs of Labor Market Entry. In J. P. Smith (Ed.), *Female Labor Supply*, pp. 327–364. Princeton, NJ: Princeton University Press.

Costa, D. L. 2000. The Wage and Length of Work Day: From the 1890s to 1991. *Journal of Labor Economics, 18*(1), 156–181.

Cowan, R. S. 1983. *More Work for Mother: The Ironies of Household Technology from the Open Hearth to the Microwave*. New York: Basic Books.

Danziger, S., R. Haveman, and R. Plotnick. 1981. How Income Transfer Programs Affect Work, Savings, and the Income Distribution: A Critical Review. *Journal of Economic Literature, 19*(1), 975–1028.

Deacon, R. E. and F. M. Firebaugh. 1988. *Family Resource Management*. Second edition. Boston: Allyn and Bacon.

Deaton, A. 1992. *Understanding Consumption*. New York: Oxford University Press.

Deaton, A., and J. Muellbauer. 1981. *Economics and Consumer Behavior*. New York: Cambridge University Press.

DeCicca, P., D. Kenkel, and A. Mathios. 2002. Putting Out the Fires: Will Higher Taxes Reduce the Onset of Youth Smoking? *Journal of Political Economy, 110*(1): 114–169.

Dickert, S., S. Houser, and J. K. Scholz. 1995. The Earned Income Tax Credit and Transfer Programs: A Study of Labor Market and Program Participation. In J. M. Poterba (Ed.), *Tax Policy and the Economy*, pp. 1–50. Boston: National Bureau of Economic Research and the MIT Press.

Dooley, M. D. 1982. Labor Supply and Fertility of Married Women: An Analysis with Grouped and Ungrouped Data from the 1970 U.S. Census. *Journal of Human Resources, 17*, 499–532.

Duncan, G. 1984. *Years of Poverty, Years of Plenty*. Ann Arbor, MI: Survey Research Center, Institute for Social Research, University of Michigan.

Duncan, G. J., and S. D. Hoffman. 1990. Welfare Benefits, Economic Opportunities, and Out-of-Wedlock Births Among Black Teenage Girls. *Demography, 27*, 519–535.

Edwards, L. N., and M. Grossman. 1979. The Relationship between Children's Health and Intellectual Development. In S. J. Mushkin and D. W. Dunlop (Eds.), *Health: What Is It Worth? Measures of Health Benefits*, Chap. 12. New York: Pergamon Press.

Ehrenberg, R. G., and R. S. Smith. 1982. *Modern Labor Economics*. Glenview, IL: Scott, Foresman and Co.

Eissa, N., and H. W. Hoynes. 1998. The Earned Income Tax Credit and the Labor Supply of Married Couples. NBER Working Paper.

Eissa, N., and J. B. Liebman. 1996. Labor Supply Response to the Earned Income Tax Credit. *Quarterly Journal of Economics, 111*(2), 605–637.

Ermisch, J. F. 1989. Purchased Child Care, Optimal Family Size and Mother's Employment. *Journal of Population Economics, 2*(2), 79–102.

Espenshade, T. J. 1984. *Investing in Children: New Estimates of Parental Expenditures*. Washington, DC: Urban Institute.

Falvey, R. E., and N. Gemmell. 1996. Are Services Income-Elastic? Some New Evidence. *Review of Income and Wealth, 42*(3), 257–269.

Fan, J. X., and J. K. Lewis. 1999. Budget Allocation Patterns of African Americans. *Journal of Consumer Affairs, 33*(1), 134–164.

Fleisher, B. M., and G. F. Rhodes. 1979. Fertility, Women's Wage Rates, and Labor Supply. *American Economic Review, 69*(1), 14–24.

Frazis, H., and J. Stewart. 1999. Tracking the Returns to Education in the 1990s. *Journal of Human Resources, 34*(3), 629–641.

Freidan, A. 1974. The U.S. Marriage Market. In T. W. Schultz (Ed.), *Economics of the Family: Marriage, Children, and Human Capital*, pp. 352–371. Chicago: University of Chicago Press for the National Bureau of Economic Research.

Friedman, M. 1957. *A Theory of the Consumption Function*, Princeton NJ: Princeton University Press for the National Bureau of Economic Research.

Gerner, J. L., and C. D. Zick. 1983. Time Allocation Decisions in Two-Parent Families. *Home Economics Research Journal, 12*(2), 145–158.

Getzen, T. E. 2000. Health Care Is an Individual Necessity and a National Luxury: Applying Multilevel Decision Models to the Analysis of Health Care Expenditures. *Journal of Health Economics, 19*, 259–270.

Ghez, G. R., and G. S. Becker. 1975. *The Allocation of Time and Goods over the Life Cycle*. New York: National Bureau of Economic Research and Columbia University Press.

Gies, F., and J. Gies. 1987. *Marriage and the Family in the Middle Ages*. New York: Harper & Row.

Goldsmith, R. W. 1955. *A Study of Saving in the US*, Vol. 1. Princeton, NJ: Princeton University Press.

Gould, B. W. 1998. Factors Affecting the Timing of Purchasing of Butter, Margarine, and Blends: A Competing Goods Analysis. *American Journal of Agricultural Economics 80*, 793–805.

Gramm, W. L. 1974. The Demand for the Wife's Nonmarket Time. *Southern Economic Journal, 41*, 124–133.

Gronau, R. 1977. Leisure, Home Production, and Work – The Theory of the Allocation of Time Revisited. *Journal of Political Economy, 85*(6), 1099–1123.

Grossman, M. 1972. *The Demand for Health: A Theoretical and Empirical Investigation.* New York: Columbia University Press for the National Bureau of Economic Research.

Grossman, M. 1976. The Correlation between Health and Schooling. In N. Terleckj (Ed.), *Household Production and Consumption*, Vol. 40, pp. 147–211. New York: Columbia University Press for the National Bureau of Economic Research.

Grossman, M. 2000. The Human Capital Model. In A. J. Culyer, and J. P. Newhouse (Eds.), *Handbook of Health Economics*, Volume 1A, pp. 348–408. Amsterdam: Elsevier.

Hall, R. E. 1988. Intertemporal Substitution in Consumption. *Journal of Political Economy, 96*(2), 339–357.

Harris, J. E., and S. W. Chan. 1999. The Continuum-of-Addition: Cigarette Smoking in Relation to Price Among Americans Aged 15–29. *Health Economics, 8*(1), 81–86.

Haveman, R., and B. Wolfe. 1995. The Determinants of Children's Attainments: A Review of Methods and Findings. *Journal of Economic Literature, 33*(4), 1829–1878.

Hayashi, F. 1985. The Effects of Liquidity Constraints on Consumption: A Cross-sectional Analysis. *Quarterly Journal of Economics, 100*, 183–206.

Henderson, J. M., and R. E. Quandt. 1958. *Microeconomic Theory*. New York: McGraw-Hill.

Herman, A. M. 1999. *Report on the American Workforce.* Washington, DC: U.S. Department of Labor.

Hersch, J., and L. S. Stratton. 1997. Housework, Fixed Effects, and Wages of Married Women. *Journal of Human Resources, 32*(2), 285–307.

Hicks, J. R. 1946. *Value and Capital.* Second edition. Oxford: Clarendon Press.

Hill, M. S. 1985. Patterns of Time Use. In F. T. Juster and F. P. Stafford (Eds.), *Time, Goods, and Well-being*, pp. 133–176. Ann Arbor, MI: Survey Research Center, Institute for Social Research, University of Michigan.

Hirshleifer, J. 1976. *Price Theory and Applications.* Englewood Cliffs, NJ: Prentice-Hall.

Hofferth, S. L., and J. Sandberg. 1999. *Changes in American Children's Time, 1981–1997.* Paper presented at the Annual Meeting of the American Sociological Association, Chicago, IL.

Hoffman, S. D. and G. J. Duncan. 1995. The Effect of Incomes, Wages, and AFDC Benefits on Marital Disruption. *Journal of Human Resources, 30*(1), 19–41.

Hotz, V. J., J. A. Klerman, and R. J. Willis. 1997. The Economics of Fertility in Developed Countries. In M. R. Rosenzweig, and O. Stark (Eds.), *Handbook of Population and Family Economics*, Vol. 1A, pp. 275–348. New York: Elsevier.

Imbens, G. W., D. B. Rubin, and B. Sacerdote. 1999. Estimating the Effect of Unearned Income on Labor Supply, Earnings, Savings and Consumption: Evidence from a Survey of Lottery Players. National Bureau of Economic Research, NBER Working Paper 7001.

Institute of Medicine, National Cancer Policy Board. 1998. *Taking Action to Reduce Tobacco Use.* Washington DC: National Academic Press.

Ironmonger, D. 1997, November. National Accounts of Household Productive Activities. In Papers presented at the Conference on Time Use, Non-Market

Work, and Family Well-Being. Washington, DC: Bureau of Labor Statistics and the MacArthur Foundation.

Ironmonger, D., and F. Soupourmas. 2003. Married Households and Gross Household Product. In S. Grossbard-Schechtman (Ed.), *Marriage and the Economy: How Marriage Affects Work, Spending and the Macro-Economy*. New York: Cambridge University Press.

Jaeger, D. A., and M. E. Page. 1996. Degrees Matter: New Evidence on Sheepskin Effects in the Returns to Education. *Review of Economics & Statistics, 78*(4), 733–740.

Juster, F. T., P. Courant, G. J. Duncan, et al. 1978. *Time Use in Economic and Social Accounts*. Ann Arbor, MI: Survey Research Center, University of Michigan, Manuscript.

Kahn, J. R., R. R. Rindfuss, and D. K. Guilkey. 1990. Adolescent Contraceptive Method Choices. *Demography, 27*(3), 323–335.

Katz, L. F., and K. M. Murphy. 1992. Changes in Relative Wages, 1963–1987: Supply and Demand Factors. *Quarterly Journal of Economics, 107*(1), 35–78.

Kenkel, D. S. 1996. New Estimates of the Optimal Tax on Alcohol. *Economic Inquiry, 34*, 296–319.

Keynes, N. M. 1936. *The General Theory of Employment, Interest, and Money*. London: Macmillan.

Killingsworth, M. R., and J. J. Heckman. 1986. Female Labor Supply: A Survey. In O. C. Ashenfelter and R. Layard (Eds.), *Handbook of Labor Economics* Vol. 1, pp. 103–198. New York: North-Holland Publishing Co.

Kimmel, J., and T. J. Kniesner. 1998. New Evidence on Labor Supply: Employment Versus Hours Elasticities by Sex and Marital Status. *Journal of Monetary Economics, 42*(2), 289–301.

Kooreman, P., and A. Kapteyn. 1987. A Disaggregated Analysis of the Allocation of Time within the Household. *Journal of Political Economy, 95*(2), 223–249.

Kotlikoff, L. J. 1988. Intergenerational Transfers and Savings. *Journal of Economic Perspectives, 2*, 41–58.

Kraft, J. M., and J. E. Coverdill. 1994. Employment and the Use of Birth Control by Sexually Active Single Hispanic, Black, and White Women. *Demography, 31*(4), 593–602.

Kuznets, S. S. 1942. *Uses of National Income in Peace and War*. New York: National Bureau of Economic Research.

Lazear, E. P., and R. T. Michael. 1988. *Allocation of Income within the Household*. Chicago: University of Chicago Press.

Lebergott, S. 1968. Labor Force and Employment Trends. In E. Sheldon and W. E. Moore (Eds.), *Indicators of Social Change: Concepts and Measurement* Chapter 4. New York: Russell Sage Foundation.

Lehrer, E. L. 1996a. The Determinants of Marital Stability: A Comparative Analysis of First and Higher-Order Marriages. *Research in Population Economics, 8*, 91–121.

Lehrer, E. L. 1996b. Religion as a Determinant of Marital Fertility. *Journal of Population Economics, 9*(2), 173–196.

Lehrer, E. L. 2004. The Role of Religion in Union Formation: An Economic Perspective. *Population Research and Policy Review, 23,* 161–185.

Leigh, D. E., and A. M. Gill. 1997. Labor Market Returns to Community Colleges. *Journal of Human Resources, 32*(2), 334–353.

Lichter, D. T., R. N. Anderson, and M. D. Hayward. 1995. Marriage Markets and Marital Choice. *Journal of Family Issues, 16*(4), 412–431.

Lichter, D. T., F. B. LeClere, and D. K. McLaughlin. 1991. Local Marriage Markets and the Marital Behavior of Black and White Women. *American Journal of Sociology, 96*(4), 843–867.

Lichter, D. T., D. K. McLaughlin, G. Kephart, and D. J. Landry. 1992. Race and the Retreat from Marriage: A Shortage of Marriageable Men? *American Sociological Review, 57*(6), 781–799.

Liebman, J. 1997. The Impact of the Earned Income Tax Credit on Incentives and Income Distribution. *Tax Policy and the Economy, 12,* 83–119.

Lino, M. 2001. *Expenditures on Children by Families: 2001 Annual Report.* U.S. Department of Agriculture, Center for Nutrition Policy and Promotion, Misc. Publication 1528–2001. Available online at http://www.usda.gov/cnpp/Crc/crc2001.pdf.

Lopoo, L. M., S. McLanahan, and I. Garfinkel. 2004. Explaining the Trend in Teenage Birth Rates from 1900 to 1999. Unpublished manuscript.

Loughran, D. S. 2002. The Effect of Male Wage Inequality on Female Age at First Marriage. *The Review of Economics and Statistics, 84*(2), 237–250.

Macunovich, D. J. 1999. The Fortunes of One's Birth: Relative Cohort Size and the Youth Labor Market in the United States. *Population Economics, 12*(2), 215–272.

MaCurdy, T., D. Green, and H. Paarsch. 1990. Assessing Empirical Approaches for Analyzing Taxes and Labor Supply. *Journal of Human Resources, 25*(3), 415–490.

Manlove, J. E., T. L. Gitelson, A. R. Papillo, and S. Russel. 2000. Explaining Demographic Trends in Teenage Fertility, 1980–1995. *Family Planning Perspectives, 32,* 166–75.

Mann, J. S., and G. E. St. George. 1978. *Estimates of Elasticities for Food Demand in the United States.* Washingtion, DC: U.S. Department of Agriculture.

Manser, M., and M. Brown. 1979. Bargaining Analyses of Household Decisions. In C. B. Lloyd, E. S. Andrews, and C. L. Gilroy (Eds.), *Women in the Labor Market,* Chapter 1. New York: Columbia University Press.

Manser, M., and M. Brown. 1980. Marriage and Household Decision-Making: A Bargaining Analysis. *International Economic Review, 21*(1), 31–44.

Mansfield, E. 1982. *Microeconomics: Theory and Applications.* Fourth edition. New York: W. W. Norton Co.

Mare, R. D. and C. Winship. 1991. Socioeconomic Change and the Decline of Marriage for Blacks and Whites. In C. Jencks and E. Peterson (Eds.), *The Urban Underclass,* pp. 175–202. Washington, DC: The Brookings Institution.

Mayer, T. 1972. *Permanent Income, Wealth and Consumption.* Berkeley and Los Angeles: University of California Press.

McCarthy, P. S. 1996. Market Price and Income Elasticities of New Vehicle Demands. *The Review of Economics and Statistics, 78*(3), 543–547.

McElroy, M. and M. Horney. 1981. Nash-bargained Decisions: Toward a Generalization of the Theory of Demand. *International Economic Review, 22*, 333–349.

McInnis, E. 1959. *Canada: A Political and Social History*. Rev. ed. New York: Rinehart & Co.

Meyer, B. D. and D. T. Rosenbaum. 2000. Making Single Mothers Work: Recent Tax and Welfare Policy and its Effects. *National Tax Journal, 53*(4, part 2), 1027–1061.

Michael, R. T. 1988. Why Did the U.S. Divorce Rate Double Within a Decade? *Research in Population Economics, 6*, 367–399.

Mincer, J. 1963. Market Prices, Opportunity Costs, and Income Effects. In C. F. Christ (Ed.), *Measurement in Economics: Studies in Mathematical Economics and Econometrics in Memory of Yehuda Grunfeld*, pp. 75–79. Stanford, CA: Standford University Press.

Mincer, J. 1974. *Schooling, Experience, and Earnings*. New York: Columbia University Press for NBER.

Mitchell, W. C. 1912. The Backward Art of Spending Money. *American Economic Review, 2*, 269–281.

Modigliani, F., and R. Brumberg. 1954. Utility Analysis and the Consumption Function: An Interpretation of Cross-Section Data. In K. K. Kurihara (Ed.), *Post-Keynesian Economics*. New Brunswick, NJ: Rutgers University Press.

Moffit, R. 1984. The Estimation of Fertility Equations on Panel Data. *Journal of Human Resources, 19*(1), 22–34.

Mroz, T. A. 1987. The Sensitivity of an Empirical Model of Married Women's Hours of Work to Economic and Statistical Assumptions. *Econometrica, 55*(4), 765–799.

Murphy, K. M., and F. Welch. 1992. The Structure of Wages. *Quarterly Journal of Economics, 107*(1), 285–326.

Murray, C. 1984. *Losing Ground*. New York: Basic Books.

Olson, L. 1983. *Cost of Children*. Lexington, MA: Lexington Books.

O'Neill, B. M. 1978. *Time-Use Patterns of School-Age Children in Household Tasks: A Comparison of 1967–68 Data and 1977 Data*. Unpublished Master's Thesis, Cornell University.

Owen, J. D. 1970. *The Price of Leisure*. Montreal: McGill-Queens University Press.

Owen, S. J. 1987. Household Production and Economic Efficiency: Arguments for and against Domestic Specialization. *Work, Employment, and Society, 1*(2), 157–178.

Pencavel, J. 1986. Labor Supply of Men: A Survey. In O. Ashenfelter and R. Layard (Eds.), *Handbook of Labor Economics*, Vol. 1, pp. 3–102. New York: North-Holland Publishing Co.

Pencavel, J. 1998. The Market Work Behavior and Wages of Women, 1975–94. *Journal of Human Resources, 33*(4), 771–804.

Pencavel, J. 2002. A Cohort Analysis of the Association Between Work Hours and Wages Among Men. *Journal of Human Resources, 37*(2), 251–274.

Peters, H. E. 1986. Marriage and Divorce: Informational Constraints and Private Contracting. *American Economic Review, 76*(3), 437–454.

Pollak, R. A. 1988. Tied Transfers and Paternalistic Preferences. *American Economic Review, 78*(2), 240–244.

Puller, S. L., and L. A. Greening. 1999. Household Adjustment to Gasoline Price Change: An Analysis Using 9 Years of US Survey Data. *Energy Economics, 21,* 37–52.

Reid, M. 1934. *The Economics of Household Production.* New York: John Wiley and Sons.

Ressler, R. W., and M. S. Waters. 2000. Female Earnings and the Divorce Rate: A Simultaneous Equations Model. *Applied Economics, 32,* 1889–1898.

Rindfuss, R. R., S. P. Morgan, and K. Ofutt. 1996. Education and the Changing Age Pattern of American Fertility. *Demography, 33*(3), 277–290.

Robinson, J. P., and G. Godbey. 1997. *Time for Life: The Surprising Ways Americans Use Their Time.* University Park, PA: Pennsylvania State University Press.

Rosenzweig, M. R., and O. Stark. 1997. *Handbook of Population and Family Economics,* Vol. 1A and 1B. New York: Elsevier.

Ryder, N. B., and C. F. Westoff. 1971. *Reproduction in the United States.* Princeton: Princeton University Press.

Saffer H., and F. J. Chaloupka. 1995. The Demand for Illicit Drugs. NBER Working Paper No. 5238. New York: National Bureau of Economic Research.

Santos, F. P. 1972. *Some Economic Determinants of Marital Status.* Unpublished Ph.D. dissertation, Columbia University.

Schultz, T. W. 1974. *Economics of the Family.* Chicago: University of Chicago Press for the National Bureau of Economic Research.

Schultz, T. P. 1994. Marital Status and Fertility in the United States: Welfare and Labor Market Effects. *Journal of Human Resources, 29*(2), 637–669.

Seskin, E. P., and R. P. Parker. 1998. A Guide to the NIPA's. *Survey of Current Business, 78*(3): 26–68.

Slutsky, E. 1915. Sulla Teoria del Bilancio del Consumatore. *Giornale deglo Economisti, 51,* 19–23.

Solberg, E., and D. C. Wong. 1992. Family Time Use: Leisure, Home Production, Market Work, and Work Related Travel. *Journal of Human Resources, 27*(3), 485–510.

South, S. J., and K. M. Lloyd. 1992. Marriage Markets and Nonmarital Fertility in the United States. *Demography, 29*(2), 247–264.

Spence, A. M. 1974. *Market Signaling: Informational Transfer in Hiring and Related Screening Processes.* Cambridge, MA: Harvard University Press.

Stafford, F. T. and G. J. Duncan. 1985. The Use of Time and Technology by Households in the United States. In T. Juster and F. P. Stafford (Eds.), *Time, Goods, and Well-being,* pp. 245–289. Ann Arbor, MI: Survey Research Center, Institute for Social Research, University of Michigan.

Strauss, J. and D. Thomas. 1995. Human Resources: Empirical Modeling of Household and Family Decisions. In J. Behrman and T. N. Srinivasan (Eds.), *Handbook of Development Economics,* Vol. IIIA, pp. 1885–2023. New York: Elsevier.

Taylor, L. D. 1975. The Demand for Electricity: A Survey. *Bell Journal of Economics, 6*(1), 74–110.

Thomson, E. 1997. Couple Childbearing Desires, Intentions, and Births. *Demography, 34*(3), 343–354.

Triest, R. K. 1990. The Effect of Income Taxation on Labor Supply in the United States. *Journal of Human Resources, 25*(3), 491–516.

Tyrell, T. J., and T. D. Mount. 1987. Analysis of Food and Other Expenditures Using a Linear Logit Model. In R. Rauniker and C. L. Huang (Eds.), *Food Demand Analysis: Problems, Issues, and Empirical Evidence*, pp. 143–153. Ames, IA: State University Press.

U.S. Bureau of the Census. 1982. *Statistical Abstract of the United States: 1982–83*, 103rd ed. Washington, DC: GPO.

U.S. Bureau of the Census. 1999. *Statistical Abstract of the United States: 1999*, 119th ed. Washington, DC: GPO.

U.S. Bureau of the Census. 2000a. Educational Attainment in the United States March 2000. *Current Population Survey*, pp. 20–236. Washington, DC: GPO.

U.S. Bureau of the Census. 2000b. *Statistical Abstract of the United States: 2000*. 120th ed. Washington, DC: GPO.

U.S. Bureau of the Census. 2003. *Statistical Abstract of the United States: 2002*, 123rd ed. Washington, DC: GPO.

U.S. Bureau of the Census. 2004–2005. *Statistical Abstract of the United States: 2004–05*. Available at http://www.census.gov/prod/2004pubs/04statab/labor.pdf.

U.S. Bureau of Economic Analysis, U.S. Department of Commerce. 1986. *The National Income and Product Accounts of the United States, 1929–82*. Washington, DC: GPO.

U.S. Bureau of Economic Analysis. 2004. *National Income and Product Accounts Tables*. Available at http://www.bea.doc.gov/bea/dn/nipatbls/NIP2-2.HTM.

U.S. Bureau of Labor Statistics. 2004a. Consumer Expenditures in 2002. Report 974, February.

U.S. Bureau of Labor Statistics 2004b. Time-Use Survey – First Results Announced by BLS. Press Release, September 14.

U.S. National Center for Education Statistics. 2003. *Digest of Education Statistics, 2003*. Washington, DC. Available at http://nces.ed.gov//programs/digest/do3/tables/dt249.asp

U.S. National Center for Health Statistics. 1997. *Monthly Vital Statistics Report, 45*(10), Supplement.

Wachtel, P. 1977. Inflation, Uncertainty and Saving Behavior Since the Mid-1950s. *Explorations in Economic Research*, (fall), 558–578.

Wagner, J., and M. Mokhtari. 2000. The Moderating Effect of Seasonality on Household Apparel Expenditure. *Journal of Consumer Affairs, 34*(2), 314–329.

Walden, M. L. 1996. Implicit Tax Rates of the Expanded Earned Income Tax Credit for Welfare Recipients in North Carolina. *Journal of Consumer Affairs, 30*(2), 348–372.

Weber, W. E. 1975. Interest Rates, Inflation and Consumer Expenditures. *American Economic Review, 65*(5), 843–858.

Weiss, Y. 1997. The Formation and Dissolution of Families: Why Marry? Who Marries Whom? And What Happens Upon Divorce. In M. R. Rosenzweig, and O. Stark (Eds.), *Handbook of Population and Family Economics*, Vol. 1A, pp. 81–125. New York: Elsevier.

Weiss, Y., and R. J. Willis. 1985. Children as Collective Goods and Divorce Settlements. *Journal of Labor Economics, 3*(3), 268–292.

Weiss, Y., and R. J. Willis. 1997. Match Quality, New Information, and Marital Dissolution. *Journal of Labor Economics, 15*(1, part 2), S293–S329.

Whittington, L. A. 1992. Taxes and the Family: The Impact of the Tax Exemption for Dependents on Marital Fertility. *Demogaphy, 29*(2), 215–226.

Whittington, L. A., and J. Alm. 2003. The Effects of Public Policy on Marital Status in the United States. In S. A. Grossbard-Shechtman (Ed.), *Marriage and the Economy*, pp. 75–101. New York: Cambridge University Press.

Whittington, L. A., J. Alm, and H. E. Peters. 1990. Fertility and the Personal Exemption: Implicit Pronatalist Policy in the United States. *American Economic Review, 80*(3), 545–566.

Wilder, R. P., J. E. Johnson, and R. G. Rhyne. 1992. Income Elasticity of the Residential Demand for Electricity. *Journal of Energy and Development, 16*(1), 1–13.

Williams, L. B., and W. F. Pratt. 1990. Wanted and Unwanted Childbearing in the United States: 1973–1988. *Advance Data from Vital and Health Statistics,* 189.

Willis, R. L. 1986. Wage Determinants: A Survey and Reinteroretation of Human Capital Earnings Functions. In O. C. Ashenfelter and R. Layard (Eds.), *Handbook of Labor Economics*, Vol. 1, pp. 525–602. Amsterdam: North-Holland Publishing Co.

Wilson, W. J. 1987. *The Truly Disadvantaged.* Chicago: University of Chicago Press.

Wilson, W. J., and K. M. Neckerman. 1986. Poverty and family structure: The Widening Gap Between Evidence and Public Policy Issues. In S. H. Danziger and D. H. Weinberg (Eds.), *Fighting Poverty: What Works and What Doesn't*, pp. 232–259. Cambridge, MA: Harvard University Press.

Wolf, E. 1999. Joint Labour Supply Decisions of Couples. In J. Mertz and M. Ehling (Eds.), *Time Use – Research, Data, and Policy*, pp. 269–291. Baden-Baden, Germany: NOMOS Verlagsgesellschaft.

Wood, R. G. 1995. Marriage Rates and Marriageable Men: A Test of the Wilson Hypothesis. *Journal of Human Resources, 30*(1), 194–204.

Wright, C. 1969. Saving and the Rate of Interest. In A. C. Harberger and M. J. Bailey (Eds.), *The Taxation of Income from Capital*, pp. 275–300. Washington, DC: Brookings Institution.

Yen, S. T., and H. H. Jensen. 1996. Determinants of Household Expenditures on Alcohol. *Journal of Consumer Affairs, 30*(1), 48–67.

Zabel, J. E. 1993. The Relationship Between Hours of Work and Labor Force Participation in Four Models of Labor Supply Behavior. *Journal of Labor Economics, 11*(2), 387–416.

Zick, C. D., and W. K. Bryant. 1996. A New Look at Parents' Time Spent in Child Care: Primary and Secondary Time Use. *Social Science Research, 25,* 260–280.

Zick, C. D., and J. L. McCullough. 1991. Trends in Married Couples' Time Use: Evidence from 1977–78 and 1987–88. *Sex Roles, 24*(7/8), 459–487.

Index